HE'S STILL COMING

A CAPTIVATING BIBLICAL STUDY OF THE LAST DAYS

A 40-Year Update and Greatly Expanded Revision of the Book
THE KING IS COMING
1974-2014

H. L. WILLMINGTON

**Best-selling Author of *Willmington's Guide to the Bible* and
Dean, Willmington School of the Bible & Liberty Home Bible Institute**

publishers
SOLUTION
The Key to Publishing and Printing Possibilities

978-1-937925-18-5   **Paperback**

publishers
SOLUTION
The Key to Publishing and Printing Possibilities

P. O. Box 2184
Forest, VA 24551
Phone (434) 219-0398
www.PublishersSolution.com

Cover & Interior Design by Heather Kirk of the Publishers Solution Design Team

SPECIAL DEDICATION

Shortly after coming to Liberty University as dean of our Bible School in 1972, I received a call that literally changed my life! It was from Dr. Wendell Hawley, an executive at the Tyndale House Publishing Company in Carol Stream, Illinois, informing me that Tyndale had received and accepted for publication my first book, entitled, *The King is Coming*.

In the ensuing years, God has allowed me to author a number of other books. However, it is my opinion that had Dr. Hawley not recommended the book (which frankly had been turned down by several other publishers), my writing outreach ministry probably would be only a fraction of what it is today. So, dear friend, thank you for believing in me, and for your continued encouragement to this author!

CONTENTS

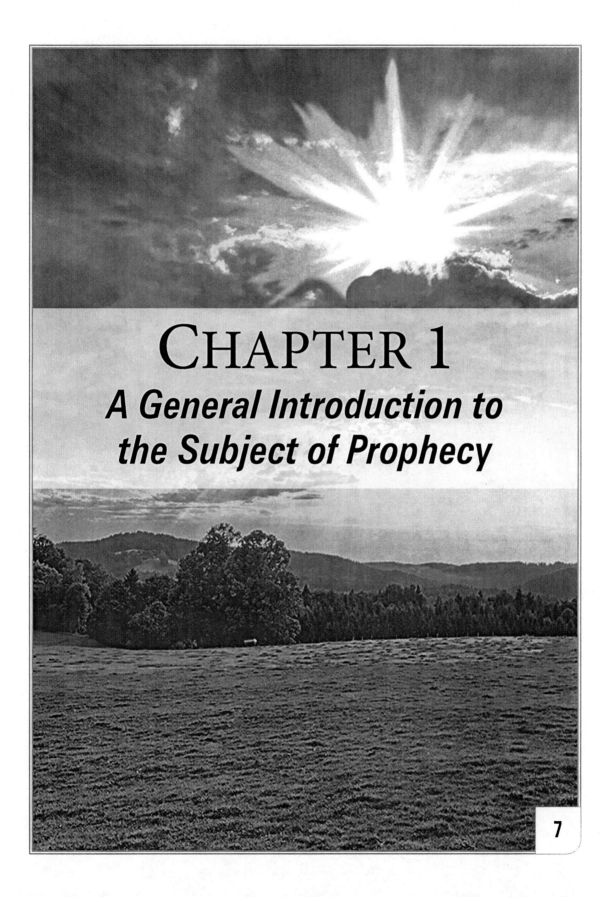

CHAPTER 1
A General Introduction to the Subject of Prophecy

MAJOR THEMES IN PROPHECY

There are some 38 key areas. The following chart overviews these:

NO.	TITLE	SUBJECT
1	Millions of Instant Astronauts	The "Catching Up" Rapture of All Believers
2	Gold, Silver, Precious Stones Wood, Hay, Stubble—Which?	The Judgment Seat of Christ
3	When the Angels Will Sing, "Here Comes the Bride"	The Wedding Between Christ & His Church
4	Everything He Has Done, Is Doing, or Will Do	Praising God for His Work in Creation & His Work in Redemption
5	Seven Years of Pure Hell on Earth	An Introduction to The Coming Great Tribulation
6	A Man Sent by Satan	The Rise & Reign of the Antichrist
7	A Hellish John the Baptist	The Antichrist's False Prophet
8	Remember Humpty Dumpty? Well … He's Back!	The Revival of the Old Roman Empire
9	The Valley of Dry Bones & The Year 1948	The Rebirth of the Nation Israel & Its Significance
10	When the Northern Bear Comes Over the Mountain	The Gog and Magog Invasion Into Israel
11	Don't Sign! It's From Hell! But They Will	Satan's Seven-Year Covenant With Israel
12	A Living Statue and the Mark of a Man	The Abomination of Desolation & the Number 666
13	The Persecution & Protection of the Woman Wearing a Crown of Twelve Stars	Satan's Past & Future Attempts to Destroy Israel
14	Refuge in Rock City	Petra—Where the Jews Will Hide Out from the Antichrist
15	Hell's Version of the Cross and Empty Tomb	The Assassination and Resurrection (?) of the Antichrist

NO.	TITLE	SUBJECT
16	Praise God, He's Gone!	The Casting Out of Satan from Heaven
17	A Harlot & A Queen: Two Sisters in the City of Satan	Representing the False Church & the Merchants of Greed in Babylon
18	When the Man of Son Kills the Woman of Sin	The Murder of the False Church by the Antichrist
19	Both Preach the Gospel But Neither are Human	An Angel and An Eagle
20	12,000 x 12 = New Births Without Number	Ministry of the 144,000
21	Light to Direct the Feet Oil to Heal the Soul	The Olive Tree and Lampstand Ministry of God's Two Witnesses
22	Universal Rejoicing Over Their Dead Bodies But Suddenly the Party's Over	The Martyrdom and Resurrection Of the Two Witnesses
23	First the Seals, Then the Trumpets Then the Bowls—Will it Ever Stop?	God's Twenty-One Fold Punishment Upon Man
24	The Secret of the Seven Thunders & Completion of the Mystery of God	God's Explanation in Regards to the Presence of Evil & That of Human Suffering (??)
25	Two in the Past, Two in the Future, One Now in Heaven	A History of Former, Future, & Present Temples
26	Annihilated in a Single Hour	The Destruction of Babylon
27	Last Time: The Lamb of God Next Time: The Lion of Judah	The Second Coming of Jesus Christ
28	The Biggest & Bloodiest Conflict of All	Overviewing the Battle of Armageddon
29	Your Invitation to Attend the Most Important Meal Since the One in the Upper Room	The Marriage Supper of the Lamb
30	He Once Said, "Come Unto Me," He Will Say, "Depart From Me"	Jesus's Words at the Sheep & Goats Judgment To Determine Who Will Enter the Millennium
31	The Rapture Was the First This Will Be the Second	The Resurrection of O. T. Believers & Those Who Were Martyred During The Great Tribulation

NO.	TITLE	SUBJECT
32	365,000 Days in Solitary Confinement	Length of Satan's Time in the Bottomless Pit
33	Just Think of It! Ten Centuries of Peace & Prosperity	The Glorious Millennium
34	First, Destruction by Fire Then Eternity in the Fire	Satan's Final Revolt is Crushed and He is Cast into Hell
35	The Most Fearful Judgment Known to Man	Events at the Great White Judgment Throne
36	Purging of the Old, Presenting of the New	Former Creation Nevermore: Future Creation Forevermore
37	That Shining City Among the Stars	The New Jerusalem
38	Worlds Without End	Eternity

Meaning of the word *prophecy*—twofold

1. To forthtell in regards to the present (Isa. 1:2-6; 1 Cor. 3:1-4)
2. To foretell in regards to the future (Isa. 2:2-4; 1 Cor. 15:51-57)

Reasons for and benefits of studying prophecy

1. Because one third (over 8,000 verses) are given over to the subject
2. Because the study will comfort and reassure us (1 Thess. 4:13-18; 1 Peter 1:7-9)
3. Because it will promote holy living (1 Thess. 3:13; 5:23; Titus 2:12, 13; James 5:7-9; 2 Peter 3:10-14; 1 John 3:3).
4. Because God desires to reveal the future to us (Psa. 25:14; Dan. 2:28; Amos 3:7; Matt. 11:25; Luke 8:10; Rev. 1:1).
5. Because Jesus is the subject, source, and spirit of prophecy (Luke 24:44; Acts 10:43; Rev. 19:10).
6. Because more prophecy will be revealed as we approach the last days (Dan. 12:8-10).
7. Because it supports the certainty of those prophecies yet to come. This is simply to say that inasmuch as all the O. T. prophecies in regards to the first coming of Christ have been literally fulfilled, we have every reason to rightly assume all the N. T. prophecies regarding His second coming will all likewise occur.

Requirements for understanding prophecy_____

In general it may be said …

1. One must know Jesus as Savior. This is to say he/she must be born again (John 3:3, 6; 1 Cor. 2:14)

2. One must know Jesus as Lord. This is to say he/she must be Spirit-controlled (1 Cor. 2:10, 15).

3. The bottom line of all this means a godly believer, though he might scarcely be able to read and write, can, on his knees with an open Bible, see and understand the future far more clearly than an unsaved Ph.D. can view and comprehend it standing on his tip toes!

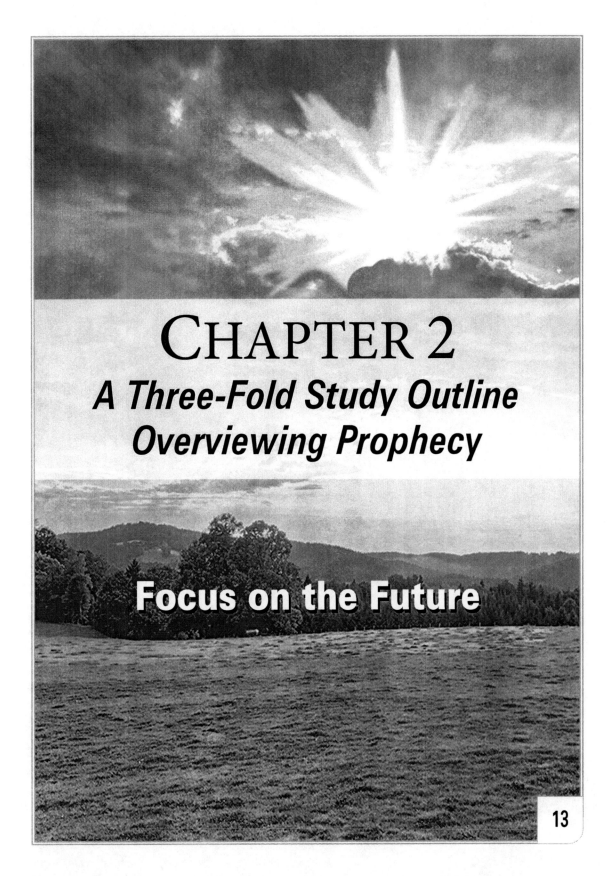

CHAPTER 2
A Three-Fold Study Outline Overviewing Prophecy

Focus on the Future

A Three-Fold Study in Regards to Prophecy

Part One

    I.   From: The Trump of God

    II. To: The Wrath of God

Part Two

    I.   From: The Wrath of God

    II. To: The Coming of the Son of God

Part Three

    I.   From: The Coming of the Son of God

    II. To: The Celestial City of God

PART ONE

I. From: The Trump of God (1 Thess. 4:16)

II. To: The Wrath of God (Matt. 24:21)

- Key Personalities Involved
  - A. The Father: Seen sitting upon a throne (Dan. 7:9-10; Rev. 4:2, 3; 5:1)
  - B. The Son: Introduced as the Lion of the Tribe of Judah, the Root of David; seen as a slain lamb (Rev. 5:5, 6)
  - C. The Holy Spirit: The One who ushers John into the heavenlies (Rev. 4:2)
  - D. Twenty-four elders: Sitting upon twenty-four smaller thrones (Rev. 4:4)
  - E. Four living creatures: Who day and night praise God for His holiness (Rev. 4:6-8)
  - F. A universal choir of the redeemed, praising God (Rev. 5:9, 10, 13)
  - G. Untold millions of angels praising God (Rev. 5:11, 12)

- Key Events Involved
  - A. The Rapture of the Church (1 Thess. 4:13-17; 1 Cor. 15:51-54)
  - B. The Judgment Seat of Christ (Rom. 14:10-12; 1 Cor. 3:11-15; 2 Cor. 5:10)
  - C. The Two Hymns of Praise (Rev. 4:11; 5:10)
  - D. The Marriage Service of Jesus to His Church (2 Cor. 11:2; Eph. 5:25-27)

PART TWO

I. From: The Wrath of God

II. To: The Coming of the Son of God

- ▪ Key Personalities Involved
  A. The Father (Psa. 2:6-8; Dan. 7:9, 10, 13, 14; Rev. 14:1-5)
  B. The Son (Rev. 6:1; 7:9, 17; 14:1)
  C. The Holy Spirit (Rev. 14:13; 17:3)
  D. The 144,000 (Rev. 7:4-7)
  E. The two witnesses—Moses and Elijah (Mal. 4:4-6; Rev. 11:3-12)
  F. The elect angels (Rev. 7:11)
  G. Michael, the archangel (Rev. 12:7)
  H. The evil angels (Rev. 9:11, 14; 16:13, 14)
  I. The martyred souls under the altar (Rev. 6:9-11)
  J. A great unnumbered multitude of the redeemed (Rev. 7:9, 10)
  K. Satan (Rev. 12:3, 4, 9)
  L. The Antichrist (Rev. 13:1)
  M. The false prophet (Rev. 13:11)
  N. Leader of the armies of Magog (Ezek. 38:1-4)
  O. Ten kings who will aid the Antichrist in his rise to power (Rev. 17:12-18)
  P. The kings of the east (Rev. 16:12)
  Q. An army of locusts—like demons from the bottomless pit (Rev. 9:1-11)
  R. An army of horse and rider demons from the Euphrates River (Rev. 9:13-19)
  S. The king of the bottomless pit whose name is Abaddon in the Hebrew language and Apollyon in the Greek (Rev. 9:11)
  T. Three symbolic women
     1. A persecuted woman: Israel (Rev. 12:1, 2)
     2. A religious harlot: the false church (Rev. 17:3-6)
     3. An arrogant and greedy queen: the world's economic systems (Rev. 18:7)
- ▪ Key Events Involved
  A. Those occurring during the first three and a half years of the Great Tribulation
     1. The appearances of the Antichrist and his false prophet (2 Thess. 2:3; Rev. 13:1-18)
     2. The revival of the old Roman Empire (Dan. 2:31-43; 7:4-14)
     3. The organization of the super harlot church (1 Tim. 4:1; 2 Tim. 3:1-5; Rev. 17:1-6)

4. The mass return of the Jews to Israel (Isa. 43:5, 6; Ezek. 37:1-14; 34:11-13; 36:24)
5. The ministry of the two witnesses (Rev. 11:3-6)
6. The ministry of the 144,000 (Rev. 7:1-8)
7. The rebuilding of Babylon (Isa. 13:19, 20; Jer. 50:40; 51:7, 8)
8. The pouring out of the first six seal judgments (Rev. 6:1-17)

B. Those events occurring during the middle part (a brief, undetermined time) of the Great Tribulation
1. The Gog and Magog invasion into Israel (Ezek. 38-39)
2. The destruction of the false church (Rev. 17:14-18)
3. The casting of Satan from heaven (Rev. 12:7-12)
4. The martyrdom of the two witnesses (Rev. 11:7-9)

C. Those events occurring during the final three and a half years of the Great Tribulation
1. The preaching of the gospel by two non-human messengers
   a. By an angel (Rev. 14:6, 7)
   b. By an eagle (Rev. 8:13)
2. The vision of the tabernacle in heaven (Rev. 11:19; 15:5)
3. The singing of two special songs
   a. The song of the 144,000 (Rev. 14:1-5)
   b. The song of Moses (Rev. 15:3)
4. The wicked activities of the Antichrist and his false prophet
   a. Those of the Antichrist (Rev. 13:5-7; 2 Thess. 2:4)
      (1) Blaspheming God
      (2) Claiming to be God
      (3) Demanding to be worshipped as God
      (4) Waging war against the saints of God
   b. Those of the false prophet (Rev. 13:8, 12-18; Matt. 24:15; Dan. 9:27)
      (1) Forcing the unsaved world to worship the Antichrist
      (2) Deceiving the unsaved world by his satanic miracles
      (3) Placing a statue of the Antichrist into the Jewish Holy of Holies
      (4) Giving power to the statue, causing it to speak
      (5) Creating his mark (666) which must be displayed by all in the unsaved world to buy, sell, take a job, leave a job, etc.
5. The assassination and resurrection (?) of the Antichrist (Rev. 13:3, 14)
6. The worldwide worship of both the Antichrist and Satan himself (Rev. 13:4)

7. The universal persecution of Israel (Dan. 12:1; Zech. 11:16; Matt. 24:21; Rev. 12:13)

8. The deliverance of a Jewish remnant (Micah 2:12; Rev. 12:13-17)

9. The last seal judgment, consisting of seven trumpets (Rev. 8:1-13; 9:1-21; 11:15-19)

10. The most frightening description of eternal hell in the entire Bible (Rev. 14:9-11)

11. The pouring out of the seven vial or bowl judgments (Rev. 15:1, 6; 16:1-21)

12. The secret of the seven thunders and the completion of the mystery of God (Rev. 10:1-7)

13. The destruction of commercial Babylon (Rev. 18:1-24)

PART THREE

I. From: The Coming of the Son of God

II. To: The Celestial City of God

■ Key Personalities Involved

A. A great heavenly choir (Rev. 19:1-6)

B. The Lamb's wife (Rev. 19:7)

C. John the apostle (Rev. 19:10)

D. Jesus Christ

1. As a sovereign soldier (Rev. 19:11-16)

2. As a judge (Rev. 20:11, 12)

3. As the Alpha and Omega (Rev. 22:13)

4. As the root of David (Rev. 22:16a)

5. As the bright and morning star (Rev. 22:16b)

E. An angel with a key and chain (Rev. 20:1)

F. Satan

1. In prison (Rev. 20:2)

2. On the battlefield (Rev. 20:7)

3. In the lake of fire (Rev. 20:10)

4. A multitude of martyrs (Rev. 20:4)

5. A gathering of all the unsaved (Rev. 20:11-15)

6. The Holy Spirit (Rev. 22:17)

■ Key Events

A. The Marriage Supper of the Lamb (Rev. 19:7-9)

B. John the apostle's attempts to worship an angel
     1. First attempt (Rev. 19:10)
     2. Second attempt (Rev. 22:8, 9)
C. The Return of Jesus Christ (Rev. 19:11-16)
D. The Battle of Armageddon (Rev. 19:17, 18, 21)
E. The Antichrist and False Prophet cast into hell (Rev. 19:20)
F. Satan is cast into the bottomless pit (Rev. 20:1-3)
G. The glorious Millennium (Rev. 20:4-6)
H. Satan is loosed from the bottomless pit (Rev. 20:7)
I. The final revolt in the Bible (Rev. 20:8, 9)
J. Satan is cast into hell (Rev. 20:10)
K. The Great White Throne Judgment (Rev. 20:11-15)
L. Appearance of the Holy City, New Jerusalem (Rev. 21:1-8)
M. Description of the Holy City (Rev. 21:9-22:5)
N. Scripture's final:
     1. Invitation (Rev. 22:16, 17)
     2. Warning (Rev. 22:18, 19)
     3. Promise (Rev. 22:20, 21)

CHAPTER 3
The First Four Events in Prophecy

EVENT 1 THE RAPTURE OF THE CHURCH_____

INTRODUCTION TO THE RAPTURE

It occurred late Thursday night in a secluded place during the month of April some 2000 years ago. A meal accompanied by a meeting was in progress with twelve being in attendance which included eleven followers and their leader. The leader had already dropped a bombshell when he quietly and sadly announced that one of his followers would betray him. Soon, the traitor, realizing the leader had him in mind, quickly left the room.

Immediately the tension lessened, resulting in the leader issuing yet another announcement, but this time a glorious one. It would include both a note of reassurance and that of a special two-fold revelation:

- **The reassurance**

  "Let not your heart be troubled; ye believe in God, believe also in me" (John 14:1).

- **The two-fold revelation**

  "In My Father's house are many mansions; if it were not so, I would have told you. I go to prepare a place for you. And if I go and prepare a place for you, I will come again and receive you to Myself; that where I am, there you may be also. And where I go you know, and the way you know" (John 14:2, 3).

  This of course all transpired in an upper room in the city of Jerusalem. The leader was Jesus, the eleven, his disciples, and the traitor, Judas Iscariot.

  These eleven were no doubt reassured, but could not, at first, comprehend his two-fold promise to (1) leave this earth to build a city, and, (2) return and transport them to that city!

  Most Bible students feel this marks the first biblical reference regarding a controversial event known as the Rapture! Thus this chapter will attempt to expand and clarify Jesus' words.

- During the summer of 1975 I signed up for a course in Historical Geography, which was offered by the American Institute of Holy Land Studies, located on Mt. Zion in Jerusalem, Israel.

  This was also the time when the American Secretary of State, Henry Kissinger, was flying in and out of Jerusalem, Damascus, Ammon, and Cairo, attempting to secure a peace treaty for that troubled part of the world.

  One afternoon during that summer I stood at a bus stop near the Jaffa Gate along with some Israeli citizens, seeking transportation to downtown Jerusalem. As we waited, a car suddenly sped by with a sign on its bumper that read:

  GUESS WHO'S COMING TO JERUSALEM SOON?

All of us saw this sign, prompting one of the citizens to address a rabbi who was also waiting for the bus as follows:

"Did you see that sign? You know, I haven't read the *Jerusalem Post* this morning, but is Henry coming again?"

The rabbi responded that he did not know. Well, ignoring Alexander Pope's wise insight that fools rush in where angels fear to tread, I approached the rabbi, introduced myself and suggested to him the strong possibility, indeed probability, that the sign writer may not have had Henry in mind! "Oh," said the rabbi, "If not Henry, then who?"

Taking a deep breath I told him that he probably wouldn't believe my answer, and sure enough, he didn't!

James Walker Whitcomb's beautiful song offers the probable correct answer to the sign maker's question:

Jesus may come today, Glad day! Glad day!
And I would see my Friend;
Dangers and troubles would end
If Jesus should come today.

Chorus

Glad day! Glad day! Is it the crowning day?
I'll live for today, nor anxious be, Jesus my Lord, I soon shall see;
Glad day! Glad day! Is it the crowning day?

I may go home today, Glad day! Glad day!
Seemeth I hear their song;
Hail to the radiant throng!
If I should go home today.

Why should I anxious be? Glad day! Glad day!
Lights appear on the shore,
Storms will affright never more,
For He is at hand today.

Faithful I'll be today, Glad day! Glad day!
And I will freely tell
Why I should love Him so well,
For He is my all today.

THE MEANING OF THE WORD RAPTURE

Actually, the word 'rapture' is from *rapere*, found in the expression "caught up" in the Latin translation of 1 Thess. 4:17. However, if one so desires, the Rapture could be scripturally referred to as the *harpazo*, which is the Greek word translated "caught up" in 1 Thess. 4:17. The identical phrase is found in Acts 8:39, where Philip was caught away by the Holy Spirit, and in 2 Cor. 12:2, 4, when Paul was caught up into the third heaven. Or if you'd rather, the Rapture could be known as the *allasso*, from the Greek translated "changed" in 1 Cor. 15:51, 52. *Allasso* is also used in describing the final renewal and transformation of the heavens and the earth. (See Heb. 1:12.) So then, use whatever name suits your fancy. Of course, the important thing is not what you name it, but rather, can you claim it? That is, will you participate in it?

Thus, the next scheduled event predicted in the Word of God will take place where the Savior Himself appears in the air to catch up His own!

THE CERTAINTY OF THE RAPTURE

Question: How can we be sure concerning any future event which is predicted in the Bible such as Christ's return, the Great Tribulation, the rise of the Antichrist, the Battle of Armageddon, the glorious Millennium, etc.?

Well, consider the following: In the Old Testament there are over forty prophecies in regards to the first coming of Jesus Christ (His virgin birth, where it would occur, His dual nature, sufferings, death, and resurrection), all of which have been literally fulfilled! In light of this, is it not logical to assume each prophecy concerning His second coming will likewise be fulfilled? After all, up to this point God enjoys a perfect track record!

AN ILLUSTRATION OF THE RAPTURE

A man is cleaning out his garage and discovers a small box filled with a mixture of tiny iron nails, wooden splinters, sawdust, and pieces of paper. Suppose he desires to save the nails. How could he quickly separate them from the wooden splinters? If a magnet was available, the task would be quite simple. He would simply position the magnet over the box. Immediately all those objects possessing the same physical nature would be caught up to meet the magnet in the air.

If his wife were watching all this, spotting a particular object in the box, she might say: "Look at the sharp point on that! I bet the magnet will zap that up!" But unknown to her, that tiny item might be a sharp sliver of wood which would not be taken up. Or, she might conclude: "That fragment over there is a piece of wood for sure." However, in reality it could be a "back-slidden" nail with some rust on it. But in both cases the magnet would quickly and accurately discern the character of the piece and act accordingly.

When Christ appears, He will not come especially for black or white people, for Catholics or Protestants, for Jews or Gentiles, but only for those individuals who possess the same nature as Himself. One of the most thrilling things God does for each repenting sinner is to give him or her the very mind of Christ and a brand new creation! (See 1 Cor. 2:16; 2 Cor. 5:17; Eph. 4:24; 2 Pet. 1:4).

THE HOLY SPIRIT AND THE RAPTURE

There is a common misconception that the Holy Spirit first made His appearance at Pentecost (Acts 2:4) and that He will depart following the Rapture, based on Paul's words in 2 Thess. 2:1-8 (NIV). Wrong on both counts!

- He came long before Pentecost.

   In fact, the *second* verse in the Bible marks His *first* appearance! *"The earth was without form, and void; and darkness was on the face of the deep. And the Spirit of God was hovering over the face of the waters"* (Gen. 1:2).

- He will *not* depart at the Rapture!
   A. He will offer comfort to the martyrs during the Great Tribulation (Rev. 14:13).
   B. He explains the mystery of Babylon the Great, the mother of harlots, to John the apostle (Rev. 17:3).
   C. Through His convicting ministry, a great multitude come to Christ (Rev. 7:9, 13, 14).
      1. Jesus tells us the *fact of* this ministry:
         "Nevertheless I tell you the truth. It is to your advantage that I go away; for if I do not go away, the Helper will not come to you; but if I depart, I will send Him to you. And when He has come, He will convict the world of sin, and of righteousness, and of judgment: of sin, because they do not believe in Me; of righteousness, because I go to My Father and you see Me no more; of judgment, because the ruler of this world is judged" (John 16:7-11).
      2. Paul explains the *need for* this ministry:
         "Now we have received, not the spirit of the world, but the Spirit who is from God, that we might know the things that have been freely given to us by God. These things we also speak, not in words which man's wisdom teaches but which the Holy Spirit teaches, comparing spiritual things with spiritual. But the natural man does not receive the things of the Spirit of God, for they are foolishness to him; nor can he know them, because they are spiritually discerned" (1 Cor. 2:12-14).

- Question: Are these truly the last days? If so, could it be possible that the Antichrist himself is, at this very moment, walking among us, but unrecognized by us? Of course no one can say. But according to Paul, if this be the case, his evil plans are blocked at every turn by the Holy Spirit! Note His words:

"Concerning the coming of our Lord Jesus Christ and our being gathered to him, we ask you, brothers, not to become easily unsettled or alarmed by some prophecy, report or letter supposed to have come from us, saying that the day of the Lord has already come. Don't let anyone deceive you in any way, for that day will not come until the rebellion occurs and the man of lawlessness is revealed, the man doomed to destruction. He will oppose and will exalt himself over everything that is called God or is worshiped, so that he sets himself up in God's temple, proclaiming himself to be God. Don't you remember that when I was with you I used to tell you these things? And now you know what is holding him back, so that he may be revealed at the proper time. For the secret power of lawlessness is already at work; but the one who now holds it back will continue to do so till he is taken out of the way. And then the lawless one will be revealed, whom the Lord Jesus will overthrow with the breath of his mouth and destroy by the splendor of his coming" (2 Thess. 2:1-8, NIV).

In summary, then, the influence and ministry of the Holy Spirit, indwelling and working through His people in this present age, is the power that holds back the dark flood of evil, which is ready to be released and sweep across our world.

Dr. Donald Grey Barnhouse offers a very practical application in regard to all this:

> Well, what is keeping the Antichrist from putting in his appearance on the world stage? *You* are! You and every other member of the body of Christ on earth.
>
> The presence of the church of Jesus Christ is the restraining force that refuses to allow the man of lawlessness to be revealed. True, it is the Holy Spirit who is the real restrainer. But as both 1 Cor. 3:16 and 6:19 teach, the Holy Spirit indwells the believer. The believer's body is the temple of the Spirit of God. Put all believers together then, with the Holy Spirit indwelling each of us, and you have a formidable restraining force.
>
> For when the church is removed at the Rapture, the Holy Spirit goes with the church insofar as His restraining power is concerned. His work in this age of grace will be ended. Henceforth, during the Great Tribulation, the Holy Spirit will still be here on earth, of course—for how can you get rid of God?—but He will not be indwelling believers as He does now. Rather, He will revert to His Old Testament ministry of "coming upon" special people. (*Thessalonians: An Expositional Commentary*, Grand Rapids, MI, Zondervan, 1977, pp. 99, 100)

■ A final thought based on the words of the prophet Isaiah:

"...when the enemy shall come in like a flood, the Spirit of the Lord shall lift up a standard against him (Isa. 59:19).

One of the truly great construction accomplishments in American history is Hoover Dam, located on the border of Arizona and Nevada, completed in 1935 to control and harness the mighty waters of the Colorado River. It rises 726 feet above the lowest part of its foundation. This is equivalent to a 72-story office building! 3,250,000 cubic yards of concrete were used to form the dam. This would pave a standard highway from San Francisco to New York City. Its thickness ranges from 45 feet at the crest to 660 feet at its base. The length is 1244 feet.

This powerful dam thus holds back literally billions and billions of angry, swirling waters, allowing only a controlled amount to escape through its exits. If the unthinkable ever happened and the dam broke, portions of several western states would literally be inundated, drowning scores of thousands of people!

With all of this in mind, it can be stated the Holy Spirit functions in the real sense of the word as a divine dam, both restraining and controlling the waters of sin and iniquity, allowing only a portion to pass through the exits involved.

THE ORDER OF THE RESURRECTION AT THE RAPTURE

Paul discusses this in two key passages:

■ 1 Thessalonians 4:13-17

    A. The revelation by the apostle

        1. We are not to be ignorant regarding this glorious event. This is but one of four key areas that Paul would not have us to be ignorant. The other three are:

            a. The events in the Old Testament (1 Cor. 10:1)

            b. The restoration of Israel (Rom. 11:25)

            c. The manifestation of spiritual gifts (1 Cor. 12:1)

        Special Note: The year was around 850 B.C. and the place may have been the city of Samaria. The prophet was Hosea, son of Beeri. At that time ten of the twelve tribes of Israel had turned from the true God, resulting in the land being filled with gross immorality and pagan idolatry. Because of all this a heart-broken Hosea pronounced divine judgment upon its people. But the most tragic sin which would soon lead to the cruel Assyrian Captivity, was *not* immorality, *or* idolatry, but rather the sin regarding ignorance of God's Word! Heed his words:

        "My people are destroyed for lack of knowledge. Because you have rejected knowledge, I also will reject you from being priest for Me; Because you have forgotten the law of your God, I also will forget your children" (Hosea 4:6).

        Some eight centuries later the Savior would remind a group of wicked Pharisees in regards to this very thing:

        "Jesus answered and said to them, 'You are mistaken, not knowing the Scriptures nor the power of God'" (Matt. 22:29).

        2. The Rapture will involve a two-fold process:

            a. First, concerning the bodies of departed believers:

"...them who sleep in Jesus," "...the dead in Christ." Their bodies will be raised first. The death of a believer is looked upon as a peaceful sleep. (See Matt. 27:52; John 11:11; Acts 7:60; 13:36; 1 Cor. 15:6, 18, 20, 51; 2 Pet. 3:4.)

However, it should be quickly stated that this verse in no way teaches soul sleep. That unscriptural doctrine is refuted by Matt. 17:3 and Rev. 6:9-11.

    B.   Second, concerning the bodies of living believers:

"For this we say unto you by the word of the Lord, that we which are alive and remain unto the coming of the Lord shall not prevent (precede) them which are asleep" (1 Thess. 4:15). Note Paul's usage of the pronoun "we."

The apostle apparently hoped at this time to be here when Christ came. He would later know otherwise:

"For I am already being poured out as a drink offering, and the time of my departure is at hand" (2 Tim. 4:6).

    3.   A three-fold sound will be heard at the Rapture:

        a.   A shout

        b.   The voice of the archangel

        c.   The trump of God

    4.   In regards to the shout:

It is often supposed that Michael will be this archangel on the basis of Dan. 12:1, 2. However, it is not unreasonable to suggest that Gabriel will be the angel involved at this time because of the vital part he played in those events surrounding the first coming of Christ. (See Luke 1:19, 26; Matt. 1:20; 2:13.) This is the final of three instances in which Christ shouted. On each occasion a resurrection took place!

        a.   The shout at Bethany

"And when he thus had spoken, he cried with a loud voice, Lazarus, come forth. And he that was dead came forth, bound hand and foot with grave clothes: and his face was bound about with a napkin. Jesus saith unto them, Loose him, and let him go" (John 11:43, 44).

        b.   The shout at Calvary

"Jesus, when he had cried again with a loud voice, yielded up the ghost. And, behold, the veil of the temple was rent in twain from the top to the bottom; and the earth did quake, and the rocks rent: And the graves were opened; and many bodies of the saints which slept arose. And came out of the graves after his resurrection, and went into the holy city, and appeared unto many" (Matt. 27:50-53).

    5.   When this occurs, all of us will be with the Lord forever.

    B.   The exhortation by the apostle

"Wherefore, comfort one another with these words" (1 Thess. 4:18).

■ **1 Corinthians 15:51-57**

"Behold, I shew you a mystery; We shall not all sleep, but we shall all be changed. In a moment, in the twinkling of an eye, at the last trump: for the trumpet shall sound, and the dead shall be raised incorruptible, and we shall be changed. For this corruptible must put on incorruption, and this mortal must put on immortality. So when this corruptible has put on incorruption, and this mortal has put on immortality, then shall be brought to pass the saying that is written: Death is swallowed up in victory. O Death, where is your sting? O Hades, where is your victory? The sting of death is sin, and the strength of sin is the law. But thanks be to God, who gives us the victory through our Lord Jesus Christ" (1 Cor. 15:51-57).

A. The revelation by the apostle

Observe some phrases from this passage:

1. "I shew you a mystery."

What is this mystery or secret concerning the Rapture? Let us suppose you began reading the Bible in Genesis chapter 1, and read through 1 Corinthians chapter 14. If you stopped your reading there, you would already have learned about many important facts, such as creation, man's sin, the flood, Bethlehem, Calvary, the resurrection, and the existence of heaven and hell. But you would be forced to conclude that a Christian could get to heaven only after physically dying. You would of course note the two exceptions of Enoch (Gen. 5:24) and Elijah (2 Kings 2:11), but apart from these it would be clear that believers have to travel the path of the grave to reach the goal of glory. But now the secret is out, and here it is: Millions of Christians will someday reach heaven without dying! *"Behold, I shew you a mystery; We shall not all sleep, but we shall all be changed"* (1 Cor. 15:51). This, then, is the mystery of the Rapture!

H. L. Turner's gospel hymn, *Christ Returneth*, speaks eloquently of Christ's sudden return, especially verse four which is, in essence, a musical summary regarding the mystery of the Rapture!

> *It may be at morn, when the day is awaking,*
> *When sunlight thru darkness and shadow is breaking,*
> *That Jesus will come in the fullness of glory*
> *To receive from the world His own.*
>
> *It may be at midday, it may be at twilight,*
> *It may be, perchance, that the blackness of midnight*
> *Will burst into light in the blaze of His glory,*
> *When Jesus receives His own.*
>
> *While hosts cry Hosanna, from heaven descending,*
> *With glorified saints and the angels attending,*

With grace on His brow, like a halo of glory,
Will Jesus receive His own.

O joy! O delight! Should we go without dying,
No sickness, no sadness, no dread and no crying,
Caught up thru the clouds with our Lord into glory,
When Jesus receives His own.

<u>Chorus</u>
O Lord Jesus, how long, how long
Ere we shout the glad song
Christ returneth! Hallelujah! Hallelujah! Amen,
Hallelujah! Amen.

2. "We shall be changed … in the twinkling of an eye."

   The twinkling (or blinking) here is calculated to occur at one fifth of a second! It is thus the third fastest thing in the universe!

   a. The *first* is the speed of light, 186,284 m.p.h.

   b. The *second* is the time it takes for the driver in back of you to begin to lay on his horn when the traffic light in front of you turns green! And that, my friend, is fast!

3. "For the trump shall sound"

   In at least three biblical passages concerning the Rapture a trumpet is mentioned (1 Cor. 15:52; 1 Thess. 4:16; Rev. 4:1). How are we to understand this?

   Dr. J. Dwight Pentecost writes, "the phrase 'the trump of God' is significant, for in the Old Testament the trumpet was used for two things—to summon to battle and to summon to worship." (*Prophecy for Today*, Zondervan, p. 30).

   Which of the two meanings, however, is involved at the Rapture? Dr. Pentecost suggests that both meanings are in mind, one directed toward angels and the other to believers.

   a. To angels the trumpet blast will mean "Prepare for battle!"

   According to various New Testament passages (John 14:30; Eph. 6:12; 1 John 5:19) this present world lies in the hands of the evil one, the devil, and the very atmosphere is filled with his wicked power and presence. Satan will obviously resist believers being caught up through his domain and becoming freed from his wicked worldly system. Therefore, the trumpet commands the angels, "Prepare for battle! Clear the way for the catching up of those resurrected bodies and those living believers!"

   b. To all believers the trumpet blast will mean "Prepare to worship!" In Num. 10:1-3 we read, "And the Lord spake unto Moses, saying, Make thee two trum-

pets of silver ... that thou mayest use them for the calling to the assembly and when they shall blow with them, all the assembly shall assemble themselves to thee at the door of the tabernacle ..."

Regarding the Rapture trumpet, Num. 10:4 seems to be especially significant: "*If they blow but with one trumpet, then the princes, which are heads of the thousands of Israel, shall gather themselves unto thee.*" At the Rapture only one trumpet is sounded, suggesting that in God's sight all believers occupy a place of utmost importance. We are all "head princes" in the mind of God.

4. "*For this corruptible must put on incorruption, and this mortal must put on immortality*" (1 Cor. 15:53).

   a. Corruptible: that supernatural act whereby the bodies of departed believers will be resurrected.

   b. Mortal: that supernatural act whereby the bodies of living believers will be transformed.

   To grasp this concept, let us compare a human being to an automobile. In this illustration the car will represent the body and the driver will represent the soul. Although the driver/soul, car/body are all closely related, they are nevertheless *not* one and the same! The driver *has* a car, but he *is* a person. The soul *has* a body, but he *is* a person. To continue the analogy, when the car breaks down, the driver makes his exit, resulting in his automobile being placed in a junkyard. When the body breaks down (physical death), the soul (person) makes his exit, resulting in his flesh being placed in a grave yard. In the body/soul illustration the believer departs to be with Christ, awaiting the resurrection of a new body. In fact, there is some scriptural suggestion he may receive a temporary body until the old one is resurrected. See 2 Cor. 5:1; Rev. 6:9-11.

   Thus to summarize the promise of future Rapture resurrection, consider the following:

   (1) The situation requiring this promise (1 Cor. 15:50): Flesh and blood cannot inherit God's Kingdom.

   (2) The secret associated with this promise (1 Cor. 15:51): All believers alive at Christ's coming will go to heaven without dying.

   (3) The suddenness of this promise (1 Cor. 15:52a): This will occur in the amount of time it takes to blink an eye.

   (4) The signal introducing this promise (1 Cor. 15:51b): The last trumpet will signify the fulfillment of this promise.

   (5) The schedule of this promise (1 Cor. 15:52c, 53):

      (a) Departed believers will exchange their corrupted bodies for incorruptible ones (1 Cor. 15:53).

HE'S STILL COMING

(b) Living believers will exchange their mortal bodies for immortal ones (1 Cor. 15:53).

(6) The Scriptures predicting this promise (1 Cor. 15:54-57): Old Testament prophets Isaiah and Hosea wrote of this (Isa. 25:8; Hos. 13:14).

B. The exhortation by the apostle

"Therefore, my beloved brethren, be steadfast, immovable, always abounding in the work of the Lord, knowing that your labor is not in vain in the Lord" (1 Cor. 15:58).

OLD TESTAMENT BELIEVERS AND THE RAPTURE

It is the view of this book that only those individuals saved from Pentecost to the Rapture (i.e., the body and bride of Christ, the church) will be raised at that time. Thus, all Old Testament saints and those martyred during the Great Tribulation will be raised at the beginning of the Millennium. This resurrection is referred to as the first resurrection in Rev. 20:6, contrasting it to the second resurrection (at which time the unsaved dead will be raised) which occurs at the end of the Millennium (Rev. 20:11-15).

Question: If true, why is this the case? Would it seem more appropriate for God to include the bodies of all departed beginning with Adam? Of course the Lord alone has the full answers. This much, however, we do know: that He has chosen two institutions to accomplish His divine purpose. Thus:

- In past time it *was* the nation Israel, as seen in the Old Testament (Deut. 4:37; 7:6; 14:2; Psa. 33:12; Acts 13:17). But Israel failed God because of her sin (Hos. 10:1; John 1:11).

- At the present time it *is* the church of God (2 Thess. 2:13; Eph. 1:4; 1 Peter 2:9)

  A. The church was promised in Matthew 16.

  B. The church was birthed in Acts 2.

- So then, in the fullness of time Jesus appeared, not only to die for our sins, but also to introduce phase two in the story of redemption:

  A. He came to *set aside* the nation Israel (Mt. 21:43; 23:37-39). However, it must be understood that this setting aside was *not* permanent! Paul emphasizes this:

  " ... I say then, hath God cast away his people? God forbid ... God hath not cast away his people whom he foreknew ... " (Rom. 11:1-2)!

  In fact, during three all-important biblical chapters the apostle summarizes the entire divine plan for Israel:

  1. In Romans 9, we read of Israel's past selection.

  2. In Romans 10, we read of Israel's present rejection.

  3. In Romans 11, we read of Israel's future restitution!

  So then, save that silver denarius, for Israel's going to rise again!

B. He came to *build up* the church of God! But how does all the above answer the original question? Why not include both O. T. and N. T. individuals at the Rapture?

Simply this: God has some unfinished business with Israel, namely, the rejection of His Son. This unbelief will be purged from the nation during the Great Tribulation, causing them to gladly accept Jesus as their Messiah!

"He will swallow up death forever, and the Lord God will wipe away tears from all faces; the rebuke of His people He will take away from all the earth; for the Lord has spoken. And it will be said in that day: 'Behold, this is our God; we have waited for Him, and He will save us. This is the Lord; we have waited for Him; we will be glad and rejoice in His salvation'" (Isa. 25:8-9).

"For I say to you, you shall see Me no more till you say, 'Blessed is He who comes in the name of the Lord!' And as they were eating, Jesus took bread, blessed and broke it, and gave it to the disciples and said, 'Take, eat; this is My body.'"

"Then He took the cup, and gave thanks, and gave it to them, saying, 'Drink from it, all of you. For this is My blood of the new covenant, which is shed for many for the remission of sins. But I say to you, I will not drink of this fruit of the vine from now on until that day when I drink it new with you in My Father's kingdom'" (Mt. 23:39; 26:26-29).

On a personal note, I believe it possible that this "unfinished business" will be accomplished in the ancient city of Petra when Jesus meets with the remnant of Jewish people who have fled there to escape the wrath of the Antichrist.

A ONE-WORD SUMMARY OVERVIEWING THE RAPTURE

This word, found only in 1 Corinthians 16:22 is the word, *Maranatha*. It is part of an Aramaic formula, meaning, "our Lord is coming."

It was probably used not only for one Christian to greet another believer, but may have been shouted out in the Roman arena by those about to become martyrs as an encouragement to others soon to experience the same fate.

Some years ago during a prophecy conference in upstate New York, Lehman Strauss, well-known Bible teacher, had just finished his sermon on the Rapture, concluded by encouraging his listeners to greet their friends with these words: "Dear friend, God's word for you today is Maranatha." The next morning, en route to breakfast, Dr. Strauss was met by two ladies, who, remembering his challenge, cried out—"Dr. Strauss, this is God's word for you today—Maranatha!" Well…maybe not!

SALVATION AFTER THE RAPTURE

As we have previously noted, many thousands of individuals will indeed be saved during the Great Tribulation as revealed in the book of Revelation: *"After these things I looked, and behold, a great multitude which no one could number, of all nations, tribes, peoples, and tongues, standing before the throne and before the Lamb, clothed with white robes, with palm branches in their hands, Then one of the elders answered, saying to me, 'Who are these arrayed in white robes, and where did they come from?' And I said to him, 'Sir, you know.' So he said to me, 'These are the ones who come out of the great tribulation, and washed their robes and made them white in the blood of the Lamb'"* (Rev. 7:9, 13, 14).

However, verse nine seems to indicate these persons will constitute those who had never heard the gospel message prior to the Great Tribulation. See also Matthew 24:14.

Thus, the following questions:

- What about that individual who had heard but not responded before the Rapture? Will he have, as it were, a second chance to be saved? Three views have been advocated:
  A. Yes, based on Acts 2:21; Rom. 10:13; 1 Tim. 2:4; 2 Pet. 3:9; Rev. 7:9-14.
  B. No, based on 2 Thess. 2:8-12.
  C. Conditional. This view would distinguish between those who, for whatever reason, had simply neglected to receive Christ, as opposed to those who had categorically rejected Him! (See 2 Peter 3:5.)

- What about the unborn, babies, and young children?
  A. Concerning the unborn:
     These scriptures clearly teach that God views the unborn as true human beings! See Psa. 139:13-16; Jer. 1:5; Lk. 1:41-44; Gal. 1:15.
  B. Concerning babies:
     David testified to the salvation of infants. Compare the last phrase of 2 Sam. 12:23 with the last phrase of Psa. 23:6.
  C. Concerning young children:
     Jesus both recognized and praised the spiritual perception of little children. See Matt. 18:1-6, 10; 19:13-15; 21:15, 16.
     The common consensus among most Bible students is that all babies and children will participate in the Rapture! This would include those still in the womb of saved mothers.

TWO OLD TESTAMENT FORESHADOWS OF THE RAPTURE

While the Rapture is of course an exclusive New Testament doctrine, there are nevertheless two Old Testament events which illustrate it.

Seen in Enoch, who was taken from the world before the flood judgment (Gen. 5:24).

Seen in Lot, who was taken from Sodom before the fire judgment (Gen. 19:22-24).

CONTRASTING THE RAPTURE WITH THE REVELATION

Although these two are inseparably linked together, they are not the same. In essence, the Rapture introduces the Great Tribulation, while the Second Coming will conclude it. Other distinguishing features are:

■ **The Rapture:**

A. Christ comes in the air (1 Thess. 4:16, 17).

B. He comes for His saints (1 Thess. 4:16, 17).

C. The Rapture is a mystery, i.e., a truth unknown in Old Testament times (1 Cor. 15:51).

D. Christ's coming for His saints is never said to be preceded by signs in the heavens.

E. The Rapture is identified with the day of Christ (1 Cor. 1:8; 2 Cor. 1:14; Phil. 1:6, 10).

F. The Rapture is presented as a time of blessing (1 Thess. 4:18).

G. The Rapture takes place in a moment, in the twinkling of an eye (1 Cor. 15:52).

H. The Rapture seems to involve the church primarily (Jn. 14:1-4; 1 Cor. 15:51-58; 1 Thess. 4:13-18).

I. Christ comes as the bright and morning star (Rev. 22:16).

■ **The Second Coming:**

A. He comes to the earth (Zech. 14:4).

B. He comes with His saints (1 Thess. 3:13; Jude 14).

C. The revelation is not a mystery; it is the subject of many Old Testament prophecies (Psa. 72; Isa. 11; Zech. 14).

D. Christ's coming with His saints will be heralded by heavenly signs (Matt. 24:29, 30).

E. The revelation is identified with the day of the Lord (2 Thess. 2:1-12, ASV).

F. The main emphasis of the revelation is on judgment (2 Thess. 2:8-12).

G. The revelation will be visible worldwide (Matt. 24:27; Rev. 1:7).

H. The revelation involves Israel primarily, then also the Gentile nations (Matt. 24:1; 25:46).

I. Christ comes as the sun of righteousness with healing in his wings (Mal. 4:2).

THE FOUR VIEWS IN REGARD TO THE NATURE OF THE RAPTURE

■ **The Partial Rapture View (also known as the "Spiritual Only" View)**

This says the Rapture will be limited to those spirit-filled believers who are faithfully working and waiting for Christ's return, thus leaving carnal Christians behind to endure a seven-year "Protestant purgatory" of some sort. It is true, of course, that the vast bulk of giving, praying and serving in most evangelical churches is done by 15 percent of the membership. These are the true spiritual pillars who uphold their church. And what of the remaining 85 percent? These may be likened to sluggish caterpillars that crawl in and out of the church once every six weeks or so! Thus, according to the Partial Rapture View, only the pillars will be caught up, leaving the caterpillars behind! Scriptures said to support this view are: Matt. 24:40-51; 25:1-13; Luke 20:35; Phil. 3:10-14; 1 Thess. 5:4-6; Heb. 9:28; Rev. 3:10.

The partial Rapture theory is to be rejected for the following three reasons:

    A. First, it confuses grace with rewards.

    B. Second, it divides the bride of Christ. How can the Marriage of the Lamb take place if part of the bride is left on earth?

    C. Third, it ignores the clear scriptural teaching to the contrary. (See 1 Thess. 1:9, 10; 2:19; 4:14-16; 5:4-11; Rev. 22:12.) Perhaps the most conclusive evidence against the partial Rapture theory is 1 Cor. 15:51. This church was one of the most carnal in the history of Christianity, yet Paul declares in this verse that if the Rapture occurred in their day, *all* of the saved in that church would be raptured.

The Mid-Tribulation Rapture View

This position holds the entire church will go through the first three and a half years of the Tribulation and will be caught up with the two martyred witnesses (Rev. 11:12). Here a distinction is made between the wrath of Antichrist (first part of the Tribulation) and the wrath of God (final three and a half years). Thus, the first half is described by Jesus as the "beginning of sorrows" (Matt. 24:5-20, especially verse 21). Scriptures said to support this view are: Dan. 12:6, 7, 11; Rev. 11:3; 12:3, 6, 14.

A common argument of the mid-trib position is: "It is egotistical for us to believe the church in our day will escape suffering and judgment. Where was the Rapture for the multitudes of Chinese believers murdered by the Japanese during World War II, or the Russian Christians slaughtered by the godless Communists?" The shallowness of this argument should be immediately evident, for it confuses satanic wrath with divine wrath. Nowhere are we promised we will escape suffering or even martyrdom. But we are assured we will escape divine wrath, for this is the very essence of the Great Tribulation, when God will punish the world. (Compare Isa. 24:1; 63:3-6; Rev. 6:17 with 1 Thess. 1:10; 5:9.)

The New Testament pictures the church as the body and bride of Christ. If the mid-tribulation or post-tribulation view were correct, then a part of His body would suffer amputation, and a section of the bride would be left behind! In addition to this, one would be forced to conclude that all bodies of carnal departed Christians would likewise be left in the grave. This simply is not the clear teaching of the Word of God. In addition to this there are two serious problems connected with the mid-tribulation position.

First, it destroys the imminence of Christ's return, for, according to its view the Savior could not possibly come until at least three and a half years after the time of this writing.

Second, it creates a date-setting chronology, for if it is known when the Tribulation begins (usually thought to occur when the Antichrist makes his seven-year covenant with Israel) and if Christ appears during the middle of the seven years, then one can know the dates of both the Rapture and Second Coming. But Jesus said this information would not be revealed. (See Matt. 24:36.)

The Post-Tribulation Rapture View

This view says the church will have to endure the entire seven year Tribulation, arguing that the Bible presents but one general resurrection, and that resurrection occurs at the end of the

Great Tribulation as described in Dan. 12:1, 2; John 6:39, 40; 11:23-25; Rev. 20:6. Other scriptures said to support this view are: Matt. 13:24-30; 24:29-31, 40, 41. Some wag has suggested that if the mid-trib or post-trib positions on the Rapture be correct, then the words to that beautiful Christian song, *Is It The Crowning Day?*, be changed to read as follows:

Jesus can't come today, sad day, sad day.

And I won't see my friend,

Danger and troubles won't end,

For Jesus can't come today.

Chorus

Sad day, sad day, it's not the crowning day!

I'll live for today and anxious be,

The false prophet and antichrist I soon shall see,

Sad day, sad day, for it's not the crowning day.

Personally, I much prefer the original words!

■ **The Pre-Tribulation Rapture View**

This view holds that all believers will be caught up to meet Jesus in the air just prior to the Great Tribulation. The author of this book holds to the pre-trib view for the following reasons:

A. The angel Gabriel explains the prophecy of the seventy weeks to Daniel (9:24-27), connecting this period of time (490 years, with the final seven years being the Great Tribulation) to the nation Israel! Inasmuch as the New Testament Church has not replaced Old Testament Israel (Rom. 11:1, 2, 26, 27; 1 Cor. 10:32), it can be concluded God will use these seven tribulational years to deal with His unfaithful wife (Old Testament Israel, see entire book of Hosea), while the pure, chaste bride of Christ (New Testament Church, 2 Cor. 11:2) will be in the heavenlies, having no need of forgiveness and cleansing (Eph. 5:25-27).

B. Paul affirms in 1 Thess. 1:10 and 5:9 that the church is to escape God's wrath.

C. Jesus says the same thing in Rev. 3:10.

D. John seems to place the Rapture in Rev. 4:1 and the beginning of the Great Tribulation in Rev. 6:1.

E. Jesus promised to return and remove His people from the earth (John 14:1-3), whereas the Old Testament predicts Him returning to the earth (Zech. 14:4), thus indicating there will be two separate appearances in regards to His return.

F. Paul reaffirms Jesus' promise in 1 Thess. 4:16, 17, saying we will be caught up in the clouds.

Perhaps the strongest proof of this statement is the fact that up to chapter 6 of Revelation the church is mentioned many times, but from chapter 6 to chapter 19 (the period of the Tribulation) there is no mention whatsoever of the church on earth. In fact, the only godly group Satan can find to persecute is the nation Israel. (See Rev. 12.) In Rev. 4:1 John declares, "*After this I looked, and, behold, a door was opened in heaven: and the first voice which I heard was as it were of a trumpet talking with me; which said, 'Come up hither …'*"

Consider an illustration from U. S. history at this point:

> On Sunday, Dec. 7, 1941, the Japanese bombed Pearl Harbor, inflicting great damage upon American forces stationed there. On Monday, Dec. 8, President Franklin Roosevelt delivered his "Day of Infamy" speech before Congress, which body then declared war upon Japan, Germany and Italy. On Tuesday, Dec. 9, FDR sent telegrams to the U.S. ambassadors serving in Tokyo, Berlin, and Rome, ordering them to leave for home immediately. It is of course standard procedure for a king or president to call his ambassadors home before waging war. With all this in mind, it may be said that some day God will declare an all out war on planet earth, known as the Great Tribulation! But, before He does, He will call His ambassadors home!

> "*Now, then we are ambassadors for Christ, as though God did beseech you by us: we pray you in Christ's stead, be ye reconciled to God*" (2 Cor. 5:20).

> "*For which I am an ambassador in bonds: that therein I may speak boldly, as I ought to speak*" (Eph. 6:20).

CHALLENGES OF THE BELIEVER IN LIGHT OF THE RAPTURE

■ **We are to heed the admonition given in the book of Hebrews:** "*Not forsaking the assembling of ourselves together, as is the manner of some, but exhorting one another, and so much the more as you see the Day approaching*" (Heb. 10:25).

A. This verse informs us just *what* we are to do, and *where* we are to do it.

    1. The *what* involved

       " *… exhorting one another*"

       Here are some elements in this exhortation:

       a. Live a godly life in the godless generation (Acts 2:40)

       b. Remain faithful to the faith (Acts 11:23; 14:22)

       c. Be both thankful and prayful (1 Tim. 2:1)

       d. Teach sound doctrine and be able to defend what you teach (2 Tim. 4:2; Titus 1:9; Jude 3)

       e. Do not make light of God's discipline or lose heart when He rebukes you (Heb. 12:5)

       f. Warn concerning the deceitfulness of sin (Heb. 3:13)

g. For all those in leadership (1 Peter 5:1-3)

    1) Be anxious to serve as a leader

    2) Be a role model leader to those you serve

2. The *where* involved

" ... the assembling of ourselves together ... "

This would include:

a. Church services

b. Bible study groups

c. Prayer sessions

d. Sunday school classes, etc.

■ **We are to observe the Lord's Supper with the Rapture in mind.**

A. Question: Why do most evangelical Christians observe the ordinance of baptism only once, but partake of the Lord's Supper many times?

B. Answer: Because of what these ordinances stand for. Baptism depicts the death, burial, and resurrection of Christ, all of which only occurred but once (Rom. 6:3-5). But what of Communion? Did not Paul also connect it to Christ's death? He did indeed, then added three all-important words.

Note: *"For as often as ye eat this bread, and drink this cup, ye do show the Lord's death till he come."* (1 Cor. 11:26). In other words, the Lord's Table should serve as a reminder of *both* the historical *cross* and of the prophetical *crown*!

■ **We are to be patient.**

"Be ye also patient, stablish your hearts: for the coming of the Lord draweth nigh" (James 5:8).

> Patience is a virtue,
> Possess it if you can,
> Rarely found in women,
> And never found in man.

Be that as it may, the importance of patience in the Christian life is underlined by the following verses:

A. It is better to possess patience and self-control than to capture a strong city (Prov. 16:32).

B. The bitter root of suffering, if allowed, will later bring forth the blessed fruit of patience (Rom. 5:3-5).

C. This kind of patience leads to knowing God's perfect will for your life (Heb. 10:36).

D. Thus, the ultimate goal of patience is spiritual maturity (James 1:2-4).

Katharina Amalia von Schlegel's beautiful Christian hymn composed three centuries ago expresses this noble goal as follows:

Be still, my soul! The Lord is on thy side;
Bear patiently the cross of grief or pain;
Leave to thy God to order and provide;
In every change He faithful will remain.
Be still, my soul! Thy best, thy heavenly Friend
Through thorny ways leads to a joyful end.

Be still, my soul: thy God doth undertake
To guide the future, as He has the past.
Thy hope, thy confidence let nothing shake;
All now mysterious shall be bright at last.
Be still, my soul: the waves and winds still know
His voice Who ruled them while He dwelt below.

Be still, my soul: the hour is hastening on
When we shall be forever with the Lord.
When disappointment, grief and fear are gone,
Sorrow forgot, love's purest joys restored.
Be still, my soul: when change and tears are past
All safe and blessèd we shall meet at last.

So then, suffering saint, in light of the Rapture, we can well afford to be patient, with the glorious knowledge that the story has a happy ending—the Bridegroom gets the Bride (Rev. 21)!

■ **We are to live separated lives.**

"… we know that, when he shall appear, we shall be like him; for we shall see him as he is. And every man that hath this hope in him purifieth himself …" (1 John 3:2, 3).

"… denying ungodliness and worldly lusts, we should live soberly, righteously, and godly, in this present world: Looking for that blessed hope, and the glorious appearing of the great God and our Saviour Jesus Christ" (Titus 2:12, 13).

"And now, little children, abide in him; that, when he shall appear, we may have confidence, and not be ashamed before him at his coming" (1 John 2:28).

"Love has been perfected among us in this: that we may have boldness in the day of judgment; because as He is, so are we in this world" (1 John 4:17).

This does not mean of course that we are to live isolated lives but separated ones!

I (HLW) began smoking at the age of 12 and continued on even after my conversion four years later in August of 1948. Back then it seemed to me that everyone smoked. After all, this was southern Illinois, tobacco country! The pastor of the church I attended smoked a pipe and I thought one of the requirements for being a deacon was to smoke—(well, not really).

But soon after accepting Christ I became increasingly convicted of my habit, in part after hearing for the first time a powerful sermon on the Rapture! How terrible I imagined would it be to go up blowing smoke! I did honestly attempt to stop, but tobacco had too much a hold on me. However, things would soon change. One day, immediately after lighting a cigarette I heard my name being called from a nearby car. It was my godly Sunday school teacher who had led me to Christ. How embarrassed I was. Not able to drop the offending object without him seeing it, I kept both hands behind my back as we talked. Well, the more we conversed, the more uncomfortable I became. In fact, I think he may have smelled burning flesh for he soon ended the conversation and drove away.

Even though this all happened nearly 60 years ago, I can still remember standing there on that street corner in Mt. Vernon, Illinois, thinking:

"This is crazy! Here I am, desperately attempting to hide my dirty little habit from my Sunday school teacher, when Jesus my Savior sees every single time I light up!" Needless to say, this event would soon play a big part in abandoning tobacco!

■ **We are to refrain from judging others.**

"Therefore judge nothing before the time, until the Lord come, who both will bring to light the hidden things of darkness, and will make manifest the counsels of the hearts: and then shall every man have praise of God" (1 Cor. 4:5).

Surely few words are more important to understand in regards to the Rapture than that of judging! In essence, there are two extremes in judging, and both are equally and totally unscriptural. These are: (1) ever judging, and (2) never judging. Consider:

> **Ever Judging:** This is legalism, which demands that others must abide by my standards, that is, what I personally think is truth!

> **Never Judging:** This is post-modernism, which denies one must live by any set of standards, for there is no absolute truth!

We now overview each position in some detail:

A. **Ever judging**—American churches suffered much from the terrible virus of legalism during the 1960s and 1970s. Permit me now to offer two examples of this "my way or the highway" philosophy from our own ministry here in Lynchburg, Virginia.

1. Our college choir was invited to conduct a concert in a certain large church, which invitation they accepted. However, just prior to the set date, the choir leader received a letter from the host pastor listing three restrictions which had to be met. These were:

> **No slacks!** All young ladies must wear dresses.

> **No tracks!** No pre-recorded music would be allowed.

> **No blacks!** (Comment not necessary)

> Our church (the Thomas Road Baptist Church) responded as follows:

"Sir, regarding your 'no slacks, no tracks, and no blacks'—no thanks!"

2. The late Dr. Jerry Falwell was scheduled to preach in another church, and was talking with the host pastor just before the morning worship service when he noticed a brief confrontation occurring in the church lobby. It seemed a group of "Jesus People" (as they were known back then) had been stopped from entering the auditorium. When he inquired about this, the pastor explained:

"Brother Jerry, we have strict rules in this church! No male is allowed to enter with long hair, and just look at these street vagabonds! However, in the goodness of our heart we have made a barber shop in the basement, and if they agree to have a decent haircut they will be allowed to enter the auditorium, but must sit in the very back pews."

Well, after a moment of sheer frustration and unbelief, Dr. Falwell responded:

"Preacher, here's how this salvation thing works—*first*, you get them **saved**, *then* if need be, you get them **shaved**!" Really!

B. **Never judging**—A religious poll, taken some years ago found the most quoted verse in the Bible was John 3:16. No surprise. However, a more recent poll revealed that among young people, the verse was Matthew 7:1: *"Judge not, that ye be not judged."*

This has been interpreted to mean that no Christian has the right to judge any other believer for any course of action. If this be the case then a church member who was openly sleeping with a woman who was not his wife would be as welcome in a Bible fellowship group as a man who dearly loved and was faithful to his wife! I think not! In fact the apostle Paul soundly condemns this perverted thinking in the strongest way possible. Note his rebuke to the leaders in the Corinthian church who were tolerating gross sin on the part of a church member:

"It is actually reported that there is sexual immorality among you, and such sexual immorality as is not even named among the Gentiles—that a man has his father's wife! And you are puffed up, and have not rather mourned, that he who has done this deed might be taken away from among you. For I indeed, as absent in body but present in spirit, have already judged (as though I were present) him who has so done this deed. In the name of our Lord Jesus Christ, when you are gathered together, along with my spirit, with the power of our Lord Jesus Christ, deliver such a one to Satan for the destruction of the flesh, that his spirit may be saved in the day of the Lord Jesus.

Your glorying is not good. Do you not know that a little leaven leavens the whole lump? Therefore purge out the old leaven, that you may be a new lump, since you truly are unleavened. For indeed Christ, our Passover, was sacrificed for us. Therefore let us keep the feast, not with old leaven, nor with the leaven of malice and wickedness, but with the unleavened bread of sincerity and truth" (1 Cor. 5:1-8).

But back to the Matthew 7:1 verse. What exactly did Jesus mean? Who was He addressing? Here *context* is all-important. Actually He had in mind the wicked Pharisees, as identified by the following words—

"For with what judgment you judge, you will be judged; and with the measure you use, it will be measured back to you. And why do you look at the speck in your brother's eye, but do not consider the plank in your own eye? Or how can you say to your brother, 'Let me remove the speck from your eye'; and look, a plank is in your own eye? Hypocrite! First remove the plank from your own eye, and then you will see clearly to remove the speck from your brother's eye" (Matt. 7:2-5).

It should be observed He did *not* condemn judging as such, but stipulated that the one passing judgment must first judge himself! As an example: Imagine a man condemning another person for slipping a 25-cent washcloth into his suitcase upon leaving a hotel room, when the critic was at the same time driving a $250,000 Rolls Royce that he had stolen!

C. Having said all this, consider this overall summary in regards to judging:

  1. We must always remember that God and God alone is the ultimate Judge (Psa. 75:7).

  2. This means that someday He will judge each of us (Rom. 14:10-12; 1 Cor. 5:12).

  3. We are to refrain from judging the motive of another believer who may have done something we could not fully accept, or hold some theological view slightly different from our own view. An example of this might be the mode of baptism.

> *"When you get to heaven, you will likely view,*
> *Folks up there whose presence will be a shock to you.*
> *But, keep it very quiet, do not even stare,*
> *For, there will be many folks surprised to see you there!"*

  Allow me (HLW) to offer a final illustration at this point. Over the years it has been, and continues to be, my theological position that the gift of tongues, along with the other sign gifts (prophecy, healing, miracles, etc.) has been phased out with the completion of the perfect gift—the Bible itself.

  Why, though, do many sincere Christians feel these gifts are for today? I simply do not know, but I have long since determined *never* to question the *motive* of those dedicated believers who do!

  And the bottom line? Just this—we are to give the same benefit of doubt to those we disagree with that we would expect from them!

  4. We must judge in the spirit of meekness, lest we also be tempted to do the same thing (Gal. 6:1).

  5. We are not called upon to judge unbelievers for their sins of drinking, immorality, etc., but rather to present the claims of Christ (1 Cor. 5:12, 13)!

■ **We are to love believers and all men.**

"And the Lord make you to increase and abound in love one toward another, and toward all men ... To the end he may stablish your hearts ... at the coming of our Lord Jesus Christ with all his saints" (1 Thess. 3:12, 13).

We note Paul does not admonish us to like all believers, but to love them. Love may be defined as that act of one Christian seeking the highest good for another Christian. Thus, it is possible to love those we might not especially like!

An unknown poet has observed:

> To live above with those we love,
> Oh, that will then be glory.
> But to live below with those we know;
> Well, that's a different story!

During one of his confrontations with the Pharisees, Jesus was asked the following: *"Then one of them, a lawyer, asked Him a question, testing Him, and saying, 'Teacher, which is the great commandment in the law?'"* (Mt. 22:35-36).

The Savior then answered: *"'You shall love the Lord your God with all your heart, with all your soul, and with all your mind.' This is the first and great commandment. And the second is like it: 'You shall love your neighbor as yourself.' On these two commandments hang all the Law and the Prophets"* (Mt. 22:37-40).

So then, up to this point biblical love involved loving others as you love yourself. But shortly after this event, in the upper room, Jesus elevates this love to the absolute highest degree possible. Note His words: *"A new commandment I give to you, that you love one another; as I have loved you, that you also love one another. By this all will know that you are My disciples, if you have love for one another"* (Jn. 13:34-35).

Thus, two kinds of love: (1) I love you as I love myself, and (2) I love you as Christ loves me! This degree of love is only possible through the indwelling Holy Spirit (Rom. 5:5).

The love described here is *agapao*, which love is not dependent upon the beauty of the object being loved! There is a make-believe story which serves to illustrate this incredible divine love. It involved a young girl who was beautiful, brilliant and talented, but also very bitter. The reason for this bitterness? She was blind!

A young man, however, had fallen deeply in love with this young woman and desired very much to marry her. But his many proposals were always rejected. "Why?" he wanted to know. "Because I'm blind," she replied. "Yes, I know but please believe me, I love you even more and long to take care of you." "I'm sure you do, but because of my blindness, I'd make a very poor wife and mother." And so it was.

But then, miracle of all miracles, someone donated their eyes to her! Now, she could see! Unbounded joy soon filled her heart. All traces of bitterness were gone! However, suddenly she discovered an amazing thing—her lover was also blind. He had never told her about this. But no matter. Soon the proposals began again.

"Dear one, now that you can see, let's set a date for the wedding." "Yes, I do have my eyesight but I didn't realize you were also blind. I'm so sorry but we still cannot be married, for every time I look at you, I'll be reminded of my former terrible blindness." The heartbroken young man understood her rejection and agreed the marriage was not to be. Soon the couple went their separate ways.

A year later he received a wedding invitation from her, along with a note stating she had met and fallen in love with a wonderful man and asked if her former lover could be an honored guest at their wedding.

He quickly responded, explaining this would not be possible as it was becoming more difficult for him to find a guide to lead him around. He then reassured her of his continued prayers that God would grant many years of glorious happiness to both the new bride and groom! Before sealing the letter, he added the following postscript: "I would ask but one small favor. Please take special care … of my eyes!"

Some years ago, a group of theologians were asked what they thought was the greatest gospel hymn ever written. The men, almost to a man, chose Isaac Watt's musical masterpiece as seen below. Note the word *love* appears three times!

> *When I survey the wondrous cross*
> *On which the Prince of glory died,*
> *My richest gain I count but loss,*
> *And pour contempt on all my pride.*
>
> *Forbid it, Lord, that I should boast,*
> *Save in the death of Christ my God!*
> *All the vain things that charm me most,*
> *I sacrifice them to His blood.*
>
> *See from His head, His hands, His feet,*
> *Sorrow and love flow mingled down!*
> *Did e'er such love and sorrow meet,*
> *Or thorns compose so rich a crown?*
>
> *Were the whole realm of nature mine,*
> *That were a present far too small;*
> *Love so amazing, so divine,*
> *Demands my soul, my life, my all.*

■ **We are to comfort the bereaved.**

"For the Lord himself shall descend from heaven with a shout, with the voice of the archangel, and with the trump of God: and the dead in Christ shall rise first: Then we which are alive and remain shall be caught up together with them in the clouds, to meet the Lord in the air: and so shall we ever be with the Lord. Wherefore comfort one another with these words" (1 Thess. 4:16-18).

"Praise be to the God and Father of our Lord Jesus Christ! In his great mercy he has given us new birth into a living hope through the resurrection of Jesus Christ from the dead, and into

an inheritance that can never perish, spoil or fade. This inheritance is kept in heaven for you, who through faith are shielded by God's power until the coming of the salvation that is ready to be revealed in the last time. In all this you greatly rejoice, though now for a little while you may have had to suffer grief in all kinds of trials. These have come so that the proven genuineness of your faith—of greater worth than gold, which perishes even though refined by fire—may result in praise, glory and honor when Jesus Christ is revealed" (1 Peter 1:3-7, NIV).

Henry Wadsworth Longfellow (Feb. 27, 1807-Mar. 24, 1882), was one of America's most celebrated poets and educators. He authored great literary works including *Paul Revere's Ride, Evangeline, The Village Blacksmith,* and other poems. But the famous author was deeply troubled. Some sadness no doubt could be traced back to the tragic deaths of both his first and second wife.

    A. In 1835, Mary Potter died after suffering a miscarriage.

    B. In 1861, Frances Appleton was burned to death in an accidental fire.

In addition to these tragedies, he was grieved over an ongoing event which might well divide and even destroy the nation itself, namely, the brutal and bloody American Civil War. Some of all this would provide the background for his much loved Christmas hymn, *I Heard the Bells on Christmas Day.* The words are printed below.

Note the attitude change which occurs in this song:

    A. In stanzas 1-3 he pours out his grievous hurt.

    B. In stanzas 4-5 he lifts up his glorious hope.

> *I heard the bells on Christmas day*
> *Their old familiar carols play,*
> *And wild and sweet the words repeat*
> *Of peace on earth, good will to men.*
>
> *I thought how, as the day had come,*
> *The belfries of all Christendom*
> *Had rolled along the unbroken song*
> *Of peace on earth, good will to men.*
>
> *And in despair I bowed my head:*
> *'There is no peace on earth, ' I said*
> *'For hate is strong, and mocks the song*
> *Of peace on earth, good will to men.'*
>
> *Then pealed the bells more loud and deep:*
> *'God is not dead, nor doth He sleep;*
> *The wrong shall fail, the right prevail,*
> *With peace on earth, good will to men.'*

Till, ringing, singing on its way,
The world revolved from night to day
A voice, a chime, a chant sublime,
Of peace on earth, good will to men.

Thus, when Christ returns, He will solve all problems, answer all questions, heal all hurts, and right all wrongs! Oh yes, John the apostle realized all this, causing him to end the word of God by writing, *"even so, come Lord Jesus!"* (Rev. 22:21)

We are to center our thoughts on heaven.

"If then you were raised with Christ, seek those things which are above, where Christ is, sitting at the right hand of God. Set your mind on things above, not on things on the earth. For you died, and your life is hidden with Christ in God. When Christ who is our life appears, then you also will appear with Him in glory" (Col. 3:1-4).

"Do not lay up for yourselves treasures on earth, where moth and rust destroy and where thieves break in and steal; but lay up for yourselves treasures in heaven, where neither moth nor rust destroys and where thieves do not break in and steal. For where your treasure is, there your heart will be also" (Mt. 6:19-21).

"Well, thinking about heaven? I guess that is okay, but isn't it a fact a person can be so heavenly minded that he's no earthly good?" Have you ever heard this? But probably, if the truth were known, for every Christian in this category, there are at least ten other believers who are so earthly minded that they are no heavenly good!

Actually, it is not only proper but actually spiritually profitable to ponder our glorious destination! In the spring of 1971 I was pastoring a Baptist church in northern Indiana when my wife began to do certain things which, from an outsider, seemed very strange indeed! First, from an Atlas she located a city in the southern part of our country. She then sent letters to the city officials, requesting detailed information about this place:

A. What was the average weather like?
B. The cost of living?
C. The population?
D. The number and quality of elementary schools?
E. The cost of homes?
F. What were the shopping facilities (oh yes, especially this)?

But what would possibly prompt her to suddenly become very interested in a city she had only previously never even heard of, nor did she know anyone living there? In truth, these actions were not strange in the least if one knew the background. And the explanation? Well, the city was Lynchburg, Virginia, where several weeks prior to all this, I had been invited to conduct a week of Bible studies for the students enrolled in a newly-founded school, known as Lynchburg Baptist College.

It was during that week that its founder and pastor of Thomas Road Baptist Church, Dr. Jerry Falwell, offered me a position to come and create a two-year Bible program for those who only wanted to study the scriptures. So, as a result, both Sue and I had been diligently seeking God's will in this matter!

Thus, my wife's actions were perfectly natural. In a nutshell she desired to learn as much as possible concerning what became her future home. How much more should believers desire to know in regards to their eternal heavenly home!

"For here we have no continuing city, but we seek the one to come" (Heb. 13:14).

Samuel Stennett's beautiful hymn aptly summarizes this longing of the soul:

> *On Jordan's stormy banks I stand,*
> *and cast a wishful eye*
> *to Canaan's fair and happy land,*
> *where my possessions lie.*

> <u>**Refrain:**</u>
> *I am bound for the promised land,*
> *I am bound for the promised land;*
> *oh, who will come and go with me?*
> *I am bound for the promised land.*

> *O'er all those wide extended plains*
> *shines one eternal day;*
> *there God the Son forever reigns,*
> *and scatters night away.*

> *No chilling winds or poisonous breath*
> *can reach that healthful shore;*
> *sickness and sorrow, pain and death,*
> *are felt and feared no more.*

> *When I shall reach that happy place,*
> *I'll be forever blest,*
> *for I shall see my Father's face,*
> *and in his bosom rest.*

FOUR COMMANDS TO KEEP WHILE AWAITING THE RAPTURE

Believers in the early church were consistently told to be on the lookout for the coming of Christ. They were also given clear, practical instructions on what they should be doing in light of this imminent event. The most straightforward passage in the New Testament concerning what we should be doing if we believe Jesus is coming soon is in Peter's first letter:

"The end of all things is near; therefore, be of sound judgment and sober spirit for the purpose of prayer. Above all, keep fervent in your love for one another, because love covers a multitude of sins. Be hospitable to one another without complaint. As each one has received a special gift, employ it in serving one another as good stewards of the manifold grace of God" (1 Peter 4:7-10).

Notice the word *therefore* in verse 7. Peter is saying that the end of the world is coming, *therefore* here's what we should be doing. This passage emphasizes four things we should do if we believe that the end is coming soon. Dr. Mark Hitchcock suggests:

KEEP YOUR HEAD CLEAR: PRAY FOR OTHERS
As we approach the coming apocalypse, more and more people are going to get caught up in the prophetic frenzy. People will be tempted to quit their jobs, sell all their possessions, and go wait on a mountaintop in their pajamas for Jesus to come.

But the Word tells us that in view of the end of all things we are to be "earnest." This word literally means "not drunk." In other words, we are to be sober-minded, clearheaded, and mentally alert for the purpose of prayer. Believing that Christ could come back today should spur us on to a sober, disciplined prayer life.

KEEP YOUR HEART WARM: LOVE OTHERS
The badge of Christianity is love (John 13:34-35). As we see the end approaching we are to love one another with a "deep love." The word translated *deep* was used in ancient times of a horse at full gallop when its muscles were stretched to the limit. Peter is saying that our love for one another is to be stretched out but never reaching its breaking point.

KEEP YOUR HOME OPEN: SHOW HOSPITALITY TO STRANGERS
One of the signs of the second coming of Christ according to Jesus is that *"the love of many will grow cold"* (Matt. 24:12, NLT). In light of this, believers are called to show their love in a concrete way by reaching out in Christian love to strangers. This beautiful Christian virtue is mentioned specifically six times in the New Testament (Rom. 12:13; 1 Tim. 3:2; 5:9-10; Titus 1:8; Heb. 13:1-3; 1 Peter 4:9). As this world becomes a colder and more isolated place, we are to keep our homes open and show the warmth of Christ to strangers.

KEEP YOUR HANDS BUSY: USE YOUR SPIRITUAL GIFTS
Every believer in Jesus Christ has at least one spiritual gift. Spiritual gifts are supernatural empowerments that God has given to His children to serve the body of Christ.

As we see the curtain about to rise on the final act of history, we hear the Lord calling us to keep our hands busy, using for His service the gifts He has given us.

AN EVENT WHICH COULD WELL TRIGGER THE RAPTURE
Does anything have to happen before the Rapture can take place?

The surprising answer seems to be yes! One final event must transpire and that event is the adding of the last repenting sinner into the body of Christ by the Holy Spirit. Thus when the body is complete, the Head will appear, or, to use another scriptural analogy, the Bridegroom will come for His beloved bride. The entire book of Ephesians seems to suggest this. See especially 1:10, 22, 23; 2:21; 4:4, 13, 16; 5:22-33.

A very practical truth may be seen here. According to Acts 2, the first convert was added to the body of Christ at Pentecost. What an occasion that must have been, with 3,000 answering Peter's "altar call." And God had provided 120 "personal workers" to deal with them (Acts 1:15; 2:1). We know that God Himself keeps all records. Perhaps someday at the judgment seat of Christ one of these 120 will hear the Master say: "Well done, thou good and faithful servant. You led the first individual into that spiritual body!" If this be true, and if Christ's coming is at hand, it is entirely possible that a soul winner reading these very words might one day hear similar words from Jesus: "Well done, thou good and faithful servant. You led the last individual into that spiritual body!" At any rate, someday a soul winner will point some seeking sinner to the Savior and it will all be over!

POSSIBLE REACTIONS FOLLOWING THE RAPTURE

In his well-known book *The Late Great Planet Earth*, Hal Lindsey suggests several possible conversations at the moment of the Rapture:

- "There I was, driving down the freeway and all of a sudden the place went crazy … cars going in all directions … and not one of them had a driver. I mean it was wild! I think we've got an invasion from outer space!"

- "It was the last quarter of the championship game and the other side was ahead. Our boys had the ball. We made a touchdown and tied it up. The crowd went crazy. Only one minute to go and they fumbled—our quarterback recovered—and he was about a yard from the goal when—zap—no more quarterback—completely gone, just like that!"

- "It was puzzling—very puzzling. I was teaching my course in the Philosophy of Religion when all of a sudden three of my students vanished. They simply vanished! They were quite argumentative—always trying to prove their point from the Bible. No great loss to the class. However, I do find this disappearance very difficult to explain."

- "As an official spokesman for the United Nations I wish to inform all peace-loving people of the world that we are making every human effort to assist those nations whose leaders have disappeared. We have issued a general declaration of condemnation in the General Assembly concerning these heads of state. Their irresponsibility is shocking."

- "My dear friends in the congregation, bless you for coming to church today. I know that many of you have lost loved ones in this unusual disappearance of so many people. However, I believe that God's judgment has come upon them for their continued dissension and quarreling with the great advances of the church in our century. Now that the reactionaries are removed, we can progress toward our great and glorious goal of uniting all mankind into a brotherhood of reconciliation and understanding."

■ "You really want to know what I think? I think all that talk about the Rapture and going to meet Jesus Christ in the air wasn't crazy after all. I don't know about you, brother, but I'm going to find myself a Bible and read all those verses my wife underlined. I wouldn't listen to her while she was here, and now she's—I don't know where she is." (Zondervan Publishers, pp. 136, 137, 1972)

Certainly the believers will be missed. It is evident from the Bible that the sudden disappearance of both Enoch and Elijah (two Old Testament types of the Rapture) caused considerable confusion and alarm among their friends.

"By faith Enoch was translated that he should not see death; and was not found, because God had translated him" (Heb. 11:5).

Especially interesting are the words, *"and was not found."* Enoch was doubtless the object of a great manhunt!

The Scriptures describe the later translation of Elijah in even greater detail, as the citizens of Jericho ask Elisha about the disappearance of his master:

"Sir," they said, "just say the word and fifty of our best athletes will search the wilderness for your master; perhaps the Spirit of the Lord has left him on some mountain or in some ravine." "No," Elisha said, "don't bother." But they kept urging until he was embarrassed, and finally said, "All right, go ahead." Then fifty men searched for three days, but didn't find him" (2 Kings 2:16, 17, TLB).

How much more confusion and alarm will come from the sudden and mysterious disappearance of literally millions of men and women, boys and girls.

Many years ago, I (HLW) experienced firsthand just a taste of this future confusion and alarm in regard to the Rapture.

It all began when a close friend of mine invited me to join him in a vacation to Estes Park, Colorado, which I did. After driving many long and hot (no air conditioning) hours we finally arrived at our destination, nestled high in the Rocky Mountains. Back then (in the mid-fifties) two things could have been said about Estes Park—first, by day it was one of the most beautiful spots in America, and, two, by night it proved to be the most desolate area in the universe!

After grabbing a bite to eat we secured a motel at the edge of the little town and settled down for the night.

Now my friend in those days had two bad habits—first, he smoked, and second, he snored. At any rate, about midnight he began indulging his second bad habit. Never had I heard such snoring. I made several vain attempts to arouse him. Finally, after enduring this for a while, I decided enough was enough! So, I quietly slipped out of bed and clothed only in my Fruit of the Looms, made my way to the back seat of our car and soon was fast asleep. Inasmuch as the night was dark and the car only a few feet from the motel, I had no concern about modesty.

Meanwhile, back in the room, my friend awakened to indulge in his first bad habit. Of course he soon noticed my bed was empty and a quick check revealed that I was not in the bathroom either!

He thought this disappearance was strange indeed, but realizing I was a student at the Moody Bible Institute preparing for the ministry concluded I might have been out witnessing to a hoot owl, for all he knew.

But suddenly he spotted my trousers, shirt, shoes, watch and wallet. Suffice to say my friend got his trousers on pretty fast and began looking for me. Leaving the motel room he peered into the car but for some reason, did not see me. According to his testimony, the next hour and a half were the most terrifying 90 minutes of his entire life!

After leaving the car he walked the entire length of Estes Park, a distance of some two miles, attempting to find me. He said later there was absolutely no one on the street, no service station open, not a single car that drove by, and, not a dog that barked.

Upon reaching the edge of the city he turned to retrace his steps and was suddenly struck with a paralyzing fear—the Rapture had taken place and he had been left behind!

What would he do? What should he do? Indeed, what could he do? In his own words:

"I thought the best thing for me to do was to get back to the motel room as quickly as possible and call my godly wife in Quincy, Illinois. If she didn't answer the phone, I knew I was in big trouble!"

So, he began to run, shaking, shivering, and sweating, all at the same time. But as he stumbled past our car he looked in again, and this time, saw me. Of course, I was totally unaware of what had just transpired, but I vividly recall the car door opening, and being seized by two big hands, and hearing both a desperate and pitiful cry:

"ALL RIGHT, HAROLD, LET'S SETTLE THIS THING RIGHT HERE AND NOW!"

I got out of the car utterly stunned. What on earth was he babbling about? Was I just dreaming? I would soon find out a few minutes later as we sat on the edge of my bed. No, I was not dreaming, but he slowly related to me the details of his very real nightmare:

"Harold," he began, "I have been suffering the torments of the damned for the past 90 minutes. I honestly believed the Rapture had happened and that I was doomed!"

With shaking voice he continued, "Even though being raised in a Christian home, I'm not sure where I stand before God. But I do know I want to get things straight right now! So, you explain what has to be done. Go back to Adam and Eve if you must, but I'm not leaving this room until I know I'm ready for the Rapture!"

So, as briefly and clearly as possible, I explained God's simple plan of salvation. All the above transpired over fifty years go. But how could I possibly forget kneeling beside that bed in a darkened motel room in Estes Park, Colorado, and hearing my dad ask Christ to come into his heart!

A GRAND AND GLORIOUS CONCLUSION IN REGARD TO THE RAPTURE

In closing this chapter on the Rapture, consider the words of a prominent German theologian, Erich Sauer:

> The present age is Easter time. It begins with the resurrection of the Redeemer (Matt. 28), and ends with the resurrection of the redeemed (1 Thess. 4; 1 Cor. 15).
>
> Between lies the spiritual 'resurrection' of those called into life (Rom. 6:4-11; Col. 3:1). So we live between two Easters, as those who have been raised between two resurrections, as burning and shining lights … And in the power of the first Easter we go to meet the last Easter. The resurrection of the Head guarantees the resurrection of the members. The tree of life of the resurrection bears fully ripe fruit. (*The Triumph of the Crucified*, Eerdmans, 1955, p. 101)

EVENT 2 THE JUDGMENT SEAT OF CHRIST

INTRODUCTION

As a boy I had a totally erroneous view concerning the subject of judgment. In my mind I pictured a celestial courtroom located somewhere beyond the stars where all the world's inhabitants would line up single file in front of a towering throne. An angel would then appear with a set of balancing scales. Each name would be solemnly called out: "John Jones, born 1900, died 1950 step forward!"

As Jones stood there, all his recorded good works would be placed on one side of the scales and his bad deeds on the opposite side. If the good works outweighed the bad, then a much-relieved Jones would enter a door marked "heaven"; but if the reverse were true, poor Jones was designated to the door marked "hell."

Let it be stated here that one will find this concept of future judgment in the same biblical chapter that talks about Rudolph the Red-Nosed Reindeer!

Of course nothing could be further from the truth. In reality, there are a number of biblical judgments, some already past, some going on at the present time, and others yet to occur.

We begin by looking at some of these judgments.

BIBLICAL JUDGMENTS IN GENERAL

■ Past Judgments
  There were three all-important and absolutely unique ones:
  A. First Judgment
    Its uniqueness can be seen in the place, parties, punishment and promise involved:

1. The place

   It occurred in the most beautiful "courtroom" ever to exist on planet Earth—the Garden of Eden!

2. The parties

   There were five defendants. Four were guilty of disobeying God's first command—*"Don't eat of the tree of the knowledge of good and evil."* The fifth was not directly involved but was grouped with the four. These five were:

   a. Adam

   b. Eve

   c. The serpent

   d. Satan

   e. Mother Nature

3. The punishment

   a. Regarding Adam

      Backbreaking labor in his efforts to till the soil of a cursed area of ground

   b. Regarding Eve

      To experience pain in childbirth

   c. Regarding the serpent

      To crawl upon its belly through the dust and dirt

   d. Regarding the devil

      To have his head crushed by the coming Messiah

   e. Regarding Mother Nature

      Even though innocent of the crime, her domain would nevertheless be subjected to dust storms, ice storms, earthquakes, tsunamis, tornadoes, hurricanes, etc.

4. The promise

   Someday the Messiah (seed of the woman) would appear to:

   a. Redeem all sinners

   b. Restore Mother Nature's domain to its former glory

B. Second Judgment

   The Flood in Noah's day—this was the most destructive judgment in human history.

C. Third Judgment

   The Calvary judgment—note its uniqueness:

   1. The one "on the bench" was also the Father of the one being judged.

   2. Both Father (Judge) and defendant (Jesus) had previously agreed that even though the Son had nothing whatsoever to do with the original sinners (Adam and Eve), He, who knew no sin, would become sin and die for all sinners throughout human history.

■ **Present-Day Judgments**

According to the Scriptures, there are two ongoing judgments, one corporate, and the other personal.

A. Corporate

The book of Revelation opens up with a vision of Jesus, dressed in His Great High Priestly garments in heaven, both commending, and if need be, condemning the activities of His local churches.

B. Personal

Let us suppose the Holy Spirit has convicted a believer of a certain sin in his/her life. The following action will then transpire:

1. The believer's positive reaction

As a result of this conviction, the decision is made to, as it were, "settle out of court." This is quietly accomplished by first admitting the sin and then abandoning it. If and when this happens, case closed!

2. The believer's negative reaction

"Thanks, but no thanks! Unlike Moses of old, I'd rather enjoy the pleasures of sin for a season!'" Oh? Big mistake!

3. The Lord's reaction

For we know Him who said, "Vengeance is Mine, I will repay," says the Lord. And again, "The Lord will judge His people." It is a fearful thing to fall into the hands of the living God" (Heb. 10:30, 31).

■ **Future Judgments**

A number of key judgments will take place in the future. These will include that of the Sheep and Goats, ten virgins, judgments upon the antichrist, fallen angels, and Satan himself.

But let it be said the two most important divine judgments in the future are: (1) the Great White Throne Judgment, and, (2) the Judgment Seat of Christ.

Every individual on earth today and the millions who have gone before will someday appear before one of these throne judgments. The decision is therefore not whether one is to be judged, but rather where this judgment will take place.

Details concerning the Great White Throne judgment can be seen in Rev. 20:11-15. In passing, however, let it be said that only the unsaved will stand before this throne, the purpose and results being to determine degrees of punishment in hell.

We now will discuss the most important one to Christians.

THE JUDGMENT SEAT OF CHRIST IN PARTICULAR

During many of my forty-plus teaching years here at Liberty University, I often began each new semester with the following announcement:

"Just to alert you up front, there will be two final tests in this course! No, I was not referring to a mid-term and final exam. Yes, there will be a mid-term one, but again I repeat, *two* final tests! Now let me explain: I'll conduct the first final and we'll know just how much you learned. Professor Jesus will conduct the second final exam and discover what you *did* with what you *learned*."

THE MEANING AND BACKGROUND OF THE BEMA JUDGMENT SEAT OF CHRIST

The Greek word *bema* (translated "judgment seat" in the KJV) was a familiar term to the people of Paul's day. Dr. Lehman Strauss writes:

> "In the large Olympic arenas, there was an elevated seat on which the judge of the contest sat. After the contests were over, the successful competitors would assemble before the *bema* to receive their rewards or crowns. The bema was not a judicial bench where someone was condemned; it was a reward seat. Likewise the Judgment Seat of Christ is not a judicial bench. The Christian life is a race, and the divine umpire is watching every contestant. After the church has run her course, He will gather every member before the *bema* for the purpose of examining each one and giving the proper reward to each." (Lehman Strauss, *God's Plan for the Future*, Grand Rapids: Zondervan, p. 111, used by permission).

The apostle Paul seemed to have such an Olympic arena in mind when he penned Hebrews 12:1:

"Wherefore seeing we also are compassed about with so great a cloud of witnesses, let us lay aside every weight, and the sin which doth so easily beset us, and let us run with patience the race that is set before us."

This amazing human being was many things. He was a missionary, a soul winner, a pastor, a great theologian, a tentmaker, etc. But in his spare time he also seemed to be a sports lover. Often in his writings Paul uses sports as an analogy to get his point across. For example:

Wrestling. *"For we wrestle not against flesh and blood, but against principalities, against powers, against the rulers of the darkness of this world, against spiritual wickedness in high places"* (Eph. 6:12).

Boxing. *"I have fought a good fight …"* (2 Tim. 4:7). *"… So fight I, not as one that beateth the air"* (1 Cor. 9:26).

Racing. *"Know ye not that they which run in a race run all, but one receiveth the prize? So run that ye may obtain … I therefore so run …"* (1 Cor. 9:24, 26).

Here in Hebrews 12 Paul chooses the third analogy—that of a footrace. This chapter may be titled "God's Superbowl." J. Vernon McGee writes:

> "The Christian life is likened to a Greek race. Along the way the Christian as a soldier is to stand, as a believer he is to walk, and as an athlete he is to run. One day he will fly—space travel to the New Jerusalem" (*Studies in Hebrews*, p. 240).

At the time Paul wrote, King Herod had built a throne like seat in the theater at Caesarea (his headquarters) where he sat to view the games and make speeches to the people.

THE TIME, PLACE AND JUDGE AT THE BEMA JUDGMENT

- **The Time**
  Dr. J. Dwight Pentecost observes:

The event herein described takes place immediately following the translation of the church out of this earth's sphere. There are several considerations that support this. (1) In the first place, according to Luke 14:14 reward is associated with the resurrection. Since, according to 1 Thess. 4:13-17, the resurrection is an integral part of the translation, reward must be a part of that program. (2) When the Lord returns to the earth with His bride to reign, the bride is seen to be already rewarded. This is observed in Rev. 19:8, where it must be observed that the "righteousness of the saints" is plural and cannot refer to the imparted righteousness of Christ, which is the believer's portion, but the righteousness which have survived examination and have become the basis of reward. (3) In 1 Cor. 4:5; 2 Tim. 4:8; and Rev. 22:12 the reward is associated with "that day," that is, the day in which He comes for His own. Thus it must be observed that the rewarding of the church must take place between the Rapture and the revelation of Christ to the earth. (*Things to Come*, p. 220, Zondervan)

■ **The Place**

It is scarcely necessary to point out that this examination must take place in the sphere of the heavenlies. It is said in 1 Thess. 4:17 that *"we shall be caught up … in the clouds, to meet the Lord in the air."* Since the bema follows this translation, the "air" must be the scene of it. This is further supported by 2 Cor. 5:1-8, where Paul is describing events that take place when the believer is *"absent from the body, and … present with the Lord."* Thus this event must take place in the Lord's presence in the sphere of the "heavenlies." (Ibid.)

■ **The Judge**

There are four key verses that clearly state the divinely appointed judge at the bema is the Lord Jesus Christ Himself! Note:

"For the Father judgeth no man, but hath committed all judgment unto the Son" (John 5:22).

"Because he hath appointed a day, in the which he will judge the world in righteousness by that man whom he hath ordained; whereof he hath given assurance unto all men, in that he hath raised him from the dead" (Acts 17:31).

"But why dost thou judge thy brother? or why dost thou set at nought thy brother? for we shall all stand before the judgment seat of Christ" (Rom. 14:10).

"For we must all appear before the judgment seat of Christ; that every one may receive the things done in his body, according to that he hath done, whether it be good or bad" (2 Cor. 5:10).

THE PURPOSE OF THE BEMA JUDGMENT

■ **Negative considerations:**

The purpose of the bema judgment is not to determine whether a particular individual enters heaven or not, for every man's eternal destiny is already determined before he leaves this life.

The purpose of the bema judgment is not to punish believers for sins committed either before or after their salvation. The scriptures are very clear that no child of God will have to answer for his sins after this life.

"He hath not dealt with us after our sins; nor rewarded us according to our iniquities. For as the heaven is high above the earth, so great is his mercy toward them that fear him. As far as the east is from the west, so far hath he removed our transgressions from us" (Psa. 103:10-12).

"… Thou hast in love to my soul delivered it from the pit of corruption: for thou hast cast all my sins behind thy back" (Isa. 38:17).

"I have blotted out … thy transgressions, and … thy sins …" (Isa. 44:22).

"… Thou wilt cast all their sins into the depths of the sea" (Micah 7:19).

"For I will be merciful … and their sins and their iniquities will I remember no more" (Heb. 8:12).

"… The blood of Jesus Christ his Son cleanseth us from all sin" (1 John 1:7).

■ **Positive considerations:**

What then is the purpose of the bema judgment? In 1 Cor. 4:2 Paul says that all Christians should conduct themselves as faithful stewards of God: *"Moreover it is required in stewards, that a man be found faithful."*

The apostle Peter later writes a similar way: *"Minister … as good stewards of the manifold grace of God"* (1 Pet. 4:10).

In the New Testament world, a steward was the manager of a large household or estate. He was appointed by the owner and was entrusted to keep the estate running smoothly. He had the power to hire and fire and to spend and save, being answerable to the owner alone. His only concern was that periodic meeting with his master, at which time he was required to account for the condition of the estate up to that point.

With this background in mind, it may be said that someday at the bema judgment all stewards will stand before their Lord and Master and be required to give an account of the way they have used their privileges and responsibilities from the moment of their conversion.

In conclusion, it can be seen that:

    A. In the past, God dealt with us as sinners (Rom. 5:6-8; 1 Cor. 6:9-11; Eph. 2:1-3)

    B. In the present, God deals with us as sons (Rom. 8:14; Heb. 12:5-11; 1 John 3:1, 2)

    C. In the future, God will deal with us (at the bema) as stewards.

THE MANNER IN WHICH CHRIST WILL JUDGE HIS PEOPLE AT THE BEMA JUDGMENT

Dr. Mark Hitchcock observes:

BELIEVERS WILL BE JUDGED FAIRLY.

The Lord will take into account how long we have been saved as well as the opportunities and abilities he has given us. The parable of the workers in the vineyard (Matt. 20:1-16) teaches that those who enter the Lord's service later in life can receive the same reward as the "all-day" workers. The righteous judge will make no mistakes. He bases his rewards on what we did with the resources and time at our disposal.

BELIEVERS WILL BE JUDGED THOROUGHLY.

The Lord will virtually turn us inside out at the Judgment Seat. He will expose every hidden motive, thought, and deed (1 Cor. 4:5). Nothing will escape the scrutinizing eye of the Savior (Heb. 4:13).

BELIEVERS WILL BE JUDGED IMPARTIALLY.

The Lord is no respecter of persons. *"God does not show favoritism"* (Rom. 2:11). *"God has no favorites who can get away with evil"* (Col. 3:25). The only difference in God's standard of judgment is that those who teach God's Word and lead the Lord's people will be held to a higher degree of accountability (James 3:1; Heb. 13:17).

BELIEVERS WILL BE JUDGED INDIVIDUALLY.

Every believer will stand alone before the Lord. *"Each of us will stand personally before the Judgment Seat of God. Yes, each of us will have to give a personal account to God"* (Rom. 14:10, 12).

Erwin Lutzer captures something of the drama of this scene: "Imagine staring into the face of Christ. Just the two of you, one-on-one! Your entire life is present before you. In a flash you see what He sees. No hiding. No opportunity to put a better spin on what you did. No attorney to represent you. The look in His eyes says it all. Like it or not, that is precisely where you and I shall be someday."

BELIEVERS WILL BE JUDGED GRACIOUSLY.

The fact that we will receive any reward or praise at all is a testimony to God's grace. Jesus is a kind and gracious judge who will reward us all with much more than we could ever imagine (Matt. 20:13-15).

AREAS IN OUR LIVES TO BE TESTED AT THE BEMA JUDGMENT

■ **A General Consideration:**

One of the key passages in this area is that written by the apostle Paul to church in Corinth:

For no one can lay any foundation other than the one already laid, which is Jesus Christ. If anyone builds on this foundation using gold, silver, costly stones, wood, hay or straw, their work will be shown for what it is, because the Day will bring it to light. It will be revealed with fire, and the fire will test the quality of each person's work. If what has been built survives, the builder will receive a reward. If it is burned up, the builder will suffer loss but yet will be saved—even though only as one escaping through the flames" (1 Cor. 3:11-15, NIV).

Let us now attempt to answer the following questions which have been raised regarding these verses.

A. What is the nature of this foundation? What exactly does it consist of? Consider:

A believer has just accepted Christ as Savior. According to this passage, he/she is now placed upon the world's safest, most secure and strongest foundation, consisting of the death, burial and resurrection of Jesus Christ! Jesus concluded His sermon on the Mount by contrasting a man who built his house on sandy soil with the man who built his upon a rock. As long as the weather remained calm and clear both fared well, but when the storm came the first house was washed away, while the second remained! (Mt. 7:24-27)

So it is for those who construct their houses on philosophy, riches, fame, religion, etc. All may fare well while the sun is shining but when the dark clouds of pain, persecution, death, etc. descend, only the rock foundations survive. Hymn writer Robert Keene summarizes this in his beautiful song, *How Firm A Foundation*:

> *How firm a foundation, ye saints of the Lord,*
> *Is laid for your faith in His excellent Word!*
> *What more can He say than to you He hath said,*
> *You, who unto Jesus for refuge have fled?*
>
> *Fear not, I am with thee, O be not dismayed,*
> *For I am thy God and will still give thee aid;*
> *I'll strengthen and help thee, and cause thee to stand*
> *Upheld by My righteous, omnipotent hand.*
>
> *When through the deep waters I call thee to go,*
> *The rivers of woe shall not thee overflow;*
> *For I will be with thee, thy troubles to bless,*
> *And sanctify to thee thy deepest distress.*
>
> *When through fiery trials thy pathways shall lie,*
> *My grace, all sufficient, shall be thy supply;*
> *The flame shall not hurt thee; I only design*
> *Thy dross to consume, and thy gold to refine.*

B.   What role are we to assume as we stand upon this foundation? Simply this: We are to build upon it! Nothing of course can be added or subtracted from the cross and empty tomb foundation for this is the *root* of our redemption. But now comes the *fruit*. Walls, windows, rooms and roofs need to be constructed. Note Paul's words to the church at Ephesus:

"Now, therefore, you are no longer strangers and foreigners, but fellow citizens with the saints and members of the household of God, having been built on the foundation of the apostles and prophets, Jesus Christ Himself being the chief cornerstone, in whom the whole building, being fitted together, grows into a holy temple in the Lord, in whom you also are being built together for a dwelling place of God in the Spirit" (Eph. 2:19-22).

C.   What does the gold, silver, precious stones, wood, hay, stubble represent?

From verse 12 it is apparent that God classifies the works of believers into one of the following six areas: gold, silver, precious stones, wood, hay, stubble. There has been much speculation about the kinds of work down here that will constitute gold or silver up there. But it seems more appropriate to note that the six objects can be readily placed in two categories:

1. Those indestructible and worthy objects which will survive and thrive in the fires. These are the gold, silver, and precious stones.

2. Those destructible and worthless objects which will be totally consumed in the fires. These are the wood, hay, and stubble. Thus, what the fire cannot purify, it destroys, and what the fire cannot destroy, it purifies.

D. Does this passage teach the doctrine of purgatory?

Purgatory is a Roman Catholic belief which says that after death most members of the Roman Church will be required to spend a certain amount of time suffering for their unconfessed sins in a "half-way house" as it were, located somewhere between earth and heaven. This dogma was declared official at the Council of Trent in 1545 A.D.

But what say the Scriptures?

1. First, it must be observed the 1 Cor. 3 passages record the believer's house of service, not the believer himself/herself which will be tested by fire.

2. Second, one of Jesus's final sayings on the cross was the Greek word, *tetelestai*, translated, "it is finished," referring to the plan and price of salvation (Jn. 19:30).

3. Third, the author of Hebrews testified to this completed redemption when he wrote: *"Day after day every priest stands and performs his religious duties; again and again he offers the same sacrifices, which can never take away sins. But when this priest had offered for all time one sacrifice for sins, he sat down at the right hand of God, and since that time he waits for his enemies to be made his footstool. For by one sacrifice he has made perfect forever those who are being made holy"* (Heb. 10:11-14, NIV).

4. Fourth, the supposed biblical passage supporting purgatory is found in a non-canonical book, 2nd Maccabees, which reads, "It is therefore a good and holy thing to pray for the dead that they might be loosed from their sins" (2 Macc. 12:45).

■ **A Specific Consideration:**

In my many years of teaching Bible at Liberty University, I have discovered the following announcement from the professor will guarantee the immediate and undivided attention from the students: "Please note pages 110-125 in your textbook, for your final exam will be taken from the information found there!"

The students quickly mark those pages, grateful that their teacher has alerted them to some basic material that will appear on the last test! With this background in mind, one may view the blessed Father as a kindly disposed "heavenly professor" who has graciously provided us with some key questions which will be asked of us at the final exam, the Judgment Seat of Christ!

As has been previously noted (1 Cor. 3:12, 13) the fire of God will reveal the amount of gold, silver, precious stones, wood, hay, and stubble in our ministry for Him.

Though it is difficult to know just what goes to make up a "golden work" or a "stubble work," we are nevertheless informed of certain general areas in which God is particularly interested. Here then are some of these areas:

A. How we treat other believers

"For God is not unrighteous to forget your work and labour of love, which ye have shewed toward his name, in that ye have ministered to the saints, and do minister" (Heb. 6:10).

"He that receiveth a prophet in the name of a prophet shall receive a prophet's reward; and he that receiveth a righteous man in the name of a righteous man shall receive a righteous man's reward. And whosoever shall give to drink unto one of these little ones a cup of cold water only in the name of a disciple, verily I say unto you, he shall in no wise lose his reward"(Matt. 10:41, 42).

It is tragic but all too factual that often the shabbiest treatment suffered by a believer comes from the hand of another believer.

B. How we exercise our authority over others

"Obey them that have the rule over you, and submit yourselves: for they watch for your souls, as they that must give account, that they may do it with joy, and not with grief ..." (Heb. 13:17).

"Let not many of you become teachers, my brethren, knowing that as such we shall incur a stricter judgment" (James 3:1, NASB).

Almost every Christian at one time or another has had a measure of authority over another believer. This leadership role may have been that of a parent, pastor, teacher, employer, etc. It has been remarked that while some grow under authority, others simply swell.

C. How we employ our God-given abilities

"Now there are varieties of gifts, but the same Spirit ... But one and the same Spirit works all these things, distributing to each one individually just as He wills" (1 Cor. 12:4, 11, NASB).

"Wherefore I put thee in remembrance that thou stir up the gift of God which is in thee ..." (2 Tim. 1:6).

"As each one has received a special gift, employ it in serving one another, as good stewards of the manifold grace of God" (1 Pet. 4:10, NASB).

To these verses can be added the overall teaching of Jesus' parables of the ten pounds (Luke 19:11-26) and the eight talents (Matt. 25:14-29). A spiritual gift is a super-natural ability to glorify God, given by the Holy Spirit to the believer at the moment of salvation. Each Christian has at least one gift (1 Cor. 7:7; 12:7, 11; Eph. 4:7; 1 Pet. 4:10). There are eighteen of these gifts (Rom. 12; 1 Cor. 12; Eph. 4). Thus, it is vital for every child of God to discover and employ his own gift, in light of the bema.

D. How we use our money

"Upon the first day of the week let every one of you lay by him in store, as God hath pros-pered him ..." (1 Cor. 16:2).

"But this I say, He which soweth sparingly shall reap also sparingly; and he which soweth bountifully shall reap also bountifully. Every man according as he purposeth in his heart, so let him give; not grudgingly, or of necessity: for God loveth a cheerful giver" (2 Cor. 9:6, 7).

"Charge them that are rich in this world, that they be not highminded, nor trust in uncertain riches, but in the living God, who giveth us richly all things to enjoy; That they do good, that they be rich in good works, ready to distribute, willing to communicate; Laying up in store for themselves a good foundation against the time to come, that they may lay hold on eternal life" (1 Tim. 6:17-19).

Perhaps the most accurate barometer to measure the spiritual condition of a Christian is to observe his or her relationship concerning money. Jesus himself often dealt with money matters, because money matters! In the New Testament there are some thirty-eight parables. Twelve of them are about money. How much of our money belongs to God? According to 1 Cor. 6:20 it all belongs to him, because we are his, purchased with an awesome price (1 Pet. 1:18, 19). What does all this mean? It means that if I gross $500 per week, I am not only responsible for the tithe ($50) but will, at the bema, be held accountable concerning the remaining $450!

E. How we spend our time

"So teach us to number our days, that we may apply our hearts unto wisdom" (Psa. 90:12). *"Redeeming the time, because the days are evil"* (Eph. 5:16).

"Walk in wisdom … redeeming the time" (Col. 4:5). *"And if ye call on the Father, who without respect of persons judgeth according to every man's work, pass the time of your sojourning here in fear"* (1 Pet. 1:17).

Of course I, (HLW) have no way of knowing how much money each reader of this book earned last week, or what portion of that amount was saved. But I can accurately state (to the second) how much time you started out with, and what portion was saved. Each began with 168 hours and spent every single one of the 604,800 seconds involved! Someday at the bema, each of us will give an account just how we spent that time.

By the way, do you believe in tithing? Many would answer in the affirmative. But just *what* do you tithe? Of course the expected answer is—my money! Well and good, but have you considered tithing of your *time*? Consider: there are 168 hours given us each week, which would entail setting aside approximately 17 hours per week for church attendance, Bible study, prayer, Christian service, etc. Only eternity could reveal how many local churches might well double their activities for God if even a portion of the members practiced faithful stewardship in regard to both their treasure and time!

F. How much we suffer for Jesus

"Blessed are ye, when men shall revile you, and persecute you, and shall say all manner of evil against you falsely, for my sake. Rejoice, and be exceeding glad: for great is your reward in heaven …" (Matt. 5:11, 12).

"And Jesus answered and said, Verily I say unto you, There is no man that hath left house, or brethren, or sisters, or father, or mother, or wife, or children, or lands, for my sake, and

the gospel's, But he shall receive an hundredfold now in this time, houses, and brethren, and sisters, and mothers, and children, and lands, With persecutions; and in the world to come eternal life" (Mark 10:29, 30).

"For I reckon that the sufferings of this present time are not worthy to be compared with the glory which shall be revealed in us" (Rom. 8:18).

"For our light affliction, which is but for a moment, worketh for us a far more exceeding and eternal weight of glory" (2 Cor. 4:17).

"Beloved, think it not strange concerning the fiery trial which is to try you, as though some strange thing happened unto you: But rejoice, inasmuch as ye are partakers of Christ's sufferings; that, when his glory shall be revealed, ye may be glad also with exceeding joy" (1 Pet. 4:12, 13).

I would like to insert a personal memory here:

> During my first semester at the Moody Bible Institute in 1952, I purchased a beautiful wall plaque which bore the imprint of Phil. 3:10: "That I may know him, and the power of his resurrection." I was so proud of and inspired by the words on this sign. It became the first object I looked at upon rising, and the last sight before retiring. In fact, I had decided to make this passage my life's verse. One day a friend came in my room, saw the plaque, admired it, but informed me that the entire verse was not printed upon it. Somewhat shocked, I hurriedly turned to look it up. Upon discovering the entire message, I suddenly became less sure I wanted this verse as my life's verse. What I read was: "That I may know him, and the power of his resurrection, and the fellowship of his sufferings, being made conformable unto his death."

You see, I had been tremendously inspired by the first part of the verse, but was definitely less excited about the second section. I wanted the power of the resurrection without the fellowship of the sufferings, but this is impossible! One simply cannot have the first apart from the second! The second is the root, and the first the fruit.

G. How we run that particular race which God has chosen for us

"Know ye not that they which run in a race run all, but one receiveth the prize? So run, that ye may obtain" (1 Cor. 9:24).

"… that I may rejoice in the day of Christ, that I have not run in vain …" (Phil. 2:16).

"Brethren, I count not myself to have apprehended: but this one thing I do, forgetting those things which are behind, and reaching forth unto those things which are before, I press toward the mark for the prize of the high calling of God in Christ Jesus" (Phil. 3:13, 14).

"… Let us lay aside every weight, and the sin which doth so easily beset us, and let us run with patience the race that is set before us" (Heb. 12:1).

Especially to be observed are the words found in Heb. 12:1. Note the implications of this statement: Every believer has been entered in this race by God Himself. It is not just for pastors and missionaries. Note: The usual word for race (dromos) is not used here, but rather the Greek word agon, from which we get our English word agony.

This is a serious race. The pace of each runner is set by God.

The object of the race is to please God and win rewards. Its goal is not heaven. Every runner is expected to win.

"*Looking unto Jesus*" (Heb. 12:2). The phrase here speaks of a steadfast, intent and continuous gaze. How easy it is to get our eyes off Him and look to the left or right.

Perhaps to our left we see another runner behind us. Or it may be that there is a runner far ahead of us on the right. This can produce pride (as we view the left runner) and envy (as we see the runner on the right). Both are sin and cause us to slow down. Instead, we are to keep looking at Jesus. We are therefore to run down here in such a way that we might rejoice up there.

H. How effectively we control the old nature

"*And every man that striveth for the mastery is temperate in all things. Now they do it to obtain a corruptible crown; but we an incorruptible. I therefore so run, not as uncertainly; so fight I, not as one that beateth the air: But I keep under my body, and bring it into subjection: lest that by any means, when I have preached to others, I myself should be a castaway*" (1 Cor. 9:25-27).

The Greek word *castaway* here (*adokimos*) means disapproved. Without the prefix it of course speaks of approval. A key passage where *dokimazo* is used can be seen in 2 Tim. 2:15: "*Study to show thyself approved unto God …*" (See also 1 Cor. 16:3; Phil. 1:10; 1 Thess. 2:4; where the identical word is used.)

The point of the above is that Paul desired above all things to keep his old nature in check, lest he be disapproved of, reward wise, at the bema.

The Bible is replete with tragic stories of those believers who did not effectively control their old nature. This would include Noah, Aaron, Gideon, Samson, and Solomon, to name but a few.

I. How many souls we witness to and win to Christ

"*The fruit of the righteous is a tree of life; and he that winneth souls is wise*" (Prov. 11:30).

"*And they that be wise shall shine as the brightness of the firmament; and they that turn many to righteousness as the stars for ever and ever*" (Dan. 12:3).

"*For what is our hope, or joy, or crown of rejoicing? Are not even ye in the presence of our Lord Jesus Christ at his coming? For ye are our glory and joy*" (1 Thess. 2:19, 20).

J. How we react to temptation

"*My brethren, count it all joy when ye fall into divers temptations. Knowing this, that the trying of your faith worketh patience*" (James 1:2, 3).

"*… behold, the devil shall cast some of you into prison, that ye may be tried; and ye shall have tribulation ten days: be thou faithful unto death, and I will give thee a crown of life*" (Rev. 2:10).

K. How much the doctrine of the Rapture means to us

"Henceforth there is laid up for me a crown of righteousness, which the Lord, the righteous judge, shall give me at that day: and not to me only, but unto all them also that love his appearing" (2 Tim. 4:8).

L. How faithful we are to the Word of God and the flock of God

"Wherefore I take you to record this day, that I am pure from the blood of all men. For I have not shunned to declare unto you all the counsel of God. Take heed therefore unto yourselves, and to all the flock, over the which the Holy Ghost hath made you overseers, to feed the church of God, which he hath purchased with his own blood" (Acts 20:26-28).

"I charge thee therefore before God, and the Lord Jesus Christ, who shall judge the quick and the dead at his appearing and his kingdom; Preach the word ..." (2 Tim. 4:1, 2).

"Feed the flock of God which is among you, taking the oversight thereof, not by constraint, but willingly; not for filthy lucre, but of a ready mind: Neither as being lords over God's heritage, but being ensamples to the flock. And when the chief Shepherd shall appear, ye shall receive a crown of glory that fadeth not away" (1 Pet. 5:2-4).

M. How we react to persecution

"Blessed are ye, when men shall revile you, and persecute you, and shall say all manner of evil against you falsely, for my sake. Rejoice, and be exceeding glad: for great is your reward in heaven: for so persecuted they the prophets which were before you" (Matt. 5:11, 12).

"And Jesus answered and said, Verily I say unto you, There is no man that hath left house, or brethren, or sisters, or father, or mother, or wife, or children, or lands, for my sake, and the gospel's, But he shall receive an hundredfold now in this time, houses, and brethren, and sisters, and mothers, and children, and lands, with persecutions; and in the world to come eternal life" (Mark 10:29, 30).

"But love ye your enemies, and do good, and lend, hoping for nothing again; and your reward shall be great, and ye shall be the children of the Highest: for he is kind unto the unthankful and to the evil" (Luke 6:35).

The Christian is to destroy as many of his/her enemies as possible! Really? The best way to do this is to make them his friends.

"For I reckon that the sufferings of this present time are not worthy to be compared with the glory which shall be revealed in us" (Rom. 8:18).

"For our light affliction, which is but for a moment, worketh for us a far more exceeding and eternal weight of glory" (2 Cor. 4:17).

"Beloved, think it not strange concerning the fiery trial which is to try you, as though some strange thing happened unto you: But rejoice, inasmuch as ye are partakers of Christ's sufferings; that, when his glory shall be revealed, ye may be glad also with exceeding joy" (1 Peter 4:12, 13).

N. How faithful we are to our vocation

"Servants, obey in all things your masters according to the flesh; not with eyeservice, as menpleasers; but in singleness of heart, fearing God: And whatsoever ye do, do it heartily, as to the Lord, and not unto men; Knowing that of the Lord ye shall receive the reward of the inheritance: for ye serve the Lord Christ" (Col. 3:22-24).

O. How we use our tongue

"But I say unto you, That every idle word that men shall speak, they shall give account thereof in the day of judgment. For by thy words thou shalt be justified, and by thy words thou shalt be condemned" (Matt. 12:36, 37).

An Egyptian king named Amasis once sent a sacrifice to his god and requested the priest to send back the best and worst part of the animal. The priest sent back the tongue, which organ, said he, represented both demands. It has been said that the Christian should so live that he would not hesitate to sell his talking parrot to the town gossip.

THE RESULTS OF THE BEMA JUDGMENT

■ **Some will receive rewards:**

"If any man's work abide which he hath built thereupon, he shall receive a reward" (1 Cor. 3:14).

The Bible mentions at least five rewards:

A. The incorruptible crown—given to those who master the old nature (1 Cor. 9:25-27).

B. The crown of rejoicing—given to soul winners (Prov. 11:30; Dan. 12:3; 1 Thess. 2:19, 20).

C. The crown of life—given to those who successfully endure temptation (James 1:2, 3; Rev. 2:10).

D. The crown of righteousness—given to those who especially love the doctrine of the Rapture (2 Tim. 4:8).

E. The crown of glory—given to faithful preachers and teachers (Acts 20:26-28; 2 Tim. 4:1, 2; 1 Pet. 5:2-4).

It has been suggested that these "crowns" will actually be talents and abilities with which to glorify Christ. Thus, the greater the reward, the greater the ability. Who down here has not longed to be able to sing like a George Beverly Shea or to preach like a Billy Graham? It may be that this blessing will be possible up there.

E. E. Hewitt poses this question regarding our crowns in his gospel song:

> **Will There Be Any Stars?**
> I am thinking today of that beautiful land
> I shall reach when the sun goeth down;
> When through wonderful grace by my Savior I stand,
> Will there be any stars in my crown?
>
> In the strength of the Lord let me labor and pray,
> Let me watch as a winner of souls;

That bright stars may be mine in the glorious day,
When His praise like the sea-billow rolls.

Oh, what joy it will be when His face I behold,
Living gems at His feet to lay down;
It would sweeten my bliss in the city of gold,
Should there be any stars in my crown.

<u>Refrain</u>:
Will there be any stars, any stars in my crown,
When at evening the sun goeth down?
When I wake with the blest in the mansions of rest,
Will there be any stars in my crown?

■ **Some will suffer loss:**

"If any man's work shall be burned, he shall suffer loss ..." (1 Cor. 3:15). This word "suffer" is *zemioo* in the Greek New Testament, and is used again by Paul in Phil. 3, where he describes those things which were the greatest source of pride to him prior to salvation. He tells us, *"For I went through the Jewish initiation ceremony when I was eight days old, having been born into a pureblooded Jewish home that was a branch of the old original Benjamin family. So I was a real Jew if there ever was one!"*

"What's more, I was a member of the Pharisees who demand the strictest obedience to every Jewish law and custom. And sincere? Yes, so much so that I greatly persecuted the church; and I tried to obey every Jewish rule and regulation right down to the very last point" (Phil. 3:5, 6, TLB).

But after his conversion, Paul writes, *"... for whom I have suffered the loss of all things ... that I may win Christ"* (Phil. 3:8).

The point of all these teachings is simply this: At the bema judgment the carnal Christian will suffer the loss of many past achievements, even as Paul did, but with one important exception—Paul was richly compensated, since he suffered his loss to win Christ, while the carnal believer will receive nothing to replace his burned-up wood, hay, and stubble. Before leaving this section the question may be asked, "Is it possible for someone who has earned certain rewards down here to lose them somehow through carnality?" Some believe this to be tragically possible on the basis of the following verses:

"Let no man beguile you of your reward ..." (Col. 2:18).

"Look to yourselves, that we lose not those things which we have wrought, but that we receive a full reward" (2 John 1:8).

"Behold, I come quickly: hold that fast which thou hast, that no man take thy crown" (Rev. 3:11).

However, knowing the fairness and justice of God, it is far more probable that these verses refer to potential rewards, that is, rewards a believer *could have* earned, had he (or she) remained faithful.

Having now discussed the main areas to be proved at the bema, it should be said that a major concern will center in not only the *action* performed, but that attitude which prompted it. In other words, God is vitally interested in both the *what* and *why* of my deeds.

Offering a personal—and painful—illustration, I (HLW) am convinced that some of my sermons and teaching lessons which were theologically correct will nevertheless go up in flames as wood, hay, and stubble. Perhaps the Holy Spirit even used the sermon in question to convict sinners and exhort saints, for God always honors His word; but my attitude ruined any possible reward. My intent behind the sermon may have been to tickle the ears or impress the minds of those who heard.

In Isaac Watts' time, much persecution was inflicted upon the English Dissenters—those who had split from the official, state Anglican Church. Such dissenting churches were known as the Free Churches. Many of these seventeenth and eighteenth-century believers were imprisoned for their convictions. Isaac Watts' father, a learned deacon in a dissenting Congregational church in Southampton, England, was in prison at the time of his son's birth, because of his non-conformist beliefs. Stalwarts such as Isaac Watts became resolute and fearless in their proclamation of the gospel.

One of his most beloved hymns was taken from the words of two New Testament verses:

"Watch ye, stand fast in the faith, quit you like men, be strong" (1 Cor. 16:13).

"Thou therefore endure hardness, as a good soldier of Jesus Christ" (2 Tim. 2:3).

In this hymn, Mr. Watts asks three penetrating questions and concludes with a renewed dedication to become indeed both a faithful and fearless soldier of the cross!

At this point may I ask the reader to ponder these questions and respond accordingly.

TITLE: *Am I A Soldier of the Cross?*

Watts' three questions:

1. *Am I a soldier of the cross? A foll'wer of the Lamb?*
   And shall I fear to own His cause Or blush to speak His name?

2. *Must I be carried to the skies on flow'ry beds of ease,*
   While others fought to win the prize and sailed thru bloody seas?

3. *Are there no foes for me to face? Must I not stem the flood?*
   Is this vile world a friend to grace, To help me on to God?

Watts' answer:

4. *Sure I must fight if I would reign—Increase my courage, Lord!*
   I'll bear the toil, endure the pain, Supported by Thy Word.

EVENT 3 THE SINGING OF TWO SPECIAL SONGS_____

AN INTRODUCTION PREVIEWING THE TWO SONGS

Suppose you have been enrolled in a Bible survey course and are about to take the final test. The professor hands you a sealed envelope containing the test, which he says, consists of but one question. Furthermore, he adds, how well you answer will lead to either passing or failing the course.

Upon first reading of the question, you are stunned! Here is what it says:

> LIST EVERYTHING THAT GOD <u>HAS</u> EVER DONE, EVERYTHING HE'S DOING <u>NOW</u>, AND EVERYTHING HE EVER <u>WILL</u> DO!

Soon your initial shock turns to confusion, then unbelief, and finally to utter despair. Is this some kind of sick joke? Has the prof lost his mind? Even Michael the archangel could not do this.

But wait, all is not lost! Suddenly recalling the instructor's lectures on Revelation 4 and 5 you quickly and confidently ace that test in less than thirty seconds with the writing of but two words—CREATION and REDEMPTION! Two glorious words aptly describing two glorious works!

Perhaps in no other two chapters in the entire Bible are these two works more central and celebrated than in Revelation 4 and 5. Thus:

- Revelation 4 provides the background for the singing of the first song, praising God for His work in CREATION!
- Revelation 5 provides the background for the singing of the second song, praising God for His work in REDEMPTION!

AN OUTLINE OVERVIEWING THE TWO SONGS

CHAPTER FOUR:
I. **The Summons to Heaven** (4:1)
   A. The vision (4:1a): John sees a door standing open in heaven.
   B. The voice (4:1b): A voice says, "Come up here."
II. **The Sights in Heaven** (4:2-8)
   A. John sees someone seated on a throne (4:2-3a): He has the appearance of a jasper and carnelian stone.
   B. John sees an emerald rainbow above the throne (4:3b).
   C. John sees many creatures surrounding the throne (4:4, 5b, 6b-8).
      1. Twenty-four elders (4:4): They are dressed in white and wear golden crowns.
      2. Seven spirits of God (4:5b)
      3. Four living creatures (4:6b-8)
         a. Their description (4:6b-8)
            (1) They are covered with eyes (4:6b)

        (2) The first has the appearance of a lion; the second, an ox; the third, a man; and the fourth, a flying eagle (4:7).

        (3) Each has six wings (4:8a).

      b. Their duties (4:8b)—Day and night they proclaim the holiness of God.

   D. John sees a crystal sea of glass in front of the throne (4:6a).

   E. John sees a storm developing from the throne (4:5a).

III. **The Song of Heaven** (4:9-11)

   A. The singers (4:9-10): All the inhabitants of heaven

   B. The song (4:11): They worship God for His great work in creating all things.

CHAPTER FIVE:

John continues his description of his heavenly vision. The Lamb is declared worthy to open the seven-sealed scroll.

   I. **The Observation** (5:1): John sees a seven-sealed scroll in the right hand of the One upon His throne.

   II. **The Proclamation** (5:2): A mighty angel asks if anyone is able to break the seals and open the scroll.

   III. **The Investigation** (5:3): An unsuccessful three-fold search is made.

      A. In heaven (5:3a)

      B. On earth (5:3b)

      C. Under the earth (5:3c)

   IV. **The Lamentation** (5:4): John weeps over this.

   V. **The Consolation** (5:5c): He is told someone is indeed worthy to do this.

   VI. **The Manifestation** (5:5a-5b, 6, 7): This someone now steps forward.

      A. Who He is (5:5a-b, 6): Jesus Christ

        1. He is called the Lion of Judah (5:5a-b).

        2. He is called the Lamb of Jehovah (5:6).

      B. What He does (5:7): He takes the scroll from the right hand of the enthroned one.

   VII. **The Supplication** (5:8): The twenty-four elders fall down before the Lamb, holding gold bowls filled with the prayers of God's people.

   VIII. **The Exaltation** (5:9-14)

      A. The song (5:9, 10, 12, 13d-14): The lyrics praise God for His wonderful work of redemption.

      B. The singers (5:11-14)

        1. Their diversity (5:11)

          a. All of heaven's elect angels (5:11a)

          b. All of heaven's redeemed sinners (5:11b)

2. Their universality (5:13, 14)
   a. Every creature in heaven (5:13a)
   b. Every creature on earth (5:13b)
   c. Every creature under the earth (5:13c)

AN ANALYSIS REVIEWING THE TWO SONGS

CHAPTER FOUR:

I. **The Sights Involved** (Rev. 4:1-10)

"After this I looked, and there before me was a door standing open in heaven. And the voice I had first heard speaking to me like a trumpet said, 'Come up here, and I will show you what must take place after this'" (Rev. 4:1).

John was summoned to have a look into heaven, although he was still the old prisoner on earth; he saw and recorded a preview of coming attractions.

John wrote that he was "in the Spirit" immediately, which means that he was transformed in shape and structure into another dimension. He was sent through nineteen hundred (or more) years of time and sat down in heaven where he watched and recorded the horror of the Tribulation and the ultimate triumph of the Second Coming. What a view he had!

In Revelation 3 we saw a door closed and Christ was seeking entrance; now in chapter four we see an open door through which we can view the regal splendor of our God. Revelation 4 leads us into a throne room, where the King is sitting.

Twice in the book of Revelation we see an open door. The first time is in Rev. 4:1 when John sees *"a door standing open in heaven"* and the last time in Rev. 19:11 when he *"saw heaven standing open and there before me was a white horse."* The first time the door opens, somebody goes up, and the next time, somebody comes down.

A. John sees the glory of the Father seated upon His throne surrounded by a beautiful green rainbow.

Will we actually see the Father in heaven? These verses almost seem to suggest that we will. The only other description of the Father is found in Dan. 7:8-14.

John could distinguish no form or give no description of the awesome One upon the throne, save to say, *"He that sat was to look upon like a jasper and a sardine stone..."* (Rev. 4:3). Here the jasper, a white stone, and the sardine, a fiery red stone, may refer to God's two basic characteristics—His glory and His grace. These were also the first and last stones among the twelve that the Old Testament high priest bore upon his breastplate. These stone represented the twelve tribes of Israel, arranged according to the births of the twelve sons of Jacob (Exod. 28). Reuben was the first tribe, which name meant "behold a son," and Benjamin was the last, meaning, "son of my right hand." This then may be God's way of reminding all creatures throughout eternity of:

1. The incarnation of Christ (His humanity) via the jasper stone, Reuben—"behold a son."
2. The exaltation of Christ (His deity) via the sardine stone, Benjamin—"son of my right hand."

B. He sees twenty-four elders sitting on twenty-four smaller thrones, surrounding the Father's throne (Rev. 4).

Question: Are these elders humans or angels? Inasmuch as they are wearing stephanas crowns, given only to martyrs, rather than a diadema crown, only worn by monarchs, it must be concluded they are human beings.

Question: What group do they represent? The book of Revelation includes twelve references to this group of individuals called "the twenty-four elders" (4:4, 10; 5:5, 6, 8, 11, 14; 7:11, 13; 11:16; 14:3; 19:4). The fact that they are mentioned twelve times makes them key players in Bible prophecy.

There are four main views concerning the identity of the twenty-four elders: (1) angelic beings; (2) Israel; (3) the church; and (4) all of the redeemed—Israel and the church. Seven key clues in Revelation reveal that the twenty-four elders represent the church, or the body of Christ.

1. *The title:* They are called elders (*presbuteros*), who in Scripture are the representatives of God's people. We get our English word *Presbyterian* from this word. I am reminded of the little girl who came home from her Presbyterian Sunday school class, and her mother asked her what the lesson was about. The little girl replied, "We talked about heaven." "Well," her mother asked, "what did they say about it?" The little girl said, "The teacher told us that only twelve Presbyterians made it to heaven." (Hey—it's a joke.) In the New Testament, the elders of a church are its representatives. These twenty-four elders represent the glorified church in heaven.

2. *The number:* The Levitical priesthood in the Old Testament numbered in the thousands (1 Chron. 24). Since all of the priests could not worship in the temple at the same time, the priesthood was divided into twenty-four groups. A representative of each group served in the temple on a rotating basis every two weeks. Though the nation of Israel was a kingdom of priests (Exod. 19:6), only Aaron's sons were allowed to enter God's presence. In the church, however, *all* believers are priests unto God (1 Peter 2:5, 9). These twenty-four elders, therefore, are representative of the entire church of Jesus Christ.

3. *The position:* They are seated on thrones. Enthronement with Christ is promised to the church (Rev. 3:21).

4. *The crowns:* Angels are never pictured in Scripture wearing crowns, yet church age believers will receive crowns at the judgment seat of Christ (Rev. 2:10). These elders cannot include saved Israel because Old Testament believers will not be resurrected and rewarded until after the Tribulation is over (Dan. 12:1-3).

5. *The clothing:* The white clothing of the elders is the clothing of the redeemed in the church age (Rev. 3:5, 18; 19:8).

6. *The praise:* Only believers in the present church age can sing the song the elders sing in Rev. 5:9, 10.

7. *The distinction:* The elders are clearly distinguished from angels in Rev. 5:11.

C. He sees and hears lightnings and thunderings, which means that the awful storm of the Great Tribulation is about to unleash its fury. This fearful divine judgment will begin in Rev. 6.

D. He sees seven spirits of God (Rev. 4:5).

There are two theories concerning this verse:

1. It speaks of the seven-fold ministry of the Holy Spirit upon the Messiah as predicted by Isaiah the prophet (Isa. 11:1-3).

2. It refers to seven angels of judgment who pour out God's wrath upon the earth. These angels are mentioned no less than nine times (Rev. 5:6; 8:2, 6; 15:1, 6, 8; 16:1; 17:1; 21:9).

E. He sees a crystal sea of glass (Rev. 4:6).

Dr. Donald Barnhouse has written concerning this sea:

Before the throne there was a glassy sea, like crystal. The concordance immediately takes us to the temple built by Solomon after the model of the tabernacle. '*And he made a molten sea, ten cubits from the one brim to the other; it was round all about, and its height was five cubits*' (1 Kings 7:23). The great basin, fifteen feet in diameter, was supported on the backs of twelve oxen of brass, facing outward. Here the priests came for their cleansing. Each time before they entered the holy place they stopped for the cleansing ceremony. But, thank God, the laver will be turned to crystal. The day will come when none of the saints will ever need confession. One of the greatest joys in the anticipation of heaven is that the laver is crystal. I shall never have to go to the Heavenly Father again to tell Him I have sinned. I shall never have to meet the gaze of Christ that caused Peter to go out and weep bitterly. The laver is of crystal only because I and all the saints of the ages will have been made like unto the Lord Jesus Christ.

(Donald G. Barnhouse, *Revelation: An Expository Commentary*, Grand Rapids, Zondervan, 1971, p. 94, used by permission)

F. He sees four living beings (Rev. 4:6-9)

The first of these creatures had the characteristics of a lion, the second of a calf, the third of a man, and the fourth of an eagle. It is possible that these beings are the same as described by Ezekiel, the Old Testament prophet (see Ezek. 1). In chapter 10 he identified what he had previously seen as the cherubims (10:20-22). Some believe these four creatures may have inherited Lucifer's responsibilities after his terrible rebellion against God (see Isa. 14:12-15; Ezek. 28:11-19). At any rate, there is a definite similarity between the appearance of the four living creatures and the manner by which the four gospel writers present the earthly ministry of Christ.

For example, Matthew presents Christ as the lion of the tribe of Judah. Mark pictures Him as the lowly ox. Luke describes the Savior as the perfect man. John paints Him as the lofty eagle. Thus by their very features, these four heavenly beings may serve to remind redeemed sinners throughout all eternity of the Savior's blessed earthly ministry.

We are told that they " ... *rest not day and night, saying, Holy, holy, holy, Lord God Almighty, which was, and is, and is to come*" (Rev. 4:8).

II. The Song Involved

"*And when those beasts give glory and honour and thanks to him that sat on the throne, who liveth for ever and ever. The four and twenty elders fall down before him that sat on the throne, and worship him that liveth for ever and ever, and cast their crowns before the throne, saying, Thou art worthy, O Lord, to receive glory and honour and power; for thou hast created all things, and for thy pleasure they are and were created.*" (Rev. 4:9-11).

Thus, here is heaven's first great song praising God for His work in *creation*. Many of the psalms were written to praise God for His great work in creation. Note but a few:

"*When I consider thy heavens, the work of thy fingers, the moon and the stars, which thou hast ordained*" (Psa. 8:3).

"*The heavens declare the glory of God; and the firmament sheweth his handywork. Day unto day uttereth speech, and night unto night sheweth knowledge. There is no speech nor language, where their voice is not heard. Their line is gone out through all the earth, and their words to the ends of the world. In them hath he set a tabernacle for the sun*" (Psa. 19:1-4).

"*Know ye that the LORD he is God: it is he that hath made us, and not we ourselves; we are his people and the sheep of his pasture*" (Psa. 100:3).

"*Bless the LORD, O my soul. O LORD my God, thou art very great: thou art clothed with honour and majesty. Who laid the foundations of the earth, that it should not be removed for ever*" (Psa. 104:1, 5).

How it must grieve the Holy Spirit when all too often evangelical believers side with Darwin who claimed all life slowly evolved from a mass of muddy glob over billions of years rather than from the direct hand of the mighty God, as can be found in Genesis, chapters one and two.

In fact, Jesus may well have had this in mind when He admonished Nicodemus as follows:

"*If I have told you earthly things, and ye believe not, how shall ye believe if I tell you of heavenly things?*" (John 3:12).

CHAPTER FIVE:

I. **The Sights Involved** (Rev. 5:1-8)

A. The Observation (5:1)

John sees a seven-sealed scroll in the right hand of the One upon His throne.

B. The Proclamation (5:2)

A mighty angel asked if anyone was able to break the seals and open the scroll.

What is this book (really a rolled-up scroll), sealed so securely with seven seals? Whatever it contained, the scroll was extremely important, for history informs us that under Roman law, all legal documents pertaining to life and death were to be sealed seven times. A number of theologians believe that this is actually the legal title deed to the earth. Thus the angel's proclamation was, in effect, *"Who is worthy to reclaim the earth's title deed? Who is able to pour out the seven-sealed judgment, to purify this planet, and to usher in the long-awaited golden-age Millennium?"* Who indeed was worthy?

C. The Investigation

"And no man in heaven, nor in earth, neither under the earth, was able to open the book, neither to look thereon" (Rev. 5:3). Let us follow the angel as he begins his three-fold search.

1. The search in heaven

    Was there any among the redeemed worthy to claim the earth's title deed? There was not!

    a. *Adam* originally possessed this title deed (Gen. 1:28, 29), but was cheated out of it by the devil (Gen. 3:1-19).

    b. *Noah*, the hero of the flood, subsequently became the drunkard of the vineyard, thus disqualifying himself (Gen. 6-9).

    c. *Abraham*, the father of Israel, backslid and went to Egypt temporarily (Gen. 12).

    d. *David*, the man after God's own heart (1 Sam. 16:7), later broke God's heart through lust and murder (2 Sam. 11).

    e. *John the Baptist*, the forerunner of Christ, in a moment of weakness doubted that same Messiah (Matt. 11:3).

    f. *Peter, the "rock"*, denied his Lord in the hour of need (Matt. 26:70).

    g. *Paul*, perhaps the greatest Christian who ever lived, compromised his testimony (Acts 21).

2. The search on earth

    Who could accomplish in the sinful environment of earth what no man could achieve even in the sinless environment of heaven? Preachers and priests might minister to the earth, kings rule over sections of it, but claim it they could not.

3. The search under the earth (in hades)

    If no saint or angel could purify this earth, then certainly no sinner or demon would, if this were possible.

D. The Lamentation

"And I wept much, because no man was found worthy to open and to read the book, neither to look thereon" (Rev. 5:4).

Why did John weep? Perhaps because (among other things) he realized that the ultimate resurrection and glorification of his own body was directly connected with the removal of the curse placed upon this earth (see Rom. 8:17-23).

E. The Consolation

"And one of the elders saith unto me, Weep not: behold, the Lion of the tribe of Juda, the Root of David, hath prevailed to open the book, and to loose the seven seals thereof" (Rev. 5:5).

F. The Identification

"And I beheld, and, lo, in the midst of the throne and of the four beasts, and in the midst of the elders, stood a Lamb as it had been slain, having seven horns and seven eyes, which are the seven Spirits of God sent forth into all the earth. And he came and took the book out of the right hand of him that sat upon the throne" (Rev. 5:6, 7).

Question: Was it a LAMB or a LION that stepped forward and claimed the seven-sealed scroll?

Answer: It was both, for He is both!

Here in clearest possible language God the Father sets forth His most precious and profound secret, namely, that the Lamb and the Lion are one and the same!

How incredible to contemplate! The second member of the Trinity once came as the sacrificial Lamb of God, and that He will someday return as the sovereign Lion of Judah!

Perhaps even more amazing is the fact that Jesus is called a Lion on only one occasion (Rev. 5:5), but referred to as a Lamb on no less than thirty-two separate occasions! (See John 1:29, 36; Acts 8:32; [as quoted from Isa. 53:7]; 1 Peter 1:19; Rev. 5:6, 8, 12, 13; 6:1, 16; 7:9, 10, 14, 17; 12:11; 13:8; 14:1, 4 [twice], 10; 15:3; 17:14; 19:7, 9; 21:9, 14, 22, 23, 27; 22:1, 3).

Who is the heavenly hero who so boldly removes the scroll from the Father's right hand? We need not speculate for one second about his identity, for He is the Lord Jesus Christ Himself. The proof is overwhelming.

Thus, John sees Christ as a lamb, since He once came to redeem His people. This was His past work. John also sees Him as a lion, for He shall come again to reign over His people. This will be His future work. The source of His claim to the earth's scepter is therefore related to His slain lamb characteristics, while the strength of His claim is due to His mighty lion characteristics.

G. The Supplication

"And when he had taken the book, the four beasts and four and twenty elders fell down before the Lamb, having every one of them harps, and golden vials full of odours, which are the prayers of saints" (Rev. 5:8).

This is the first of two occasions where John witnesses the prayers of the saints being poured out like incense upon the golden altar in heaven. Note the reference: "And I saw the seven angels which stood before God; and to them were given seven trumpets. And *another angel came and stood at the altar, having a golden censer; and there was given unto him much incense, that he should offer it with the prayers of all saints upon the golden altar which was before the throne. And the smoke of the incense, which came with the prayers of the saints, ascended up before God out of the angel's hand"* (Rev. 8:2-4).

One summer while enrolled at the Moody Bible Institute in Chicago, I (H.L.W.) attended a Fourth of July celebration held at Soldiers Field. Upon entering, each person was issued a kitchen match along with the ticket and told further instructions would be given later in the program. The activities proved to be fun-filled and fast-moving. Finally, around 9:00 p.m. when darkness had settled down, an announcement came over the loud speaker system:

> "Your attention, please! All of you have received a kitchen match as you entered the stadium. Now here's what we want you to do with it. In a moment all lights will be extinguished and everyone is invited to join me in a countdown from ten to one. Then, upon reaching one, we'll all ignite our matches together."

Quickly all lights faded and a foreboding darkness settled down upon the crowd.

"Okay," the announcer cried out, "let's begin! Everyone count with me — ten … nine … eight … " At first only a few hundred joined him. Then, on count seven, six, and five, a few thousand. Finally, at count four, all ninety thousand voices could be heard chanting in unison, "four … three … two … one!" For one instant, NOTHING!

Then, a huge scratching sound was heard, as ninety thousand kitchen matches were being lit. The sight was absolutely incredible—indeed, breathtaking. It seemed that the entire Milky Way had suddenly descended from the heavens and settled upon Soldiers Field. But back to the Revelation scene. Just think of it—all the prayers of all the saints in all of redemption's history being poured out as gracious incense upon that Golden Altar.

You might believe your little prayer is as ineffective and weak as a simple kitchen match. Think so? When was the last time you witnessed ninety thousand such matches all at once? My prayers, your prayers, our prayers poured out like glowing incense. Surely the angels in glory will be as a awestruck at that event as was I at Soldiers Field.

III. The Song Involved (Rev. 5:9-14)

"And they sung a new song, saying, Thou art worthy to take the book, and to open the seals thereof: for thou wast slain, and hast redeemed us to God by thy blood out of every kindred, and tongue, and people, and nation; And hast made us unto our God kings and priests: and we shall reign on the earth. And I beheld, and I heard the voice of many angels round about the throne and the beasts and the elders: and the number of them was ten thousand times ten thousand, and thousands of thousands; Saying with a loud voice, Worthy is the Lamb that was slain to receive power, and riches, and wisdom, and strength, and honour, and glory, and blessing. And every creature which is in heaven, and on the earth, and under the earth, and such as are in the sea, and all that are in them, heard I saying, Blessing, and honour, and glory, and power, be unto him that sitteth upon the throne, and unto the Lamb for ever and ever. And

the four beasts said, Amen. And the four and twenty elders fell down and worshipped him that liveth for ever and ever."

Dr. Henry Morris observes:

> The twenty-four elders, presumably accompanied by all the saints, will then proceed to sing, and it will be a song such as the cosmos has never yet heard. Even at the creation, when all the newly-created angelic host shouted for joy as they sang together (Job 38:7), there was nothing like this. For now, the renewed voices of billions of redeemed saints will join in a mighty anthem of praise to their strong Redeemer and King. Perhaps, the song will even be heard on earth, as was the praise of angels at the birth of Christ (Luke 2:13).
>
> The song is new not only in magnitude but in words and music. A billion harps will accompany the golden voices of their singers, and the theme is that of gratitude to the worthy Lamb.
>
> That more than just twenty-four are singing is evident from the song: *"Thou has redeemed us to God by thy blood out of every kindred, and tongue, and people, and nation."* There are thousands of languages among men, and here is a gracious promise that God does have His elect hidden away in every tribe and people. (*The Revelation Record,* Tyndale House, p. 103)

Worthy is the Lamb is what they sing. The Bible is, in essence, a divine textbook on the subject of God's Lamb. In fact, the Scriptures can be aptly summarized by three statements about the Lamb: Isaac once asked, *"Where is the lamb?"* (Gen. 22:7). John the Baptist would later answer, *"Behold, the Lamb!"* (John 1:29). All creation will someday sing out, *"Worthy is the Lamb!"* (Rev. 5:12).

The words of John Kent's (1766-1843) beautiful hymn, *'Tis the Church Triumphant Singing* describes this glorious event in a moving and magnificent way:

> *'Tis the Church triumphant singing*
> *Worthy the Lamb;*
> *Heaven throughout with praises ringing*
> *Worthy the Lamb,*
> *Thrones and pow'rs before Him bending,*
> *Odours sweet with voice ascending,*
> *Swell the chorus never ending,*
> *Worthy the Lamb.*
>
> *Ev'ry kindred, tongue and nation,*
> *Worthy the Lamb;*
> *Join to sing the great salvation,*
> *Worthy the Lamb,*
> *Loud as mighty thunders roaring,*
> *Floods of mighty waters pouring,*

Prostrate at His feet adoring,
Worthy the Lamb.

Harps and songs for ever sounding
Worthy the Lamb;
Mighty grace o'er sin abounding,
Worthy the Lamb.
By His blood He dearly bought us;
Wand'ring from the fold He sought us,
And to glory safely brought us;
Worthy the Lamb.

Sing with blest anticipation
Worthy the Lamb;
Through the vale of tribulation,
Worthy the Lamb,
Sweetest notes, all notes excelling,
On the theme for ever dwelling,
Still untold, though ever telling,
Worthy the Lamb.

This then is heaven's second great hymn, that of *redemption*! Note the two-fold aspect of this celestial choir.

A. Its diversity—Both angels and humans will participate. Inasmuch as angels had previously been allowed to be present at the creation of the world (Job 38:1, 7) and its redemption (Luke 2:8-14), it is only appropriate that they be permitted to join in this celebration.

B. Its universality—We note every creature, saved and unsaved alike, will give honor to the Lamb. This of course in no way suggests that all will be saved. A similar passage is found in Phil. 2:5-11:

> *"Let this mind be in you which was also in Christ Jesus, who, being in the form of God, did not consider it robbery to be equal with God, but made Himself of no reputation, taking the form of a bondservant, and coming in the likeness of men. And being found in appearance as a man, He humbled Himself and became obedient to the point of death, even the death of the cross. Therefore God also has highly exalted Him and given Him the name which is above every name, that at the name of Jesus every knee should bow, of those in heaven, and of those on earth, and of those under the earth, and that every tongue should confess that Jesus Christ is Lord, to the glory of God the Father."*

What these verses are saying is no creature has a choice concerning whether he or she will acknowledge the glory of Christ, but only how that acknowledgment will be made. He will either be recognized as one's Savior and Lord of all on earth, or as one's Judge and Lord of all throughout eternity.

One final thought in regard to these twin songs of *creation* and *redemption*:

Do angels sing? We simply do not know, for they are never described as singing. However, *if* they do indeed sing, there is one song they will not join in! Johnson Oatman speaks of this in his hymn, *Holy, Holy, is What the Angels Sing*:

> There is singing up in heaven such as we have never known,
> Where the angels sing the praises of the Lamb upon the throne;
> Their sweet harps are ever tuneful and their voices are always clear,
> O that we might be more like them while we serve the Master here!
>
> But I hear another anthem, blending voices clear and strong,
> "Unto Him who hath redeemed us and hath bought us," is the song;
> We have come thro' tribulations to this land so fair and bright,
> In the fountain freely flowing He hath made our garments white.
>
> Then the angels stand and listen, for they cannot join that song,
> Like the sound of many waters, by that happy, blood-washed throng;
> For they sing about great trials, battles fought and vict'ries won,
> And they praised the great Redeemer, who hath said to them, "Well done."
>
> Refrain:
> Holy, holy, is what the angels sing,
> And I expect to help them make the courts of heaven ring;
> But when I sing redemption's story, they will fold their wings,
> For angels never felt the joys that our salvation brings.

EVENT 4 THE MARRIAGE SERVICE OF THE LAMB

INTRODUCTION TO THE WEDDING

A number of weddings are described in the Bible. The first wedding was performed by a very special minister. Whatever religious ceremony he may have chosen, it did not include those familiar words: "If any man can show just cause why these two should not be lawfully joined together, let him now speak or else forever hold his peace." The phrase was unnecessary, for the minister was God Himself, and the couple was Adam and Eve (Gen. 2:18-25).

Then there was a very unusual wedding in which the bridegroom found out the next morning, by light of day, that he had married the wrong girl (Gen. 29:21-25).

One of the most beautiful wedding stories began in a barley field outside the little town of Bethlehem (Ruth 2).

Perhaps the most tragic wedding was that between Ahab, King of Israel, and Jezebel, a godless Baal worshipper. This marriage would result in much sorrow and suffering for God's people (1 Kings 16:29-31).

Finally, the Savior of men chose a wedding in the city of Cana to perform his first miracle (John 2:1-11).

However, the most fantastic and wonderful wedding of all time is yet to take place.

THE WEDDING SERVICE AS CONTRASTED TO THE WEDDING SUPPER

I. **Passages relating to the wedding service**

    A. Romans 7:4—*"Therefore, my brethren, you also have become dead to the law through the body of Christ, that you may be married to another—to Him who was raised from the dead, that we should bear fruit to God."*

    B. 2 Corinthians 11:2—*"For I am jealous for you with godly jealousy. For I have betrothed you to one husband, that I may present you as a chaste virgin to Christ."*

    C. Ephesians 5:25-32—*"Husbands, love your wives, just as Christ also loved the church and gave Himself for her, that He might sanctify and cleanse her with the washing of water by the word, that He might present her to Himself a glorious church, not having spot or wrinkle or any such thing, but that she should be holy and without blemish. So husbands ought to love their own wives as their own bodies; he who loves his wife loves himself. For no one ever hated his own flesh, but nourishes and cherishes it, just as the Lord does the church. For we are members of His body, of His flesh and of His bones. 'For this reason a man shall leave his father and mother and be joined to his wife, and the two shall become one flesh.' This is a great mystery, but I speak concerning Christ and the church."*

II. **Passages relating to the wedding supper**

    A. Isaiah 61:10—*"I will greatly rejoice in the Lord, My soul shall be joyful in my God; For He has clothed me with the garments of salvation, He has covered me with the robe of righteousness, As a bridegroom decks himself with ornaments, And as a bride adorns herself with her jewels."*

       Matthew 22:2—*"The kingdom of heaven is like a certain king who arranged a marriage for his son."*

       Matthew 25:1—*"Then the kingdom of heaven shall be likened to ten virgins who took their lamps and went out to meet the bridegroom."*

    B. Luke 12:35-36—*"Let your waist be girded and your lamps burning; and you yourselves be like men who wait for their master, when he will return from the wedding, that when he comes and knocks they may open to him immediately."*

    C. Revelation 19:6-9—*"And I heard, as it were, the voice of a great multitude, as the sound of many waters and as the sound of mighty thunderings, saying, 'Alleluia! For the Lord God Omnipotent reigns! Let us be glad and rejoice and give Him glory, for the marriage of the Lamb has come, and His wife has made herself ready.' And to her it was granted to be arrayed in fine linen, clean and bright, for the fine linen is the righteous acts of the saints. Then he said to me, "Write: 'Blessed are those who are called to the marriage supper of the Lamb!'" And he said to me, "These are the true sayings of God."*

III. **Differences between the wedding service and supper**

A. The wedding *service* is a private event, taking place in heaven.

B. The wedding *supper* is a public event, taking place on earth.

C. The wedding *service* follows the Rapture.

D. The wedding *supper* follows the Revelation (Second Coming of Christ).

E. The wedding *service* presents Christ as the Lamb of God.

F. The wedding *supper* presents Christ as the Lion of Judah.

G. The wedding *service* concludes with great rejoicing

"Then I looked, and I heard the voice of many angels around the throne, the living creatures, and the elders; and the number of them was ten thousand times ten thousand, and thousands of thousands, saying with a loud voice: 'Worthy is the Lamb who was slain to receive power and riches and wisdom, and strength and honor and glory and blessing!'" (Rev. 5:11, 12).

H. The wedding *supper* concludes with great rejoicing

"Then a voice came from the throne, saying, 'Praise our God, all you His servants and those who fear Him, both small and great!' And I heard, as it were, the voice of a great multitude, as the sound of many waters and as the sound of mighty thunderings, saying, 'Alleluia! For the Lord God Omnipotent reigns! Let us be glad and rejoice and give Him glory, for the marriage of the Lamb has come, and His wife has made herself ready.'" (Rev. 19:5-7)

I. The wedding *service* introduces the Great Tribulation

"And the stars of heaven fell to the earth, as a fig tree drops its late figs when it is shaken by a mighty wind. Then the sky receded as a scroll when it is rolled up, and every mountain and island was moved out of its place." (Rev. 6:13, 14).

J. The wedding *supper* introduces the glorious Millennium

"…they [believers] shall be priests of God and of Christ, and shall reign with Him a thousand years" (Rev. 20:6).

THE TWO OLD TESTAMENT FORESHADOWS OF THE WEDDING

The institution of the church, of course, was not revealed in the Old Testament. Paul makes this clear in Eph. 3:1-12. However, there are two special brides mentioned in the Old Testament whose lives beautifully lend themselves as remarkable foreshadowing of the coming New Testament church. These two women are Eve and Rebekah.

I. **The bride Eve**

A. Eve proceeded from Adam's side as the church came from Christ's side.

1. The (literal) creation of Eve—"*And the Lord God caused a deep sleep to fall on Adam, and he slept; and He took one of his ribs, and closed up the flesh in its place. Then the rib which the Lord God had taken from man He made into a woman, and He brought her to the man*" (Gen. 2:21, 22).

2. The (symbolic) creation of the church—"*But one of the soldiers pierced His side with a spear, and immediately blood and water came out*" (John 19:34).

B. Eve became espoused to the first head of creation, while the church will be joined to the final Head of creation.

C. Both brides were to reign with their husbands over all creation.

1. Eve's joint-rule—"*Then God blessed them, and God said to them, "Be fruitful and multiply; fill the earth and subdue it; have dominion over the fish of the sea, over the birds of the air, and over every living thing that moves on the earth*" (Gen. 1:28).

2. The church's joint-rule—"*...and if children, then heirs—heirs of God and joint heirs with Christ, if indeed we suffer with Him, that we may also be glorified together*" (Rom. 8:17). "*And they lived and reigned with Christ a thousand years*" (Rev. 20:4).

D. Both brides become bone and flesh of their spouse—"*And Adam said: 'This is now bone of my bones and flesh of my flesh; She shall be called Woman, because she was taken out of Man.' Therefore a man shall leave his father and mother and be joined to his wife, and they shall become one flesh*" (Gen. 2:23, 24). "*For we are members of His body, of His flesh and of His bones. 'For this reason a man shall leave his father and mother and be joined to his wife, and the two shall become one flesh.'*" (Eph. 5:30, 31).

E. Eve was deceived *by* Satan, but the church will be delivered *from* Satan.

1. The deception—"*And the serpent said unto the woman, 'Ye shall not surely die'*" (Gen. 3:4).

2. The deliverance—"*And the God of peace shall bruise Satan under your feet shortly. The grace of our Lord Jesus Christ be with you. Amen*" (Rom. 16:20).

II. **The bride Rebekah**—Genesis 24 is the greatest single typical chapter in the entire Old Testament. The four key individuals involved in this chapter are Abraham, Isaac, the servant, and Rebekah.

A. Abraham sends his trusted servant to a distant land to fetch a bride for Isaac, his son. He becomes a type of the Father who has done the same for his Son. "*But thou shalt go unto my country, and to my kindred, and take a wife unto my son Isaac*" (Gen. 24:4). "*The kingdom of heaven is like unto a certain king, which made a marriage for his son, And sent forth his servants to call them that were bidden to the wedding: and they would not come*" (Matt. 22:2, 3).

B. Isaac, having been previously offered up on Mount Mariah, is content to await the arrival of his bride—He becomes a type of the Son who now awaits the arrival of his bride in heaven.

"*And Isaac went out to meditate in the field in the evening; and he lifted his eyes and looked, and there, the camels were coming*" (Gen. 24:63). "*But this Man, after He had offered one sacrifice for sins forever, sat down at the right hand of God, from that time wait-ing till His enemies are made His footstool. For by one offering He has perfected forever those who are being sanctified"* (Heb. 10:12-14).

C. The servant arrives in that distant land for the sole purpose of taking a bride—He becomes a foreshadow of the Holy Spirit.

1. Christ was sent by the Father—*"And I will pray the Father, and He will give you another Helper, that He may abide with you forever"* (John 14:16).

2. Christ came at Pentecost to take a bride—*"For by one Spirit we were all baptized into one body—whether Jews or Greeks, whether slaves or free—and have all been made to drink into one Spirit"* (1 Cor. 12:13).

3. God elevates Christ as the servant did Isaac—*"And Sarah my master's wife bore a son to my master when she was old; and to him he has given all that he has"* (Gen. 24:36). *"However, when He, the Spirit of truth, has come, He will guide you into all truth; for He will not speak on His own authority, but whatever He hears He will speak; and He will tell you things to come. He will glorify Me, for He will take of what is Mine and declare it to you"* (John 16:13, 14).

D. Rebekah, upon hearing about Isaac, agrees to go with the servant. She became a fore-shadow of the church.

1. Like the church and Christ, she loved her bridegroom even before seeing him— *"whom having not seen you love. Though now you do not see Him, yet believing, you rejoice with joy inexpressible and full of glory"* (1 Peter 1:8).

2. Like the church and Christ, she received an earnest from the riches of Isaac— *"Then the servant brought out jewelry of silver, jewelry of gold, and clothing, and gave them to Rebekah. He also gave precious things to her brother and to her mother"* (Gen. 24:53). *"Who hath also sealed us, and given the earnest of the Spirit in our hearts"* (2 Cor. 1:22). *"Which is the earnest of our inheritance until the redemption of the purchased possession, unto the praise of his glory"* (Eph. 1:14).

3. Like the church and Christ, she began her long pilgrimage to meet her bride-groom—*"So they sent away Rebekah their sister and her nurse, and Abraham's ser-vant and his men"* (Gen. 24:59). *"Beloved, I beg you as sojourners and pilgrims, abstain from fleshly lusts which war against the soul"* (1 Peter 2:11).

4. Like the church and Christ, she is prayed for by her bridegroom—*"And Isaac went out to meditate in the field in the evening; and he lifted his eyes and looked, and there, the camels were coming"* (Gen. 24:63). *"Who is he who condemns? It is Christ who died, and furthermore is also risen, who is even at the right hand of God, who also makes intercession for us"* (Rom. 8:34).

5. Like the church and Christ, she is received into the home of her father-in-law— *"Then Isaac brought her into his mother Sarah's tent; and he took Rebekah and she became his wife, and he loved her. So Isaac was comforted after his mother's death"*

(Gen. 24:67). *"In My Father's house are many mansions; if it were not so, I would have told you. I go to prepare a place for you"* (John 14:2).

THE UNIQUENESS OF THE WEDDING

Earthly marriages may be prevented because of various unexpected problems.

I. **In an earthly wedding there can be a last-minute refusal on the part of either the bride or groom. But not with the heavenly marriage.**

A. The Bridegroom has already expressed His great love for His bride (Eph. 5:25), and He never changes.

"This same Jesus, who was taken up from you into heaven, will so come in like manner as you saw Him go into heaven" (Acts 1:11). *"Jesus Christ is the same yesterday, today, and forever"* (Heb. 13:8).

B. The bride has already been glorified and is sinless, and therefore cannot be tempted into changing her mind or losing her love for the Bridegroom.

" ... a glorious church, not having spot or wrinkle ... but that it should be holy and without blemish" (Eph. 5:27). *"For by one offering he hath perfected for ever them that are sanctified"* (Heb. 10:14).

II. In an earthly wedding a serious legal problem might arise, such as a lack of age, or even that of a previous marriage—but not in the heavenly wedding. See Rom. 8:33-39:

"Who shall lay any thing to the charge of God's elect? It is God who justifies. Who is he who condemns? It is Christ who died, and furthermore is also risen, who is even at the right hand of God, who also makes intercession for us. Who shall separate us from the love of Christ? Shall tribulation, or distress, or persecution, or famine, or nakedness, or peril, or sword? As it is written: 'For Your sake we are killed all day long; We are accounted as sheep for the slaughter.' Yet in all these things we are more than conquerors through Him who loved us. For I am persuaded that neither death nor life, nor angels nor principalities nor powers, nor things present nor things to come, nor height nor depth, nor any other created thing, shall be able to separate us from the love of God which is in Christ Jesus our Lord."

III. **In an earthly wedding the tragedy of death might intervene—but not in the heavenly wedding.**

A. The bride will never die—*"And whosoever liveth and believeth in me shall never die ..."* (John 11:26).

B. The Bridegroom will never die—*"I am he that liveth, and was dead; and, behold, I am alive for evermore, Amen ..."* (Rev. 1:18).

One of my (H.L.W.) wife's friends was planning to be married on the first Saturday following her graduation from high school. On Tuesday of the wedding week she voiced her concern to Sue (my wife) in regard to a dental appointment she had made for Wednesday. "I'm deathly afraid of dentists," she said, "so, if I die in his chair," she joked, "just bury me in my wedding dress!" The tragic ending of this story is she did and she was! For unknown reasons she did indeed die in the dentist's office and was (as she had requested) buried in her wedding dress on the Saturday of her wedding day!

THE HOST, BRIDEGROOM, AND BRIDE INVOLVED IN THE WEDDING

I. **The Host involved**

    The New Testament very clearly presents the Father as the divine Host who gives this marriage. He is pictured as preparing it, then sending His servants out to invite the selected guests (Luke 14:16-23).

II. **The Bridegroom involved**

    The Father's beloved Son (Matt. 3:17; 17:5), the Lord Jesus Christ, is the Bridegroom.

    A. As stated by John the Baptist

        "John answered and said, 'A man can receive nothing unless it has been given to him from heaven. You yourselves bear me witness, that I said, 'I am not the Christ,' but, 'I have been sent before Him.' He who has the bride is the bridegroom; but the friend of the bridegroom, who stands and hears him, rejoices greatly because of the bridegroom's voice. Therefore this joy of mine is fulfilled. He must increase, but I must decrease" (John 3:27-30).

    B. As stated by the Lord Jesus Christ

        "I have not come to call the righteous, but sinners, to repentance. Then they said to Him, 'Why do the disciples of John fast often and make prayers, and likewise those of the Pharisees, but Yours eat and drink?' And He said to them, 'Can you make the friends of the bridegroom fast while the bridegroom is with them? But the days will come when the bridegroom will be taken away from them; then they will fast in those days'" (Luke 5:32-35).

III. **The bride involved**

    In two key passages the Apostle Paul makes crystal clear the identity of the bride:

    "For I am jealous for you with godly jealousy. For I have betrothed you to one husband, that I may present you as a chaste virgin to Christ" (2 Cor. 11:2). *"Husbands, love your wives, even as Christ also loved the church, and gave himself for it"* (Eph. 5:25).

THE SERVICE SCHEDULE OF THIS WEDDING

The marriage of Christ to the church will follow the Oriental pattern of marriage as described for us in the New Testament. It consisted of three separate stages:

I. **The betrothal stage**

    New Testament marriage contracts were often initiated when the couple was very young (sometimes even prior to birth) by the groom's father. He would sign a legal enactment before the proper judge, pledging his son to a chosen girl. The father would then offer the proper dowry payment. Thus, even though the bride had never seen the groom, she was nevertheless betrothed or espoused to him. A New Testament example of this first step is the marriage of Mary and Joseph.

"Now the birth of Jesus Christ was on this wise: When as His mother Mary was espoused to Joseph, before they came together, she was found with child of the Holy Ghost" (Matt. 1:18).

Both Mary and Joseph had come from Bethlehem and had perhaps been betrothed, or promised to each other, since childhood. But now Mary was found to be with child before the marriage could be consummated, and of course Joseph could arrive at only one conclusion—she had been untrue to him. Then the angel of the Lord explained to Joseph the glories of the virgin birth.

Thus the betrothal stage consisted of two steps—the selection of the bride and the payment of the dowry. With this in mind we can state that the marriage of the Lamb is still in its betrothal stage.

A. The bride has been selected

> *"Blessed be the God and Father of our Lord Jesus Christ, who has blessed us with every spiritual blessing in the heavenly places in Christ, just as He chose us in Him before the foundation of the world, that we should be holy and without blame before Him in love"* (Eph. 1:3, 4).

B. The dowry has been paid

> *"Or do you not know that your body is the temple of the Holy Spirit who is in you, whom you have from God, and you are not your own? For you were bought at a price; therefore glorify God in your body and in your spirit, which are God's"* (1 Cor. 6:19, 20).

> *"Knowing that you were not redeemed with corruptible things, like silver or gold, from your aimless conduct received by tradition from your fathers, but with the precious blood of Christ, as of a lamb without blemish and without spot"* (1 Peter 1:18, 19).

II. **The presentation stage**

At the proper time the father would send servants carrying the proper legal contract to the house of the bride. The bride would then be led to the home of the groom's father. When all was ready, the father of the bride would place her hand in the hand of the groom's father. He would then place her hand in that of his son's. Applying this background to the marriage of the Lamb, the church still awaits this second phase, the presentation stage, which we know as the Rapture! The following verses speak of this presentation stage:

" ...Christ also loved the church and gave Himself for her: that He might present her to Himself a glorious church, not having spot or wrinkle or any such thing, but that she should be holy and without blemish" (Eph. 5:25, 27). *"Now to Him who is able to keep you from stumbling, and to present you faultless before the presence of His glory with exceeding joy"* (Jude 24). *"Let us be glad and rejoice and give Him glory, for the marriage of the Lamb has come, and His wife has made herself ready. And to her it was granted to be arrayed in fine linen, clean and bright, for the fine linen is the righteous acts of the saints"* (Rev. 19:7, 8).

As in the betrothal stage, the presentation stage also consists of two steps: the showing of the proper legal papers and the fetching of the bride to the house of the groom's father.

Thus, the presentation stage will occur at the Rapture.

A. The proper legal papers will be shown—*"Nevertheless the foundation of God standeth sure having this seal, the Lord knoweth them that are his ... "* (2 Tim. 2:19).

B. The bride will be taken to the Father's home—"*In My Father's house are many mansions; if it were not so, I would have told you. I go to prepare a place for you. And if I go and prepare a place for you, I will come again and receive you to Myself; that where I am, there you may be also*" (John 14:2, 3).

III. The celebration stage

After the private marriage service was completed, the public marriage supper would begin. Many guests would be invited to this celebration. It was during such a supper that our Lord performed his first miracle, that of changing water into wine (see John 2:1-11). Jesus later made reference to this third step when he spoke the following words:

"*The kingdom of heaven is like a certain king who arranged a marriage for his son, and sent out his servants to call those who were invited to the wedding*" (Matt. 22:2, 3).

"*Let your waist be girded and your lamps burning; and you yourselves be like men who wait for their master, when he will return from the wedding, that when he comes and knocks they may open to him immediately. Blessed are those servants whom the master, when he comes, will find watching. Assuredly, I say to you that he will gird himself and have them sit down to eat, and will come and serve them*" (Luke 12:35-37).

"*Then He said to him, 'A certain man gave a great supper and invited many, and sent his servant at supper time to say to those who were invited, 'Come, for all things are now ready.'*" (Luke 14:16, 17).

It is no accident that the Bible describes the Millennium as occurring right after the celebration supper has begun. (The supper is described in Rev. 19 while the millennium is described in Rev. 20.) In New Testament times the length and cost of this supper was determined by the wealth of the father. Therefore, when his beloved Son is married, the Father of all grace (whose wealth is unlimited) will rise to the occasion by giving his Son and the bride a hallelujah celebration which will last for a thousand years!

THE PSALM WHICH DEPICTS TWO ROYAL WEDDINGS

Here we refer to Psalm 45. Note its contents:

[1] *My heart is overflowing with a good theme; I recite my composition concerning the King; my tongue is the pen of a ready writer.*

[2] *You are fairer than the sons of men; grace is poured upon Your lips; therefore God has blessed You forever.*

[3] *Gird Your sword upon Your thigh, O Mighty One, with Your glory and Your majesty.*

[4] *And in Your majesty ride prosperously because of truth, humility, and righteousness; and Your right hand shall teach You awesome things.*

[5] *Your arrows are sharp in the heart of the King's enemies; the peoples fall under You.*

[6] *Your throne, O God, is forever and ever; a scepter of righteousness is the scepter of Your kingdom.*

[7] *You love righteousness and hate wickedness; therefore God, Your God, has anointed You with the oil of gladness more than Your companions.*

^{8} *All Your garments are scented with myrrh and aloes and cassia, out of the ivory palaces, by which they have made You glad.*

^{9} *Kings' daughters are among Your honorable women; at Your right hand stands the queen in gold from Ophir.*

^{10} *Listen, O daughter, consider and incline your ear; forget your own people also, and your father's house;*

^{11} *So the King will greatly desire your beauty; because He is your Lord, worship Him.*

^{12} *And the daughter of Tyre will come with a gift; the rich among the people will seek your favor.*

^{13} *The royal daughter is all glorious within the palace; her clothing is woven with gold.*

^{14} *She shall be brought to the King in robes of many colors; the virgins, her companions who follow her, shall be brought to You.*

^{15} *With gladness and rejoicing they shall be brought; they shall enter the King's palace.*

^{16} *Instead of Your fathers shall be Your sons, whom You shall make princes in all the earth.*

^{17} *I will make Your name to be remembered in all generations; therefore the people shall praise You forever and ever.*

The weddings in view are (1) that of the King of Israel—Solomon, and (2) that of the King of Kings— Jesus Christ!

Dr. W. Graham Scroggie comments:

> We may safely assume that this psalm has a historical basis, and that which is most likely is the marriage of Solomon with the daughter of the King of Egypt (1 Kings 3:1). But, of course, such an event does not exhaust the significance of the psalm. No scripture is exhausted by its historical occasion; and they who see here an ideal and prophetic description of the union of the Messiah and His people, discern the psalm's chief and permanent value. It speaks of the Heavenly Bridegroom and His elect spouse.
>
> This song celebrates the Marriage of the King. After an introduction, (1) the Bridegroom is addressed (2-9), and then the Bride (10-17). The psalmist is in the grip of his subject; his heart is *"bubbling up,"* is *"boiling over"* with his theme; and his tongue is like a *quick scribe*. Thank God for all holy enthusiasm; there is none too much of it, though alas, there is much counterfeit of it! Great themes should generate in us holy passions (1).
>
> In addressing the Bridegroom attention is called first to His beauty (2); then to his victorious advent (3-5); next to His character and office (6, 7); and finally, to His glory and majesty (8, 9). Consider the application of verses 6, 7; in Hebrews 1:8 where it is seen that the Bridegroom is Christ (cf. Matt. 25:1-13).
>
> The Bride is now addressed (10-17). She is bidden *"hearken—consider—incline—forget."* God's people are beautiful with the beauty of the King, who is our Lord, and whom we should worship (11). This should make other people nobly covetous (12), and will do so if we are as we should be *"all glorious within"* (13). It is what we are *"within"* that matters first. How great are our privileges (14, 15), and how blessed should be our posterity (16, 17). Are you in this Song of love? Here is not only *union* but also *communion*.

Hebrews 1, which presents the Divine Christ, is vitally related to chapter 2, which presents the human Christ, and these two are one; and although His sufferings are not in view in this psalm, Calvary is not far away. This fact led Dr. Chapman to write his well-known hymn:

> *My Lord has garments so wondrous fine,*
> *And myrrh their texture fills;*
> *Its fragrance reached to this heart of mine*
> *With joy my being thrills.*
>
> *His life had also its sorrows sore,*
> *For aloes had a part;*
> *And when I think of the cross He bore,*
> *My eyes with teardrops start.*
>
> *His garments too were in cassia dipped,*
> *With healing in a touch;*
> *Each time my feet in some sin have slipped,*
> *He took me from its clutch.*
>
> *In garments glorious He will come,*
> *To open wide the door;*
> *And I shall enter my heav'nly home,*
> *To dwell forevermore.*
>
> **Refrain**
> *Out of the ivory palaces,*
> *Into a world of woe,*
> *Only His great eternal love*
> *Made my Savior go.*

Dr. Scroggie concludes by admonishing the Bride (the Church) to radiate the loveliness and beauty of her Bridegroom here on earth as she awaits His return:

> *"All thy garments smell of myrrh, aloes, and cassia."* 'What then?' says John Tauler, 'is it while the bride stands by that alone we know of the incense of her presence? Surely not. When she has gone past, still she leaves behind the perfume of the ivory palaces—so that men shall say, This way she went, by this path she followed her Lord's path; by this track her feet trod the rough flints and sherds of this earth, that they might merit to walk upon the golden streets of New Jerusalem." (*Psalms*, Revell Company, Old Tappan, New Jersey, 1972, pp. 259-261)

THE PREPARATION FOR THE WEDDING

One of the chief concerns of every bride-to-be is what she is going to wear at her wedding and wedding reception. The bride spends hours looking at dresses, shoes, veils, and all the accessories. The marriage of the Lamb should be no different. Revelation 19:8 reminds us that every believer will be present at the wedding feast, dressed in the finest white linen, which is the good deeds we have done. These good deeds are not works we have done to enter heaven. We cannot earn the garments of righteousness that Christ has provided for us by His death on the cross. However, we are to make ourselves ready for the wedding feast every day by preparing the garment we will wear to this occasion. How we are dressed on that day will depend on the life we have lived for Christ. I once heard Lehman Strauss say, "Has it ever occurred to you that at marriage of the bride to the Lamb, each of us will be wearing the wedding garment of our own making?" Make sure that you will be beautifully dressed on that day by living for Christ today.

The marriage of the Lamb is a certain event. Someday the Bridegroom will come to take His Bride to His Father's house. Make sure you have received your invitation and are living a pure life for your loving Groom.

Ann Ross Cousin's beautiful hymn, *The Sands of Time are Sinking*, speaks meaningfully in regard to this preparation.

Mrs. Cousin was a gifted nineteenth century writer of many hymns and poems of great beauty. Her most popular work has been this hymn which first appeared in 1857 in the *Christian Treasury*. It originally had nineteen stanzas; only four, however, are still in use today.

Mrs. Cousin became deeply engrossed in the writings of a great seventeenth century Scotch Covenanter preacher, Samuel Rutherford. He was known as an outstanding evangelical preacher. Once a friend reported, "Many times I thought he would have flown out of the pulpit when he came to speak of Jesus Christ."

After nine years of this forceful, evangelical preaching, Rutherford's opposition to the State Church of Scotland caused his banishment to Aberdeen. Here he was permitted to live in his own hired house but was forbidden to preach.

Rutherford's exile ended in 1638 with the signing of the Solemn League and Covenant, the government's recognition of the independent church's freedom. He continued to be an influential leader in the non-conformist movement until 1660 when once again, with the death of Cromwell, the end of the rule of the Commonwealth and the restoration of Charles II, the wrath of the monarchy again fell on him. Rutherford was relieved of all of his offices and summoned to answer to the next British Parliament to charges of high treason. There was every likelihood that this trial would result in his being beheaded. This citation came too late, however, for Rutherford was already on his death bed, where he calmly remarked, "I behoove to answer my first summons, and ere your day for me arrive, I will be where few kings and great folks come." He answered that first summons on March 30, 1661. It is recorded that his dying words were, "*Glory, Glory Dwelleth in Immanuel's Land.*" This triumphant exclamation was used by God to become the inspiration for Ann Cousin's hymn text two centuries later.

Here are the words of her hymn. Note especially verses three and four:

> *The sands of time are sinking, the dawn of heaven breaks;*
> *The summer morn I've sighed for—the fair, sweet morn awakes:*
> *Dark, dark hath been the midnight, but dayspring is at hand,*
> *And glory, glory dwelleth in Immanuel's land.*

O Christ, He is the fountain, the deep, sweet well of love!
The streams on earth I've tasted more deep I'll drink above:
There to an ocean fullness, His mercy doth expand,
And glory, glory dwelleth in Immanuel's land.

O I am my Beloved's, and my Beloved's mine!
He brings a poor vile sinner into His "house of wine."
I stand upon His merit—I know no other stand,
Not even where glory dwelleth in Immanuel's land.

The Bride eyes not her garment, but her dear Bridegroom's face;
I will not gaze at glory, but on my King of grace.
Not at the crown He giveth, but on His pierced hand:
The Lamb is all the glory of Immanuel's land.

HE'S STILL COMING

CHAPTER 4
17 Key Events of Prophecy to Occur During the Tribulation

GENERAL INTRODUCTION TO THE GREAT TRIBULATION

- ▓ **The names involved**

  No less than twelve titles for this blood-chilling period can be found in the Bible:

  A. The Day of the Lord—This title is used more frequently than any other. See, for example, Isa. 2:12; 13:6, 9; Ezek. 13:5; 30:3; Joel 1:15; 2:1, 11, 31; 3:14; Amos 5:18, 20; Obad. 15; Zeph. 1:7, 14; Zech. 14:1; Mal. 4:5; Acts 2:20; 1 Thess. 5:2; 2 Thess. 2:2; 2 Peter 3:10. A distinction should be made between the Day of the Lord and the day of Christ. The day of Christ is a reference to the Millennium. See 1 Cor. 1:8; 5:5; 2 Cor. 1:14; Phil. 1:6, 10; 2:16.

  B. The indignation (Isa. 26:20; 34:2)

  C. The day of God's vengeance (Isa. 34:8; 63:1-6)

  D. The time of Jacob's trouble (Jer. 30:7)

  E. The overspreading of abominations (Dan. 9:27)

  F. The time of trouble such as never was (Dan. 12:1)

  G. The seventieth week (Dan. 9:24-27)

  H. The time of the end (Dan. 12:9)

  I. The great day of his wrath (Rev. 6:17)

  J. The hour of his judgment (Rev. 14:7)

  K. The end of this world (Matt. 13:40, 49)

  L. The Tribulation (Matt. 24:21, 29)—The word *tribulation* is derived from the Latin *tribulem*, which was an agricultural tool used for separating the husks from the corn. As found in the Bible, the theological implications would include such concepts as a pressing together, an affliction, a burdening with anguish and trouble, a binding with oppression. Keeping this in mind, it would seem that of all the twelve names for the coming calamity, the last one would most accurately describe this period. Therefore, from this point on, the term tribulation will be employed.

- ▓ **The nature involved**

  Both Daniel the prophet and Jesus Himself warned of this period:

  " ... there has be a time of trouble, such as never has been since there was a nation ... " (Dan. 12:1).

  "For then there will be great tribulation, such as has not been from the beginning of the world until now, no, and never will be. And if those days had not been cut short, no human being would be saved. But for the sake of the elect those days will be cut short" (Matt. 24:21, 22).

  The following list has placed the severe nature of the Great Tribulation into fourteen general categories:

  A. Cosmic-related

     1. Fearful heavenly signs and disturbances (Joel 2:10)

2. Massive hailstones composed of fire and blood to fall upon the earth (Rev. 8:7; 16:21)

3. Huge meteorites to strike our planet (Rev. 8:8-11)

4. The stars of the heavens to rain down upon our world (Rev. 6:13)

5. Scorching solar heat (Rev. 16:8-9)

6. Terrifying periods of total darkness (Rev. 16:10)

7. Sun, moon, and stars to withhold their light (Isa. 13:10; Joel 2:30-31)

8. The moon to be turned into blood (Joel 2:31; Rev. 6:12)

9. The heavens to be rolled together like a scroll (Isa. 34:4; Rev. 6:14)

B. Land-related

1. Terrible worldwide famines (Rev. 6:5-6, 8)

2. Humans to be slaughtered by predatory wild beasts (Rev. 6:8)

3. Disastrous earthquakes (Rev. 6:12; 11:13; 16:18)

4. Universal disaster of land ecology (Rev. 8:7)

5. Unchecked citywide fires (Rev. 18:8-9, 18)

C. Water-related

1. Universal tidal waves and ocean disasters (Luke 21:25; Rev. 8:8-9; 16:3)

2. Both salt waters and fresh waters to become totally polluted (Rev. 8:8-11; 11:6, 16:3-4)

D. Underground-related

1. Subterranean eruptions (Rev. 9:1, 2)

E. Disease-related

1. A plague of cancerous sores (Rev. 16:2)

2. History's most frightful physical plague (Zech. 14:12)

F. Distress-related

1. A time of utter depression (Joel 2:2)

2. No period in history to compare to it (Jer. 30:7; Dan.12:1; Matt. 24:21-22)

G. Persecution-related

1. Vicious attacks upon believers (Matt. 24:9, 10; Rev. 16:6; 17:6)

2. An all-out, no-holds-barred attempt to destroy Israel (Rev. 12:1-17)

H. Religious deception-related

1. Rise of false messiahs and prophets (Matt. 24:11; 24:5)

I. Demonic activity-related

1. Universal idolatry and devil worship (Rev. 9:20; 13:11-17)

2. Invasion of murderous demonic creatures (Rev. 9:3-20)

J. Antichrist-related

1. The ultimate and universal reign of Satan's Superman (Rev. 13)
K. Total breakdown of morality-related
   1. Drunkenness (Matt. 24:38; Luke 17:27)
   2. Illicit sex (Rev. 9:21)
   3. Gross materialism (Rev. 18:12-14)
   4. Worldwide drug usage (Rev. 9:21)
L. Society-related
   1. Total destruction of earth's political, religious and economic systems (Rev. 17, 18)
M. War-related
   1. Bloody universal confrontations (Matt. 24:6, 7; Rev. 6:2-4; 14:20)
N. The gory and grievous bottom-line results
   1. Men to hide in caves (Isa. 2:19-21; Rev. 6:15-17)
   2. Pangs and sorrows of death to seize men, similar to the pains of women in labor (Isa. 13:8)
   3. No period in history to compare it to (Jer. 30:7; Dan. 12:1; Matt. 24:21, 22)
   4. A time of famine of the Word of God itself (Amos 8:11, 12)
   5. Survivors to be more rare than gold (Isa. 13:12)
   6. Human blood to be poured out like dust and their flesh like dung (Zeph. 1:17)
   7. The slain to remain unburied and the mountains to be covered with blood (Isa. 34:3; 66:24)
   8. The earth itself—
     a. To be moved out of its orbit (Isa. 13:13)
     b. To be turned upside down (Isa. 24:1, 19)
     c. To stagger like a drunkard (Isa. 24:20)
   9. A 200-mile river of human blood to flow (Rev. 14:20)
   10. Scavenger birds to eat the rotted flesh of entire armies of men
     a. Following the Gog and Magog battle (Ezek. 39:17-19)
     b. Following the Armageddon battle (Rev. 19:17-19)

■ **The reasons involved**

Why this terrible period? There are at least seven scriptural reasons:

A. To harvest the crop that has been sown throughout the ages by God, Satan, and mankind (Matt. 13:24-30, 47-50). Thus, as taught by this parable of Jesus through the Great Tribulation, the wheat will be separated from the tares, with the first to *"shine forth as the sun in the kingdom of their Father,"* and the second *"to be cast ... into a furnace of fire ..."*

B. To prove the falseness of the devil's claim:

Since his fall (Isa. 14:12-14), Satan has been attempting to convince a skeptical universe that he rather than Christ is the logical and rightful ruler of creation. Therefore, during the Tribulation the sovereign God will give him a free and unhindered hand to make good his boast. Needless to say, Satan will fail miserably.

C. To prepare a great martyred multitude for heaven (Rev. 7:9, 14)

D. To prepare a great living multitude for the Millennium (Matt. 25:32-34)

E. To punish the Gentiles (Rom. 1:18; 2 Thess. 2:11-12)

F. To purge Israel (Ezek. 20:37-38; Zech. 13:8-9; Mal. 3:3)

G. To prepare the earth itself for the Millennium—The Bible indicates that prior to the great flood our earth was surrounded by a watery canopy (Gen. 1:6-7; 7:11) resulting in a universal semitropical paradise of a climate. The discovery of vast oil and coal deposits in the area of both the north and south poles bears strong witness to this. In addition there were probably no deserts, ice caps, rugged mountains, or deep canyons, all of which so radically affect our weather today. But then came the flood, changing all this. (The psalmist may have written about this in Psalm 104:5-9.) However, during the Millennium, pre-flood conditions will once again prevail. (See Isa. 4:5; 30:26; 40:3-5; 60:19-20.) Mankind will once again experience longevity. (Compare Gen. 5 with Isa. 65:20.)

But by what process will all these tremendous changes come about? It is interesting that the King James Bible translators used the word regeneration on but two occasions. One is in reference to the conversion of repenting sinners (Titus 3:5), and the other describes the salvation of nature itself.

Note Jesus's words to His disciples: *"Jesus said unto them, Verily I say unto you, That ye which have followed me, in the regeneration when the Son of man shall sit in the throne of his glory, ye also shall sit upon twelve thrones, judging the twelve tribes of Israel"* (Matt. 19:28).

In other words, Mother Nature herself will be gloriously regenerated and give up her evil habits (droughts, tornadoes, floods, cyclones, earthquakes, volcanic action, etc.) at the beginning of the Millennium. Here are the conditions that will lead up to her marvelous conversion:

1. Between the sixth and seventh judgment seals the winds of heaven will be held back—*"And after these things I saw four angels standing on the four corners of the earth, holding the four winds of the earth, that the wind should not blow on the earth, nor on the sea, nor on any tree"* (Rev. 7:1).

2. During the fourth vial judgment, great solar heat will proceed from the sun—*"And the fourth angel poured out his vial upon the sun; and power was given unto him to scorch men with fire. And men were scorched with great heat, and blasphemed the name of God, which hath power over these plagues: and they repented not to give him glory"* (Rev. 16:8-9).

3. As a result of the seventh vial judgment, the mightiest earthquake yet will take place—*"And there were voices, and thunders, and lightnings; and there was a great*

earthquake, such as was not since men were upon the earth, so mighty an earth-quake, and so great.... And every island fled away, and the mountains were not found" (Rev. 16:18, 20).

4. During the Tribulation the sun will boil away great quantities of water into the upper atmosphere. However, the absence of wind will prohibit the formation of clouds, thus making it impossible for rain to fall. As a result, the original pre-flood canopy will be reestablished.

5. The world's greatest earthquake will level the mountains and fill up the deep canyons, thus the gentle geographical terrain existing before the flood.

6. What a wonderful and gracious God we have, who will use the very wrath of the Tribulation as an instrument to prepare for the glories of the Millennium. In per-forming this, God will answer a prayer once uttered by the prophet Habakkuk some six centuries B.C.

"O Lord, I have heard the report of you, and your work, O Lord, do I fear. In the midst of the years revive it; in the midst of the years make it known; in wrath remember mercy" (Hab. 3:2).

On a personal note here, many years ago, I briefly pastored a small rural church in central Illinois. Most of the members were farmers.

One day I was shown an article written by the editor in a farm magazine. In essence, it said that although the editor was not a religious man, yet he thought it a good practice for his readers to heed the scriptural admonition to work their ground for six days and let it rest on the seventh.

However, this simple (and sensible) suggestion terribly upset one of his readers who responded in a very caustic manner: "What foolishness," he began. "Listen, this year I planted my crops on Sunday; I fertilized my crops on Sunday. And guess what? Well, I have seen a greater harvest return than my church-going neighbors who took Sundays off. So now, here it is in October, and I can only conclude that God had absolutely nothing whatsoever to do with it!"

The letter was printed in the following magazine issue, with a brief observation from the editor: "Dear Sir, God does not settle all His accounts in October."

In closing this section which introduces the Great Tribulation, the words of Charles A. Beard seems to say it best: "The mills of God grind slowly, but they grind exceedingly small."

The seventy weeks involved

One of the most profound and far-reaching prophecies in all the Bible was written by Daniel the prophet just before his death in Babylon. It reveals certain facts regarding the Great Tribulation unknown until this time. Here are its contents:

"Seventy weeks are determined upon thy people and upon thy holy city, to finish the transgression, and to make an end of sins, and to make reconciliation for iniquity, and to bring in everlasting righteousness, and to seal up the vision and prophecy, and to anoint the most

Holy. Know therefore and understand, that from the going forth of the commandment to restore and to build Jerusalem unto the Messiah the Prince shall be seven weeks, and threescore and two weeks: the street shall be built again, and the wall, even in troublous times. And after threescore and two weeks shall Messiah be cut off, but not for himself: and the people of the prince that shall come shall destroy the city and the sanctuary; and the end thereof shall be with a flood, and unto the end of the war desolations are determined. And he shall confirm the covenant with many for one week and in the midst of the week he shall cause the sacrifice and the oblation to cease, and for the overspreading of abominations he shall make it desolate, even until the consummation, and that determined shall be poured upon the desolate" (Dan. 9:24-27).

Here six questions must be answered:

A. To whom does this prophecy refer?

It refers to Israel.

B. What is meant by the term "seventy weeks"?

The expression means literally "seventy sevens of years." In other words, God is here telling Daniel that he would continue to deal with Israel for another 490 years before bringing in everlasting righteousness.

C. When was the seventy-week period to begin?

It was to begin with the command to rebuild Jerusalem's walls. The first two chapters of Nehemiah inform us that this command was issued during the twentieth year of Artaxerxes' ascension. The *Encyclopedia Britanica* sets this date as March 5, 444 B.C.

D. What are the two major time periods mentioned within the seventy weeks (490 years)?

1. The first period to consist of sixty-nine weeks (483 years), from 444 B.C. to the crucifixion of Christ in 33 A.D.

2. The second period to consist of one week (seven years) from the Rapture to the earthly return of Jesus. Thus, the seventieth week of Daniel is in reality the Great Tribulation.

E. Do the seventy weeks run continuously?

This is to say, is there a gap somewhere between these 490 years or do they run without pause until they are completed?

Dispensational theology teaches that these weeks do not run continuously, but that there has been a gap or parenthesis of nearly 2,000 years between the sixty-ninth and seventieth week. This is known as the age of the Church. The chronology may be likened to a seventy-minute basketball game. For sixty-nine minutes the game has been played at a furious and continuous pace. Then the referee for some reason calls time out with the clock in the red and showing one final minute of play. No one knows for sure when the action will start again, but at some point the referee will step in and blow his whistle. At that time the teams will gather to play out the last minute of the game.

God has stepped in and stopped the clock of prophecy at Calvary. This divine "time out" has already lasted some twenty centuries, but soon the Redeemer will blow His trumpet, and the final "week" of action will be played upon this earth.

F. Does the Bible offer any other examples of time gaps in divine programs?

It does indeed. At least three instances come to mind in which gaps of many centuries can be found in a single short paragraph. See Isa. 9:6, 7; 61:1, 2; Zech. 9:9, 10.

G. How can all this be best summarized?

Thomas Ice offers the following excellent overview:

> **Explanation of Daniel's Seventy Weeks of Years**
> 69 x 7 x 360 = 173,880 days
> March 5, 444 B.C. + 173,880 = March 30, A.D. 33
>
> **Verification**
> 444 B.C. to A.D. 33 = 476 years
> 476 years x 365.2421989 days = 173,855 days
> + days between March 5 and March 30 = 25 days
> Totals = 173,880 days
>
> **Rationale for 360-Day Years**
> Half week—Daniel 9:27
> Time, times, and half a time—Daniel 7:25; 12:7; Revelation 12:14
> 1260 days—Revelation 12:6; 11:3
> 42 months—Revelation 11:2; 13:5
> Thus: 42 months = 1260 days = time, times, and half a time + half week
> Therefore: month = 30 days; year = 360 days
>> (*The Truth About the Tribulation*, Harvest House Publisher, p. 19)

EVENT 1 THE SEVEN-FOLD SEAL, TRUMPET, AND BOWL JUDGMENTS TO BE POURED OUT FROM HEAVEN UPON SINFUL MAN DURING THE GREAT TRIBULATION_____

INTRODUCTION

These fearful divine judgments will constitute the complete and ultimate fulfillment as warned by the apostle Paul: "*For the wrath of God is revealed from heaven against all ungodliness and unrighteousness of men, who suppress the truth in unrighteousness*" (Rom. 1:18).

■ The seven seal judgments

A. The first seal (Rev. 6:2)

"And I saw, and behold a white horse; and he that sat on him had a bow; and a crown was given unto him; and he went forth conquering and to conquer."

This is doubtless a symbolic picture of the Antichrist as he subdues to himself the ten nations of the revived Roman Empire. This may be thought of as the "Cold War" period. We note he carries no arrow, which may indicate conquest by diplomacy rather than shooting war.

B. The second seal (Rev. 6:3, 4)

"And when he had opened the second seal, I heard the second beast say, Come and see. And there went out another horse that was red; and power was given to him that sat thereon to take peace from the earth, and that they should kill one another; and there was given unto him a great sword."

The uneasy peace which the rider on the white horse brings to earth is temporary and counterfeit. The Antichrist promises peace, but only God can actually produce it!

As Isaiah would write, *"But the wicked are like the troubled sea, when it cannot rest, whose waters cast up mire and dirt. There is no peace, saith my God, to the wicked"* (Isa. 57:20, 21). Now open and bloody hostility breaks out among some of the nations.

C. The third seal (Rev. 6:5, 6)

"And when he had opened the third seal, I heard the third beast say, Come and see. And I beheld, and lo a black horse; and he that sat on him had a pair of balances in his hand. And I heard a voice in the midst of the four beasts say, A measure of wheat for a penny, and three measures of barley for a penny; and see thou hurt not the oil and the wine."

Dr. Charles Ryrie writes the following concerning this seal:

"The third judgment brings famine to the world. The black horse forebodes death, and the pair of balances bespeaks a careful rationing of food. Normally, a 'penny' (a Roman denarius, a day's wages in Palestine in Jesus' day, Matt. 20:2) would buy eight measures of wheat or three of barley. In other words, there will be one-eighth of the normal supply of food. The phrase 'see thou hurt not the oil and the wine' is an ironic twist in this terrible situation. Apparently luxury food items will not be in short supply, but of course most people will not be able to afford them. This situation will only serve to taunt the populace in their impoverished state. (*Revelation*, Moody Press, pp. 45-46)

D. The fourth seal (Rev. 6:7, 8)

"And when he had opened the fourth seal, I heard the voice of the fourth beast say, Come and see. And I looked, and behold a pale horse: and his name that sat on him was Death, and Hell followed with him. And power was given unto them over the fourth part of the earth, to kill with sword, and with hunger, and with death, and with the beasts of the earth."

1. The identity of these riders—John calls them "death" and "hell," apparently referring to physical and spiritual death. Thus the devil will destroy the bodies and damn the souls of multitudes of unbelievers during this fourth-seal plague.

2. The damage done by these riders—One-fourth of all humanity perishes during this plague. It is estimated that during the Second World War, one out of forty persons lost his life, but this seal judgment alone will claim one out of four persons—over one billion human beings! We note the phrase, "*with the beasts of the earth.*"

Here John Phillips has written:

> "The beasts are closely linked with the pestilence, and this might be a clue. The most destructive creature on earth as far as mankind is concerned, is not the lion or the bear, but the rat. The rat is clever, adaptable, and destructive. If ninety-five percent of the rat population is exterminated in a given area, the rat population will replace itself within a year. It has killed more people than all the wars in history, and makes its home wherever man is found. Rats carry as many as thirty-five diseases. Their fleas carry bubonic plague, which killed a third of the population of Europe in the fourteenth century. Their fleas also carry typhus, which in four centuries has killed an estimated two hundred million people. Beasts, in this passage, are linked not only with pestilence, but with famine. Rats menace human food supplies, which they both devour and contaminate, especially in the more underdeveloped countries which can least afford to suffer loss." (*Exploring Revelation*, Moody Press, 1974, p. 116)

E. The fifth seal (Rev. 6:9-11)

"And when he had opened the fifth seal, I saw under the altar the souls of them that were slain for the word of God, and for the testimony which they held: And they cried with a loud voice, saying, How long, O Lord, holy and true, dost thou not judge and avenge our blood on them that dwell on the earth? And white robes were given unto every one of them; and it was said unto them, that they should rest yet for a little season, until their fellow-servants also and their brethren, that should be killed as they were, should be fulfilled."

Here is religious persecution as never before. These three verses are loaded with theological implications.

1. They refute the false doctrine of soul-sleep.

2. They correct the error of one general resurrection—It is evident that the martyred souls did not receive their glorified bodies at the Rapture, as did the church-age saints. Therefore it can be concluded that these are Old Testament saints who will experience the glorious bodily resurrection after the Tribulation. (See Rev. 20:4-6.)

3. They suggest the possibilities of an intermediate body. (See also 2 Cor. 5:1-3.)

Dr. John Walvoord writes:

> "These martyred dead here pictured have not been raised from the dead and have not received their resurrection bodies. Yet is declared that they are given robes. The fact that they are given robes would almost demand that they have a body of some sort. A robe could not hang upon an immaterial soul or spirit. It is not the kind of body that Christians now have, that is the body of earth;

nor is it the resurrection body of flesh and bones which Christ spoke after His own resurrection. It is a temporary body suited for their presence in heaven but replaced in turn by their everlasting resurrection body given at the time of Christ's return." (*The Revelation of Jesus Christ*, Moody Press, 1966, p. 134)

F.   The sixth seal (Rev. 6:12-17)

"And I beheld when he had opened the sixth seal, and, lo, there was a great earthquake; and the sun became black as sackcloth of hair, and the moon became as blood; and the stars of heaven fell unto the earth, even as a fig tree casteth her untimely figs, when she is shaken of a mighty wind. And the heaven departed as a scroll when it is rolled together; and every mountain and island were moved out of their places. And the kings of the earth, and the great men, and the rich men, and the chief captains, and the mighty men, and every bond-man, and every free man, hid themselves in the dens and in the rocks of the mountains; and said to the mountains and rocks, Fall on us, and hide us from the face of him that sitteth on the throne, and from the wrath of the Lamb: For the great day of his wrath is come; and who shall be able to stand?"

1.   The greatest earthquake in history—There have, of course, been hundreds of severe earthquakes in man's history. The earliest recorded was in July, A.D. 365, in the Middle East. The most destructive was in January, 1556, in China, which nearly one million lost their lives. But at the end of the Tribulation there will be one even worse than the one occurring in the sixth seal. (See Rev. 16:18.)

2.   The greatest cosmic disturbances in history—This may be a result of nuclear war.

3.   The greatest prayer meeting in history—But they prayed for the wrong thing. The only object to protect the sinner from the wrath of the Lamb is the righteousness of the Lamb.

G.   The seventh seal (Rev. 8:1-5)

"And when he had opened the seventh seal, there was silence in heaven about the space of half an hour" (Rev. 8:1).

1.   The purpose of the silence—During the sixth seal, mankind seemed to weaken for the first time during the Tribulation. A merciful and patient God now awaits further repentance, but to no avail. God takes no pleasure in the death of the wicked (Ezek. 33:11).

2.   The duration of the silence—It was for thirty minutes. The number thirty in the Bible is often associated with mourning. Israel mourned for thirty days over the death of both Aaron (Num. 20:29) and Moses (Deut. 34:8).

■   **The seven trumpet judgments**

A.   The first trumpet (Rev. 8:7)

"The first angel sounded, and there followed hail and fire mingled with blood, and they were cast upon the earth: and the third part of trees was burnt up, and all green grass was burnt up" (Rev. 8:7).

It has been observed that plant life was the first to be created, and it is the first to be destroyed (Gen. 1:11, 12).

John Phillips writes:

> "Looked upon as a literal occurrence, an ecological disaster without parallel in historic times is described. The planet is denuded of a third of its trees and all of its grass. The consequences of this are bound to be terrible. The United States, for example, has already proceeded with deforestation to such an extent that the country contains only enough vegetation to produce sixty percent of the oxygen it consumes." (*Exploring Revelation*, Moody Press, 1974, p. 129)

B. The second trumpet (Rev. 8:8, 9)

> *"And the second angel sounded, and as it were a great mountain burning with fire was cast into the sea: and the third part of the sea became blood; And the third part of the creatures which were in the sea, and had life, died; and the third part of the ships were destroyed."*

Dr. Herman A. Hoyt writes:

> "Here we read of a great mountain burning with fire. This may refer to a meteoric mass from the sky falling headlong into the sea, perhaps the Mediterranean Sea. The result is to turn a third part of the sea a blood-red color and bring about the death of a third part of the life in the sea. Death may be caused by the chemical reaction in the water, such as radioactivity following atomic explosion. The third part of ships may be destroyed by the violence of the waters produced by the falling of the mass." (*Revelation*, BMH Press, 1966, p. 49)

C. The third trumpet (8:10-11)

> *"And the third angel sounded, and there fell a great star from heaven, burning as it were a lamp, and it fell upon the third part of the rivers, and upon the fountains of waters; And the name of the star is called Wormwood: and the third part of the waters became wormwood; and many men died of the waters, because they were made bitter."*

This star could refer to a meteor containing stifling and bitter gases, which might fall on the Alps or some other freshwater source. During the second trumpet, a third of the salt water was contaminated. Now a third of earth's fresh water suffers a similar fate. Many species of wormwood grow in Palestine. All species have a strong, bitter taste.

D. The fourth trumpet (8:12)

> *"And the fourth angel sounded, and the third part of the sun was smitten, and the third part of the moon, and the third part of the stars; so as the third part of them was darkened, and the day shone not for a third part of it, and the night likewise."*

Our Lord may have had this trumpet judgment in mind when he spoke the following words: *"And except those days should be shortened, there should no flesh be saved: but for the elect's sake those days shall be shortened"* (Matt. 24:22). *"And there shall be signs in the sun, and in the moon, and in the stars; and upon the earth distress of nations, with perplexity; the sea and the waves roaring"* (Luke 21:25).

The Old Testament prophecy of Amos is also significant here: *"And it shall come to pass in that day, saith the Lord God, that I will cause the sun to go down at noon, and I will darken the earth in the clear day"* (Amos 8:9).

It was on the fourth day that God created the sun, moon, and the stars (Gen. 1:14-16). They were to be for *"signs, and for seasons, and for days, and for years."* After the flood, God promised not to alter this divine arrangements (Gen. 8:22). But in the Tribulation, during the fourth trumpet, earth's very light will be limited by judgment.

E.   The fifth trumpet (Rev. 9:1-12)

1.   The ninth chapter of Revelation, which contains both fifth and sixth trumpet judgments, may be the most revealing section in all the Bible concerning the subject of demonology. Prior to this God has already made it known that there are two kinds of unfallen angels. These are the cherubim (Gen. 3:24; Ezek. 10:1-20), and the seraphim (Isa. 6:1-8). Here He may be describing for us the two kinds of fallen angels. We now note the first type as revealed in the fifth trumpet judgment.

2.   The location of these demons:

The bottomless pit (9:2). Literally this phrase is "shaft of the abyss." The word 'shaft' here indicates that there is an entrance from the surface of the earth to the heart of our planet. In this chapter we learn for the first time of a place called the bottomless pit. God mentions it no less than seven times in the book of Revelation (9:1, 2, 11; 11:7; 17:8; 20:1-3).

3.   The identity of these demons:

Some have identified these with the sons of God in Genesis 6:1, 2. Here the theory is that these demons attempted sexual relations with women, resulting in immediate confinement in the bottomless pit. We do know that some demons are already chained and others at present have access to the bodies of men.

a.   Unchained demons (Matt. 8:29; Luke 4:34; 8:27-31)

b.   Chained demons (Jude 6, 7; 1 Peter 3:18-20). Thus another name for this bottomless pit may be the *tartarus* mentioned in the Greek text of 2 Peter 2:4. Here Satan will be later confined during the Millennium (Rev. 20:3).

4.   The description of these demons (Rev. 9:7-10):

The shapes of these creatures are absolutely hideous. They are like horses prepared for battle. Crowns of gold seem to be upon their heads. Their faces are like men, their hair like women, their teeth like lions. They have on breastplates as of iron. Their tails are like those of a scorpion. The sound of their wings is like that of many chariots rushing toward battle.

5.   The king of these demons (Rev. 9:11):

His name is Apollyon, which means "destroyer." Here is Satan's hellish "Michael, the Archangel."

6. The one who releases these demons:

   This "fallen star," mentioned in 9:1, seems to be Satan himself. (See also Isa. 14:12; Luke 10:18; 2 Cor. 11:14.) Prior to this time Christ has held the key to the pit (Rev. 1:18), but he now allows the devil to use it for a specific purpose.

7. The torment of these demons (Rev. 9:3, 4)

   "Then out of the smoke locusts came upon the earth. And to them was given power, as the scorpions of the earth have power. They were commanded not to harm the grass of the earth, or any green thing, or any tree, but only those men who do not have the seal of God on their foreheads."

8. The duration of these demons (Rev. 9:5, 6)

   "And they were not given authority to kill them, but to torment them for five months. Their torment was like the torment of a scorpion when it strikes a man. In those days men will seek death and will not find it; they will desire to die, and death will flee from them."

F. The sixth trumpet (Rev. 9:13-21):

As we have already noted, it would seem John describes two kinds of demons, which will invade earth during the Tribulation. The sixth trumpet now ushers in the second invasion.

1. The leaders of this invasion (Rev. 9:14a)

   Four special Satanic angels—They may function to the devil as the four living creatures do to God (Rev. 4:6-8).

2. The army of this invasion (Rev. 9:16)

   a. Their number: Two hundred million! By normal standards this great army would occupy a territory one mile wide and eighty-seven miles long!

   b. Their description: These demons, unlike those involved in the first invasion, seem to be mounted upon some type of hellish horse. The horses' heads look much like lions' heads, with smoke, fire, and flaming sulfur billowing from their mouths. The riders wore fiery-red breastplates.

3. The source of this invasion (Rev. 9:14b)

   The Euphrates River—This is where evil began on earth (Zech. 5:8-11; Gen. 3), where false religion began (Gen. 4:3; 10:9, 10; 11:4), and where it will come to its end (Rev. 17-18).

4. The duration of this invasion (Rev. 9:15)

   "So the four angels, who had been prepared for the hour and day and month and year, were released to kill a third of mankind."

5. The damage wrought by this invasion (Rev. 9:18, 19)

   One third of humanity will perish.

6. The reaction following this invasion (Rev. 9:20, 21)

"But the rest of mankind, who were not killed by these plagues, did not repent of the works of their hands, that they should not worship demons, and idols of gold, silver, brass, stone, and wood, which can neither see nor hear nor walk. And they did not repent of their murders or their sorceries or their sexual immorality or their thefts."

At this point over one-half of the world's population has been wiped out. And what is the response of the survivors? Total unrepentance and intensified rebellion. That very year the FBI reports will probably show a thousand percent increase in idolatry, murder, drug-related crimes (the word "sorceries" is the Greek *pharmakeion*, from which we get our "pharmacy"; it is the Greek word for drugs), sex, felonies, and robbery.

G. The seventh trumpet (Rev. 10:7; 11:15-19):

Six aspects are introduced at the sounding of the seventh trumpet:

1. The mystery of God

   "But in the days of the sounding of the seventh angel, when he is about to sound, the mystery of God would be finished, as He declared to His servants the prophets" (Rev. 10:7).

   Without the slightest doubt, the single greatest accusation universally and continuously hurled against God has to do with the presence of evil and suffering in our world. It has been noted that these two terrible scourges are the rock bed foundation of atheism! If the God of the Bible is all-knowing and all-caring, why did He allow this deadly duet to corrupt His perfect world? Furthermore, if He is all-powerful why doesn't He step in and end the torture? Why indeed?

   Responding to this, it has been suggested that the mystery referred to in this verse may well involve a full and unedited disclosure by God Himself as to the *why* of the matter.

   When (and if) this happens, then all the Lamb's blood-washed sons and daughters (Rev. 1:5) will surely, in unison, utter the same words of praise which were said some 2,000 years ago by a Galilean crowd as they watched in amazement as the Savior healed the sick, restored sight to the blind, and hearing to the deaf ... *"He hath done all things well!"* (Mk. 7:37).

   A glorious testimony indeed, once heard in the past, once to be heard in the future. But what of this uncertain and ungodly present-day age we find ourselves in? The wise believers will take great comfort from the following lines, written by A. M. Overton:

   > *My Father's way may twist and turn,*
   > *My heart may throb and ache.*
   > *But in my soul I'm glad I know,*
   > *He maketh no mistake.*
   >
   > *There's so much now I cannot see,*
   > *My eyesight's far too dim;*

But come what may I'll simply trust,
And leave it all to Him.

For by and by the mist will lift,
And plain it all He'll make,
Through all the way, though dark to me,
He made not one mistake."

2. The kingdom of God

   "Then the temple of God was opened in heaven, and the ark of His covenant was seen in His temple. And there were lightnings, noises, thunderings, an earthquake, and great hail" (Rev. 11:19).

3. The worship of God

   "And the twenty-four elders who sat before God on their thrones fell on their faces and worshiped God" (Rev. 11:16)

4. The power of God

   "Saying: 'We give You thanks, O Lord God Almighty, the One who is and who was and who is to come, because You have taken Your great power and reigned'" (Rev. 11:17).

5. The wrath of God

   "The nations were angry, and Your wrath has come, And the time of the dead, that they should be judged, And that You should reward Your servants the prophets and the saints, And those who fear Your name, small and great, And should destroy those who destroy the earth" (Rev. 11:18).

6. The temple of God

   "Then the temple of God was opened in heaven, and the ark of His covenant was seen in His temple. And there were lightnings, noises, thunderings, an earthquake, and great hail" (Rev. 11:19).

■ **The seven bowl or vial judgments**

A. The first vial (Rev. 16:2)

   "And the first went, and poured out his vial upon the earth; and there fell a noisome and grievous sore upon the men which had the mark of the beast, and upon them which worshipped his image."

   J. Vernon McGee writes:

   "God is engaged in germ warfare upon the followers of Antichrist.... These putrefying sores are worse than leprosy or cancer. This compares to the sixth plague in Egypt, and is the same type of sore or boil (Exod. 9:8-12)." (*Reveling Through Revelation*, p. 36).

B. The second vial (Rev. 16:3)

   "And the second angel poured out his vial upon the sea; and it became as the blood of a dead man; and every living soul died in the sea."

Dr. Charles Ryrie writes the following concerning this plague:

> "The second bowl is poured on the sea, with the result that the waters became blood and every living thing in the sea dies. The 'as' is misplaced in the Authorized Version, the correct reading being 'became blood as of a dead man.' The vivid image is of a dead person wallowing in his own blood. The seas will wallow in blood. Under the second trumpet, one-third of the sea creatures died (8:9); now the destruction is complete. The stench and disease that this will cause along the shores of the seas of the earth are unimaginable. (*Revelation*, Moody Press, 1968, p. 97)

C. The third vial (Rev. 16:4-7)

"And the third angel poured out his vial upon the rivers and fountains of waters; and they became blood. And I heard the angel of the waters say, Thou art righteous, O Lord, which art, and wast, and shalt be, because thou hast judged thus. For they have shed the blood of saints and prophets, and thou hast given them blood to drink; for they are worthy. And I heard another out of the altar say, Even so, Lord God Almighty, true and righteous are thy judgments."

Two significant things may be noted in these verses:

1. This third vial judgment is, among other things, an answer to the cry of the martyrs under the altar at the beginning of the Tribulation. Their prayer at that time was, *"How long, O Lord, holy and true, dost thou not judge and avenge our blood on them that dwell on the earth?"* (Rev. 6:10).

2. These verses indicate that God has assigned a special angel as superintendent on earth's waterworks. When we compare this with Revelation 7:1, where we are told that four other angels control the world's winds, we realize that even during the hellishness of the Tribulation this world is still controlled by God.

D. The fourth vial (Rev. 16:8, 9)

"And the fourth angel poured out his vial upon the sun; and power was given unto him to scorch men with fire. And men were scorched with great heat, and blasphemed the name of God, which hath power over these plagues: and they repented not to give him glory." (See also Deut. 32:24; Isa. 24:6; 42:25; Mal. 4:1; Luke 21:25.)

Perhaps the two most illuminating passages in Scripture about man's total depravity can be found in Revelation 9:20-21 and 16:9. Both sections deal with the world's attitude toward God during the Tribulation.

"And the rest of the men which were not killed by these plagues yet repented not of the works of their hands, that they should not worship devils, and idols of gold, and silver, and brass, and stone, and of wood: which neither can see, nor hear, nor walk: Neither repented they of their murders, nor of their sorceries, nor of their fornication, nor of their thefts" (Rev. 9:20-21). *"And they repented not to give him glory"* (Rev. 16:9).

What do the verses prove? They prove that in spite of horrible wars, of terrible famines, of darkened skies, of raging fires, of bloody seas, of stinging locusts, of demonic persecutions, of mighty earthquakes, of falling stars, and of cancerous sores, sinful mankind still will not repent.

E. The fifth vial (Rev. 16:10, 11)

"And the fifth angel poured out his vial upon the seat of the beast; and his kingdom was full of darkness; and they gnawed their tongues for pain, and blasphemed the God of heaven because of their pains and their sores, and repented not of their deeds (Rev. 16:10, 11). (See also Isa. 60:2; Joel 2:1, 2, 31; Amos 5:18; Nah. 1:6, 8; Zeph. 1:15.)

This plague, poured out upon "the seat of the beast" (literally, his "throne"), will apparently concentrate itself upon the ten nations of the revived Roman Empire. Again we read those tragic words *"and repented not of their deeds."*

F. The sixth vial (Rev. 16:12)

"And the sixth angel poured out his vial upon the great river Euphrates; and the water thereof was dried up, that the way of the kings of the east might be prepared. And I saw three unclean spirits like frogs come out of the mouth of the dragon, and out of the mouth of the beast, and out of the mouth of the false prophet. For they are the spirits of devils, working miracles, which go forth unto the kings of the earth and of the whole world, to gather them to the battle of that great day of God Almighty" (Rev. 16:12-14).

Here the God of heaven employs psychological warfare upon his enemies, conditioning them to gather themselves together in the near future at Armageddon.

The Euphrates River is 1,800 miles long and in some places 3,600 feet wide. It is thirty feet deep. This river has been the dividing line between Western and Eastern civilization since the dawn of history. It served as the eastern border of the old Roman Empire. Thus, the Euphrates becomes both the cradle and grave of man's civilization. Here the first godless city (Enoch, built by Cain; see Gen. 4:16, 17) went up, and here the last rebellious city will be constructed (Babylon, built by the Antichrist; see Rev. 18).

G. The seventh vial judgment (Rev. 16:17-21)

"And the seventh angel poured out his vial into the air; and there came a great voice out of the temple of heaven, from the throne, saying, It is done. And there were voices, and thunders, and lightnings; and there was a great earthquake, such as was not since men were upon the earth, so mighty an earthquake, and so great. And the great city was divided into three parts, and the cities of the nations fell: and great Babylon came in remembrance before God, to give unto her the cup of the wine of the fierceness of his wrath. And every island fled away, and the mountains were not found. And there fell upon men a great hail out of heaven, every stone about the weight of a talent: and men blasphemed God because of the plague of the hail; for the plague thereof was exceeding great."

Thus ends the seal, trumpet, and vial judgments.

Three items in this last vial are worthy of observation:

The statement, *"It is done,"* is the second of three biblical occurrences in which this phrase is connected with some great event. The first event was Calvary and the last will be the threshold of eternity.

"When Jesus therefore had received the vinegar, he said, It is finished; and bowed his head, and gave up the ghost" (John 19:30).

"And he said unto me, It is done. I am the Alpha and Omega, the beginning and the end. I will give unto him that is athirst of the fountain of the water of life freely" (Rev. 21:6).

The world's greatest earthquake takes place. The intensity of an earthquake is measured on an instrument called a Richter scale. The greatest magnitude ever recorded so far has been 8.9. The greatest loss of life due to an earthquake occurred on January 23, 1556, in Shensi Province, China, and killed some 830,000 people. However, that earthquake will be but a mild tremor compared to the Tribulation earthquake, which, we are told, will level all the great cities of the world.

The world's greatest shower of hailstones comes crashing down on mankind. These gigantic icy chunks will weigh up to 125 pounds apiece.

▌EVENT 2▐ THE APPEARANCES OF THE ANTICHRIST AND HIS FALSE PROPHET

Since the days of Adam, it has been estimated that approximately forty billion human beings have been born upon our earth. Nearly seven billion of this number are alive today. However, by any standard of measurement one might employ, the greatest human (apart from the Son of God Himself) in matters of ability and achievement is yet to make his appearance upon our planet.

■ **The names and titles for the Antichrist.** The Scriptures give him various names and titles:

A. The *little horn* (Dan. 7:8)

B. The *willful king* (Dan. 11:36)

C. The *man of sin* (2 Thess. 2:3)

D. The *son of perdition* (2 Thess. 2:3)

E. The *wicked one* (2 Thess. 2:8)

F. The *beast* (Rev. 11:7) —This title is found thirty-six times in the book of Revelation.

G. However, his most descriptive title is the *Antichrist* (1 John 2:18, 22; 4:3). Note but a few scriptural references describing this satanic superman:

"And he shall speak great words against the most High, and shall wear out the saints of the most High …" (Dan. 7:25).

"And the king shall do according to his will; and he shall exalt himself, and magnify himself above every god, and shall speak marvellous things against the God of gods …" (Dan. 11:36).

" … that man of sin … the son of perdition; Who opposeth and exalteth himself above all that is called God, or that is worshipped; so that he as God sitteth in the temple of God,

shewing himself that he is God ... Even him, whose coming is after the working of Satan with all power and signs and lying wonders" (2 Thess. 2:3, 4, 9).

"Who is a liar but he that denieth that Jesus is the Christ? He is antichrist, that denieth the Father and the Son" (1 John 2:22).

"And I saw, and behold a white horse: and he that sat on him had a bow; and a crown was given unto him: and he went forth conquering, and to conquer" (Rev. 6:2).

"And I stood upon the sand of the sea, and saw a beast rise up out of the sea ... And the beast which I saw was like unto a leopard, and his feet were as [the feet] of a bear, and his mouth as the mouth of a lion: and the dragon gave him his power, and great authority. And he opened his mouth in blasphemy against God ..." (Rev. 13:1, 2, 6).

■ **Historical and modern attempts to identify the Antichrist**

A. The ink of the holy writ which spoke of the Antichrist had scarcely dried before speculation arose concerning his identity.

Some believe he will be a Gentile. Tim LaHaye writes:

> One of the most frequently asked questions about the Antichrist concerns his nationality. Revelation 13:1 indicates that he *"rises up out of the sea,"* meaning the sea of peoples around the Mediterranean. From this we gather that he will be a Gentile. Daniel 8:8, 9 suggests that he is the *"little horn"* that came out of the four Grecian horns, signaling that he will be part Greek. Daniel 9:26 refers to him as the prince of the people that shall come, meaning that he will be of the royal lineage of the race that destroyed Jerusalem. Historically this was the Roman Empire; therefore, he will be predominantly Roman. (Tim LaHaye, *Revelation*, Zondervan, 1975, p. 172).

B. Others affirm he will be a Jew, based on two Old Testament passages and one New Testament passage.

"And thou, profane wicked prince of Israel, whose day is come, when iniquity shall have an end" (Ezek. 21:25).

"Neither shall he regard the God of his fathers ..." (Dan. 11:37).

"I am come in my Father's name, and ye receive me not: if another shall come in his own name, him ye will receive" (John 5:43).

C. There are also those who feel he will come from the tribe of Dan, basing this upon the following:

1. Jacob's prophecy upon his son Dan

   "Dan shall be a serpent by the way, an adder in the path, that biteth the horse heels, so that his rider shall fall backward" (Gen. 49:17).

2. Dan was the first tribe to be guilty of idolatry.

   See Judges 18:30, 31; 1 Kings 12:29. The tribe of Dan is omitted from the list in Rev. 7. This chapter records the tribal identity of the 144,000 Hebrew evangelists who will be saved and called to special service during the Tribulation.

D. A number of overzealous Bible students have claimed he could be personally identified.

   1. The Antichrist is Judas Iscariot.

   Some believe he will be Judas Iscariot, on the basis of the following verses:

   Luke 22:3; John 13:27 — Here Satan actually enters Judas. This is never said of any other individual in the Bible.

   John 6:70, 71 — Here Jesus refers to Judas as the devil.

   John 17:12; 2 Thess. 2:3—The title "son of perdition" is found only twice in the New Testament. In the first instance Jesus used it to refer to Judas. In the second instance Paul used it to refer to the Antichrist.

   Acts 1:25 — Here Peter says that Judas after his death went "to his own place." Some have seen in this a reference to the bottomless pit, and, believe that Satan has retained Judas there for the past 2,000 years in preparation for his future role as the Antichrist!

   2. The Antichrist is Nero.

   Nero committed suicide under somewhat mysterious circumstances in A.D. 68. Rumors then began to circulate that he would rise from the dead and lead a fierce army against God's people.

   3. The Antichrist is Titus.

   Titus was the Roman general who destroyed the city of Jerusalem in A.D. 70.

   4. The Antichrist is Domitian.

   Domitian was the Roman Emperor on the throne when John wrote the book of Revelation.

   5. The Antichrist is Constantine the Great.

   He was the Roman ruler who declared Christianity to be the state religion in A.D. 325, and thereby corrupting it with gross worldliness and paganism.

   6. The Antichrist is Mohammed.

   Mohammed was born in Mecca in A.D. 570 and later became the founder of the Islamic religion.

   7. The Antichrist is various Roman Catholic Popes.

   8. The Antichrist is Napoleon.

   On the opening page of Tolstoy's famous novel *War and Peace*, there is an interesting reference to this belief that Napoleon is the Antichrist.

   9. The Antichrist is Benito Mussolini.

   10. The Antichrist is Adolf Hitler.

   11. The Antichrist is whoever you don't especially like! It seems the foolish and futile Antichrist speculation syndrome has all but reached this sorry stage.

■ **The Old Testament forerunners of the Antichrist**

Just as there are many Old Testament characters who depict the person and work of the Lord Jesus (such as Melchizedek in Gen. 14 and Isaac in Gen. 22), there are a number of Old Testament men who describe for us the coming ministry of the Antichrist:

Cain—by his murder of the chosen seed (Gen. 4:5-14; Jude 11; 1 John 3:12)

Nimrod—by his creation of Babylon and the tower of Babel (Gen. 10, 11)

Pharaoh—by his oppression of God's people (Exod. 1:8-22)

Korah—by his rebellion (Num. 16:1-3; Jude 11)

Balaam—by his attempt to curse Israel (Num. 23, 24; 2 Peter 2:15; Jude 11; Rev. 2:14)

Saul—by his intrusion into the office of the priesthood (1 Sam. 13:9-13)

Goliath—by his proud boasting (1 Sam. 17)

Absalom—by his attempt to steal the throne of David (2 Sam. 15:1-6)

Jeroboam—by his substitute religion (1 Kings 12:25-31)

Sennacherib—by his efforts to destroy Jerusalem (2 Kings 18:13-17)

Nebuchadnezzar—by his golden statue (Dan. 3:1-7)

Haman—by his plot to exterminate the Jews (Esther 3)

Antiochus Epiphanes—by his defilement of the Temple (Dan. 11:21-35)

Of all the Old Testament foreshadows of the Antichrist, by far the most pronounced type is Antiochus Epiphanes. He was a Syrian. He came to the throne in 175 B.C. and ruled until 164 B.C. He was anti-Semitic to the core. He assaulted Jerusalem, murdering over 40,000 in three days, and selling an equal number into cruel slavery.

Dr. Walter Prices writes:

> On September 6, 171 B.C., he began his evil actions toward the Temple. On December 15, 168, his Temple desecration reached its ultimate low, for on that day this Nero of the Old Testament sacrificed a giant sow on an idol altar he had made in the Jewish Temple. He forced the priests to swallow its flesh, also made a broth of it, and sprinkled all the Temple. He finally carried off the golden candlesticks, table of shewbread, altar of incense, various other vessels, and destroyed the sacred books of the law. A large image of Jupiter was placed in the Holy of Holies. All this was termed by the horrified Jews as "The abomination of desolation," and is referred to by Jesus in Matt. 24:15 as a springboard to describe the activities of the future Antichrist. (*The Coming Antichrist*)

▪ **The personal characteristics of the Antichrist**

A. He will be an intellectual genius (Dan. 8:23).

B. He will be an oratorical genius (Dan. 11:36).

C. He will be a political genius (Rev. 17:11, 12).

D. He will be a commercial genius (Dan. 11:43; Rev. 13:16, 17).

E. He will be a military genius (Rev. 6:2; 13:2).

F. He will be a religious genius (2 Thess. 2:4; Rev. 13:8).

Thus, to use various American presidents as an analogy, here is a world leader possessing:

a. The leadership of a Washington and Lincoln
b. The eloquence of a Franklin Roosevelt
c. The charm of a Teddy Roosevelt
d. The charisma of a Kennedy
e. The popularity of an Ike
f. The political savvy of a Johnson
g. The intellect of a Jefferson

G. He shall do everything according to his own selfish will (Dan. 11:36). (See also Rev. 13:7; 17:13.) He shall magnify himself and malign God (Dan. 11:36). (See also 2 Thess. 2:4; Rev. 13:6.) The word for "marvelous things" in this verse is literally "astonishing, unbelievable." The Antichrist will scream out unbelievable blasphemies against God, insults no one else could ever think of or would dare say if he could. He will be allowed by God to prosper (be given full rope) during the Tribulation (the indignation) (see Dan. 11:36). (See also Rev. 11:7; 13:4, 7, 10.) The phrase "that which is determined shall be done," however, reminds us that God is still in absolute control, even during the terrible reign of this monster.

H. He will not regard *the gods of his fathers* (Dan. 11:37). The word for God is plural. The Antichrist will carry out a vendetta against all organized religion. In fact, it is he who will destroy that great harlot, bloody Babylon, which is the super world church. (See Rev. 17:5, 16.)

I. He will not have the desire for (or of) women (Dan. 11:37). Here three theories are offered to explain this phrase.

a. The normal desire for love, marriage, and sex. (See 1 Tim. 4:3.)
b. Those things characteristic of women, such as mercy, gentleness, and kindness.
c. That desire of Hebrew women to be the mother of the Messiah (1 Tim. 2:15).

J. His god will be the god of fortresses (11:38). The Antichrist will spend all his resources on military programs.

■ **The rise to power of the Antichrist**

A. Through the power of Satan (2 Thess. 2:3, 9-12; Rev. 13:2).

B. Through the permission of the Holy Spirit. His present-day manifestation is being hindered by the Holy Spirit until the Rapture of the church. God is in control of all situations down here and will continue to be (see Job 1-2; 2 Thess. 2:6, 7).

C. Through the formation of a ten-nation organization. He will proceed from a ten-dictatorship confederation which will come into existence during the Tribulation.

D. Through the cooperation of the false religious system (Rev. 17).

E. Through his personal charisma and ability.

F. Through a false peace program, probably in the Middle East (Dan. 8:25).

G. Through a master plan of deception and trickery (Matt. 24:24; 2 Thess. 2:9; Rev. 14:14). Out of the ninety-one occurrences in the New Testament of the words meaning "to deceive," or "to go astray," twenty-two of them belong definitely to passages dealing with the Antichrist and the Tribulation. (See Matt. 24:4, 5, 11, 24; 2 Thess. 2:3, 9-11; 2 Tim. 3:13; Rev. 12:9; 18:23; 19:20; 20:3, 8, 10.) Three reasons explain this fearful deception:

a. *Universal ignorance of God's Word* (see Matt. 22:29)

b. *Fierce demonic activity* (see 1 Tim. 4:1)

c. *The empty soul* (see Luke 11:24-26)

H. Through a possible and (many believe) probable event

1. The possible event

One of the most challenging and chilling problems confronting the leaders of most European nations is the number of Muslims living in their midst. France is already at their mercy. Many of these Muslims are hardcore, western-hating fanatics with but one supreme goal—that is, to utterly destroy all existing governments and force its citizens, either through submission or sword to become willing slaves to Allah!

But could it be that in the midst of this terrible threat a statesman or perhaps soldier might rise to the occasion, promising if given the power, to rid the country of this vicious cancer? If successful, he would immediately be heralded as a heroic twenty-first century Charles Martel, who stopped the Muslim hordes at the Battle of Tours in 731 A.D.

2. The probable event

The second event has to do with the assassination and resurrection of the Antichrist. Some years ago one of America's most influential news reporters was asked what he felt would be the greatest news story in history. After some reflection he replied, "Well, if a universally well-known leader, such as a president or king, would be assassinated and shortly following his state funeral, suddenly climb out of his coffin and demand that all peoples now submit to his authority, that, my friend, would be the greatest story in human history."

■ **The attempts of the Antichrist to imitate the real Christ**

The Antichrist would surely have been a tremendously successful mimic on any late night TV talk show! Note the following areas in which he will attempt to imitate the person and work of Christ.

A. The Antichrist comes in the very image of Satan, as Christ came in the image of God (2 Thess. 2:9; Rev. 13:4; cf. Col. 1:15 and Heb. 1:3).

B. The Antichrist is the second person in the hellish trinity, as Christ is in the heavenly Trinity (Rev. 16:13; cf. Matt. 28:19).

C. The Antichrist comes up from the abyss, while Christ comes down from heaven (Rev. 11:7; 17:8; cf. John 6:38).

D. The Antichrist is a savage beast, while Christ is a sacrificial Lamb (Rev. 13:2; cf. 5:6-9).

E. The Antichrist receives his power from Satan, as Christ received his power from his Father (Rev. 13:2; cf. Matt. 28:18).

F. The Antichrist will experience a resurrection (perhaps a fake one), just as Christ experienced a true one (Rev. 13:3, 12; cf. Rom. 1:4).

G. The Antichrist will receive the worship of all unbelievers, as Christ did of all believers (John 5:43; Rev. 13:3, 4, 8; cf. Matt. 2:11; Luke 24:52; John 20:28; Phil. 2:10, 11).

H. The Antichrist will deliver mighty speeches, as did Christ (Dan. 7:8; Rev. 13:5; cf. John 7:46). Satan will doubtless give to the Antichrist his vast knowledge of philosophy, science, and human wisdom accumulated through the centuries (Ezek. 28:12).

I. The greater part of the Antichrist's ministry will last some three and a half years, about the time span of Christ's ministry (Rev. 12:6, 14; 13:5)

J. The Antichrist will attempt (unsuccessfully) to combine the three Old Testament offices of prophet, priest, and king, as someday Christ will successfully do.

K. The Antichrist's symbolic number is six, while the symbolic number of Christ is seven (Rev. 13:18; cf. 5:6, 12).

L. The Antichrist will someday kill his harlot wife, while Christ will someday glorify his holy bride (Rev. 17:16, 17; cf. 21:1, 2).

The activities of the Antichrist

Bible scholar and prophecy expert, Dr. Mark Hitchcock has, in my mind, provided for us the most concise, yet complete, listing of the Antichrist's activities ever attempted. Here is the list:

A. He will appear in "the time of the end" of Israel's history (Dan. 8:17).

B. His manifestation will signal the beginning of the Day of the Lord (2 Thess. 2:1-3).

C. His manifestation is currently being hindered by the "restrainer" (2 Thess. 2:3-7).

D. His rise to power will come through peace programs (Rev. 6:4). He will make a covenant of peace with Israel (Dan. 9:27).

E. This event will signal the beginning of the seven-year Tribulation.

F. He will break that covenant at its midpoint.

G. Near the middle of the Tribulation, the Antichrist will be assassinated or violently killed (Dan. 11:45; Rev. 13:3, 12, 14).

H. He will descend into the abyss (Rev. 17:8).

I. He will be raised back to life (Rev. 13:3, 12, 14; 17:8).

J. The whole world will be amazed and will follow after him (Rev. 13:3).

K. He will be totally controlled and energized by Satan (Rev. 13:2-5).

L. He will subdue three of the ten kings in the reunited Roman Empire (Dan. 7:24).

M. The remaining seven kings will give all authority to the beast (Rev. 17:12-13).

N. He will invade the land of Israel and desecrate the rebuilt temple (Dan. 9:27; 11:41; 12:11; Matt. 24:15; Rev. 11:2).

O. He will mercilessly pursue and persecute the Jewish people (Dan. 7:21, 25; Rev. 12:6).

P. He will set himself up in the temple as God (2 Thess. 2:4).

Q. He will be worshipped as God for three and a half years (Rev. 13:4-8).

R. His claim to deity will be accompanied by great signs and wonders (2 Thess. 2:9-12).

S. He will speak great blasphemies against God (Dan. 7:8; Rev. 13:6).

T. He will rule the world politically, religiously, and economically for three and a half years (Rev. 13:4-8, 16-18).

U. He will be promoted by a second beast who will lead the world in worship of the Beast (Rev. 13:11-18).

V. He will require all to receive his mark (666) in order to buy and sell (Rev. 13:16-18).

W. He will establish his religious, political, and economic capital in Babylon (Rev. 17).

X. He and the ten kings will then destroy Babylon (Rev. 18:16).

Y. He will kill the two witnesses (Rev. 11:7).

Z. He will gather all the nations against Jerusalem (Zech. 12:1-2; 14:1-3; Rev. 16:16; 19:19).

AA. He will fight against Christ when He returns to earth. In this campaign he will suffer total defeat (Rev. 19:19).

BB. He will be cast alive into the lake of fire (Dan. 7:11; Rev. 19:20). (From his book, *Cashless—One World Under the Antichrist*, pp. 120-122)

CC. Thus, a bottom line summary in regards to this future Satanic Superman might observe:

 1. No, he will not be born in a lowly manger from the womb of a virgin, as was the true Christ (Isa. 7:14).

 2. Yes, he will be universally worshipped by the unsaved world, unlike the true Christ who was *"despised and rejected by His own people"* (Rev. 13:11, 12; Isa. 53:3; John 1:12).

 3. Yes, he will work many miracles as did the true Christ (Rev. 13:14; John 3:2).

 4. Yes, he will make a seven-year covenant with Israel, but then break it, unlike the true Christ who has already made an eternal covenant with Israel, and will never break it! (Dan. 9:27; Jer. 31:35-37)

5. Had you lived somewhere in the Middle East some 2,000 years ago, you could have said to your children, "Kids, look at that man. He is different from all other men, *'for in him all the fullness of the Godhead lives in bodily form'* " (Col. 2:9).

6. Now fast forward in the Great Tribulation under the same circumstances: "Kids, look at that man. He is different from all other men, for in him dwells all the energy of Satan himself!" (2 Thess. 2:7, 9; Rev. 13:2)

7. Charles Dyer writes:

> The distinction by *Time* magazine as Man of the Year seemed entirely fitting. If ever a leader was destined for greatness, he fit the part. He first gained public recognition when he worked to galvanize and stabilize Europe. His new Confederation of Europe, which replaced the EEC and NATO, was a political masterstroke. With the sudden economic collapse of the United States, this European confederation stepped in to assume the mantle of world leader.
>
> Troublesome times demand strong leadership—and strong leadership was needed to impose order amid chaos. At first many countries and groups opposed his plan for economic unity. Some threatened military action to block the unification of Europe. But in the end most capitulated. However, three nations chose not to accept the inevitable, and they were crushed by the combined military might of the former NATO forces.
>
> But *Time* did not choose him as Man of the Year merely for his success in uniting Europe. His efforts to promote peace in the Middle East and to impose a settlement on Israel and her Arab neighbors diffused a potential powder keg. Everything he did seemed to prosper—as though God Himself was pleased with him.
>
> Certainly he deserved to be *Time* magazine's Man of the Year. On a globe cursed with petty despots and bickering politicians, here was an individual who carried himself with dignity and respect. He thought in global terms, and he made strategic decisions. All the world marveled at his power and influence. But who is this great leader?
>
> *Time* magazine has not yet named him Man of the Year, but 2,000 years ago the Apostle Paul identified him as the "man of lawlessness." Today most people would call him the Antichrist. If God's end-time program is near, he could already be alive and in some position of power. His actual identity will not be revealed until he signs the seven-year treaty with the nation of Israel. (*World News and Bible Prophecy*, Tyndale Publishers, p. 212)

■ **The Antichrist's False Prophet**

"And I beheld another beast coming up out of the earth; and he had two horns like a lamb, and he spake as a dragon" (Rev. 13:11).

A. His identity:

Who is this second beast of Rev. 13 who is also called on three later occasions "the false prophet?" (See Rev. 16:13; 19:20; 20:10.) Some believe he will be a Jew (while the Antichrist will be a Gentile), and that he will head up the apostate church.

B. His relationship with the Antichrist:

1. The false prophet will function as a hellish John the Baptist!
   a. Note John's relationship in regard to the true Christ (John 3:28, 30).
   b. Note the false prophet's relationship in regard to the false Christ (Rev. 13:12).

2. The false prophet will function as a hellish unholy spirit. Note:
   a. The Holy Spirit is the Third Person of the heavenly Trinity (Matt. 28:19), while the false prophet is the third person of the hellish trinity (Rev. 16:13).
   b. The Holy Spirit leads men into all truth (John 16:13), while the false prophet seduces men into all error (Rev. 13:11, 14).
   c. The Holy Spirit glorifies Christ (John 16:13-14), while the false prophet glorifies the Antichrist (Rev. 13:12).
   d. The Holy Spirit made fire to come down from heaven at Pentecost (Acts 2:3), while the false prophet will do likewise on earth in view of men (Rev. 13:13).
   e. The Holy Spirit gives life (Rom. 8:2), while the false prophet kills (Rev. 13:15).
   f. The Holy Spirit marks with a seal all those who belong to God (Eph. 1:13), while the false prophet marks those who worship Satan (Rev. 13:16-17).

C. His nature and activities

1. He will be gentle in appearance, but will possess a devilish character (Rev. 13:11b).
2. He will brutally exercise all the authority and power given him by the Antichrist (Rev. 13:12a).
3. He will force all the world to worship the Antichrist (Rev. 13:12b).
4. He will perform great miracles, such as causing fire to come down from heaven (Rev. 13:13).
5. He will deceive the entire earth (Rev. 13:14a).
6. He will build a great statue of the Antichrist and cause it to speak (Rev. 13:14-15).
7. He will kill those who refuse to worship this statue (Rev. 13:15b).
8. He will require the rest to receive the mark of the statue, which is 666 (Rev. 13:18).
9. Without the mark, no one will be able to buy or sell (Rev. 13:16-17).
10. He will be cast into the lake of fire at the end of the Great Tribulation (Rev. 19:20).

D. His mark

He causes all, both small and great, rich and poor, free and slave, to receive a mark on their right hand or on their foreheads, and that no one may buy or sell except one who has the mark or the name of the beast, or the number of his name. Here is wisdom. Let him who has understanding calculate the number of the beast, for it is the number of a man: His number is 666 (Rev. 13:16-18).

(See section under APPENDIX THREE for information regarding this mark.)

Question: Is it possible the Antichrist will not only desecrate the third temple as predicted by Paul (2 Thess. 2:4), but also the very Ark of the Covenant in the Holy of Holies?

Dr. Randall Price suggests the following:

> In the text of Dan. 9:27 we read this: 'On the wing of abominations will come one who makes desolate, even until a complete destruction, one that is decreed, is poured out on the one who makes desolate.' The word 'wing' literally translates the Hebrew term *kanaf* used in Dan. 9:27 and its construction has been such a problem for interpreters that almost every commentator has offered a different explanation. (*Jerusalem in Prophecy*, p. 260)

After reviewing several theories, Price concludes:

> " … It may be that 'wing' refers to the actual place where the abomination of desolation occurs—in this case, on the winged cherubim of the Ark itself." (Ibid, p. 261).

Prophecy teacher, Gary Frazier, paints this chilling picture:

> Somewhere at this moment there may be a young man growing to maturity. He is in all likelihood a brooding, thoughtful young man. Inside his heart, however, there is hellish rage. It boils like a cauldron of molten lead. He hates God. He despises Jesus Christ. He detests the Church. In his mind, there is taking shape the form of a dream of conquest. He will disingenuously present himself as a friend of Christ and the Church. Yet … he will, once empowered, pour out hell itself onto this world. Can the world produce such a prodigy? Hitler was once a little boy. Stalin was a lad. Nero was a child. The tenderness of childhood will be shaped by the devil into the terror of the *Antichrist*.

EVENT 3 THE REBIRTH AND MASS RETURN OF THE JEWS TO ISRAEL

INTRODUCTION

A great event indeed! However, before the glorious day celebration, there would occur two days of grievous desolation!

- Both days had to do with Israel's capital, the city of Jerusalem.
- Both days, although separated by centuries would occur on the same month of the calendar.
  A. The first happened on the 9th of Ab, (August 9) 586 B.C.
  B. The second happened on the 9th of Ab, 70 A.D.

- Each would result in Jerusalem being totally destroyed.
  - A. The temple of Solomon was burned on the first siege.
  - B. The temple of Herod on the second siege
- The Babylonian king Nebuchadnezzar led the first attack to punish the Jews for rebelling against him.
- The Roman General Titus led the second attack to punish the Jews for not paying their taxes.
- Jeremiah the prophet describes the first day, while Josephus, a Jewish governor, the second day.
  - A. Jeremiah's report:
    1. Judean King Zedekiah had joined with Egypt in rebelling against Nebuchadnezzar (2 Chron. 36:13).
    2. For this he was captured, forced to watch his sons being executed, blinded, and carried off into Babylonian Captivity (2 Kings 25:7).
    3. At this time, Seriah, the Jewish high priest, along with all nobles were also killed (Jer. 39:6).
    4. The Babylonian monarch showed no mercy whatsoever in regards to women and children (2 Chron. 36:17).
    5. In addition to the temple of Solomon, all public and private buildings were burned.
    6. Finally, he ransacked the temple, taking all its precious vessels to Babylon (Dan. 5:1-4).
  - B. Josephus's report:
    1. When the Jews refused to pay their taxes, the Roman Empire sent General Cestius to force payment.
    2. However, after surrounding Jerusalem with an army of 23,000 soldiers, for still unexplained reasons, he withdrew his troops.
    3. Nero then ordered Vespasian, one of his ablest generals to do what Cestius had failed to do.
    4. During this time, all Christians living in the city fled and settled in an area just east of the Jordan River.
    5. Vespasian commanded his son Titus to complete the job. In February of 70 A.D. his 80,000 troops set up a siege.
    6. To make matters worse for the citizens within Jerusalem, there were three Jewish factions fighting with each other. One held the upper town, one the lower, and one the temple in between.
    7. Soon, terrible starvation plagued all the inhabitants within the walls, causing some to resort to cannibalism!

8. Eventually Titus broke down the walls and entered the doomed city. To vent his anger he crucified as many as 500 per day. In fact, as the weeks went on it became difficult to enter Jerusalem because of all the crosses.

9. In the long run, over one million perished during the siege, and nearly 100,000 were carried to Babylon and sold as slaves!

Well, there you have it … persecution and pain, doom and destruction, helplessness and hopelessness, all covering Israel's landscape. Small wonder he would ask: *"Is there no balm in Gilead; is there no physician there … ?"* (Jer. 8:22)

And his conclusion—*"The harvest is past, the summer is ended, and we are not saved"* (Jer. 8:20).

But wait! The story does not end here, for about this time, a contemporary prophet, Ezekiel by name, had a vision where he witnessed Israel's great physician, *"the sun of righteousness with healing in his wings"* standing on the horizon, possessing abundant amounts of balm! The place of the vision was by the river Chebar, a large canal between the Euphrates and Tigris Rivers near ancient Babylon.

■ **The information *in* the vision**

The hand of the Lord was upon me, and he brought me out in the Spirit of the Lord and set me down in the middle of the valley; it was full of bones. And he led me around among them, and behold, there were very many on the surface of the valley, and behold, they were very dry. And he said to me, "Son of man, can these bones live?" And I answered, "O Lord God, you know." Then he said to me, "Prophesy over these bones, and say to them, O dry bones, hear the word of the Lord." Thus says the Lord God to these bones: Behold, I will cause breath to enter you, and you shall live. And I will lay sinews upon you, and will cause flesh to come upon you, and cover you with skin, and put breath in you, and you shall live, and you shall know that I am the Lord."

So I prophesied as I was commanded. And as I prophesied, there was a sound, and behold, a rattling, and the bones came together, bone to its bone. And I looked, and behold, there were sinews on them, and flesh had come upon them, and skin had covered them. But there was no breath in them. Then he said to me, "Prophesy to the breath; prophesy, son of man, and say to the breath, Thus says the Lord God: Come from the four winds, O breath, and breathe on these slain, that they may live." So I prophesied as he commanded me, and the breath came into them, and they lived and stood on their feet, an exceedingly great army (Ezek. 37:1-10).

■ **The interpretation *of* the vision**

Then he said to me, "Son of man, these bones are the whole house of Israel. Behold, they say, 'Our bones are dried up, and our hope is lost; we are indeed cut off.' Therefore prophesy, and say to them, Thus says the Lord God: Behold, I will open your graves and raise you from your graves, O my people. And I will bring you into the land of Israel. And you shall know that I am the Lord, when I open your graves, and raise you from your graves, O my people. And I will put my Spirit within you, and you shall live, and I will place you in your own land. Then you shall know that I am the Lord; I have spoken, and I will do it, declares the Lord" (Ezek. 37:11-14).

Here then is the bottom line: In the last days God will regather, regenerate, and restore His ancient people Israel! In fact many Bible scholars believe this passage predicts not *one* but *two* returns. Thus:

- The first return (Ezek. 11:7; 36:24; 37:21)

- The second return (Ezek. 11:18, 19; 36:25-27; 37:23)

- One rabbi likens these two returns to the unfolding of a flower. First, there is the bud, then the blossom. See Isaiah 27:6

Dr. Mark Hitchcock offers the following chart which summarizes both returns:

THE BUD	THE BLOSSOM
THE PRESENT (FIRST) REGATHERING	THE PERMANENT (FUTURE) REGATHERING
Worldwide	Worldwide
Return to part of the land	Return to all the land
Return in unbelief	Return in faith
Restored to the land only	Restored to the land and to the Lord
Sets the stage for the Tribulation	Sets the stage for the Millennium
Discipline	Blessing

We now consider the circumstances accompanying each return:

- The first return: Four significant dates are involved in this "Bud" return—
  A. August, 1897
    1. The location: Basel, Switzerland
    2. The man in charge: Theodor Herzl
    3. The details:
        a. Theodor Herzl (1860-1904) was a wealthy and influential Jewish playwright and political activist who became known as the father of modern Zionism. The goal of Zionism was to bring as many Jews worldwide back to the land of their fathers, Israel! Zionism was purely secular in nature, having no association with the Old Testament. In fact almost all the early Zionists were agnostics.
        b. So then, in August of 1897, Herzl organized and presided over the first Zionist conference. During his speech Herzl cried out:

"Today, there is a land without a people, and a people without a land. So then, give the land without a people to the people without a land!"

    c. All 112 of those in attendance of course knew what he was advocating—the *land* without a people was Palestine. The Turks had occupied it since 1517 and had constantly raped and abused it. It was a desolate, barren, sand-covered wilderness, cursed by poisonous snakes, ill-smelling swamps, a hot and hostile place with little life and no hope! The *people* without a land were of course the Jewish people who were scattered all throughout the world.

    d. Actually, there were 113 attending that conference. God Himself was present. In fact, God had already determined to do exactly what Herzl had demanded. In essence it can be demonstrated that He allowed, *in part* both world wars (I & II) to give the *land* without a people (WWI) to the *people* without a land (WWII).

B. December, 1917:
    1. The location: Just outside the city of Jerusalem
    2. The man in charge: Field Marshal Edmund Allenby (1861-1936)
    3. The details:

World War I was coming to a close. General Allenby, leader of the British forces in Palestine, had been ordered to take the city from the Turks who had sided up with Germany. He soon realized however that this would be no easy task, for the Turks had threatened to slash the throats of every Christian, Jew, and Arab within the holy city before surrendering.

What to do? After praying about it, the general took the following action: He sent planes over Jerusalem and instructed them to drop leaflets assuring the Turks that if they laid down their arms and left, no harm would come to them. The general then affixed his name and rank at the end of the leaflets.

Well, the reaction of the enemy was remarkable indeed. Already under much fear and uncertainty being completely surrounded, their fears turned to sheer panic! And the reason? Well, Allah is the Mid-Eastern root name for God, and Nebi for a prophet. So then, in their frightened minds, these leaflets came from the prophet of God Himself! Thus did Allenby take the city without any blood being shed. Shakespeare once asked, "What's in a name?" It would seem plenty in this one!

Thus, by Christmas of 1917, the land of Palestine which had, for 400 years, suffered under the cruel hands of the Turks, was now controlled by the British. Those few December days had witnessed the removal of it from the Muslim world to that of the Western world—or in religious terms, from Allah to Jehovah!

And the bottom line of all this? Well, the first part of Herzl's cry had been answered: the *land* was being prepared for the *people*.

C. April 30, 1945

    1. Location: An underground bunker in Berlin, Germany. On this day Adolf Hitler committed suicide by gunshot, thus ending the terrible war in Europe.

    2. The man in charge: Among many military soldiers, the key man was Supreme Commander Dwight David "Ike" Eisenhower (Oct. 14, 1890-March 28, 1969)

    3. The details:

        a. A glorious day indeed, but as his victorious troops began moving through the land, they were sickened by what they saw.

        b. The Nazis had constructed literally thousands of death camps which had held millions of innocent victims, many of which had already been murdered, and many more in the last stages of starvation.

        c. This ghastly act of genocide was soon filmed and seen by the Western Allied Nations.

        d. As a result, the gory scenes served to temporarily involve the sympathy of the entire world.

        e. This resulted in several hundred thousand death camp survivors being allowed to enter Palestine.

        f. And the bottom line of all the above? Simply this: The actions of one man, perhaps more than any other individual, which would eventually lead to the modern state of Israel four years later, was none other than … Adolf Hitler!

        Certainly no other single event in secular history more demonstrated the words of the psalmist than did this event—"*Surely the wrath of man shall praise thee* … (Psa. 76:10).

        g. Again, the bottom line: with all this, the second part of Herzl's cry had been answered—the **people** were being prepared for the **land**!

D. May 14, 1948

    1. The location: A two-story museum in Tel Aviv

    2. The man in charge: David Ben-Gurion, first prime minister of Israel

    3. The details:

        a. During the thirty-year control of Palestine (1917-1947) the British had made promises to both Jews and Arabs they could not possibly keep.

        b. Thus, on November 29, 1947, the United Nations Special Committee on Palestine advocated the partition of Palestine and the creation of statehood for Israel.

        c. As a result at dawn on May 14, 1948 the British flag, the Union Jack, was hauled down from the Governor's House in Jerusalem.

        d. At 3:45 P.M. that same day, Ben-Gurion met with 400 Jewish religious and political leaders plus many newsmen around the world.

e. After calling the meeting to order, all arose and sang the newly-written Jewish national anthem.

f. Ben-Gurion then read in Hebrew the historic 697-word Declaration of Independence in seventeen short minutes! What a day this was!

Question: Did the prophet have this day in mind when he wrote:

"*Who hath heard such a thing? Who hath seen such things? . . .shall a nation be born at once … ?*" (Isa. 66:8)

g. At 6:11 P.M. Washington, D. C., time, President Harry Truman recognized the Israeli state. On May 18, Russia did the same.

h. On May 15, 1948, Israel was invaded by Egypt, Jordan, Iraq, Syria, and Lebanon.

i. Thus, 650,000 Jews were pitted against 45,000,000 Arabs. Nevertheless, even being outnumbered 70 to 1, Israel fought back.

j. To the utter astonishment of the military world, Israel was victorious! The War of Independence ended on February 24, 1949.

k. William F. Albright, professor of Semitic languages at Johns Hopkins University, expressed his wonder at such accomplishments. He wrote:

"No other phenomenon in history is quite so extraordinary as the unique event represented by the Restoration of Israel … At no other time in world history, so far as it is known, has a people been destroyed, and then come back after a lapse of time and reestablished itself. It is utterly out of the question to seek a parallel for the occurrence of Israel's restoration after 2500 years of former history." (*Israel: Its role in Civilization*, p. 31).

■ **The second return**

Note: The following material is, admittedly, somewhat speculative in nature, but hopefully not too far off the mark.

A. Beginning of the Great Tribulation

1. Location: Jerusalem and other Israeli cities

2. The man in charge: The Western leader, a.k.a. the Antichrist!

3. Details:

a. Following the Rapture (?) a massive number of Jews coming from all over the world will make their way to the Land of Promise!

b. Two events may account for this great ingathering. One involves a treaty, the other a temple.

Note: For a detailed discussion concerning both treaty and temple, see Appendix One and Two at the end of this study (pg. 132-136).

B. The middle of the Great Tribulation

1. The location(s): At this time there would seem to be two locations, both involving Satan's persecution of Israel, and God's preservation of Israel:
   a. First location: In the holy of holies where the false prophet will attempt to force Israel to worship the Antichrist (Mt. 24:15; Rev. 13:14, 15).
   b. Second location: In the ancient city of Petra where a remnant of Jews who escape the Antichrist's wrath will hide out until the Second Coming of Christ (Mt. 24:16, 26, 27).

      Note: For more information in regards to these two locations, see Appendix Three and Four at the end of this study.
2. The man in charge: Actually, a heavenly being, Michael the archangel, and his angels! (Jude 9; Rev. 12:7).
3. Details: Prophecy expert, Dr. Mark Hitchcock, suggests the following events to transpire during this time—
   a. Antichrist will break the peace treaty at its midpoint and will invade Israel, making Jerusalem his throne (Dan. 11:40-45).
   b. Antichrist will desecrate the temple, set up the abomination of desolation in the Holy Place, and proclaim himself God (Dan. 9:27; 12:11; Matt. 24:15; 2 Thess. 2:3-4; Rev. 13:11-15).
   c. Jerusalem and all Israel will suffer terrible persecution (Jer. 30:4-7).
   d. The two witnesses will be killed by Antichrist, and their bodies will lie in the streets of Jerusalem for three and a half days (Rev. 11:7-11). (*The Key Places in Bible Prophecy*, p. 105, Tyndale House Publishers)

C. The end of the Great Tribulation
1. The location: From one end of heaven to the other end of heaven
2. The man in charge: The Lord Jesus Christ
3. The details: Again, according to Dr. Hitchcock—
   a. Antichrist will gather his allies together to come against Jerusalem (Zech. 12:1-3).
   b. Jerusalem will fall to the hands of Antichrist, and half the city will be destroyed (Zech. 14:2).
   c. Christ will return to the Mount of Olives, just east of Jerusalem (Zech. 14:4).
   d. In a final desperate move, Antichrist will gather his forces against Christ only to be destroyed in and around the city of Jerusalem (Joel 3:12-13; Rev. 19:19).
   e. A massive earthquake will split the city of Jerusalem into three parts (Zech. 14:4-5). (Ibid, p. 105)
   f. Finally, the ultimate and all inclusive regathering of the Jewish people to their land will occur!

"Immediately after the tribulation of those days the sun will be darkened, and the moon will not give its light; the stars will fall from heaven, and the powers of the heavens will be shaken. Then the sign of the Son of Man will appear in heaven, and then all the tribes of the earth will mourn, and they will see the Son of Man coming on the clouds of heaven with power and great glory. And He will send His angels with a great sound of a trumpet, and they will gather together His elect from the four winds, from one end of heaven to the other" (Matt. 24:29-31).

APPENDIX ONE: THE TREATY WITH ISRAEL

■ **The fact of their covenant**

At the beginning of the Great Tribulation the Antichrist will sign a seven-year covenant between himself and the nation of Israel. This is directly stated by both Isaiah and Daniel, and is inferred by Ezekiel.

A. The direct statements:

1. By Isaiah—*"And your covenant with death ... and your agreement with hell shall not stand ..."* (28:18).

2. By Daniel—*"And he shall confirm the covenant with many for (seven years) one week ... "* (9:27a).

B. The inference by Ezekiel:

" ... and they shall dwell safely, all of them" (38:8).

" ... to those who are at rest, who dwell safely, all of them dwelling without walls, and having neither bars or gates" (38:11).

In this chapter Ezekiel predicts Gog and Magog (Russia?) will invade Israel when the land is at peace, inferring that the Jews are basking under the assurance of the Antichrist's previous peace treaty with them.

■ **The nature of this covenant**

As previously noted, Daniel says the Antichrist will "confirm the covenant with Israel". The original Hebrew text may refer to either, the initial "making of the covenant" or the "confirming", literally, "strengthening" of a pre-existent one.

On May 19, 1993, a document called "The Jerusalem Covenant" was signed by Israeli officials and Jewish leaders worldwide. It is a reaffirmation of the historic unity of Jerusalem and a declaration of the prophetic blessings accompanying the rebuilding of the Temple on the Temple Mount. Some have considered this covenant (a copy of which is enshrined in a special exhibition at the Western Wall Tunnel) the very document the Antichrist will one day ratify with Israel. Of this we cannot be certain, but it may be a treaty like this one which guarantees Israel's sovereignty over Jerusalem and the Temple Mount.

■ **The reasons for the covenant**

A. What is the Antichrist's intent in making this treaty?

B. Several reasons may be involved:
 1. To lure the Jews back to Israel, in order to later exterminate them. At the beginning of the twenty-first century, one-fourth of the world's Jewish population dwell in the land of Israel. Their treaty however could persuade three-fourths to do so.
 2. To offer himself in place of God as Israel's strength and benefactor
  a. God had previously promised to establish a covenant of "peace" (Ezek. 37:26) with Israel in the future, but he would do it now!
  b. God had previously promised to build a temple for Israel (Haggai 2:7-9; Zech. 6:12, 13) in the future, but he would do it now!

APPENDIX TWO: THE TEMPLE OF ISRAEL

This event will be overviewed by a Q & A format—

■ *Will it be rebuilt?* In a word, *yes!*

The worship history of Israel can be aptly summarized by the study of one test structure and two permanent buildings.

A. The Tabernacle of Moses
 1. Built in 1446 B.C. by Moses (Exod. 40)
 2. Destroyed in 1100 B.C. by the Philistines (1 Sam. 4)
B. The First Temple
 1. Built in 960 B.C. by Solomon (1 Kings 5-8; 2 Chron. 2-3)
 2. Destroyed in 586 B.C. by Nebuchadnezzar (2 Kings 25; 2 Chron. 36)
C. The Second Temple
 1. Built by Zerubbabel (original building) in 516 B.C. (Ezra 6), and greatly enlarged in 4 B.C. by King Herod (John 2)
 2. Destroyed in 70 A.D. by Titus and the Roman army (Matt. 24:1, 2)

 Thus, for some 2,000 years the Jews have had no temple as predicted by Hosea, the prophet, over 2,700 years ago!

 "For the children of Israel shall abide many days without a king, and without a prince, and without a sacrifice, and without an image, and without an ephod, and without teraphim" (Hosea 3:4).

D. The Third Temple
 1. To be built by the Antichrist at the beginning of the Great Tribulation?
 2. To be destroyed at the Second Coming of Christ?
 3. At any rate, Daniel, Jesus, Paul and the apostle John spoke regarding this temple:
  a. As predicted by Daniel (Dan. 9:27)
  b. As predicted by Jesus (Matt. 24:15)

  c. As predicted by Paul (2 Thess. 2:4)

  d. As predicted by John (Rev. 11:1)

■ ***Where* will it be built?**

All agree that the Third Temple will be built somewhere on the thirty-five acre Temple Mount in Jerusalem. But precisely where the relatively small temple will be placed upon the mount is a source of great debate. What are the options?

Three sites have received the most attention as possible temple locations: the Northern site, the Traditional site, and the Southern site.

A. The view held by most religious Jews in Israel today is that the *traditional site*, as preserved by the Dome of the Rock, is where the next temple will be built. This is the view we believe to be correct. Nevertheless, it really doesn't matter what anyone thinks—other than the Jews making the decisions when the time comes.

B. While many details could be given in support of this view, it comes down to a simple fact—the Dome of the Rock preserves the rock, and thus the spot of prior temples.

C. Hebrew archaeologist Dan Bahat states:

  "I will say right now that the temple is standing exactly where the Dome of the Rock is today on the Temple Mount. I want to say explicitly and clearly that we believe that the Rock under the Dome is the precise site of the Holy of Holies. The Temple extended exactly to the place where the Dome is. The 'Foundation Stone' is actually that stone which comprised the Holy of Holies."

D. Chaim Richman of the Temple Institute says:

  "We have a tradition that has been passed down in an unbroken chain from our fathers that the Rock, the stone underneath of the Dome of the Rock, is the 'foundation stone.'"

E. Dan Bahat agrees with this when he adds:

  "If this site were not the site of the Temple, we would not have the sanctity that has been bestowed upon that stone for centuries. The Church fathers describe how the Jews were coming every year to that place, and the Muslims chose to build their sanctuary on the very same stone because they were aware of the Jewish tradition … Omar, the Muslim conqueror of Jerusalem, was brought by a Jew straight to that stone and not to another one. So the tradition is quite clear about the tradition of this place." (*The Last Days' Temple*, Harvest House, pp. 33, 35-37)

F. The Bible does not require that the Temple be built upon a specific site in Jerusalem in order to fulfill the prophecy. However, the Jewish point of view believes that it must be built where earlier temples once stood. At this time, the overwhelming belief within Jewish circles is that it will be built where the current Dome of the Rock now stands. They believe that if the Temple could be built somewhere other than the Temple Mount, it would have been constructed long ago.

G. Thus, the area now occupied by the Muslim Dome of the Rock would seem to be the place. Note the eventful history of this mount:
   1. The place where Abraham offered up Isaac (Gen. 22:2)
   2. The place where the hand of the death angel was stayed in David's time (1 Chron. 21:15-29). David then bought this area from a Jebusite named Ornan.
   3. The place where Solomon built the first temple (2 Chron. 3:1)
   4. The place where the second temple was constructed
      a. Begun by Zerubbabel (Ezra 3)
      b. Greatly enlarged by King Herod (John 2:20)
   5. In A.D. 135 Roman Emperor Hadrian built a statue of Jupiter on this spot.
   6. The earliest Christians looked upon Moriah as a place cursed by God.
   7. In A.D. 534 Emperor Justinian built a church dedicated to St. Mary.
   8. In A.D. 639 Jerusalem fell to Islam and Moriah became a Muslim shrine.
   9. In A.D. 691 the famous Dome of the Rock was completed. This shrine, the third holiest in the Muslim world, is an octagonal building, each side measuring sixty-six feet, for a total of 528 feet in circumference. The diameter is 176 feet, and the height 108 feet. The walls are thirty-six feet high. It remains standing today.
   10. In the tenth century the Crusaders captured Jerusalem and worshiped God in this building on Mt. Moriah, believing it was actually the second Temple. They called it the Lord's Temple.
   11. A century later the Arabs took it again, this time for keeps.
   12. In ancient times Moriah covered twenty-five acres. Today it occupies thirty-five acres. It is 2,425 feet above sea level.
   13. Jewish legend has it that in the beginning Moriah was suspended in midair and the rest of the world created around it. Muslim legend teaches that the rock inside their dome on Moriah is the gate to paradise. They say believers can hear the roar of the five rivers of the Garden of Eden beneath Moriah. Here they believe is the rock Adam was created upon and the spot where Noah's Ark rested. Here final judgment will take place. True believers will then be ushered by the angel Gabriel into paradise. Muslims believe Mohammed, riding on Burak (a winged horse with a woman's face and peacock's tail), accompanied by Gabriel, came from Mecca to this rock, before his ascent into the seventh heaven. Muslims also believe the souls of the dead pray there twice each week.

      What will happen to the Dome of the Rock, which must be removed to allow the construction of the third temple? Of course, no one knows. Perhaps an earthquake will destroy it, or it may be bombed or burned. It could be the Antichrist himself will relocate it on another nearby site.

■ **Why will it be built?** It would seem both the Antichrist and Israel will have a vested interest in its construction.

A. In regards to the Antichrist

It has been previously suggested that this evil man may actually play a major role in its building, so as to convince Jewish leaders that he is indeed their friend!

B. In regards to Israel

Since its destruction in 70 A.D. there has always been a desire in the Jewish soul to rebuild its beloved temple. But, in recent years a new and alarming trend has been discovered, resulting in an intensified determination to rebuild it.

This is reported by evangelical scholar Dr. Randall Price in his book (1992), *Ready to Rebuild*. According to Price:

"In 1964, nine percent of Jewish marriages were to non-Jews. By 1990 this number had jumped to nearly sixty percent. As a result of those mixed marriages, three out of four children born are being raised in non-Jewish religious setting. In light of this serious problem some Rabbis feel a Jewish temple might serve to promote Jewish values among the young people!"

Another important reason is given by various rabbis:

"We have this concept that we have six hundred and thirteen commandments to fulfill and one-third of those commandments are dependent in some way on the Temple for their fulfillment."

■ **What possible discovery may lead to the rebuilding of the third temple?**

It may involve the most important object God ever ordered constructed on the surface of planet Earth! It occurred at the base of Mt. Sinai during the summer of 1446 B.C. when Moses was instructed as follows:

"And they shall make an ark of shittim wood: two cubits and a half shall be the length thereof, and a cubit and a half the breadth thereof, and a cubit and a half the height thereof. And thou shalt overlay it with pure gold, within and without shalt thou overlay it, and shalt make upon it a crown of gold round about" (Exod. 25:10, 11).

What do we know in regards to this majestic, mysterious, and (as we will soon see) missing "God box" known as the Ark of the Covenant? Here a little background will prove helpful.

A. Description:

A five foot-long, three-foot high, three-foot wide box made of acacia wood, overlaid by gold. It contained a pot of manna, Aaron's rod that budded, and the two tablets of the Law of Moses. The lid was called the Mercy Seat. Two golden angels overlooked the Mercy Seat.

B. History:

1. It was to be placed in the Holy of Holies (Exod. 26:33, 34).
2. It was overshadowed by the Shekinah glory cloud (Exod. 40:34).
3. It was carried around the city of Jericho (Josh. 6:1-17).
4. It resided in Shiloh during the time of Joshua and Samuel (Josh. 18:1; 1 Sam. 3:3).

5. It was captured (briefly) by the Philistines (1 Sam. 4).

6. It was later returned to Israel, resting at Kirjath-jearim (1 Sam. 6, 7).

7. It was eventually brought to Jerusalem by David (2 Sam. 6).

8. It was placed in the first temple by King Solomon (1 Kings 8).

9. It is last referred to during the reign of King Josiah (2 Chron. 35:3).

C. Theories concerning its whereabouts:

Jewish historian A. Edersheim says the Ark was not in the temple of Herod, but simply a stone called the Stone of Foundation, three fingers high. So then, where is the Ark today? Various theories have been offered:

1. It was destroyed by Nebuchadnezzar and the Babylonians when they burned both Jerusalem and the temple in 586 B.C. (2 Kings 25; 2 Chron. 36; Jer. 39).

2. It was taken to Babylon by Nebuchadnezzar at that time.

3. It was hidden by Jeremiah the prophet prior to the Babylonian invasion, probably under the present Dome of the Rock. Most Christian and Jewish scholars would hold this view.

D. Here it may be asked just what all this has to do with the building of third temple. Simply, it is this: When David became king over all Israel in 1004 B.C., he did two significant things. First, he captured Jerusalem from the pagan Jebusites (1 Chron. 11:4-9). The second thing he did was to locate the Ark of the Covenant and bring it into Jerusalem (1 Chron. 13).

We then read:

"Now it came to pass, as David sat in his house, that David said to Nathan, the prophet, Lo, I dwell in a house of cedar, but the Ark of the Covenant of the Lord remaineth under curtains (in a tent)" (1 Chron. 17:1).

David then decided to build a temple to house the Ark. Of course, as things turned out, God appointed Solomon (David's son) to erect the temple rather than David. But the point to be made here is that the taking of Jerusalem and the location of the Ark resulted in the building of the First Temple! What is the situation today? The Jews now possess Jerusalem. Is the Ark still intact somewhere? If so, God may allow its discovery once again to trigger the construction of a temple—the third temple.

An old Jewish maxim states: "Jerusalem is in the center of the world, the Temple Mount is in the center of Jerusalem, and the Temple is in the center of the Mount." We might well add, "And the Ark is in the center of the Temple."

Are there any present-day activities occurring in Israel in regards to the rebuilding of the Third Temple?

There are indeed, which would include:

A. The Temple Institute, a Jewish organization located in a building near the Western wall whose sole purpose is to construct those objects needed in the Third Temple, including a silver menorah, goblets, ritual slaughtering knives, priestly garments, trumpets, etc.

B. Earnest attempts to secure an unblemished red heifer to fulfill the purification requirements as found in Numbers 19:1-10.

C. Talmudic (law) schools to train those men who believe they are of priestly descent to minister in the new temple.

D. The fashioning of musical harps based on biblical records to be used by the Levitical priests in the temple worship services.

E. The musical skills of Micah and Shoshanna Harrari who have made a number of harps, based on biblical records, to be used by the singing Levitical priests during the future Third Temple worship services.

F. Various attempts to lay a four-ton temple cornerstone, carved out in a desert area south of Israel by a special flint stone. This huge rock, carried on a flatbed truck is driven around the old city of Jerusalem yearly by the Temple Mount foundation, headed by Gershon Solomon.

G. The sudden reappearance of thousands of segulit snails on the Mediterranean sea-shore. Former chief Rabbi Isaac Herzog believes a blue dye extracted from these tiny creatures may have been used in biblical times to produce the exact blue color as specified in Num. 15:37-40 in making the priestly garments (taken from the book, *Ready to Rebuild*, Dr. Randall Price, Harvest House, 1992).

APPENDIX THREE: THE ABOMINATION OF DESOLATION IN THE JEWISH HOLY OF HOLIES

With the exception of Jesus's murder at the hands of sinful men, perhaps the most blasphemous act in all the scriptures will occur in the Holy of Holies.

■ The record involved

A. According to Daniel

"Then he shall confirm a covenant with many for one week; but in the middle of the week He shall bring an end to sacrifice and offering. And on the wing of abominations shall be one who makes desolate, even until the consummation, which is determined, is poured out on the desolate" (Dan. 9:27).

"And from the time that the daily sacrifice is taken away, and the abomination of desolation is set up, there shall be one thousand two hundred and ninety days" (Dan. 12:11).

B. According to Jesus

"Therefore when you see the 'abomination of desolation,' spoken of by Daniel the prophet, standing in the holy place (whoever reads, let him understand), then let those who are in Judea flee to the mountains" (Matt. 24:15, 16).

C. According to Paul

"Let no one deceive you by any means; for that Day will not come unless the falling away comes first, and the man of sin is revealed, the son of perdition, who opposes and exalts himself above all that is called God or that is worshiped, so that he sits as God in the temple of God, showing himself that he is God" (2 Thess. 2:3, 4).

D. According to John

"He performs great signs, so that he even makes fire come down from heaven on the earth in the sight of men. And he deceives those who dwell on the earth by those signs which he was granted to do in the sight of the beast, telling those who dwell on the earth to make an image to the beast who was wounded by the sword and lived. He was granted power to give breath to the image of the beast, that the image of the beast should both speak and cause as many as would not worship the image of the beast to be killed. He causes all, both small and great, rich and poor, free and slave, to receive a mark on their right hand or on their foreheads, and that no one may buy or sell except one who has the mark or the name of the beast, or the number of his name. Here is wisdom. Let him who has understanding calculate the number of the beast, for it is the number of a man: His number is 666" (Rev. 13:13-18).

■ **The chronology involved**

After the judgment of Russia, the destruction of the false church, and the murder of most of God's preachers (the 144,000 and the two witnesses), an unbelievable vacuum will undoubtedly settle down upon the world. The Antichrist will immediately exploit this.

Note: Details regarding these events will be discussed at a later time in the notes.

The following is but a suggestion of the chronology of events, which may take place at this critical time.

A. The Antichrist and his false prophet make their headquarters in Jerusalem after God destroys Russia.

B. Here in the holy city, perhaps during a television speech, the Antichrist is suddenly assassinated, as millions of viewers watch (Rev. 13:3, 14).

C. Before his burial, perhaps during the state funeral, he suddenly rises from the dead. The world is electrified. At any rate, the Antichrist now breaks the seven-year covenant he had previously made three and a half years before. Thus:

D. The false prophet thereupon makes a statue of the Antichrist, causes it to speak, and places it in the Holy of Holies (Matt. 24:15; Dan. 9:27; 12:11; 2 Thess. 2:4).

E. A law is passed which stipulates that no one can buy, sell, work, or obtain any necessity of life unless he carries a special mark on his right hand or his forehead to identify him as a worshiper of the beast (Rev. 13:16, 17).

■ **The mark involved**

The number of this mark is 666 (Rev. 13:18). There are (at least) two views regarding the number 666:

A. It represents the total imperfection of the Antichrist, for seven is the perfect (and divine) number.

B. It involves a numerical system known as *gematria*. By way of explanation, in many languages, including Hebrew, Greek and Latin, each alphabetical letter was assigned a numerical equivalent. Thus, it is possible the world will observe a letter/number arrangement of some sort during the Great Tribulation. If this be the case, the combined letters in the Antichrist's name or title will equal 666!

C. Whatever is involved in this hellish mark, it is apparently important, for it is referred to again no less than six times. (See Rev. 14:9, 11; 15:2; 16:2; 19:20; 20:4.)

D. The Bible speaks precisely about what the mark will be:

1. The Antichrist's mark, identified with his person the actual number 666, not a representation
2. A mark, like a tattoo
3. Visible to the naked eyes
4. On the person, not in him or her
5. Recognized, not questioned
6. Voluntary, not involuntary—not given through stealth or trickery
7. Used after the Rapture, not before
8. Used in the second half of the Tribulation
9. Needed to buy and sell
10. Universally received by non-Christians, but universally rejected by Christians
11. A show of worship and allegiance to the Antichrist promoted by the false prophet
12. The mark that leads to eternal punishment in the lake of fire

   (*Fast Facts on Bible Prophecy*, Tommy Ice, Harvest House, p. 130)

■ **The ultimate desecration involved**

Question: Is it possible the Antichrist will not only desecrate the third temple as predicted by Paul (2 Thess. 2:4), but also the very Ark of the Covenant in the Holy of Holies?

Dr. Randall Price suggests the following:

"In the text of Daniel 9:27 we read this: 'On the wing of abominations will come one who makes desolate, even until a complete destruction, one that is decreed, is poured out on the one who makes desolate.' The word 'wing' literally translates the Hebrew term Kanaf used in Daniel 9:27 and its construction has been such a problem for interpreters that almost every commentator has offered a different explanation." (*Jerusalem in Prophecy*, p. 260)

After reviewing several theories, Price concludes:

"Another view is that winged statues or emblems (like the Roman standards that bore images of the emperor) may have been placed at the site of the altar. In my opinion, this line of evidence has the greater support. However, it is not necessary to limit the desecration to the outer altar on the basis of what the apocryphal references tell us about Antiochus' abomination. Rather if the Antichrist is to take the progression of desecration a step forward, then the greater violation would have to proceed from the outside (area of lesser sanctity) to the inside (area of greater sanctity) of the Temple.

With that in mind, it may be that 'wing' refers to the actual place where the abomination of desolation occurs—in this case, on the winged cherubim of the Ark itself." (Ibid., p. 261)

APPENDIX FOUR: PERSECUTION, PROTECTION, AND A PLACE CALLED PETRA

The events recorded in Revelation 12 are somewhat challenging to place in correct chronology. Hoping to help clarify the details I have included my summary in regards to this chapter as taken from *Willmington's Outline Bible*, p. 766.

I. **Satan's former hatred for God and His people** (12:1-5)
   A. His sin at the beginning (12:3-4): This seems to refer to his original fall.
   B. His sin at Bethlehem (12:1-2, 4-5)
      1. Satan's persecution of God's nation (12:1-2)
      2. Satan's persecution of God's Son (12:4b, 5b)
         a. The birth of Jesus (12:4a, 5a)
         b. The ascension of Jesus (12:5c)

II. **Satan's future hatred for God and His people** (12:6-17)
   A. The woman in the wilderness (12:6, 13-18): The woman here is the nation of Israel.
      1. Israel will be persecuted by Satan during the Great Tribulation (12:13, 15, 17).
      2. Israel will be protected by God during the Great Tribulation (12:6, 14, 16).
   B. The war in the heavens (12:7-12): Some believe this will occur in the middle of the Great Tribulation.
      1. The results (12:7-9)
         a. The defeat of Satan (12:7-8): Michael the archangel will defeat him.
         b. The dismissal of Satan (12:9): He will be cast down to earth.
      2. The reaction (12:10-12)
         a. Satan will be filled with wrath (12:10b, 12c).
         b. Saints will be filled with joy (12:10a, 11-12a).
         c. Sinners will be filled with fear (12:12b).

With this background overview we now ask and attempt to answer six questions regarding its contents:

▪ **Does this Rev. 12 chapter record not one but two wars in heaven?** It would seem to be the case. Thus—

A. The first war, fought at the dawn of human history
   1. As referred to by Isaiah (14:12-15)
   2. As referred to by Ezekiel (28:13-17)
   3. As referred to by John (Rev. 12:4)
B. The second war, to be fought during the middle of the Great Tribulation

   "And war broke out in heaven: Michael and his angels fought with the dragon; and the dragon and his angels fought, but they did not prevail, nor was a place found for them in heaven any longer. So the great dragon was cast out, that serpent of old, called the Devil and Satan, who deceives the whole world; he was cast to the earth, and his angels were cast out with him" (Rev. 12:7-9).

■ **Who is this persecuted woman?**

"Now a great sign appeared in heaven: a woman clothed with the sun, with the moon under her feet, and on her head a garland of twelve stars. Then being with child, she cried out in labor and in pain to give birth. She bore a male Child who was to rule all nations with a rod of iron. And her Child was caught up to God and His throne" (12:1, 2, 5).

These words are unquestionably symbolic, but to whom do they refer?

A. She is not Mary. Mary never spent three and a half years in the wilderness, as does this woman (Rev. 12:6, 14). Neither was Mary personally hated, chased, and persecuted, as we see here (Rev. 12:13, 17). While Mary did give birth to that One who will someday *"rule all nations with a rod of iron"* (Rev. 12:5), the language in this chapter has a wider reference than to Mary.

B. She is not the Church. The Church did not bring the man-child into existence, as does this woman (Rev. 12:5), but rather the opposite. See Matthew 16:18.

C. She is Israel. A Jewish Christian who reads Revelation 12:1 will undoubtedly think back to the Old Testament passage in which Joseph describes a strange dream to his father and eleven brothers:

   "Behold, I have dreamed a dream ... the sun and the moon and eleven stars made obeisance to me" (Gen. 37:9).

   This was, of course, fulfilled when Joseph's eleven brothers bowed down to him in Egypt (Gen. 43:28).

■ **Who is the great red dragon that attempts to destroy the woman?** Rev. 12:9 clearly answers this question: *"...that old serpent, called the Devil and Satan...."*

■ **Why are both the woman and the dragon said to be located in heaven?**

A. In regards to the devil: Satan in heaven? No way! After all, the common idea among many today has the devil dressed in a pair of red underwear, with two horns and a tail, busily at work pitching coal in the furnace of hell! Correct? Not even close! Actually, he can usually be found near the throne of God, viciously slandering Christians! (Rev. 12:10)

B. In regards to the woman (Israel): A clue here may be seen in Rev. 1:12-20, where Jesus is described as wearing His high priestly garments, tending to seven lampstands which are said to be seven local churches. So then, could it not be concluded that if the Head of the Church does this for His congregations, the Messiah of Israel may well perform the same loving oversight to His ancient people!

In fact, the vision of an Old Testament prophet named Zechariah seems to lend support to this idea:

> "Then the angel showed me Jeshua the high priest standing before the angel of the Lord. The Accuser, Satan, was there at the angel's right hand, making accusations against Jeshua. And the Lord said to Satan, 'I, the Lord, reject your accusations, Satan. Yes, the Lord, who has chosen Jerusalem, rebukes you. This man is like a burning stick that has been snatched from the fire.' Jeshua's clothing was filthy as he stood there before the angel. So the angel said to the others standing there, 'Take off his filthy clothes.' And turning to Jeshua he said, 'See, I have taken away your sins, and now I am giving you these fine new clothes.' Then I said, 'They should also place a clean turban on his head.' So they put a clean priestly turban on his head and dressed him in new clothes while the angel of the Lord stood by" (Zech. 3:1-5).

■ **When do the woman's persecutions occur?**

Sadly, the answer involves a continuous "when:"

A. Persecutions in the *past*:

Throughout her long history, Satan has made every attempt to exterminate Israel. This he has done by resorting to:

1. Enslaving (Exod. 2)
2. Drowning (Exod. 14)
3. Starving (Exod. 16)
4. Tempting (Exod. 32, Num. 14)
5. Cursing (Num. 14)
6. Devouring (Dan. 6)
7. Hanging (Esther 3)
8. Capturing (2 Kings 17, 24)
9. Swallowing (Jonah 2)
10. Burning (Dan. 3)

B. Persecutions at the *present*:

1. Racial: Hitler's death camps
2. Political: The disdain from the United Nations
3. Religious: Coming from the Arab nations who claim Allah has mandated that all Jews and their religion be literally wiped from the earth.

C. Persecutions in the *future:* Both past and present persecutions have been severe, but the most universal and vicious time is yet to come!

John Phillips writes:

> "What a time of terror lies ahead for Israel! The world has seen dress rehearsals for this coming onslaught already—the knock on the door at the dead of night; the dreaded secret police; the swift ride through the darkened streets to the sidings where the boxcars wait; the dreadful ordeal of days and nights without food, drink or sanitation, with men and women and children herded like cattle in the dark, and with little babies flung on top of the struggling heap of humanity like so many sacks of flour; the lonely sidings; the barbed wire; the concentration camps; the callous treatment and cruel tortures; and then the gas ovens and the firing squads. It has been rehearsed already in preparation for the full-stage production of terror." (*Exploring Revelation*, Moody Press, 1974, p. 174)

> *"And at that time shall Michael stand up, the great prince which standeth for the children of thy people: and there shall be a time of trouble, such as never was since there was a nation even to that same time"* (Dan. 12:1).

> *"For, lo, I will raise up a shepherd in the land, which shall not visit those that be cut off, neither shall seek the young one, nor heal that that is broken, nor feed that that standeth still: but he shall eat the flesh of the fat, and tear their claws in pieces"* (Zech. 11:16).

> *"For then shall be great tribulation, such as was not since the beginning of the world to this time, no, nor ever shall be"* (Matt. 24:21).

W. Kac observes:

> "Next to the survival of the Jews, the most baffling historical phenomenon is the hatred which he has repeatedly encountered among the nations of the earth. This hostility to the Jews, which goes under the name anti-Semitism, is as old as Jewish existence. It is endemic; i.e., like many contagious diseases it is always with us to some degree. But under certain circumstances it assumes epidemic proportions and characteristics. It is prevalent wherever Jews reside in sufficiently large numbers to make their presence. 'The growth of anti-Semitism,' Chaim Weizmann declares, 'is proportionate to the number of Jews per square kilometer. We carry the germs of anti-Semitism in our knapsack on our backs.'" (*Rebirth of the State of Israel*, p. 306)

■ **How will individual Israelis react to this horrible persecution?**

When the Israelites see the statue of the Antichrist standing in their Holy of Holies, the words of Christ will come to their minds. He had warned them about this very thing many centuries earlier (Matt. 24:15-20). At this point the Jews of the world will travel down one of three roads:

A. Many Israelites will be killed by the Antichrist.

> *"And it came to pass that in all the land, saith the Lord, two parts therein shall be cut off and die; but the third shall be left therein"* (Zech. 13:8).

B. Some Israelites will follow the Antichrist.

> *"And then shall many be offended, and shall betray one another, and shall hate one another. Many false prophets shall rise, and shall deceive many. And because iniquity shall abound, the love of many shall wax cold"* (Matt. 24:10-12).

> *" ... I know the blasphemy of them which say they are Jews, and are not, but are the synagogue of Satan"* (Rev. 2:9).

> *"Behold, I will make them of the synagogue of Satan which say they are Jews, and are not, but do lie: behold, I will make them to come and worship before thy feet, and to know that I have loved thee"* (Rev. 3:9).

C. A remnant of Israel will be saved.

> *"And to the woman were given two wings of a great eagle, that she might fly into the wilderness, into her place, where she is nourished for a time, and times, and half a time, from the face of the serpent"* (Rev. 12:14).

> *"And I will bring the third part through the fire, and will refine them as silver is refined, and will try them as gold is tried; they shall call on my name, and I will hear them: I will say, It is my people: and they shall say, The Lord is my God"* (Zech. 13:9).

▦ **Where is this hiding place which will provide safety for the escaping remnant?**

While it is not actually specified in the scriptures, many Bible students believe this place will be the ancient city of Petra.

This is based on the following three passages:

> *"And ye shall flee to the valley of the mountains; for the valley of the mountains shall reach unto Azal: yea, ye shall flee ... and the Lord my God shall come, and all the saints with thee"* (Zech. 14:5).

>   (The "Azal" mentioned here is thought to be connected with Petra.)

> *"Who is this that cometh from Edom, with dyed garments from Bozrah?* (Isa. 63:1).

The first few verses of Isaiah 63 deal with the Second Coming of Christ. He comes to Edom (of which Petra is capital) and Bozrah (a city in Edom) for some reason, and many believe that reason is to receive his Hebrew remnant who are hiding there.

> *"He shall enter also into the glorious land, and many countries shall be overthrown: but these shall escape out of his hand, even Edom"* (Dan. 11:41).

Thus, for some reason the land of Edom will not be allowed to fall into the hands of the Antichrist. It is assumed by some that the reason is to protect the remnant. This city, located in modern Southwest Jordan, was once the capital of Edom.

Petra has been called "the rainbow city," and once had 267,000 inhabitants. It was a large market center at the junction of a great caravan route. The city is inaccessible except through the gorge or canyon in the mountains, which is wide enough for only two horses abreast. The perpendicular walls of the gorge are from 400 to 700 feet high and are brilliant in splendor, displaying every color of the rainbow. The old buildings, cut from the solid rock of the mountain, still stand. A clear spring bubbles over rose-red rocks. Wild figs grow on the banks. Everything awaits Israel!

Thomas Ice aptly summarizes all this by the following overview:

"Bozrah, sheepfold in Hebrew, is located in the mount range of Mount Seir in the southern part of the modern state of Jordan. It will be to this location that the Jewish remnant will flee from the Antichrist in the middle of the tribulation (Matthew 24:15-21). Revelation 12:6, 14 also speak of this mid-tribulation flight of the Jews living in Israel to 'a place prepared by God, so that there she (Israel) might be nourished for one thousand two hundred and sixty days' (verse 6). A number of Old Testament passages (Isaiah 33:13-16; 41:17-20); Micah 2:12), when gleaned and harmonized, teach that Israel's mid-tribulational flight will be:

- In the mountains
- In the wilderness
- A place prepared in advance
- Very defensible

(*Footsteps*, Fruchtenbaum, p. 202)

"Daniel 11:40-45 indicates that three areas, designated by their ancient names of Edom, Moab, and Ammon, will escape the worldwide rule of Antichrist. This is the exact area where the Jewish remnant will be nurtured by the Lord through the second half of the Tribulation. The city of Bozrah will be the sheepfold that will protect the Jewish remnant.

"Jeremiah 49:13, 14 indicates that the end of the Tribulation the Antichrist will find the Jews in Bozrah and send his armies to attack them. Hosea 6:1-3 teaches that the threatened Jewish remnant will plead in faith for Messiah to return. He will do this in order to protect the remnant, and this will lead to the eventual Second Coming to the Mount of Olives in Jerusalem. But the Second Coming will not occur until Messiah stops by His sheepfold to rescue His people. Most likely the exact location of Bozrah is the abandoned city of Petra." (*Fast Facts on Bible Prophecy*, Harvest House, pp. 39, 40)

Many years ago the noted Bible scholar W. E. Blackstone, on the basis of these verses, hid thousands of copies of the New Testament in and around the caves and rocks of Petra. He felt that someday the terrified survivors of the Antichrist's bloodbath will welcome the opportunity to read God's Word.

On October 14, 1974, I visited Petra for the first time. Before leaving America my students were asked to sign their names, along with their favorite Scripture verse, in the front pages of a large Bible. I then included the following letter:

"Attention to all of Hebrew background: This Bible has been placed here on October 14, 1974, by the students and Dean of the Thomas Road Bible Institute of Lynchburg, Virginia, USA. We respectfully urge its finder to prayerfully and publicly read the following Bible chapters. They are Daniel 7 and 11; Matthew 24; 2 Thessalonians 2; and Revelation 12 and 13."

We then wrapped the Bible in heavy plastic and placed it in one of the remote caves among the thousands in Petra.

EVENT 4 THE PRESENT REVIVAL OF THE OLD ROMAN EMPIRE

INTRODUCTION

At long last, after nearly 800 years of terrible cruelty, that hideous monster beast with huge iron teeth, used to crunch and swallow its untold victims, was officially pronounced dead! What a relief! Well, not quite.

The problem was the creature kept trying to crawl out of its grave! On each occasion it was re-buried, but soon the plot covering it would slowly open up, once again revealing the decaying features of this zombie-like beast.

The most recent appearance occurred in 1932 when the evil tyrant who had raised it up, boasting this time the beast would live and reign for a thousand years! But a scant thirteen years later the creature would die with its master in a Berlin bunker, resulting in the entire world celebrating its passing. Surely, this time there would be no resurrection. But to the contrary, a few short years later the representatives of several nations not only carefully exhumed the rotting corpse and cleaned it up, but also gradually gave it authority to oversee the citizens living in those nations! Strange indeed the workings of fate ... or was it fate?

****

Question: What on earth did a nightmare dream of an ancient Babylonian monarch 2600 years ago have to do with the modern countries of Europe? Read on!

Upon awakening the monarch, Nebuchadnezzar, summoned all his political and religious leaders into the royal bedroom, demanding two things from them. *First*, that they tell him the details of the dream, and *second*, the meaning involved. Upon learning they were unable to do so, he orders all be put to death! This included Daniel the prophet who was not there. Soon, during Daniel's prayer time God revealed both the information and interpretation of the dream to him!

■ The details in the dream
   The king had seen a huge and powerful statue of a man, made up of various materials:
   A. The head was gold

B. The breast and arms were silver

C. Its belly and thighs were brass

D. Its legs and feet were part iron and clay

This statue was then utterly pulverized into small powder by a special rock, supernaturally cut from a mountainside which fell upon it. The rock grew until it filled the entire earth.

The meaning of the dream

A. Regarding the statue

In essence it had to do with four Gentile world powers, or empires

   1. The gold stood for Babylon (605-539 B.C.)
   2. The silver stood for Persia (539-331- B. C.)
   3. The brass stood for Greece (331-323 B. C.)
   4. The iron and clay stood for Rome (322 B.C. to 476 A.D.)

B. Regarding the huge rock which fell upon the statue and crushed it

This stood for the ultimate power, Jesus Christ Himself, who would someday fall upon and crush all world Gentile powers!

The difficulty regarding the dream

Houston, we've got a problem! This is indeed the case! And the problem? Well … .

A. Babylon was indeed the head of gold, ruled over by Nebuchadnezzar.

B. Persia was the chest and arms of silver, ruled over by Cyrus the Great who took over the Babylonian Empire in October of 539 B.C.

C. Greece was the stomach and thighs of brass, ruled over by Alexander the Great who defeated the Persians.

D. Rome was the iron and clay who took over the entire Middle East powers in 322 B.C.

E. As predicted, the Messiah (represented by the huge rock) was born and raised during the reign of Caesar. But now the problem — Did Jesus destroy the Gentile statue of world power? To the contrary, He Himself was put to death by an official representing the Roman Empire!

Actually there is a three-fold suggested solution to the problem:

   1. Daniel never wrote these predictions in the first place (or)
   2. Daniel wrote them, but was on some ancient drugs at the time (or)
   3. "Save those Euros for Rome's going to rise again! Oh yes, the devil's version of 'The Empire Strikes Back' will soon be shown in your local theater!"

The bottom line

In a nutshell the Bible predicts that in the last days the Old Roman Empire will be indeed revived and headed up by a powerful Western leader, none other than the Antichrist himself! This Empire will consist of ten nations, all of which will be utterly destroyed by the Rock, King Jesus, at the Battle of Armageddon!

■ **Question:** Whatever happened to the ancient Rome of the Caesars? Well, after some six hundred years of rule it fell apart in 476 A.D. But even today it is busily engaged in changing the little poem:

> *Humpty Dumpty sat on a wall,*
> *Humpty Dumpty had a great fall.*
> *All the king's horses and all the king's men*
> *Couldn't put Humpty together again!*

Sadly, this poem may well describe our own country, the United States, but is not the case regarding the European powers. The truth is, Old Humpty will indeed be put back together with such power which would surely have amazed the Caesars! Consider the following dates:

A. From Rome's fall in 476 A. D. to 1949

1. Christmas Day, 800 A.D., Charlemagne, King of the Franks, was crowned by the pope as "Emperor of the Romans," but his rule fell apart after his death in 814 A.D.

2. 962 A. D.—Otto the Great, a powerful German ruler, attempted unsuccessfully to do this.

3. December 8, 1804—Napoleon crowned himself Emperor, saying, "I am a Roman Emperor in the best line of the Caesars." But his empire melted like snow following his defeat at the Battle of Waterloo in 1815.

4. 1870—Bismarck, the iron Chancellor of Germany, conquered France and named his victory, the Second Reich. But it ended with Germany's surrender to the Allies in 1918.

5. 1938—Hitler boasted to the world that he had created the Third Reich which would endure for a thousand years! Not even close! A mere seven years later he committed suicide in a Berlin bunker!

B. From 1949 to the present

1. April 4, 1949—The North Atlantic Treaty Organization (NATO) came into being.

2. March 25, 1957—The treaty of Rome was signed in Rome, paving the way for the present-day European Common Market.

3. December 28, 1958—The Treaty of Rome was formally ratified.

   Two national magazines described this meeting as follows:

   "On Capitoline Hill in Rome, nearly 2,000 years ago, Caesar's legions went forth to bring the first unified rule to Europe's warring tribes. Since the Roman Empire's fall the unification of Europe has been a dream which neither the sword of Napoleon nor Hitler could realize. But on Rome's Capitoline Hill last week six statesmen, with the peaceful stroke of a pen, took the biggest step yet made toward this dream of centuries" (*Life Magazine*, 9 January 1959).

"When the history of the 20th century is written, last week is likely to prove one of its water-sheds. For in the seven days which spanned 1958 and 1959, Western Europe began to flex its economic muscles for the first time in a decade, and took its biggest step toward unity since the death of Charlemagne 1,145 years ago" (*Time Magazine*, 12 January 1959, p. 23).

4. November 9, 1989—The hated twenty-eight mile Berlin Wall, built by Eastern Berlin in 1961, was torn down.

5. October 3, 1990—The two Germanys merged to form a new united country. The importance of this merge cannot be overstressed, for without it, the Common Market would not have been what it is today!

6. January 1, 1993—On this date Western Europe became a single economic market, linking 345 million people in twelve nations, and eliminating tariffs and custom barriers!

7. January 1, 2002—Euro currency was officially issued.

With this in mind, consider this shocking statement made by Paul Henri Spaak, first President of the Council of Europe, former president of the U. N. General Assembly, and one of the chief architects of the European Common Market:

"Send us a man who can hold the allegiance of all the people, and whether he be God or the devil, we will receive him!" (*Moody Monthly Magazine*, March 1974).

EVENT 5 THE FALSE CHURCH

INTRODUCTION

It was during my senior year in a very liberal college affiliated with a major religious denomination when I first met a number of young men training for the ministry. One spring afternoon near Easter, I was sitting quietly in the college sweet shop enjoying a cup of coffee when I witnessed and heard the following scene. It involved five students, all of whom were pastoral majors. Four were sitting in a booth when the fifth walked up, and, extending his hand, exclaimed, "Hey guys, shake hands with Jesus Christ! Whoops, look out for the holes!"

Then one of the four asked if the others had heard of the new do-it-yourself Easter kit. It seemed no one had. "Well," he continued, "it's a rather bulky package containing two boards and three nails!" This resulted in loud laughter. After remaining silent for a few minutes, I finally mustered up the nerve to say something to the two joke tellers. I mean it's one thing to tell a smutty story, but another thing to attack the Atonement!

"Excuse me," I began, "I couldn't help overhearing your conversation and was just wondering if you really understood the nature concerning that Person you were ridiculing, and, even more important, how and why He got those wounds?" Well, in an instant the pair exploded! You might have thought I'd questioned the integrity of their mothers.

"Look," said the one, "both my grandfather and father were preachers, so lay off!" "Yeah," said the other, "we don't need some holy Joe preaching to us! Mind your own business!" End of conversation!

Later that semester I met and became friends with another pastoral major (not one of the five) named Terry. As I was soon to discover, he, too, held the same theological position of the five. This came out as we sat in that same sweet shop. Terry informed me he would be preaching his first funeral for one of the members of his church. When asked what he planned to say, I was told it would be basically the same things I probably would say.

"But, Terry, I believe saved people go to heaven at death, and you're not at all sure there is an afterlife of any kind! I mean, isn't that hypocrisy?"

"No," he replied, "I compare this to what I tell my kids about Santa, the tooth fairy, and the Easter bunny! Sure, none of it is true, but, hey, if it makes them feel good for a while at least, why not?"

In the ensuing years, I've thought about these incidents (along with others similar in nature) and sadly concluded that unless there was a radical change in their thinking, these young men are, if still alive, religious spokesmen for the harlot church! As Paul once classified them as "*having a form of godliness, but denying the power thereof …* " (2 Tim. 3:5).

THE SUPER HARLOT CHURCH, AS DESCRIBED

John the apostle writes about a bloodshedding, God-hating, gold-loving prostitute, calling her "mystery Babylon" (Rev. 17:5). This brutal, bloody, and blasphemous harlot is none other than the universal false church, the wicked wife of Satan. God had no sooner begun His blessed work in preparing for Himself a people than the devil did likewise. In fact, the first baby to be born on earth later became Satan's original convert. (See Gen. 4:8; 1 John 3:12). We shall now consider the historical, current, and future activities of this perverted prostitute.

- ■ **The harlot viewed historically**
  - A. Satan's church began officially at the Tower of Babel in Genesis 11:1-9, nearly twenty-four centuries B.C. Here, in the fertile plain of Shinar, probably very close to the original Garden of Eden, the first spade of dirt was turned for the purpose of devil-worship.
  - B. The passage in Genesis 11 does not teach that early mankind stupidly attempted to build a tower which would reach into outer space! Especially to be noted are the words in verse four "may reach." They are in italics to show they are supplied by

the translators and therefore not in the original Hebrew text. In reality, the phrase should read, "whose top is heaven."

C. Archaeological evidence suggests that the Tower of Babel was in reality a building given over to astrology, or the heathen worship of the heavens. Among the ruins of ancient Babylon is a building 153 feet high with a 400-foot base. It was constructed of dried bricks in seven stages, to correspond with the known planets to which they were dedicated. The lowermost was black, the color of Saturn, the next orange, for Jupiter, the third red, for Mars, and so on. These stages were surmounted by a lofty tower, on the summit of which were the signs of the Zodiac.

Dr. Barnhouse writes:

> "It was an open, definite turning to Satan and the beginning of devil worship. This is why the Bible everywhere pronounces a curse on those who consult the sun, the moon and the stars of heaven."

The first full-time minister of Satan was Nimrod, Noah's wicked and apostate grandson (Gen. 10:8-10).

D. Secular history and tradition tell us that Nimrod married a woman who was as evil and demonic as himself. Her name was Semerimus. Knowing God's promise of a future Savior (Gen. 3:15), Semerimus brazenly claimed that Tammuz, her first son, fulfilled this prophecy.

Semerimus thereupon instituted a religious system which made both her and her son the objects of divine worship. She herself became the first high priestess. Thus began the mother-child cult which later spread all over the world.

E. What was the teaching of Semerimus' satanic church? That Semerimus herself was the way to God. She actually adopted the title "Queen of Heaven." Adherents believed that she alone could administer salvation to the sinner through various sacraments, such as the sprinkling of holy water. They believed that her son Tammuz was tragically slain by a wild bear during a hunting trip—that he was, however, resurrected from the dead forty days later. Thus, each year afterward the temple virgins of this cult would enter a forty-day fast as a memorial to Tammuz' death and resurrection.

After the forty-day fast, a joyful feast called Ishtar took place. At this feast colored eggs were exchanged and eaten as a symbol of the resurrection. An evergreen tree was displayed and a Yule log was burned. Finally hot cakes marked with the letter 'T' (to remind everybody of Tammuz) were baked and eaten. About 2000 B.C. God called Abraham away from all this (see Josh. 24:2, 3) and led him into the Promised Land. But by the ninth century B.C., Israel had returned to this devil worship under the influence of wicked Jezebel (see 1 Kings 16:30-33). At this time the cult was worshipped under the name of Baal.

F. Both Jeremiah and Ezekiel warned against this hellish thing.

1. "The children gather wood, and the fathers kindle the fire, and the women knead their dough, to make cakes to the queen of heaven, and to pour out drink offerings unto her . . ." (Jer. 7:18; 44:25).

2. "Then he brought me to the door of the gate of the LORD'S house which was toward the north; and, behold, there sat women weeping for Tammuz" (Ezek. 8:14).

By the time of Christ this cult had so influenced Roman life that the Caesars were not only crowned as Emperors of Rome but also bore the title Pontifex Maximus, meaning, "high priest." They were high priests of the Babylonian satanic church.

The harlot viewed currently

Is mystery Babylon at work today? She is indeed, stronger and more sinful than ever. At least three New Testament writers and two modern ones describe her latter-day activities and characteristics.

A. Paul

"This know also, that in the last days perilous times shall come. For men shall be lovers of their own selves, covetous, boasters, proud, blasphemers, disobedient to parents, unthankful, unholy, Without natural affection, trucebreakers, false accusers, incontinent, fierce, despisers of those that are good, Traitors, heady, highminded, lovers of pleasures more than lovers of God; Having a form of godliness, but denying the power thereof: from such turn away" (2 Tim. 3:1-5).

"For the time will come when they will not endure sound doctrine; but after their own lusts shall they heap to themselves teachers, having itching ears; and they shall turn away their ears from the truth, and shall be turned unto fables" (2 Tim. 4:3, 4).

B. Peter

"But there were false prophets also among the people, even as there shall be false teachers among you, who privily shall bring in damnable heresies, even denying the Lord that bought them ..." (2 Peter 2:1).

C. John

"I know thy works, that thou art neither cold nor hot: I would thou wert cold or hot. So then because thou art lukewarm, and neither cold nor hot, I will spue thee out of my mouth. Because thou sayest, I am rich, and increased with goods, and have need of nothing; and knowest not that thou art wretched, and miserable, and poor, and blind, and naked" (Rev. 3:15-17).

D. Chuck Templeton

1. In the 1940s two of the most well-known and respected evangelical evangelists were Chuck Templeton and Billy Graham. They were friends, both powerful and effective preachers.

2. In the opinion of many of their peers, Templeton was the more talented of the two. He often preached to huge crowds numbering up to 30,000 nightly. Some 130-150 would walk the aisle to accept Jesus following each of his sermons.

3. In 1946 Templeton was ranked one of the most successful soul-winners by the National Association of Evangelicals.

4. In addition to all this he became the pastor of a rapidly growing church in Toronto.

5. Finally, he was one of three vice-presidents of Youth for Christ International.

6. But then, in 1948 he enrolled in Princeton Theological Seminary where his faith was destroyed by unbelieving professors. As a result some nine years later in 1957, Templeton publically announced he was a full-fledged agnostic.

   Following this defection he tried, unsuccessfully, to convince Billy Graham to also renounce his faith.

   "Billy, you will be committing intellectual suicide if you continue to proclaim the deity of Jesus, the virgin birth, the resurrection of Christ and the inspiration of the scriptures," he warned. "No rational and enlightened scholar now believes these fairy tales, myths, and fables."

8. To his everlasting credit, however, Billy stood firm and earnestly contended *"for the faith which was once delivered unto the saints"* (Jude 3).

9. Shortly before his death he published a book titled, *Farewell to God: My Reasons for Rejecting the Christian Faith* in which he traced his painful journey from light into spiritual darkness. Templeton died in 2001 at the age of 86. The lines of an unknown poet aptly summarize his life—

> *Oh, to have no Christ, no Bible,*
> *How lonely life must be.*
> *Like a sailor lost and driven,*
> *On a wild and stormy sea;*
>
> *Oh, to have no Christ, no Bible*
> *No hand to clasp thine own,*
> *Through the dark veil of shadows,*
> *Thou must press thy way alone.*

E. Bart Ehrman
   1. Bart was born on October 5, 1955 and professed Jesus as his Savior at an early age.
   2. He graduated from the Moody Bible Institute and Wheaton College.
   3. During those years he became a very well-known youth worker.
   4. In 1985 he completed his Ph.D. at Princeton Seminary. Tragically, however, as was the case regarding Chuck Templeton, his professors robbed him of his faith.
   5. He now is the distinguished professor of New Testament Studies at the University of North Carolina at Chapel Hill. The supreme teaching goal of this professor as demonstrated in his classroom is to likewise destroy the faith of his students as his own faith had once been destroyed.

6. Dr. Ehrman is a prolific writer, authoring or editing over 24 published books, most of which attack and ridicule the faith he once proclaimed.

7. But how could this cause a once close friend to become a sworn enemy in regards to the Bible? Dr. Randall Price, distinguished professor of Jewish Studies at Liberty University explains:

   " ... in his book, *Misquoting Jesus*, Ehrman credits the cause of his spiritual doubt and declension to a moment of realization that occurred in an exegetical course at Princeton Theological Seminary."

   Ehrman discovered that Mark appeared to have made a historical error in his Gospel when he had Jesus state that David went to "Abiathar the high priest" (Mark 2:26). However, according to 1 Samuel 21:1-6 Abiathar was not yet the high priest—his father Ahimelech was. Ehrman, then still clinging to his belief in inerrancy, tried in a course paper to harmonize the two texts and explain the error. He next describes the "turning point" that moved him away from a belief in inerrancy:

   > I was pretty sure Professor [Cullen] Story would appreciate the argument, since I knew him as a good Christian scholar who obviously (like me) would never think there could be anything like a genuine error in the Bible. But at the end of my paper he made a simple one-line comment that for some reason went straight through me. He wrote: "Maybe Mark just made a mistake." I started thinking about it, considering all the work I had put into the paper, realizing that I had to do some pretty fancy exegetical footwork to get around the problem, and that my solution was in fact a bit of a stretch. I finally concluded, 'Hmm ... maybe Mark *did* make a mistake.'

   > Once I made that admission, the floodgates opened. For if there could be one little, picayune mistake in Mark 2, maybe there could be mistakes in other places as well. (*Searching for the Original Bible*, Harvest House Publishers, Eugene, Oregon)

8. So then, Chuck Templeton and Bart Ehrman, former shining torches, then (Chuck) and now (Bart) reduced to smoking candles. How can this be explained? John the apostle provides the tragic answer: "*They went out from us, but they were not of us; for if they had been of us, they would no doubt have continued with us: but they went out, that they might be made manifest that they were not all of us*" (1 John 2:19).

9. Finally, there is a simple solution to Ehrman's problem:

   Again, to quote from Dr. Price –

   > If we look more closely at what Mark actually wrote in chapter two, we find he did not say, "*when Abiathar was the high priest,*" as Bart Ehrman quotes it, but "*in the time of Abiathar the high priest.*" It was this very argument that Ehrman had made to his professor—a rational and reasonable argument, within the context, that follows a proper principle of interpretation.

What is ironic is that in Ehrman's account in *Misquoting Jesus* he unwittingly makes the very same "mistake" (twice) he came to believe Mark had made. On page 9 he writes of "what the great King David had done when he and his men were hungry, how they went into the Temple *'when Abiathar was the high priest'* . . ." However, David was not yet *king* when this occurred and no *Temple* yet existed, only the Tabernacle!

Now, if a world-class scholar like Ehrman can make anachronistic statements like this and expect his readers to understand what he *really* means without accusing him of error, why couldn't Mark (actually, Jesus) do the same? (Ibid., p. 242)

Dr. J. Dwight Pentecost observes:

The New Testament pictures the conditions within the professing church at the end of the age by a system of denials:

- Denial of *God*—Lk. 17:26; 2 Tim. 3:4, 5
- Denial of *Christ*—1 Jn. 2:18; 4:3; 2 Pet. 2:6
- Denial of *Christ's return*—2 Pet. 3:3, 4
- Denial of *the faith*—1 Tim. 4:1, 2; Jude 3, 4
- Denial of *sound doctrine*—2 Tim. 4:3, 4
- Denial of *the separated life*—2 Tim. 3:1-7
- Denial of *Christian liberty*—1 Tim. 4:3, 4
- Denial of *morals*—2 Tim. 3:1-8, 13; Jude 18
- Denial of *authority*—2 Tim. 3:4

(Pentecost, *Things to Come*, p. 155)

■ **The harlot viewed prophetically**

Her wicked actions will result in—

A. An increase of false prophets (Mt. 24:11, 24)

B. A decrease in biblical faith (Lk. 18:8)

John the apostle summarizes this wretched satanic system as follows—

So he carried me away in the spirit into the wilderness: and I saw a woman sit upon a scarlet coloured beast, full of names of blasphemy, having seven heads and ten horns. And the woman was arrayed in purple and scarlet colour, and decked with gold and precious stones and pearls, having a golden cup in her hand full of abominations and filthiness of her fornication: And upon her forehead was a name written, MYSTERY, BABYLON THE GREAT, THE MOTHER OF HARLOTS AND ABOMINATIONS OF THE EARTH. And I saw the woman drunken with the blood of the saints, and with the blood of the martyrs of Jesus: and when I saw her, I wondered with great admiration. (Rev. 17:3-6)

Here is the conclusion of the matter:

> Mystery Babylon is composed of apostate masses from Protestantism, the cults, Catholicism, Judaism, and every other major world religion.

THE SUPER HARLOT CHURCH, AS DESTROYED

Who destroys this vicious vixen and why?

"And the ten horns which thou sawest upon the beast, these shall hate the whore, and shall make her desolate and naked, and shall eat her flesh, and burn her with fire" (Rev. 17:16).

■ The *who* involved

One of the most ironic moments in all recorded history has to do with the destruction of this filthy prostitute, the false religious system. It is not the fact involved but rather the source, for the Antichrist himself will literally annihilate her!

■ The *why* involved

Two factors will lead to the destruction.

A. The hatred of the Antichrist

Apparently after helping him obtain his vast power the false church will then attempt to control the Antichrist. But he will have none of it!

History gives us many examples of the Roman Catholic Church (and indeed other religious systems) attempting to control kings and rulers.

Note the edict of Pope Gregory VII in the eleventh century:

> "It is laid down that the Roman Pontiff is universal bishop, that his name is the only one of its kind in the world. To him alone it belongs to dispose or reconcile bishops … He alone may use the ensigns of empire; all princes are bound to kiss his feet; he has the right to depose emperors, and to absolve subjects from their allegiance. He holds in his hands the supreme mediation in questions of war and peace, and he alone may adjudge contested succession to kingdoms—all kingdoms are held in fiefs—under Peter … the Roman church has never erred … the Pope is above all judgment" (*Short Paper on Church History*, p. 355).

B. The sovereignty of God

"For God hath put in their hearts to fulfil his will, and to agree, and give their kingdom unto the beast, until the words of God shall be fulfilled" (Rev. 17:17).

In closing this study, Jesus may well have had in mind the leaders of the false church at the end of His Sermon on the Mount when he warned:

> *"A good tree cannot bring forth evil fruit, neither can a corrupt tree bring forth good fruit. Not every one that saith unto me, Lord, Lord, shall enter into the kingdom of heaven; but he that doeth the will of my Father which is in heaven. Many will say to me in that day, Lord, Lord, have we not prophesied in thy name? and in thy name*

have cast out devils? and in thy name done many wonderful works? And then will I profess unto them, I never knew you: depart from me, ye that work iniquity" (Matt. 7:18, 21-23).

EVENT 6 GOD'S TWO WITNESSES

"And I will give power to my two witnesses, and they will prophesy one thousand two hundred and sixty days, clothed in sackcloth. These are the two olive trees and the two lampstands standing before the God of the earth" (Rev. 11:3, 4).

INTRODUCTION

During the early part of the Great Tribulation, God will raise up two choice spokesmen, bold and brave individuals, who, like those warriors from the tribe of Issachar in the Old Testament, will be as they were, *"men who had understanding of the times, to know what Israel ought to do"* (1 Chron. 12:32).

We will overview this "dynamic duo" in a seven-fold fashion:

■ **Their number**

As has already been noted, there will be two. The number two plays an important role in the Bible.

A. Isaiah called two honest men, Uriah and Zechariah, to witness a document he was signing! (Isa. 8:1, 2)

B. According to the Law of Moses only on the testimony of two (or three) witnesses could a guilty man be put to death (Deut. 17:6; 19:15). See also Heb. 10:28.

C. Two false witnesses were involved in the death of Naboth, who wrongly accused him of blasphemy (1 Kings 21:10).

D. During His earthly ministry Jesus sent out seventy disciples, two by two, with instructions to proclaim the Gospel (Lk. 10:1).

E. During His unfair trials, two false and lying witnesses accused the Savior of planning to destroy the temple (Mt. 26:61).

F. Two witnesses had to be present before a church elder could be accused of any wrong-doing (1 Tim. 5:19).

G. King Solomon aptly summarized the wisdom and need of all the above with the following words— *"Two are better than one, because they have a good return for their labor: If either of them falls down, one can help the other up. But pity anyone who falls and has no one to help them up"* (Eccles. 4:9, 10).

■ **Their character**

Three characteristics define these two men—

A. Integrity! They will function as witnesses who are faithful *to* God's truth.

B. Light bearers! They will function as lampstands who shed light *upon* God's truth.

C. Anointed ones! They will function as olive trees who are empowered *by* God's truth.

■ **Their counterparts**

Both the O.T. and N.T. record many examples in regards to the effectiveness seen by and through various two-man teams.

A. In the O. T.
   1. Joshua and Caleb
   2. Ezekiel and Daniel
   3. Ezra and Nehemiah
   4. Haggai and Zechariah

B. In the N. T.
   1. Peter and John
   2. Paul and Barnabas
   3. Paul and Silas

■ **Their identity**

A. Some hold that they are Elijah and Enoch. Hebrews 9:27 states that all men are appointed to die, and since these two men did not experience physical death, they will be sent back to witness and to eventually die a martyr's death.

   However, Hebrews 9:27 should be regarded as a general statement for someday an event will occur which will allow all living Christians to enter heaven without dying! This event is known as the Rapture! Paul gives us the details in two passages:
   1. 1 Cor. 15:51-55
   2. 1 Thess. 4:13-18

B. Some hold that they are Elijah and Moses.
   1. Elijah
      a. Because of Malachi 4:5, 6 which predicts that God will send Elijah during the great and dreadful day of the Lord
      b. Because Elijah appeared with Moses on the Mount of Transfiguration to talk with Jesus (Mt. 17:3)
      c. Because Elijah's Old Testament ministry of preventing rain for some three years will be repeated by one of the witnesses during the Tribulation. (Compare 1 Kings 17:1 with Rev. 11:6.)
      d. Because the witnesses will be able to destroy their enemies by fire (Rev. 11:5), as Elijah once did (2 Kings 1:10-12).

The Jews definitely felt Elijah would come again. When the Sanhedrin sent out a delegation from Jerusalem to check out the preaching and baptizing ministry of John the Baptist, the second question they asked was: *"Art thou Elijah?"* (John 1:21)

The Jewish work, *The Twelve Prophets*, is a commentary on the Hebrew text of the Old Testament. It also advocates Elijah's return:

> "Elijah the prophet ... the messenger who will prepare the way for the coming of the Lord ... is to later generations the helper and healer, the reconciler and peace-bringer, the herald of the days of the Messiah ..." (*Books of the Bible*, London, Soncino Press, 1948, p. 356).

Even today at every Passover meal in Jewish homes there is an empty chair set in place for the prophet Elijah.

2. Moses

   a. Because of Jude 9, where we are informed that after the death of Moses Satan attempted to acquire his dead body, so that God would not be able to use him against the Antichrist during the Tribulation

   b. Because Moses' Old Testament ministry of turning water into blood will be repeated by one of the witnesses during the Tribulation (compare Exod. 7:19 with Rev. 11:6).

   c. Because Moses appeared with Elijah on the Mount of Transfiguration (Matt. 17:3).

   d. Because of the very nature of the Great Tribulation itself. According to Dan. 9:24-27 God will use this period to both punish and purify Israel. In Matt. 5:17, Jesus summarized the entire Old Testament by referring to the law (the first five books), and the prophets (the remaining Old Testament books). Thus, inasmuch as God will deal with Israel in Old Testament fashion during the Great Tribulation, what better men could he use to minister through than Moses, a representative of the law, and Elijah, greatest of the prophets?

■ **Their ministry (Rev. 11:4-6)**

A. To prophesy in sackcloth before men as God's anointed lampstands

B. To destroy their enemies in the same manner that their enemies would attempt to destroy them

C. To prevent rain for three and a half years

D. To turn waters into blood

E. To smite the earth with every kind of plague

F. To (perhaps) lead the 144,000 Jewish evangelists to the Lord (Rev. 7:4)

■ **Their martyrdom**

"When they finish their testimony, the beast that ascends out of the bottomless pit will make war against them, overcome them, and kill them. And their dead bodies will lie in the street of the great city which spiritually is called Sodom and Egypt, where also our Lord was crucified. Then those from the peoples, tribes, tongues, and nations will see their dead bodies three-and-a-half days, and not allow their dead bodies to be put into graves. And those who dwell on the earth will rejoice over them, make merry, and send gifts to one another, because these two prophets tormented those who dwell on the earth" (Rev. 11:7-10).

To show his contempt for them, he refused to permit their dead bodies to be buried, but leaves them to rot in the streets of Jerusalem (Rev. 11:8). It is called Sodom because of its immorality, and Egypt because of its worldliness. It is interesting to note that this prophecy (Rev. 11:9) could not have been fulfilled until the middle sixties.

The following article explains why:

> The first link in a worldwide, live television system was taken on May 2, 1965, when the Early Bird Satellite, hovering 22,300 miles in space between Brazil and Africa, united millions of American and European viewers in an international television exchange (*Reader's Digest Almanac*, 1966 edition).

Let us consider two questions at this point:

A. Why will God allow the Antichrist to murder these two faithful and fearless messengers? The sovereign answer is quite simple: because they had accomplished their assigned ministries!

In other words they could not be killed until "they shall have finished their testimony." Satan cannot touch one hair of the head of the most humble saint until God gives him specific permission (see Job 1:12; 2:6). These two, like Paul, finished their testimonies (2 Tim. 4:7). Contrast this with Belshazzar's sad death (Dan. 5:26-30).

The supreme example of this of course can be readily seen in both the earthly life and death of Jesus Christ Himself!

1. In life

   "But I have a greater witness than John's; for the works which the Father has given Me to finish—the very works that I do—bear witness of Me, that the Father has sent Me" (John 5:36). *"I have glorified You on the earth. I have finished the work which You have given Me to do"* (John 17:4).

2. In death

   "So when Jesus had received the sour wine, He said, "It is finished!" And bowing His head, He gave up His spirit" (John 19:30).

B. Have you ever earnestly and continuously besought God to do something for months on end but are still waiting for an answer? Well, take heart: Consider the desperate and despondent request of an Old Testament man who prayed some 2700 years ago which still awaits an answer!!! The man in question was Elijah the prophet. He had invoked the fury of a godless Baalite queen for killing a large number of her devilish religious leaders. Here is the biblical record:

> *"And Ahab told Jezebel all that Elijah had done, also how he had executed all the prophets with the sword. Then Jezebel sent a messenger to Elijah, saying, 'So let the gods do to me, and more also, if I do not make your life as the life of one of them by tomorrow about this time.' And when he saw that, he arose and ran for his life, and went to Beersheba, which belongs to Judah, and left his servant there. But he himself went a day's journey into the wilderness, and came and sat down under a broom tree. And he prayed that he might die, and said, 'It is enough! Now, Lord, take my life, for I am no better than my fathers!'"* (1 Kings 19:1-4).

Thus, the prayer. However, sometime during the Great Tribulation, God will answer that twenty-seven-centuries-long prayer! And the moral of the story? Simply this— Be careful what you ask God for, as it may be answered in ways you never expected!

■ **Their resurrection**

"But after the three and a half days the breath of life from God entered them, and they stood on their feet, and terror struck those who saw them. Then they heard a loud voice from heaven saying to them, 'Come up here.' And they went up to heaven in a cloud, while their enemies looked on. At that very hour there was a severe earthquake and a tenth of the city collapsed. Seven thousand people were killed in the earthquake, and the survivors were terrified and gave glory to the God of heaven" (Rev. 11:11-13).

Author John Phillips describes this event as only he can:

> "Death cannot hold them, and they arise from the grave. John tells us that they have a triumphant resurrection. He says, 'And after three days and a half the Spirit of life from God entered into them and they stood upon their feet; and great fear fell upon them which saw them.' Picture the scene: the sun-drenched streets of Jerusalem, the holiday crowds flown in from the ends of the earth for a firsthand look at the corpses of these detested men, the troops in the beast's uniform, the temple police. There they are: devilish men from every kingdom under heaven, come to dance and feast at the triumph of the beast. And then it happens! As the crowds strain at the police cordon to peer curiously at the two dead bodies, there comes a sudden change.
>
> Their color changes from a cadaverous hue to the blooming, rosy glow of youth. Those stiff, stark limbs—they bend, they move! Oh, what a sight! They rise! The crowds fall back, break, and form again.
>
> They also have a triumphant rapture. John says, 'And they heard a great voice from heaven saying unto them, Come up hither. And they ascended up to heaven in a cloud; and their enemies beheld them.' But will these evil men repent when faced with this, the greatest of miracles! Not a bit of it! 'Father, Abraham!' cried the rich man from the flames of a lost eternity. 'Father Abraham … if one went unto them from the dead, they will repent.' Back came the solemn reply, 'If they hear not Moses

and the prophets, neither will they be persuaded though one rose from the dead' (Luke 16:30, 31). And here not just one, but two arise, and repentance is the farthest thing from the minds of men." (*Exploring Revelation*, Moody Press, 1974, p. 158).

EVENT 7 MINISTRY OF THE ONE HUNDRED AND FORTY-FOUR THOUSAND

INTRODUCTION

"And I heard the number of those who were sealed. One hundred and forty-four thousand of all the tribes of the children of Israel were sealed: Then I looked, and behold, a Lamb standing on Mount Zion, and with Him one hundred and forty-four thousand, having His Father's name written on their foreheads" (Rev. 7:4; 14:1).

- Revelation 7 is the final of seven scriptural passages which list by name the twelve tribes of Israel. The first six are:
  A. Genesis 49
  B. Numbers 1 and 26
  C. Deuteronomy 33
  D. Joshua 13-19
  E. Ezekiel 48

- Actually, fourteen names are associated with the twelve tribes, as recorded by Genesis 48 and 49:
  A. The first two tribes appear in Genesis 48.
  B. Their names are Manasseh and Ephraim, Jacob's two favorite grandsons, who were Joseph's sons. In fact the old patriarch blessed these two prior to doing the same for his own sons as recorded in Genesis 48.
  C. However, the number 12 is still retained in all the lists through some unique rearranging. Examples:
    1. Some include Ephraim and Manesseh, but omit Joseph, or Dan, or Levi (two of these).
    2. Other lists leave out Jacob's grandson.
  D. None of the lists are identical. We are not told why this is the case.
  E. At any rate, Jacob blesses his two grandsons as follows—
    "Then Jacob said to Joseph: 'God Almighty appeared to me at Luz in the land of Canaan and blessed me, Your offspring whom you beget after them shall be yours; they will be called by

the name of their brothers in their inheritance.' So Joseph brought them from beside his knees, and he bowed down with his face to the earth. And Joseph took them both, Ephraim with his right hand toward Israel's left hand, and Manasseh with his left hand toward Israel's right hand, and brought them near him. Now when Joseph saw that his father laid his right hand on the head of Ephraim, it displeased him; so he took hold of his father's hand to remove it from Ephraim's head to Manasseh's head. And Joseph said to his father, 'Not so, my father, for this one is the firstborn; put your right hand on his head.' But his father refused and said, 'I know, my son, I know. He also shall become a people, and he also shall be great; but truly his younger brother shall be greater than he, and his descendants shall become a multitude of nations.' So he blessed them that day, saying, 'By you Israel will bless,' saying, 'May God make you as Ephraim and as Manasseh!' And thus he set Ephraim before Manasseh.

"*Then Israel said to Joseph, 'Behold, I am dying, but God will be with you and bring you back to the land of your fathers. Moreover I have given to you one portion above your brothers, which I took from the hand of the Amorite with my sword and my bow'*" (Gen. 48:3, 6, 12, 13, 17-22).

■ **Identity of the Twelve Tribes**

A. As the text clearly states, all 144,000 are Jewish men, totally refuting the claims of—

   1. The Jehovah Witnesses, who believe that through good works down here, they can be counted as one of the select group.

   2. The Seventh-Day Adventists, who identify this group as 144,000 SDA's whom Jesus will find worshipping God on the Sabbath when He returns!

■ **Spiritual Condition of the Twelve Tribes**

An amazing contrast can be seen by comparing the twelve tribes in the Old Testament with that of the twelve tribes appearing in the Great Tribulation. Thus:

A. The grievous spiritual condition of the twelve Old Testament tribes—

   1. The tribe of *Dan* was predicted by Jacob to become as a treacherous serpent, lurking beside the highway biting the horses' heels, thus causing the rider to tumble backward (Gen. 49:17).

   2. The tribe of *Benjamin* was almost all but exterminated during a tribal war, which pitted eleven against the one (Judges 20:44, 46, 47).

   3. Only the tribe of *Levi* stood with God during the terrible Golden Calf episode (Exod. 32:26).

   4. The tribe of *Ephraim* was guilty of gross idolatry (Hosea 4:17, 18; 6:4).

   5. All but two tribes (*Judah* and *Benjamin*) rebelled against the house and dynasty of King David (1 Kings 12:1-16).

B. The glorious spiritual condition of the twelve Great Tribulational tribes—

   1. All will be saved and indwelt by the Holy Spirit (Rev. 7:1). See also Eph. 1:13; 4:30; 2 Cor. 1:22.

2. Protected from all harm (Rev. 7:3)

3. Fellowshipping with Jesus (Rev. 14:1)

4. Pure in body and spirit (Rev. 14:4a)

5. Following Jesus wherever He went (Rev. 14:4b)

6. Serving as firstfruits of the redeemed before God (Rev. 14:4c)

7. Enjoying the music of heaven (Rev. 14:3a)

8. Personally singing a new song which only they could sing (Rev. 14:3b)

Ministry of the Twelve Tribes

Jesus himself during his Mt. Olivet sermon predicted the tremendous scope of their ministry: *"And this gospel of the kingdom shall be preached in all the world for a witness unto all nations . . ."* (Mt. 24:14). In other words these future evangelists will accomplish in a few short years that which the Christian church has not been able to do in the past twenty centuries, namely, fulfill the Great Commission: *"Go ye therefore, and teach all nations, baptizing them in the name of the Father, and of the Son, and of the Holy Ghost: Teaching them to observe all things whatsoever I have commanded you: and lo, I am with you always, even unto the end of the world. Amen"* (Mt. 28:19, 20).

While the church is never instructed to bring the world to Christ, it is commissioned to bring Christ to the world!

This passage does not mean that God will save only Jews during the Tribulation, for in Revelation 7:9-17, the Bible declares that a great multitude from every nation will be saved. What this chapter does teach, however, is that God will send out 144,000 "Hebrew Billy Sundays" to evangelize the world.

A tremendous contrast can be seen by comparing Numbers 31 with Revelation 7:

1. In Numbers 31, God sends out 12,000 Israelite warriors to consume their enemies.

2. In Revelation 7, God will send out 144,000 Israelite witnesses to convert their enemies.

Judah heads up this list, and not Reuben, the firstborn. Both Dan and Ephraim are missing. Both tribes were guilty of going into idolatry (Judges 18; Hosea 4). The tribes of Levi and Manasseh here take their place. However, both are listed in Ezekiel's millennial temple (Ezek. 48), so they simply forfeit their chance to preach during the Tribulation. Some have concluded on the basis of Genesis 49:17 and Jeremiah 8:16 that the Antichrist will come from the tribe of Dan.

Fruit of the Twelve Tribes

I believe it may be concluded by most Bible students that, up to this time, history's greatest revival occurred around 760 B.C. in the pagan and cruel capital of the Assyrian Empire, the city of Nineveh. The Old Testament book of Jonah records this for us:

> *Now the word of the LORD came to Jonah the second time, saying, "Arise, go to Nineveh, that great city, and preach to it the message that I tell you." So Jonah arose and went to Nineveh, according to the word of the LORD. Now Nineveh was an exceedingly great city, a*

three-day journey in extent. And Jonah began to enter the city on the first day's walk. Then he cried out and said, "Yet forty days, and Nineveh shall be overthrown!"

So the people of Nineveh believed God, proclaimed a fast, and put on sackcloth, from the greatest to the least of them. Then word came to the king of Nineveh; and he arose from his throne and laid aside his robe, covered himself with sackcloth and sat in ashes. And he caused it to be proclaimed and published throughout Nineveh by the decree of the king and his nobles, saying, Let neither man nor beast, herd nor flock, taste anything; do not let them eat, or drink water. But let man and beast be covered with sackcloth, and cry mightily to God; yes, let every one turn from his evil way and from the violence that is in his hands. Who can tell if God will turn and relent, and turn away from His fierce anger, so that we may not perish? Then God saw their works, that they turned from their evil way; and God relented from the disaster that He had said He would bring upon them, and He did not do it (Jonah 3:1-10).

But this turning to God event, however glorious it was, pales into insignificance when compared with the Great Tribulation revival! Here is the Apostle John's account:

After these things I looked, and behold, a great multitude which no one could number, of all nations, tribes, peoples, and tongues, standing before the throne and before the Lamb, clothed with white robes, with palm branches in their hands, and crying out with a loud voice, saying, "Salvation belongs to our God who sits on the throne, and to the Lamb!" All the angels stood around the throne and the elders and the four living creatures, and fell on their faces before the throne and worshiped God, saying: "Amen! Blessing and glory and wisdom, Thanksgiving and honor and power and might, Be to our God forever and ever. Amen."

Then one of the elders answered, saying to me, "Who are these arrayed in white robes, and where did they come from? And I said to him, "Sir, you know." So he said to me, "These are the ones who come out of the great tribulation, and washed their robes and made them white in the blood of the Lamb (Rev. 7:9-14).

At this time God will wonderfully answer the prayer of Habakkuk: "*O LORD, revive thy work in the midst of the years … in wrath, remember mercy*" (Hab. 3:2).

EVENT 8 THE GOG AND MAGOG INVASION INTO THE LAND OF ISRAEL

WHEN THE BEAR COMES OVER THE MOUNTAIN

Chapters 36-39 in the book of Ezekiel are closely related:

- Chapters 36 and 37 tell us how God will, in the future, *direct* His people *to* the land of Israel!
- Chapters 38 and 39 tell us how God will, in the future, *protect* His people *in* the land of Israel!

166   HE'S STILL COMING

The following is an outline summary regarding this protection. Ezekiel predicts that Israel will someday be attacked by an enemy confederation led by a warrior named Gog, from the land of Magog.

- **The abhorrence of Gog** (38:1-3): God states his anger concerning the evil plans of Gog.
- **The allies of Gog** (38:4-7): Ezekiel identifies these nations as Persia, Ethiopia, Libya, Gomer, and Beth-togarmah.
- **The attack by Gog** (38:8-16)
  - A. When Gog will attack (38:8-11): The invasion will occur "in the latter days" when Israel is at peace in their own land.
  - B. Why Gog will attack (38:12-16): This will be done to plunder and loot.
- **The annihilation of Gog** (38:17-39:24)
  - A. As foretold in the former days (38:17-18): This destruction was predicted by the prophets long ago.
  - B. As fulfilled in the final days (38:19-39:24)
    1. The plan (38:19-22): God will accomplish this annihilation by a threefold method:
       - a. A mighty earthquake (38:19-20): All living things will quake in terror at God's presence.
       - b. Mutiny among the enemy troops (38:21): Their men will turn against each other.
       - c. The use of sword, disease, floods, hailstorms, fire, and brimstone (38:22)
    2. The place (39:1-6): This will occur on the mountains of Israel.
    3. The purpose (38:23; 39:7-8, 21-24)
       - a. In regard to the Gentile nations (38:23; 39:21, 23-24): Upon witnessing this destruction, the pagan nations will acknowledge the person and power of the true God.
       - b. In regard to the Jewish nation (39:7-8, 22): They also will know that Israel's God is indeed the only true God!
    4. The purifying (39:9-16)
       - a. Seven years of fuel (39:9-10): There will be sufficient war debris to serve as fuel for the people of Israel for seven years.
       - b. Seven months of funerals (39:11-16): It will take Israel seven months to bury the dead.
    5. The proclamation (39:17-20): God will personally invite the wild birds and animals to consume the flesh of the fallen enemy warriors.
- **The assembling after Gog** (39:25-29): God will then regather, regenerate, and restore his people to their land.

(Taken from *Willmington's Outline Bible*, Tyndale House Publishers, 1999, pp. 406, 407)

Now for some details, presented in Q and A format:

- ▓ **Where is the land of Magog located?**

    Many believe this is a reference to the land of Russia. There seems to be geographical, historical, and linguistic evidence that this is the case.

    A. Geographical evidence

    Ezekiel tells us in three distinct passages (38:6, 15; 39:2) that this invading nation will come from the "uttermost part of the north" (as the original Hebrew renders it). A quick glance at any world map will show that only Russia can fulfill this description.

    Dr. Mark Hitchcock observes:

    > " ... there is considerable historical evidence that a place known as Rosh was very familiar in the ancient world. While the word has a variety of forms and spellings, it is clear that the same people are in view.
    >
    > "In Egyptian inscriptions, Rosh (Rash) is identified as a place that existed as early as 2600 B.C. There is a later Egyptian inscription from about 1500 B.C. that refers to a land called Reshu that was located to the north of Egypt.
    >
    > "The place-name Rosh (or its equivalent in the respective language) is found at least twenty times in other ancient documents. It is found three times in the Septuagint, ten times in Sargon's inscriptions, once in Assurbanipal's cylinder, once in Sennacherib's annals, and five times in Ugaritic tablets.
    >
    > "Clearly, Rosh was a well-known place in Ezekiel's day. In the sixth century B.C., the time when Ezekiel wrote his prophecy, several bands of the Rosh people lived in an area to the north of the Black Sea. Many scholars have traced a direct connection between these people and the people from which Russia derives its name. John Ruthven, after an in-depth investigation into the issue, says:
    >
    > "But other indications, such as geographical location, ethnography, and the general descriptions of the culture, provide us with some confidence that there is a direct connection between the *Rosh* of Ezekiel and the tribal Rus from which the modern Russia derives its name. Indeed this is the suggestion of one Russian historian, who states: 'The first reference to the ... *Russ*, the ancestors of the Russian rulers, is found in Ezekiel 38:2f.'"

    After providing extensive, overwhelming evidence of the origin and early history of the Rosh people, and then tracing them through the centuries, Clyde E. Billington Jr. concludes:

    > Historical, ethnological, and archaeological evidence all favor the conclusion that the Rosh people of Ezekiel 38-39 were the ancestors of the Rus/Ros people of Europe and Asia ... the Rosh people who are mentioned in Ezekiel 38-39 were well-known to ancient and medieval writers by a variety of names which all derived from the names of Tiras and Rosh ... Those Rosh people who lived to the north of the Black Sea in ancient and medieval times were called the Rus/

Ros/Rox/Aorsi from the early times . . From this mixture with Slavs and with the Varangian Rus in the 9th century, the Rosh people of the area north of the Black Sea formed the people known today as the Russians.

(*The Truth Behind Left Behind*, Doubleday Religious Publishing Group, 2004, pp. 52, 53)

B. Historical Evidence

The ancient Jewish historian Josephus (first century A.D.) assures us that the descendants of Magog (who was Japheth's son and Noah's grandson) migrated to an area north of Palestine. But even prior to Josephus, the famous Greek historian Herodotus (fifth century B.C.) writes that Meshech's descendants settled north of Palestine.

C. Linguistic Evidence

" ...Wilhelm Gesenius who died in 1852 and is considered by modern Hebrew scholars as one of the greatest scholars of the Hebrew language, unquestionably believed that Rosh in Ezekiel was a proper noun identifying Russia. Gesenius says that *Rosh* in Ezekiel 38:2-3; 39:1 is a 'northern nation, mentioned by the Byzantine writers of the tenth century, under the name *the Ros*, dwelling to the north of Taurus ... as dwelling on the river Rha (*Wolga*).'

"This identification by Gesenius cannot be passed off lightly. Gesenius, as far as we know, was not a pretribulationalist or even a premillennialist. He had no eschatological, end time ax to grind. Yet objectively he says without hesitation that Rosh in Ezekiel 38-39 is Russia." (Ibid., p. 51)

▧ **Just how big is Russia?**

In a nutshell, it is the world's largest country embracing 8,649,496 square miles, some one-sixth of the earth's total land area. This is nearly two and a half times the size of the United States!

▧ **How long have evangelical Christians held the view that Magog is Russia?**

Many have criticized all this, accusing Bible believers of simply waiting to see what happens and then twisting current events into their own peculiar prophetical scheme. To answer this, the following quotes are given. It will be observed by the dates that both statements were written long before Russia became the power she is today.

"Russia is evidently destined to become the master of Asia. Her frontier line across Asia will be 5,000 miles in length. We believe, from the place assigned to Russia in the Word of God, that her legions will sweep over the plains and mountains of Asia and will become the dominant power over all the East." (*The Prophetical News and Israel's Watch*, Walter Scott, June, 1888).

"This king of the North I conceive to be ... Russia. Russia occupies a momentous place in the prophetic word." (John Cumming, Bible teacher, 1864)

▧ **When and how did Russia become what she is today?**

Some years back, Dr. Joshua Kunitz, a professor at London University, wrote a book about Russia and titled it, *Russia, the Giant That Came Last*. No better words could have been chosen to describe the U.S.S.R. The rise of Russia has been nothing less than phenomenal: Even though her land began to be peopled by the Slavs as early as the fifth century A.D., Russia remained a geographical void for the next thousand years. Then came Peter the Great and the world began to take notice. In 1712 he transferred the capital from Moscow to St. Petersburg. After this, Catherine the Great appeared upon the scene (1762-1796) with her attempts to westernize Russia. Russia's place in world history was now assured.

But how clumsy she was in those days. She was soundly defeated by tiny Japan in 1905. In 1914 she entered World War I, only to suffer crushing defeat. In October of 1917 the Communist Lenin took over all of Russia with some 40,000 followers.

Following World War II, she became the second most powerful nation on earth!

■ **But what is her status today?**

Note the boasts of a former Russian president:

> "If anyone believes that our smiles involve abandonment of the teaching of Marx, Engles, and Lenin, he deceives himself. Those who wait for that must wait until a shrimp learns to whistle." (Nikita Khrushchev, speech in Moscow, September 17, 1955)

On Thursday, December 21, 1991, the shrimp learned to whistle. The unthinkable occurred! The mighty Soviet Union as we had known it for seventy years no longer existed. The empire had fallen! All that remains of the mighty Soviet Empire is a loose commonwealth of the former republics. In the place of the world's most powerful communist state, there are now fifteen new countries with individual economic, political, and cultural agendas.

So then, where does this leave us? Does it mean the Magog/Russia connection should be rejected as just another fanciful claim held by sincere, but uneducated believers? Not even close!

However, it must be admitted that her power, riches, and influence have dropped drastically since the days of the Cold War. She is not among the ten richest nations in the world and only ranks number 47 in the GDP per capita.

So then, what or who will fuel her rise once again to the glory of former days? I believe two men back then were responsible, namely, Vladimir Lenin and Joseph Stalin. But that was then. What about today? Is there a man who is able to pick up their fallen mantles? It is now time to introduce the second most powerful man to appear in the Great Tribulation, second only to the Antichrist Himself!

■ **Who is this mysterious Gog, referred to by Ezekiel no less than seven times in chapters 38 and 39?**

The King James Version calls him "the chief prince" in these references with the footnote "or prince of Rosh." Almost all other translations do the same.

■ **So, what do we know regarding his activities?**

Frankly, very little, as compared with the recorded information describing the activities of the coming Antichrist! But consider the following:

A. He will be able to control not only Russia but the surrounding nations, i.e., Iran, Turkey, Libya, etc.

B. This may be his attempt to create an Eurasian Union, patterned somewhat like the European Union of the Antichrist's.

C. He will probably attack Israel for at least three reasons:

  1. To cash in on the riches of Palestine (Ezek. 38:11, 12)

  2. To control the Middle East—Ancient conquerors have always known that he would control Europe, Asia, and Africa, must first control the Middle East bridge which leads to these three continents.

  3. To challenge the authority of the Antichrist (Dan. 11:40-44)

D. All this activity on his part will be fueled by the age-long hellish hatred Satan has for the nation Israel. Thus, he will join hands with the radical Muslims whose animosity for Israel is unnatural, unremitting and unprecedented among the nations of the world. Note but a few examples of their horrible hostility:

> "We are announcing a war against the sons of apes and pigs (the Jews) which will not end until the flag of Islam is raised in Jerusalem" (Hamas leaflet, September 1, 1993).

> "Our first goal is the liberation of all occupied territories ... and the establishment of a Palestinian state whose capital is Jerusalem ... it is the only basis for interim solution and the forerunner to a final settlement, which must be based on complete withdrawal from all occupied Palestinian lands ... The Palestinian state is within our grasp. Soon the Palestinian flag will fly on the walls, the minarets, and the cathedrals of Jerusalem" (Yasser Arafat, January, 1994, and repeated frequently ever since). "We Palestinians will take over everything, including all of Jerusalem ... We plan to eliminate the State of Israel and establish a Palestinian state" (Yasser Arafat to Arab ambassadors in Stockholm, January 30, 1996). "The Muslims say to Britain, to France and to all the infidel nations that Jerusalem is Arab. We shall not respect anyone else's wishes regarding her" (Sheikh Ekrima Sabri, Palestinian Mufti of Jerusalem at the Al-Aksa Mosque, July 11, 1997). (*Jerusalem in Prophecy*, Randall Price, p. 146)

■ **Is there a man even now, having been chosen to assume the role of Gog, waiting his cue to enter the spotlight of prophecy? Or perhaps at this present hour actually on the stage itself?** I write the following material with a disclaimer: No one on earth today knows the identity of either the Antichrist or the leader of Magog except those two men themselves. But allow me to suggest an individual who may possibly be a forerunner of Gog, if not Gog himself.

■ **What do we know about Russia's current president, Vladimir Putin?**

A. He has been in power since May 7, 2000, and will continue until at least May 7, 2018, at which time his term expires.

B. For sixteen years (1975-1991) he was a KGB agent, rising to the rank of lieutenant colonel.

C. He is an accomplished martial arts athlete and holds a black belt.

D. He is a great sports enthusiast, bringing various Olympic games to Russia, including the 2013 world championships in athletics, plus the Grand Prix in 2014.

E. He has flown military jets and supersonic heavy bombers in air shows.

F. He has fought raging wildfires in piloting a Beriev Be-200 aircraft to dump water on the fire.

G. He loves to fish and swim in a cold Siberian river.

H. In his spare time he rides Harley-Davidson vehicles, resulting in the Russian bikers voting him as a member of the Hell's Angels, with the name of Abaddon.

I. Putin also enjoys testing race cars. In November, 2000, in St. Petersburg he reached a speed of 240 km per hour in a Formula One auto.

J. He once participated in a scuba diving project at an ancient archaeological site on a Greek island.

K. On one occasion he descended in deep water and submerged hundreds of feet to the bottom of Lake Baikal, the world's deepest lake.

L. He has at times lent his support to protect the endangered animals, such as polar bears, the Siberian tigers and other wild creatures.

M. He sees himself as a painter and musician, once playing and singing Blueberry Hill at a charity concert! In fact one of his paintings, featuring a winter scene, became the top lot at the charity auction in St. Petersburg, raising thirty seven million rubles!

N. There are reports that his personal wealth is around forty billion dollars!

O. In September of 2006 France's President Jacques Chirac awarded Putin the Grand Cross, France's highest decoration.

P. On February 12, 2007, Saudi King Abdullah presented him with his country's top civilian decoration.

Q. On November 15, 2011, China gave him the Confucius Peace Prize.

R. He was *Time* magazine's Person of the Year for 2007.

S. In April of 2008, Putin was listed as one of the most influential people in the world.

T. All the above information pictures Vladimir Putin as a man of all seasons, with a reckless passion for adventure, living each day to its fullest! Some have even viewed him as a Russian Teddy Roosevelt, America's most energy-driven political leader!

But there is a dark side to this fun-loving man:

HE'S STILL COMING

1. He has been accused of brutally murdering his enemies.
2. He certainly is no friend of the U. S.
    a. Putin has accused America of murdering Muammar Gaddafi.
    b. He enjoyed friendly relationships with Iran, and Hugo Chavez of Venezuela, two of our most hostile enemies.
3. He, in the past two or three years, has sold $1.5 billion worth of military weapons to Syria, whose president has, in the past twenty-four months, systematically slaughtered over 100,000 of his own people!
4. He longs for the "good old days" during the Stalin era. On April 25, 2005, Putin went on national television and told his nation that the destruction of the Soviet Union was "the greatest geopolitical catastrophe of the twentieth century."
5. Under his leadership Russia has become the most crime-ridden, gang-led, politically-corrupt country in the civilized world. Mother Russia has degenerated into a virtual mafia state.
6. The Communist Party is the only legal party, and the rights of political association are forbidden to any other group.
7. The printed word is controlled by the government, which also regulates education and all means of communication—telephone, telegraph, and radio.
8. News going out to foreign countries is subject to censorship.
9. In recent months Putin has attempted to place all religious groups in Russia under the control of the government.

■ **So then, does all this prove that Vladimir Putin is the Gog of Ezekiel 38, 39?**

In a word—*no*! But might it indicate that he could serve as a forerunner, as it were, of Gog? In a word—*possibly*! But whatever the case, it is entirely possible that in the not-too-distant future the headlines of the *New York Times* (or *Washington Post*) might read:

SHOWDOWN BETWEEN GOG AND GOD *(Report dispatch somewhere north of Israel)*

"In a surprise move, Gog (ruler, or chief) of Magog (Russia?) apparently attempted a lightning attack against Israel, but was soundly turned back, supposedly by the very God of Israel Himself! Whoever, or whatever, the case, it was evident a supernatural source was at work, for the invading troops were not only defeated, but utterly destroyed by weapons of war, frightful floods, massive hailstones, and even, reportedly, fire and brimstone falling from the sky. When the smoke had cleared, nearly 85 percent of the enemy warriors lay dead on the battlefield! What will transpire next is anyone's guess. One thing is crystal clear: Israel's God is not to be trifled with!"

■ **One final question: Is the Gog and Magog invasion and the Battle of Armageddon one and the same?**

They are not, as seen by the following contrasts:

GOG AND MAGOG	ARMAGEDDON
Invasion is led by Gog.	Invasion is led by the Antichrist.
Gog is destroyed.	The Antichrist and the false prophet are destroyed. No mention of Gog.
Israel is at peace at the time of the invasion.	There is no mention of Israel's peace.
Armies gather to plunder Israel.	Armies gather to fight against Christ.
Occurs during the first half of the Tribulation.	Occurs at the end of the Tribulation.
Russia and her allies invade Israel.	All nations invade Israel.
Occurs so that all the nations will know that He is God.	Occurs to destroy the nations.

EVENT 9 THE RISE, GLORY, AND FALL OF BOTH ANCIENT AND FUTURE BABYLON

THE RISE AND FALL OF *ANCIENT* BABYLON
THE RISE AND FALL OF *FUTURE* BABYLON

In 1859 Charles Dickens, an English author, began writing a serialized weekly novel which he called, *A Tale of Two Cities*, that soon became a classic in English literature. The action in his novel took place in London and Paris.

Some 1400 years B. C., the Supreme Author of the universe began (through His scribes) writing, which soon became and still is, the masterpiece of all literature! A subtitle of His book might also be thought of as A Tale of Two Cities. Those are Babylon and Jerusalem! One is associated with anarchy, rebellion and evil, the other with peace and goodness. The first became the capital of Satan (Rev. 18:2), and the other, the capital of God (Deut. 12:21; 14:24).

Babylon is referred to 280 times in sixteen biblical books.

Jerusalem is referred to nearly 1000 times (various other titles such as City of David, Zion, etc.) in 38 biblical books.

THE RISE AND FALL OF *ANCIENT* BABYLON

- **Ancient Babylon—The Rise**
  The ancient city of Babylon was the capital of ten dynasties in Mesopotamia, considered one of the earliest cradles of civilization and the birthplace of writing and literature. Note the biblical account:

A. *"Cush begot Nimrod; he began to be a mighty one on the earth. He was a mighty hunter before the Lord; therefore it is said, 'Like Nimrod the mighty hunter before the Lord.' And the beginning of his kingdom was Babel, Erech, Accad, and Calneh, in the land of Shinar"* (Gen. 10:8-10).

This is the first reference to Nimrod, Ham's grandson, and Noah's great-grandson. Here we are told Nimrod was (1) a mighty warrior, (2) a great hunter, and, (3) a kingdom builder. However, as the next chapter suggests (chap. 11), he apparently got off to a bad start in regards to the building role:

B. *"Now the whole earth had one language and one speech. And it came to pass, as they journeyed from the east, that they found a plain in the land of Shinar, and they dwelt there. Then they said to one another, 'Come, let us make bricks and bake them thoroughly.' They had brick for stone, and they had asphalt for mortar. And they said, 'Come, let us build ourselves a city, and a tower whose top is in the heavens; let us make a name for ourselves, lest we be scattered abroad over the face of the whole earth.*

"But the Lord came down to see the city and the tower which the sons of men had built. And the Lord said, 'Indeed the people are one and they all have one language, and this is what they begin to do; now nothing that they propose to do will be withheld from them. Come, let Us go down and there confuse their language, that they may not understand one another's speech.' So the Lord scattered them abroad from there over the face of all the earth, and they ceased building the city. Therefore its name is called Babel, because there the Lord confused the language of all the earth; and from there the Lord scattered them abroad over the face of all the earth" (Gen. 11:1-9).

Many Bible students feel Nimrod was the driving force behind this fiasco.

C. At any rate, he was both confused and angry. For a while, his grand plan to build the city of Babylon had proceeded without a hitch. Actually, it was meant to be (1) a project to feed the massive ego of its builder, and (2) to serve as a universal religious, political, and economic center of the universe! The crowning jewel of this city on the Euphrates River was to be a lofty and majestic tower which would seem to lift its noble head among the stars! So far, so good. But upon near completion unusual and totally unexpected things began to happen. The first sign of trouble was that of an unearthly sound, not unlike that made by the buzzing coming from a huge swarm of angry bees! But these sounds proceeded from frightened and frustrated workmen, trying desperately to communicate with fellow laborers in various languages that only they could understand. What on earth, Nimrod wondered, was going on? In reality, the trouble was not on earth at all, but was coming down from heaven itself!

D. So, this proposed Gate of God (meaning of the word *Babel*) had become the city of confusion!

■ **Ancient Babylon—The Glory**

Here are some key dates and events contributing to the splendor of ancient Babylon.

A. **3000 B.C.**—Babylon is established as a small settlement on the fertile banks of the Euphrates River. This is recognized as one of the first civilizations on earth.

B. **2250 B.C.**—Building of the Tower of Babel

C. **1700 B.C.**—Babylon was ruled by Hammurabi, one of the most famous kings in ancient history, and the author of Hammurabi's legal code, including over 300 laws, covering many social and economic relationships.

D. **605-562 B.C.**—Nebuchadnezzar, the greatest military figure of his day, began building Babylon, causing it to become the most splendid city in the ancient world and one of its seven wonders! This was known as the Golden Age of Babylon.

Bible teacher Lehman Strauss has aptly described this shining city on the sands:

> Babylon was founded by Nimrod, the great-grandson of Noah (Genesis 10:8-10). Surviving a series of conflicts, it became one of the most magnificent and luxurious cities in the known world. Superbly constructed, it spread over an area of fifteen square miles, the Euphrates River flowing diagonally across the city. The famous historian Herodotus said the city was surrounded by a wall 350 feet high and 87 feet thick, wide enough for six chariots to drive abreast. Around the top of the wall were 250 watchtowers placed in strategic locations. Outside the huge wall was a large ditch, or moat, which surrounded the city and was kept filled with water from the Euphrates River. The large ditch was meant to serve as an additional protection against attacking enemies, for any attacking army would have to cross this body of water first before approaching the great wall. The cost of constructing this military defense was estimated to be in excess of one billion dollars. When we consider the value of a billion dollars in those days, plus the fact that it was all built with slave labor, one can imagine something of the wonder and magnificence of this famous city.
>
> But in addition to being a bastion for protection, Babylon was a place of beauty. The famous hanging gardens of Babylon are on record yet today as one of the seven wonders of the world. Arranged in an area 400 feet square, and raised in perfectly-cut terraces one above the other, they soared to a height of 350 feet. Viewers could make their way to the top by means of stairways which were ten feet wide. Each terrace was covered with a large stone slab, topped with a thick layer of asphalt, two courses of brick cemented together, and finally, plates of lead to prevent any leakage of water. On top of all this was an abundance of rich, fertile earth planted with vines, flowers, shrubs, and trees. From a distance these hanging gardens gave the appearance of a beautiful mountainside, when viewed from the level plains of the valley. The estimated cost to build this thing of beauty ran into hundreds of millions of dollars.

HE'S STILL COMING

The tower of Babel with its temples of worship presented an imposing sight. The tower itself sat on a base 300 feet in breadth and rose to a height of 300 feet. The one chapel on the top contained an image alone reported to be worth $17,500,000 and sacred vessels, used in worshiping Babylonian gods, estimated at a value of $200,000,000. In addition to this wealth and grandeur the temple contained the most elaborate and expensive furniture ever to adorn any place of worship. Every student should read a good history and a reliable encyclopedia on the city of Babylon, and he will be convinced that this ancient city surpassed anything that man has built on earth in its military fortifications, its beauty and wealth, its religious pomp and extravagance. Nebuchadnezzar indeed had been an ambitious builder, and his own words fit well his accomplishments when he said, "Is not this great Babylon, that I have built?" (Daniel 4:30) (*Commentary on Daniel*, Loizeaux Brothers, Neptune, New Jersey, pp. 147-148)

Note: Dr. Strauss wrote these words in the mid-1960s, so the costs he refers to would probably be five-fold higher today!

E. **539 B.C.**—The Persians under King Cyrus conquered Babylon in 539 B.C., but the city wasn't destroyed. The Persians simply captured the city.

F. **450 B.C.**—Herodotus, "the father of history," visited the city of Babylon. He described it in grand terms. He said the inner walls were 85 feet thick and 340 feet high with 100 gates. Obviously, at the time of his depictions, the city of Babylon—even nearly one hundred years after its fall to the Persians—was still a flourishing city of unbelievable grandeur.

G. **331 B.C.**—Alexander the Great conquered the city and it became the center of his empire for the twelve-year campaign against the Persians and India. His death in 323 saw the beginning of the city's glory.

H. **312 B.C.**—After his death, Alexander's empire was divided among four of his generals. One of those generals, Seleucus, seized Babylon in 312.

I. **25 B.C.**—The famous geographer Strabo visited Babylon. He described the hanging garden as one of the Seven Wonders of the World. He also described the bountiful crops of barley produced in the surrounding country.

▧ **Ancient Babylon—The Fall**

In a very real sense of the word, ancient Babylon never really fell, but was like the old soldiers of the military song who "never die but just fade away."

THE RISE AND FALL OF *FUTURE* BABYLON

▧ **Future Babylon—The Rise**

It is truly amazing that for some twelve centuries following the death of Alexander the Great, the world's attention turned from the Middle East to Europe in the west, especially to Rome.

But key events transpiring during the nineteenth and twentieth centuries shifted the world's attention back to the Middle East, particularly to the city of Babylon.

Now we come to the key issue in regard to Babylon. Does this ancient city have any role to play in prophecy? If so, what will be the nature of this role? The following series of Q & A will attempt to explain this:

A. Will Babylon rebuild? Many Bible students (including this one) would answer with an emphatic *yes!*

B. What scriptures do we employ in advocating this position?

The prophecies of both Isaiah (13, 14), and Jeremiah (51, 52) in regard to ancient Babylon—these men foretell the following:

1. That Babylon would be suddenly and supernaturally destroyed, probably by fire from heaven (Isa. 13:19; Jer. 50:40)
2. That it would never be rebuilt (Isa. 13:20; Jer. 50:39; 51:29, 37, 62)
3. That this destruction would occur during the Great Tribulation (Isa. 13:10, 11, 13)
4. Especially to be noted in the phrase "Day of the Lord" (Isa. 13:6, 9), a common Old Testament title for the Great Tribulation.
5. That Israel's repentance will follow the city's destruction (Jer. 50:4, 5)
6. That the glorious Millennium will follow Israel's repentance (Isa. 14:1-3, 7; Jer. 50:19, 20)

C. Have all or any of these prophecies been fulfilled? Actually, not one of them has, to this date!

What happened to the glittering city of Daniel and Nebuchadnezzar? Was it suddenly destroyed by supernatural fire? To the contrary, it continued for yet another 600 years before it completely dropped from the scene. Thus, we have but two conclusions to explain this:

1. Both Isaiah and Daniel are wrong, or—
2. Babylon will be rebuilt, thus permitting these prophecies to be fulfilled.

D. Are there biblical passages which predict that future Babylon will become a satanic city? In a word, *yes*, as described by Zechariah in the Old Testament and John in the New Testament.

1. Zechariah's vision:

Then the angel who talked with me came out and said to me, "Lift your eyes now, and see what this is that goes forth." So I asked, "What is it?" And he said, "It is a basket that is going forth." He also said, "This is their resemblance throughout the earth: Here is a lead disc lifted up, and this is a woman sitting inside the basket"; then he said, "This is Wickedness!" And he thrust her down into the basket, and threw the lead cover over its mouth. Then I raised my eyes and looked, and there were two women, coming with the wind in their wings; for they had wings like the wings of a stork, and they lifted up the basket between earth and heaven. So I said to the angel who talked with me, "Where are they carrying the basket?" And he said to me, "To build a house for it in the land of Shinar; when it is ready, the basket will be set there on its base" (Zech. 5:5-11).

Dr. Mark Hitchcock aptly summarizes this remarkable vision as follows:

a. An ephah, or basket, is seen going forth.

b. A woman is in the basket.

c. A lid of lead is on the basket.

d. Two flying women are described as carrying off the basket with the woman in it.

e. The basket is carried to Babylon (Shinar) by the flying women so that a house can be built there for the woman they're carrying inside it.

Let's look briefly at each of these five points so we can understand what this vision is all about.

First, what did Zechariah see? The main thing that Zechariah sees in his vision is "a basket for measuring grain," or an ephah. An ephah was the largest measure in the Old Testament, comprising about ten gallons (1.05 American bushels). It was a dry measure used for measuring flour and barley.

Second, who did Zechariah see? In this vision he saw a woman in the basket who symbolizes evil or wickedness. Referring to the woman, the angel says, "This is Wickedness!" In other words, the commerce he sees will be *corrupted* or evil.

Third, the woman is being held back by something. Interestingly, the wickedness is pushed down into the basket and a heavy lid is closed on top of her. In other words, she is held back in the basket until the time is ready for it to be opened. God is in control. He will not let it out *until He is ready*.

Fourth, how is the basket transported? The two women with wings take the basket away. Some see the two women as demonic forces on an evil mission, seeking to protect the wicked woman and enshrine her for worship. But I believe it's best to identify the women as agents of God's providence and power, demonstrating that God is in total control of wickedness. That the two women have wings also seems to indicate that the basket is transported quickly to its new destination.

Fifth, where is the basket taken? Where will this vision be fulfilled? Notice Zechariah's question, "Where are they taking the ephah?" The answer is very specific. "To build a temple for her in the land of Shinar (Babylon)." But this will only occur when everything is ready, Zechariah is told, "and when it is prepared, she will be set there on her own pedestal."

In other words, this will transpire only when everything is ready. Then the basket will be taken to the land of Babylon.

After the flood, the first outbreak of evil in the world occurred at Babylon. Everything will come full circle. The world's first capital city will be the place of its final city, Babylon. I believe this means that, in the end times, Babylon will become the world capital of an evil world economic system run by Antichrist. (*The Second Coming of Babylon*, pp. 96-99, Multnomah Press.)

2. John's vision:

After these things I saw another angel coming down from heaven, having great authority, and the earth was illuminated with his glory. And he cried mightily with a loud voice, saying, "Babylon the great is fallen, is fallen, and has become a dwelling place of demons, a prison for every foul spirit, and a cage for every unclean and hated bird!" (Rev. 18:1, 2)

E. What significant historical dates support this position? Dr. Mark Hitchcock writes:

1. **1805-1810:** In the French Department of War in Paris, there are records of surveys and maps of Babylon made by Napoleon. It is believed that he intended to rebuild the ancient city into a "New Babylon," making it his capital in recognition of its strategic position as a governmental and commercial center. (*The Second Coming of Babylon*, p. 125, Multnomah Press)

2. **December, 1917:** As World War I draws to a close the victorious British forces drive the Turks from the city of Jerusalem which had occupied it since 1517. This resulted in new states being organized in the Middle East.

3. **1932:** Among these states was Iraq, which received its independence that year.

4. **1927:** Huge oil fields were discovered near Kirkuk in Iraq. Today nearly sixty percent of the world's oil reserves are located in the Middle East.

   Question: How much oil reserves does Iraq possess? While estimates vary wildly, the general consensus is in the neighborhood of 300 billion barrels. If true, then this land may lie on top of the world's largest ocean of "black gold!"

5. **1979:** Saddam Hussein gains control over Iraq.

6. **September, 1987:** First International Babylon Festival

7. **September, 1988:** Second International Babylon Festival. Prophecy expert Dr. Charles Dyer attended this festival. Note his amazing account:

   It is a cloudless September summer night, and the moon casts its shining image on the banks of the gentle Euphrates River. Thousands of guests and dignitaries walk by torch light to Babylon's Procession Street and enter the city from the north. Instructed to line the streets along the massive walls, the guests obediently follow orders. When the audience is in place, the dark-eyed man in charge nods, and the procession begins.

   Rows and rows of soldiers parade in, dressed in Babylonian tunics and carrying swords, spears, and shields. Interspersed among the ranks of soldiers are groups of musicians playing harps, horns, and drums. Clusters of children carry palm branches, and runners bear bowls of incense. Then come soldiers and still more soldiers in a seemingly endless line of men and weapons. After the procession, the guests attend a ceremony paying tribute to Ishtar, the mother goddess of Babylon.

Have I just described a scene of pagan worship from the time of Daniel? Perhaps, but it is also exactly what I witnessed when I returned to Babylon in 1988 for the second International Babylon Festival held under the patronage of Saddam Hussein …

When I attended the Babylonian Festivals in 1987 and 1988, guests from all over the world gathered there. There were ballet troupes from the Soviet Union and France, opera singers from Italy, folk dancers from Greece, Turkey, Poland and Yugoslavia, flamenco artists from Spain, a symphony from the Soviet Union, and Bedouin dancers from Saudi Arabia. The Iraqis even invited Madonna, who didn't show. (*The Rise of Babylon*, pp. 16, 17, 30, Tyndale House Publishers, Wheaton, IL)

By the beginning of the twentieth century, as Babylon crumbled into the shifting sands of the desert, it seemed unlikely that it would ever rise from the mounds that had entombed it for so long.

As recently as fifteen years ago, all that existed on the site of ancient Babylon were dusty ruins, or ruins of ruins. Babylon's walls, made from clay bricks, were not as strong as the still-imposing stone structures of Egypt. Barely a wall was intact.

But as of February 1990, over sixty million bricks had been laid in the reconstruction of Nebuchadnezzar's fabled city. Saddam Hussein has ignored the objections of archaeologists who consider it a crime to build over ancient ruins. He has scrapped a plan to rebuild Babylon on a nearby site across the Euphrates River. On the exact site of ancient Babylon, he has reconstructed the Southern Palace of Nebuchadnezzar, including the Procession Street, a Greek theater, many temples, what was once Nebuchadnezzar's throne room, and a half-scale model of the Ishtar Gate. (Ibid., pp. 26, 27)

8. **August 2, 1990:** Iraq invades Kuwait.
9. **August 7, 1990:** Operation Desert Storm begins.
10. **March 19, 2003:** Operation Iraqi Freedom begins (Second Persian war).

F. If ancient Babylon is rebuilt, who will do it and why?

It is possible the Antichrist will rebuild it for the following reasons:

1. Because of its history. Babylon once served as Satan's first headquarters (Gen. 11:1-9) and may well become his final capital. It was built by Nimrod, wicked and apostate great-grandson of Noah (Gen. 10:10).

2. Because of its location. The Euphrates River is 1800 miles long and in some places 3600 feet wide. It is thirty feet deep. This river has been the dividing line between Western and Eastern civilization since the dawn of history. It served as

the eastern border of the old Roman empire. It has always been a line of separation between the people living east of it and those living west of it.

After defeating his enemies the Persians some three centuries B.C. the great western conqueror Alexander the Great made Babylon his headquarters. In the future the Antichrist may do the same, following his victories in the west (Dan. 7:24; Rev. 17:12, 13) and the destruction of Gog and Magog in the north (Ezek. 38, 39).

G.   Is the idea of a new Babylon an old idea? Dr. Mark Hitchcock observes:

Here is just a small sampling of writers from the past who taught about a literal rebuilt city of Babylon in the end times—long before the rest of us had ever heard of Saddam Hussein or the Gulf War crisis.

1.   J. A. Seiss—a Lutheran pastor and scholar born in 1823.

2.   Benjamin Wills Newton—originally wrote about the rebuilt city of Babylon around 1850.

3.   G. H. Pember—wrote in 1888.

4.   Clarence Larkin—wrote in 1919.

5.   Arthur W. Pink—In his excellent 1923 summary of the biblical teaching on the Antichrist, he supported the view of a rebuilt Babylon in the end times.

6.   F. E. Marsh—1925.

7.   William R. Newell—1935.

None of these men possibly could have dreamed that Iraq, the land of ancient Babylon, would move to the center of the world stage as it has today. Yet they believed what they saw in the Scriptures. And amazingly, what these men saw in the Word of God and accepted by faith we are now witnessing with our own eyes. These scholars didn't develop their views on Babylon by looking at the headlines. There weren't any such headlines when they wrote! (*The Truth Behind Left Behind*, p. 102, Tyndale House Publishers, Wheaton, IL)

H.   What seems to be the two main objections in regards to a new Babylon?

1.   *First objection*: Babylon, as found in the book of Revelation, is in reality a secret code word referring to Rome! However there is not the slightest evidence to support this. Actually, the word Babylon is mentioned some 280 times in the Bible, and in practically every case it refers to the literal city of Babylon, or the Babylonian Empire! Why would this not be the case in the book of Revelation? Furthermore, in the last biblical book the author (John the Apostle) writes of—

a.   A literal island: Patmos (Rev. 1:9)

b.   A literal river: The Euphrates (9:14)

c.   A literal mountain: Mt. Zion (14:1)

d.   Seven literal cities: Ephesus, Smyrna, Pergamos, Thyatira, Sardis, Philadelphia, and Laodicea (Rev. 2-3). Why should he not do the same regarding Babylon?

2. *Second objection:* In my thinking this is the more serious of the two. Simply speaking, it has to do with the limited amount of time involved. Here is the problem: At best, the Antichrist would have less than seven years (probably closer to four years) to construct this great world-famous city. It can be shown that New York, Paris, London, and Tokyo took decades to complete. After all, Rome wasn't built in a day!

I. Is there an answer to this second argument? There is indeed and it involves two present-day cities—

1. *First city:* Oak Ridge, Tennessee

   a. Oak Ridge has been nicknamed, "the secret city", "the city behind a fence", "the atomic city."

   b. In 1942 this sleepy little Tennessee town of 3000 souls would, by 1945, swell to 100,000.

   c. During these short years, army engineers had secured and developed 60,000 acres of land, built 300 miles of roads, laid 55 miles of railroad track and constructed the longest building in the world at that time to house the uranium separating process.

   d. Finally, ponder this: Apart from a dozen or so top scientists, a few military and political individuals, one of human history's greatest changing events was accomplished without any of the actual workers, or even the members of Congress who voted to fund it, having the slightest knowledge of it!

2. *Second City:* Dubai

   A city in the United Arab Emirates, located on the southeast coast of the Persian Gulf. Here are some amazing facts about Dubai –

   a. Its population as of January 1, 2013 was 2,106,177.

   b. Dubai is truly a global city serving as a business and cultural hub of the Middle East and the Persian Gulf region.

   c. The city is known for its skyscrapers and high rise buildings. It now boasts of more high-rise structures than any other city.

   d. In fact, the world's tallest building, the Burj Khalifa, reaching 2,722 feet is located in Dubai. It is some two and a half times higher than the Empire State building in New York City.

   e. It is the current home of the famous former Cunard Ocean Liner, Queen Elizabeth 2.

   f. Dubai's airport is one of the busiest in the world.

   g. Dubai is the seventh most visited city in the world with 7.6 million visitors a year.

   h. The city has been called the "shopping capital of the Middle East," boasting of more than seventy shopping malls, including the largest one on earth.

i. At the height of its building activities, Dubai was home to 20 percent (one out of five) of the world's 125,000 construction cranes!

j. But now for the most amazing fact of all—just a few years ago Dubai existed only in the minds of its planners, for at that time the very ground of the present city was to be located at the bottom of the Persian Gulf!

Special note regarding these two cities: If both could come into being in such a short amount of time, the one under the cover of darkness, the other covered by the waters of the Gulf, then what kind of a city could the dictator of the western world build with untold billions of dollars at his disposal?

■ **Future Babylon—The Glory**

Note the following two testimonies:

In that day Babylon will dominate and rule the world. The capital of Antichrist will be Babylon, and he will have the first total dictatorship. The world will be an awful place. In that day everything will center in Babylon. The stock market will be read from Babylon—not New York. Babylon instead of Paris will set the styles for the world. A play, to be successful, will have to be a success in Babylon, not London. Everything in the city will be in rebellion against almighty God, and it centers in Antichrist. (J. V. McGee, quoted by Dr. Hitchcock in his book, *The End*, p. 366, Tyndale House Publishers)

Babylon is indeed a prime prospect for rebuilding, entirely apart from any prophetic intimations. Its location is the most ideal in the world for any kind of international center. Not only is it in the beautiful and fertile Tigris-Euphrates plain, but it is near some of the world's richest oil reserves. Computer studies for the Institute of Creation Research have shown, for example, that Babylon is very near the geographical center of all the earth's land masses. It is within navigable distances to the Persian Gulf and is at the crossroads of the three great continents of Europe, Asia, and Africa. Thus there is no more ideal location anywhere for a world trade center, a world communications center, a world banking center, a world educational center, or especially, a world capital! The greatest historian of modern times, Arnold Toynbee, used to stress to all his readers and hearers that Babylon would be the best place in the world to build a future world cultural metropolis. With all these advantages, and with the head start already made by the Iraqis, it is not far-fetched at all to suggest that the future capital of the "United Nations Kingdom," the ten-nation federation established at the beginning of the tribulation should be established there. (Henry Morris, *The Revelation Record*, pp. 348, 349)

A. How does the Bible itself refer to future Babylon?

John the apostle on nine occasions calls it "that great city," or, "Babylon the Great."

B. What are the facts as given in Revelation 17?

1. The main theme: Religion without God

2. Represented by a cruel harlot

3. Features
    a. She is in bed with the rulers of earth.
    b. She is the mother of all prostitutes and abominations.
    c. She is drunk on the blood of the martyrs of Jesus.
    d. Her religion has become a home for every evil demonic spirit.
    e. Her sins are piled up to heaven.
    f. She holds a gold chalice in her hand, brimming with vile obscenities.
    g. She is dressed in purple and scarlet, adorned with gold, gems, and pearls.

C. What are the features as given in Revelation 18?
   1. The main theme: Riches without God
   2. Represented by an arrogant queen
   3. Features
    a. She revels in her riches, and boasts, saying, "I sit as queen, I am not a widow, I will never mourn."
    b. Her total wealth is beyond belief, consisting of the following:
      (1) Cargos of gold, silver, precious gems, and pearls
      (2) Bolts of fine linen, purple silk, and scarlet cloth
      (3) Perfumed and precious wood, vessels of ivory, bronze, iron, and marble
      (4) The finest cinnamon and spices, incense, myrrh, and frankincense
      (5) Wine, oil, flour, wheat
      (6) Cattle, sheep, horses, chariots
      (7) Human slaves
      (8) The most talented harpists, singers, flutists, and trumpeters
      (9) Special artisans of every kind

D. How can the present New York City be compared to the future New Babylon City? Simply speaking, both cities are based on, and universally known by, two basic institutions:
   1. New York City
    a. Wall Street, symbolizing the financial aspect
    b. Madison Avenue, symbolizing the advertising aspect
   2. New Babylon City
    a. The harlot, symbolizing false religions
    b. The Queen, symbolizing uncontrolled greed

Future Babylon—The Fall

A. The destruction of Babylon's religious institution:
   1. The *who* involved:

Who was behind this terrible destruction? It was caused by the Antichrist and his western leaders! *"The beast and the ten horns [ten western kings] you saw will hate the prostitute. They will bring her to ruin and leave her naked: they will eat her flesh and burn her with fire"* (Rev. 17:16, NIV).

2. The *why* involved:

Why this hatred? It may well be that the religious leaders, who no doubt had helped the Antichrist's rise to power, now, at this time, will demand more power and a bigger share in his reign, but he will have none of it!

3. The *when* involved:

When, during the Great Tribulation, will this transpire? It seems safe to place it at the middle of the seven years.

4. The *how* involved:

How does religious Babylon's destruction unfold?

a. It begins with the most severe earthquake in human history (Rev. 16:18).

b. This results in the city being split into three parts (Rev. 16:19).

c. Then, from the sky huge hailstones of about a hundred pounds each fell upon man (Rev. 16:21).

5. *The response* involved:

What was the reaction to all this? In essence, the response was two-fold:

a. "Hallelujah, for there goes the harlot!" (Rev. 19:1-4)

b. "Hallelujah, for here comes the bride!" (Rev. 19:6-9)

B. The destruction of Babylon's financial institution

1. The *who* involved:

" ...*for mighty is the Lord who judges her*" (Rev. 18:8).

2. The *why* involved:

"...*for her sins are piled up to heaven and God has remembered her crimes*" (Rev. 18:5).

3. The *when* involved:

At the very end of the Great Tribulation

4. The *how* involved:

a. It begins with a series of plagues (Rev. 18:8)

b. It is completed in one hour, as great sheets of fire are hurled down from heaven upon the doomed city (Rev. 18:8, 10, 17, 19).

5. *The response* involved: Two reactions –

a. Worshipping! Coming from heaven's saints, apostles, and prophets (Rev. 18:20)

b. Weeping! Coming from earth's –

1. Monarchs (Rev. 18:9)

2. Merchants (Rev. 18:11, 15)
3. Mariners (Rev. 18:15-20)

■ **Now for the great, grand, and glorious conclusion**

Sometime in the near future, Satan's New Babylon City will give way to God's New Jerusalem City!

A. The first will never more blight saved humanity!

B. The second will evermore bless saved humanity!

"Now I saw a new heaven and a new earth, for the first heaven and the first earth had passed away. Also there was no more sea. Then I, John, saw the holy city, New Jerusalem, coming down out of heaven from God, prepared as a bride adorned for her husband. And I heard a loud voice from heaven saying, 'Behold, the tabernacle of God is with men, and He will dwell with them, and they shall be His people. God Himself will be with them and be their God. And God will wipe away every tear from their eyes; there shall be no more death, nor sorrow, nor crying. There shall be no more pain, for the former things have passed away" (Rev. 21:1-4).

"Then one of the seven angels who had the seven bowls filled with the seven last plagues came to me and talked with me, saying, 'Come, I will show you the bride, the Lamb's wife. And he carried me away in the Spirit to a great and high mountain, and showed me the great city, the holy Jerusalem, descending out of heaven from God, having the glory of God. Her light was like a most precious stone, like a jasper stone, clear as crystal" (Rev. 21:9-11).

EVENT 10 THE BATTLE OF ARMAGEDDON

"And they gathered them together to the place called in Hebrew, Armageddon" (Rev. 16:16).

On the headquarters of the United Nations in New York there are inscribed the words of Micah 4:3:

> *". . . and they shall beat their swords into plowshares and their spears into pruninghooks: nation shall not lift up a sword against nation, neither shall they learn war any more."*

This, of course, will literally be realized some glorious day, but not until the Prince of Peace comes to reign on this earth! Until that day, both Daniel (Dan. 9:26) and Jesus (Mt. 24:6) warned of continual war. It has been pointed out by the Society of International Law at London that there have been only 268 years of peace during the last 4,000 years of human history, despite the signing of more than 8,000 peace treaties!

In February of 1914 a prophecy conference was held in Los Angeles, sponsored by Bible-believing people. When the sessions were completed, a liberal religious magazine, *The Christian Advocate*, sneeringly dubbed it a "pathetic conference" because the conference held that the Bible-taught wars would continue and intensify until the advent of Christ. But the sneers soon disappeared, for in August of that very year guns of World War I commenced their deadly thunder, and threats of wars continue to this day! Until the coming of Christ, the U. N. would have more correctly inscribed the fearful words of Joel 3:9-10:

> "Proclaim ye this among the Gentiles; Prepare war, wake up the mighty men, let all the men of war draw near; let them come up; Beat your plowshares into swords, and your pruning-hooks into spears."

It has been calculated by a former president of the Norwegian Academy of Sciences, aided by historians from England, Egypt, Germany, and India, that since 3600 B.C., over 14,531 wars have been waged in which 3,640,000 people have been killed. This figure is over ten times the entire population of the United States. The value of this destruction would pay for a golden belt around the world some ninety miles in width and thirty-three feet thick.

James Boice writes:

> One of the earliest of all historical records, a Sumerian bas-relief from Babylon (c. 3000 B.C.), shows soldiers fighting in close order, wearing helmets and carrying shields. Wars fill the history of every ancient culture—Babylon, Syria, Assyria, Egypt, Phoenicia. (*The Last and Future World*, Grand Rapids: Zondervan Press, 1979, p. 99)

Michael Lee Lanning, Lt. Col. (Ret.) U. S. Army has written a very enlightening article which is entitled, *The Top Ten Battles of All Time*. Before listing the ten, he explains: "The following list is not a ranking of decisive engagements, but rather a ranking of battles according to their influence on history …" He begins with the least significant (number ten) and concludes with the most significant (number one). Here are these battles from ten to one:

- ▪ **#10 Austria—Ottoman Battle of Vienna — 1529**
  This battle stopped the advance of Islam into Central and Western Europe.

- ▪ **#9 Battle of Waterloo—1815**
  During this battle the English General Wellington soundly defeated Napoleon Bonaparte.

- ▪ **#8 The Huai-Hai Chinese War—1948**
  This final major fight between Nationalist Leader Chiang Kai-Shek and the Communist leader Mao Tse-tung for control over all of China, with Mao being victorious.

- ▪ **#7 Atomic Bombings Upon Two Japanese Cities, Hiroshima (August 6, 1945), and Nagasaki (August 9)**, which resulted in ending World War II.

- ▪ **#6 The Battle at Cajamarca in 1532,** when Spanish military leader Francisco Pizarro defeated the Inca Empire.

- ▪ **#5 The American Civil War Battle of Antietam** fought at Antietam Creek in Maryland on September 17, 1862. Although it ended in a stalemate, the North would later be seen as the winner for three reasons:
  A. It was the first battle in which the North was not totally routed by the South.

B. All hope that the South might be recognized by the British and French was gone.

C. Following the battle President Abraham Lincoln felt the time had come to issue the Emancipation Proclamation.

#4 The Battle of Leipzig (October, 1813)

At this time the combined alliance of Prussia, Russia, Sweden, Great Britain, the Netherlands and Bavara, often called the Battle of the Nations met and routed Napoleon's armies. Like the Battle of Antietam, there are three factors underlying the significance of this battle:

A. It serves as a forerunner in regards to Armageddon, at which time all of earth's nations will assemble in the Valley of Megiddo in an attempt to destroy God Himself.

B. Leipzig led to the fall of Paris.

C. The defeat of Napoleon's troops at Leipzig helped weaken his army thus contributing to the final defeat of Napoleon by Wellington at Waterloo some six months later.

#3 The World War II Battle of Stalingrad (1942, 1943)

This battle was the final great offensive by the German Nazis on the eastern front who had invaded Russia in June, 1941. It was the turning point in the war which would, some 27 months later, result in the suicide of Adolf Hitler, the capture of Berlin, and the end of the war in Europe.

#2 The Battle of Hastings (1066)

William, Duke of Normandy, defeated his foes at Hastings and on Christmas Day, he was crowned King of England. He would soon be known as William the Conquerer. Thus began the British monarchy, which one thousand years later, is still very much alive and well.

#1 The Battle of Yorktown (1781)

It would seem impossible to overstate the importance regarding this battle which resulted in the defeat of the British occupying forces by the American colonists, led by General George Washington, and the independence of the United States of America! One can only imagine what the world would look like today, had British General Henry Clinton won that battle! Only God Himself knows just how much blood has been shed, how many bones were broken, how many bodies have been shattered, the sheer agony endured and the number of deaths involved.

But as terrible as the butcher's bill will eventually amount to in human lives regarding these ten battles, along with all wars in history put together, it will not even remotely compare with the final and most frightful all-out slaughter which still awaits sinful man!

It is known as the Battle of Armageddon! This indeed will be the big one! Unique, universal, unequaled!

A. It will include soldiers coming from 192 of the 193 nations on earth, from Afghanistan to Zimbabwe, with Israel alone being the one exception.

B. These troops will be led by the Antichrist and his false prophet.

C. Their all-consuming goal will not be for territory, or fame, or wealth, but solely motivated by a satanic hatred for Israel.

D. The warriors will be subjected to the most severe plague in human history.

"And this shall be the plague with which the Lord will strike all the people who fought against Jerusalem: Their flesh shall dissolve while they stand on their feet, Their eyes shall dissolve in their sockets, And their tongues shall dissolve in their mouths" (Zech. 14:12).

■ **Facts concerning the Battle of Armageddon**

A. The word "Armageddon" literally means, "the mountain of Megiddo." The city of Megiddo is located on the south side of the plain of Jezreel, and is often referred in the Old Testament as a military stronghold (Josh. 12:21; 17:11; 2 Kings 9:27; 23:29). A number of O. T. battles and events occurred at Megiddo:

1. Deborah and Barak defeated the Canaanites at Megiddo (Judges 4:10-24; 5:19).

2. The godly Judean King Josiah was killed during a battle of Megiddo (2 Kings 23:29, 30).

3. During the tenth century B.C., Solomon rebuilt and fortified Megiddo, making it one of his chariot cities (1 Kings 9:15).

4. In 1918 (A.D.), the British allied forces under General Allenby entered northern Palestine through the Megiddo Pass en route to do battle with the Turkish forces.

B. Five key Old Testament and New Testament authors predict this bloody battle:

1. David (Psa. 2)

2. Isaiah (13:6-13; 24:1; 24:19, 20; 26:21; 34:1-4)

3. Joel (3:2, 9-16)

4. Zechariah (12:2-4, 9; 14:12)

5. John (Rev. 14:14, 20; 16:16; 19:17-21)

C. Some of the key passages are as follows:

1. From David

Why do the nations rage, And the people plot a vain thing? The kings of the earth set themselves, And the rulers take counsel together, Against the Lord and against His Anointed, saying "Let us break Their bonds in pieces And cast away Their cords from us." He who sits in the heavens shall laugh; The Lord shall hold them in derision. Then He shall speak to them in His wrath, And distress them in His deep displeasure (Psa. 2:1-5).

2. From Isaiah

I will punish the world for its evil, and the wicked for their iniquity; I will halt the arrogance of the proud, and will lay low the haughtiness of the terrible (Isa. 13:11). *For behold, the Lord comes out of His place to punish the inhabitants of the earth for their iniquity; the earth will also disclose her blood, and will no more cover her slain* (Isa. 26:21).

3. From Zechariah

   It shall be in that day that I will seek to destroy all the nations that come against Jerusalem (Zech. 12:9).

4. From Joel

   I will also gather all nations, And bring them down to the Valley of Jehoshaphat; and I will enter into judgment with them there on account of My people, My heritage Israel, Whom they have scattered among the nations; They have also divided up My land (Joel 3:2).

   Let the nations be wakened, and come up to the Valley of Jehoshaphat; For there I will sit to judge all the surrounding nations. Put in the sickle, for the harvest is ripe. Come, go down; For the winepress is full, The vats overflow—For their wickedness is great." Multitudes, multitudes in the valley of decision! For the day of the Lord is near in the valley of decision (Joel 3:12-14).

   Especially to be noted are the two references regarding the Valley of Jehoshaphat (3:2, 12). Although the exact location of this valley is unknown, some have identified it with the N. T. Kidron Valley mentioned in John 18:1. If true it could be placed between the walled city of Jerusalem on the west and the Mount of Olives on the east. More about this later.

D. Armageddon is not the same as the Russian invasion of Ezekiel 38. Note the differences: Russia invades from the north, but at Armageddon the nations come from all directions. Russia invades to capture Israel's wealth, but this invasion is to destroy the Lamb and His people. Gog leads the Russian invasion, but the Antichrist leads this one.

E. Armageddon is not the final war in the Bible. The final war occurs after the Millennium (Rev. 20:7-9); Armageddon takes place at the end of the Tribulation.

F. The geography of this battle will total some 20,000 square miles!

G. The dimensions are as follows: From Megiddo in the north to the Sinai in the south, to the Mediterranean Sea in the west, to Jordan in the east.

   1. Marvin Vincent writes concerning Armageddon and its location:

      "Megiddo was in the plain of Esdraelon, which has been the chosen place for encampment in every contest carried on in Palestine from the days of . . Assyria unto the disastrous march of Napoleon Bonaparte from Egypt into Syria. Jews, Gentiles, Saracens, Christian Crusaders, and anti-Christian Frenchmen; Egyptians, Persians, Druses, Turks, and Arabs, warriors of every nation that is under heaven, have pitched their tents on the plains of Esdraelon, and have beheld the banners of their nation wet with the dews of Mt. Tabor and Mt. Hermon." (*Word Studies in the New Testament, p. 542*)

   2. Dr. Herman A. Hoyt aptly describes the location:

      "The staggering dimensions of this conflict can scarcely be conceived by man. The Battlefield will stretch from Megiddo on the north (Zech. 12:11; Rev. 1:16) to

Edom on the south (Isa. 34:5, 6; 63:1), a distance of sixteen hundred furlongs—approximately two hundred miles. It will reach from the Mediterranean Sea on the west to the hills of Moab on the east, a distance of almost one hundred miles. It will include the Valley of Jehoshaphat (Joel 3:2, 12) and the Plains of Esdraelon. At the center of the entire area will be the city of Jerusalem (Zech. 14:1, 2).

"Into this area the multiplied millions of men, doubtless approaching 400 million, will be crowded for the final holocaust of humanity. The kings with their armies will come from the north and the south, from the east and from the west … In the most dramatic sense this will be the 'valley of decision' for humanity (Joel 3:14) and the great winepress into which will be poured the fierceness of the wrath of Almighty God (Rev. 19:15)." (*The End Times*, p. 163)

H. As has been previously observed, Joel predicts the final phase of Armageddon will take place in the Valley of Jehoshaphat, a valley perhaps known as the Kidron Valley in the New Testament.

He writes, "*Multitudes, multitudes, in the valley of decision . . .*" (Joel 3:14). Two questions arise at this point:

1. When one considers the sheer number of troops (multiplied millions) involved, how could even a tiny fraction be fitted into this narrow valley? The answer of course is that they won't be. A reasonable possibility is that the Antichrist might gather his key military men there to plan for one last attempt to destroy Israel and his hated enemy, Jesus Christ!

2. But why this area in the first place? The nearby Mount of Olives might provide the answer. Consider: God had already informed His people in the Old Testament of the exact location of both His Son's first and second coming!

   a. The first coming

      But you, Bethlehem Ephrathah, Though you are little among the thousands of Judah, Yet out of you shall come forth to Me The One to be Ruler in Israel, Whose goings forth are from of old, From everlasting (Micah 5:2).

   b. The second coming

      And in that day His feet will stand on the Mount of Olives, Which faces Jerusalem on the east. And the Mount of Olives shall be split in two, From east to west, Making a very large valley; Half of the mountain shall move toward the north And half of it toward the south (Zech. 14:4). See also Acts 1:9-11.

3. So then, how does the Mount of Olives work into Satan's battle plan? Well, he almost succeeded in having Jesus murdered at His first coming, but the soldiers arrived in Bethlehem a little too late. But this time he will personally arrange and witness the destruction of the hated Son of God!

I. There are at least three main reasons for this battle.

What will draw all the nations of the world into the area of Armageddon? They will gather themselves there for various reasons. It would seem that the following are three of the more important reasons.

1. Because of the sovereignty of God. In at least five distinct passages we are told that God Himself will gather the nations here.

    He hath delivered them to the slaughter (Isa. 34:2).

    I will also gather all nations, and will bring them down into the valley of Jehoshaphat (Joel 3:2).

    For I will gather all nations against Jerusalem to battle (Zech. 14:2).

    For my determination is to gather the nations, that I may assemble the kingdoms, to pour upon them mine indignation, even all my fierce anger (Zeph. 3:8).

    And he gathered them together into a place called in the Hebrew tongue Armageddon (Rev. 16:16).

2. Because of the deception of Satan (Rev. 16:13-14). In this passage we are told that three special unclean spirits will trick the nations into gathering at Armageddon.

3. Because of the hatred of the nations for Christ. A number of passages tell us of this devilish hatred (Psa. 2:1-3; Rev. 11:18). The nations, led by the Antichrist, will doubtless realize the imminent return of Christ (Rev. 11:15; 12:12). They will also be aware of his touching down on the Mount of Olives (Zech. 14:4; Acts 1:9-12). Thus it is not unreasonable to assume they will gather in that area to try to destroy Christ at the moment of His return to earth.

J. There will be two final events leading to this battle.

1. The drying up of the Euphrates River (Rev. 16:12)

    Dr. Donald Barnhouse quotes Seiss in describing this:

    > "From time immemorial the Euphrates with its tributaries has been a great and formidable boundary between the peoples east of it and west of it. It runs a distance of 1,800 miles, and is scarcely fordable anywhere or any time. It is from three to twelve hundred yards wide, and from ten to thirty feet in depth; and most of the time it is still deeper and wider. It was the boundary of the dominion of Solomon, and is repeatedly spoken of as the northeast limit of the lands promised to Israel.... History frequently refers to the great hindrance the Euphrates has been to military movements; and it has always been a line of separation between the peoples living east of it and those living west of it." (*Revelation*, p. 301)

    Thus when this watery barrier is removed, tens of millions of soldiers from China, India, and other Asian nations will march straight for Armageddon and destruction.

2. The destruction of Jerusalem—Perhaps the saddest event during the Tribulation will be the siege and destruction of the Holy City. This will be the forty-seventh and

last takeover of the beloved city of David. The following passages bear this out:

> Behold, I will make Jerusalem a cup of trembling unto all the people round about, when they shall be in the siege both against Judah and against Jerusalem (Zech. 12:2).

> For I will gather all nations against Jerusalem to battle; and the city shall be taken, and the houses rifled, and the women ravished; and half of the city shall go forth into captivity, and the residue of the people shall not be cut off from the city (Zech. 14:2).

> And when ye shall see Jerusalem compassed with armies, then know that the desolation thereof is nigh (Luke 21:20).

When these two events transpire, both the angels in paradise and the demons in perdition will surely hold their breath.

K. God will laugh concerning man's puny efforts to fight against Him at Armageddon (Psa. 2:4).

L. God will punish the nations in an unprecedented way (Micah 5:15).

M. The most horrible plagues ever known will fall upon them (Zech. 12:4; 14:12-15).

N. They will be crushed as overripe grapes (Isa. 63:6).

O. Their blood will flow out in a stream 200 miles long and as high as a horse's bridle (Rev. 14:20).

P. Vultures will then be summoned to feast upon the dead bodies of the warriors (Isa. 66:24; Mt. 24:28; Lk. 17:37; Rev. 19:17, 18).

Two authors aptly describe this battle for us:

1. Palestine is to be given a blood bath of unprecedented proportions which will flow from Armageddon at the north down through the valley of Jehoshaphat, will cover the land of Edom, and will wash over all Judea and the city of Jerusalem. John looks at this scene of carnage and he describes it as blood flowing to the depths of the horses' bridles. It is beyond human imagination to see a lake that size that has been drained from the veins of those who have followed the purpose of Satan to try to exterminate God's chosen people in order to prevent Jesus Christ from coming to reign. (Dwight Pentecost, *Prophecy for Today*, p. 118)

2. The Battle of Armageddon will result in wholesale carnage among the legions of the beast. The brilliance of Christ's appearing will produce a trembling and demoralization in the soldiers (Zech. 12:2; 14:13). The result of this demoralization and trembling will be the desertion from the Antichrist and the rendering of him inoperative (2 Thess. 2:8). This tremendous light from heaven will produce astonishment and blindness in animals and madness in men (Zech. 12:4).

A plague will sweep through the armies from this light and men will not fight where they stand (Zech. 14:12). The blood of animals and men will form a lake two hundred miles long and bridle deep (Rev. 14:19, 20). The stench of this rotting mass of flesh and blood will fill the entire region (Isa. 34:3). The mangled forms of men and beasts will provide a feast for the carrion birds (Rev. 19:17, 18, 21). The beast and the false prophet will then be cast alive into the lake of fire forever (Rev. 19:20). (Herman A. Hoyt, *The End Times*, p. 165)

EVENT 11 THE SECOND COMING OF CHRIST _____

INTRODUCTION TO JESUS'S RETURN

Jesus is coming to earth again; what if it were today?
Coming in power and love to reign; what if it were today?
Coming to claim His chosen Bride, all the redeemed and purified,
Over this whole earth scattered wide; what if it were today?

<u>Chorus:</u>
Glory, glory! Joy to my heart 'twill bring.
Glory, glory! When we shall crown Him King.
Glory, glory! Haste to prepare the way;
Glory, glory! Jesus will come some day.

Thus wrote the songwriter Lelia Morris at the beginning of the twentieth century. The Second Coming of Jesus is indeed a major biblical theme. Prophecy expert Dr. Mark Hitchcock has compiled the following facts:

- **Jesus' return is mentioned 1,845 times in the scriptures.**
- **Twenty-three Old Testament and twenty-seven New Testament books refer to it.**
- **The Second Coming is mentioned eight times to every first coming reference.**
- **It is the first and final prophecy:**
  A. The first
     Now Enoch, the seventh from Adam, prophesied about these men also, saying, "Behold, the Lord comes with ten thousands of His saints" (Jude 14).
  B. The final
     He who testifies to these things says, "Surely I am coming quickly." Amen. Even so, come, Lord Jesus! (Rev. 22:20)
- **Christ Himself calls attention to it on twenty-one occasions.**
- **Jesus warned His enemies and promised His friends He would return.**
  A. The warning (given to the wicked high priest Caiaphas during one of the Savior's unfair trials):

But Jesus kept silent. And the high priest answered and said to Him, "I put You under oath by the living God: Tell us if You are the Christ, the Son of God!" Jesus said to him, "It is as you said. Nevertheless, I say to you, hereafter you will see the Son of Man sitting at the right hand of the Power, and coming on the clouds of heaven" (Matt. 26:63, 64).

B. The promise:

Then Jesus said to them, "Do not be afraid. Go and tell My brethren to go to Galilee, and there they will see Me" (Matt. 28:10).

(*101 Answers*, p. 200, Multnomah Publishers, 2001)

■ **Here are key Old Testament and New Testament passages which describe Jesus' return:**

A. Old Testament
1. Isaiah 11:12; 25:9; 40:5, 10; 59:20
2. Ezekiel 43:2, 4
3. Daniel 7:13, 14
4. Habakkuk 3:3-6, 10-11
5. Haggai 2:6-7
6. Zechariah 8:3; 14:4, 8
7. Malachi 3:1

B. New Testament
1. Matthew 24:29-30; 26:64
2. Acts 1:11; 3:20-21; 15:16
3. Romans 11:26
4. 1 Corinthians 15:24
5. 2 Thessalonians 1:7-8
6. Revelation 1:7; 19:11-14

FACTS REGARDING JESUS' RETURN

■ **Contrasted with His Rapture return—they are *not* one and the same.**

A. At the Rapture, He comes to claim His bride. At the Second Coming, He comes to claim His crown.

B. The Rapture introduces the Great Tribulation. The Second Coming will conclude it.

■ **The signs preceding and accompanying the Second Coming**—*"And then shall appear the sign of the Son of Man in heaven ... "* (Matt. 24:30).

A. The light from the sun, moon, and stars shall be dimmed, resulting in great cosmic disturbances (Matt. 24:29).

B. The sound of a deafening trumpet will be heard (Matt. 24:31).

C. The Shekinah Glory Cloud of God will appear in the east (Ezek. 43:2, 4).

D. The God-Man Jesus Christ will appear:
1. Displaying a dazzling brilliance and majesty (Isa. 40:5; Ezek. 43:2; Mk. 14:62)
2. In blazing fire, accompanied by powerful angels (2 Thess. 1:7)
3. Riding a white horse (Rev. 19:11)
4. Wearing many royal crowns and possessing a secret name known only by Him (Rev. 19:12)
5. Clothed with a robe dipped in blood (Rev. 19:13)
6. Followed by heaven's armies, all dressed in finest linen, white and clean (Rev. 19:14)
7. Wielding a mighty sword for the purpose of destroying His enemies (Rev. 19:15)
8. Bearing on His robe and thigh the title, KINGS OF KINGS AND LORD OF LORDS (Rev. 19:16)
9. Causing sheer terror in the hearts of all nations (Matt. 24:30)
10. Resulting in being recognized by the Jewish nation (Zech. 12:10; Rev. 1:7)

▨ The place of the Second Coming

It will be on the Mount of Olives.

A. Because of the prophecies involved
1. Zechariah predicted this would be the place (Zech. 14:4).
2. Angels predicted this would be the place (Acts 1:10-12).
B. Because there is a tradition that Christ first spoke the Lord's Prayer on the Mount of Olives (Matt. 6:9-13). Note especially the phrase in 6:10, *"thy kingdom come."* Here our Lord instructs us to pray for the millennial kingdom to be established! In light of this, it would seem appropriate that the Savior would appear on this same spot to do that very thing He told us to pray for!
C. Because this would seem to be the ideal place to defeat His assembled enemies in the Valley of Jehoshaphat (also known as the Kidron Valley) located just below the Mount of Olives (Joel 3:2, 12; John 18:1).

▨ The dating (?) of the Second Coming

Some have advocated Jesus will return during the Jewish Feast of Trumpets. Leviticus 23 lists Israel's great religious festivals. Some believe these feasts also serve as prophetical statements concerning the future work of Christ. For example:

A. The Passover Sabbath feast (Lev. 23:44)
This speaks of Calvary (1 Cor. 5:7).
B. The Feast of Firstfruits (Lev. 23:9-14)
This speaks of the Resurrection (1 Cor. 15:23).
C. The Feast of Pentecost (Lev. 23:15-22)
This speaks of the coming of the Holy Spirit (Acts 2:1).

D. The Feast of Trumpets (Lev. 23:23-25)

This speaks of the Rapture and Second Coming (1 Thess. 4:18; Rev. 11:15).

E. The Day of Atonement Feast (Lev. 23:26-32)

This speaks of the coming Great Tribulation (Rev. 6-19).

F. The Feast of Tabernacles (Lev. 23:33-44)

This speaks of the Millennium (Rev. 20:6).

While it is true that Jesus was crucified in the same month (April) that the Old Testament Passover Lamb was slain (Exod. 12), and that the Holy Spirit came upon the disciples at New Testament Pentecost in the same month (June) when Old Testament Pentecost was to be celebrated (Lev. 23:15), it does not necessarily follow that He must return during the month of October, the time when the Feast of Trumpets is to be celebrated (Lev. 23:24). The fact is, no one knows the exact time of His return! Jesus Himself made this very clear. Note His warning:

> *"But of that day and hour no one knows, not even the angels in heaven, nor the Son, but only the Father. Take heed, watch and pray; for you do not know when the time is. It is like a man going to a far country, who left his house and gave authority to his servants, and to each his work, and commanded the doorkeeper to watch. Watch therefore, for you do not know when the master of the house is coming—in the evening, at midnight, at the crowing of the rooster, or in the morning—lest, coming suddenly, he find you sleeping. And what I say to you, I say to all: Watch!"* (Mark 13:32-37)

■ **The itinerary of the Second Coming**

A. It begins with fearful manifestations in the skies.

> *"Immediately after the tribulation of those days the sun will be darkened, and the moon will not give its light; the stars will fall from heaven, and the powers of the heavens will be shaken"* (Matt. 24:29).

> *"And there will be signs in the sun, in the moon, and in the stars; and on the earth distress of nations, with perplexity, the sea and the waves roaring; men's hearts failing them from fear and the expectation of those things which are coming on the earth, for the powers of the heavens will be shaken."* (Luke 21:25-26).

B. In the midst of this, the heavens open and Jesus comes forth.

> *"Then the sign of the Son of Man will appear in heaven, and then all the tribes of the earth will mourn, and they will see the Son of Man coming on the clouds of heaven with power and great glory"* (Matt. 24:30). *"...the Lord Jesus is revealed from heaven with His mighty angels"* (2 Thess. 1:7).

> *"Behold, he cometh with clouds; and every eye shall see him ..."* (Rev. 1:7).

> *"And I saw heaven opened, and behold a white horse; and he that sat upon him was called Faithful and True ..."* (Rev. 19:11).

HE'S STILL COMING

C. The returning Savior touches down upon the Mount of Olives, causing a great earthquake (Zech. 14:4, 8). The Mount of Olives is one of the most important mountains in both biblical history and prophecy.

1. It towers over Mt. Moriah by 318 feet.

2. It rises to a height of 2,743 feet above sea level.

3. Its name derives from the olives grown there.

4. Sometimes it was called the Mount of Lights (designating the beginning of a new month, year, etc.).

5. David paused here, wept, and worshipped God after being driven from Jerusalem by Absalom his son (2 Sam. 15:30, 32).

6. Tradition says that Christ first spoke the Lord's Prayer on this mountain.

7. The Church of the Lord's Prayer, built in 1868, has the prayer engraved in thirty-two languages on thirty-two marble slabs, each three feet wide and six feet long. The Bible says Jesus often visited here.

8. *"And he came out, and went, as he was accustomed, to the Mount of Olives; and his disciples also followed him"* (Luke 22:39).

9. From here He sent for a colt to ride during the triumphal entry on Palm Sunday (Matt. 21:1).

10. Here He delivered the Mount Olivet Discourse (Matt. 24-25).

11. He visited here after leaving the upper room and may have uttered his high priestly prayer (John 17) from this spot (Matt. 26:30).

12. He slept here on occasion during the passion week (Luke 21:37).

13. He ascended from here (Acts 1).

14. He will touch down here at the Second Coming (Zech. 14).

15. After touching down on the Mount of Olives, Christ proceeds to Petra and Bozrah, two chief cities in Edom.

    While it is impossible to be dogmatic here, it would seem that He goes to Edom to gather the hiding Israelite remnant. Accompanied by the holy angels, the church, and the remnant, Christ marches toward Armageddon (Isa. 34:6; 63:1).

■ **The planning and price involved in the Second Coming**

In the spring of 1990 the late Dr. Jerry Falwell invited a special guest to deliver the commencement address at Liberty University here in Lynchburg. However, nearly a year prior to the May graduation, an advance party of officials arrived in the city, took up an extended residence and began preparing for the guest's arrival. Finally he came, spoke, and left barely an hour later. But as we eventually learn, that trip had cost eleven million dollars, which was, thankfully, paid for by an outside source.

At first glance it might seem all this has a classic case of gross overkill! Why all the fuss for a mere visitor? Well, this guest was anything but a mere visitor. Actually, the advance party consisted of highly trained Secret Service men, all sworn to protect this guest. George H. W. Bush—President of the United States! So then, the most important man in America deserved nothing but the best.

Now, if all this was done for a mortal leader of a single country, what should be done when the Supreme Creator of the Universe and Coming King of Planet Earth pays us a visit? Consider:

A. In regard to the planning

Some six centuries B.C., the Old Testament prophet Zechariah discloses the place of His appearance, the Mount of Olives (Zech. 14:4). Thus the Father has been anticipating His beloved Son's visit not for just a year, but for twenty-five centuries!

B. In regards to the price

The New Testament apostle Peter has calculated the cost for this visit:

> "… knowing that you were not redeemed with corruptible things, like silver or gold, from your aimless conduct received by tradition from your fathers, but with the precious blood of Christ, as of a lamb without blemish and without spot" (1 Peter 1:18-19).

■ **The reasons involved in regards to the Second Coming**

A. To defeat the Antichrist and the world's nations assembled at Armageddon (Rev. 19:17-21)

B. To regather, regenerate, and restore faithful Israel

Perhaps the most frequent promise in all the Old Testament concerns God's eventual restoration of Israel. The prophets repeat this so often that it becomes a refrain, a chorus of confidence. Note the following:

> "Fear not: for I am with thee: I will bring thy seed from the east, and gather thee from the west; I will say to the north, Give up; and to the south, Keep not back; bring my sons from far, and my daughters from the ends of the earth" (Isa. 43:5-6).

> "For I will set mine eyes upon them for good, and I will bring them again to this land: and I will build them, and not pull them down . . ." (Jer. 24:6).

> "… thus saith the Lord God, I will even gather you from the people, and assemble you out of the countries where ye have been scattered, and I will give you the land of Israel" (Ezek. 11:17).

> "And ye shall dwell in the land that I gave to your fathers; and ye shall be my people, and I will be your God" (Ezek. 36:28).

> "And I will bring again the captivity of my people of Israel, and they shall build the waste cities, and inhabit them; and they shall plant vineyards, and drink the wine thereof; they shall also make gardens, and eat the fruit of them. And I will plant them upon their land, and they shall no more be pulled up out of their land which I have given them, saith the Lord thy God" (Amos 9:14, 15).

Perhaps the most sublime song of praise concerning Israel's restoration is sung by the prophet Micah:

> "Who is a God like You, Pardoning iniquity and passing over the transgression of the remnant of His heritage? He does not retain His anger forever, because He delights in mercy. He will again have compassion on us, and will subdue our iniquities. You will cast all our sins into the depths of the sea" (Micah 7:18-19).

In the New Testament our Lord also speaks about this during one of his last sermons:

> "And he shall send his angels with a great sound of trumpet, and they shall gather together his elect from the four winds, from one end of heaven to the other" (Matt. 24:31).

Thus will our Lord gather Israel when He comes again and, as we have already observed, He will begin by appearing to the remnant hiding in Petra. Here we note:

1. Their temporary sorrow

> "And I will pour on the house of David and on the inhabitants of Jerusalem the Spirit of grace and supplication; then they will look on Me whom they pierced. Yes, they will mourn for Him as one mourns for his only son, and grieve for Him as one grieves for a firstborn. In that day there shall be a great mourning in Jerusalem, like the mourning at Hadad Rimmon in the plain of Megiddo. And the land shall mourn, every family by itself: the family of the house of David by itself, and their wives by themselves; the family of the house of Nathan by itself, and their wives by themselves" (Zech. 12:10-12).

> " And one will say to him, 'What are these wounds between your arms?' Then he will answer, 'Those with which I was wounded in the house of my friends' " (Zech. 13:6).

> "Behold, He is coming with clouds, and every eye will see Him, even they who pierced Him. And all the tribes of the earth will mourn because of Him" (Rev. 1:7).

2. Their ultimate joy

> "He will swallow up death forever, And the Lord God will wipe away tears from all faces; The rebuke of His people He will take away from all the earth; For the Lord has spoken. And it will be said in that day: "Behold, this is our God; We have waited for Him, and He will save us. This is the Lord; We have waited for Him; We will be glad and rejoice in His salvation" (Isa. 25:8-9).

> "Moreover the light of the moon will be as the light of the sun, And the light of the sun will be sevenfold, As the light of seven days, In the day that the Lord binds up the bruise of His people and heals the stroke of their wound" (Isa. 30:26).

> "He will feed His flock like a shepherd; He will gather the lambs with His arm, And carry them in His bosom, And gently lead those who are with young" (Isa. 40:11).

> "I, even I, am He who blots out your transgressions for My own sake; And I will not remember your sins" (Isa. 43:25).

> "Can a woman forget her nursing child, and not have compassion on the son of her womb? Surely they may forget, yet I will not forget you" (Isa. 49:15).

"For the Lord will comfort Zion, He will comfort all her waste places; He will make her wilderness like Eden, and her desert like the garden of the Lord; joy and gladness will be found in it, thanksgiving and the voice of melody" (Isa. 51:3).

"For you shall go out with joy, and be led out with peace; the mountains and the hills shall break forth into singing before you, And all the trees of the field shall clap their hands" (Isa. 55:12).

C. To judge and punish faithless Israel

In the book of Romans the great Apostle Paul makes two significant statements concerning his beloved nation Israel. He writes:

Negative statement: *"For they are not all Israel, which are of Israel"* (Rom. 9:6).

Positive statement: *"And so all Israel shall be saved: as it is written, There shall come out of Zion the Deliverer, and shall turn away ungodliness from Jacob"* (Rom. 11:26).

By the positive statement, Paul of course meant that all faithful Israel would be saved. As we have previously seen, this blessed event will occur during the Tribulation.

By the negative statement, Paul writes concerning faithless Israel. In other words, all that glitters is not gold. From the very moment God began working through Abraham (the first Hebrew), Satan also began working through members of that same race. Thus, as the Bible has been advanced by faithful Israel throughout history, it has likewise been opposed by faithless Israel.

Therefore, when the Master of all Israel returns, He will be especially gracious to true Israel but especially harsh with false Israel. Note the tragic record of false Israel.

1. Her sins against the Father
   a. Rebelling (Num. 14:22-23)
   b. Rejecting (1 Sam. 8:7)
   c. Robbing (Mal. 3:8-9)
2. Her sins against the Son
   a. She refused him (John 1:11).
   b. She crucified him (Acts 2:22-23; 3:14-15; 4:10; 1 Thess. 2:14-16).
3. Her sins against the Holy Spirit—stubborn resistance. (See Acts 7:51.)

The Apostle Paul dearly loved his nation, and doubtless wrote the following description of faithless Israel and her future judgment with a heavy and weeping heart:

"Who killed both the Lord Jesus and their own prophets, and have persecuted us; and they do not please God and are contrary to all men, forbidding us to speak to the Gentiles that they may be saved, so as always to fill up the measure of their sins; but wrath has come upon them to the uttermost" (1 Thess. 2:15-16).

Thus the tragic prophecy of Ezekiel will someday be fulfilled upon faithless Israel:

"But as for those whose hearts follow the desire for their detestable things and their abominations, I will recompense their deeds on their own heads," says the Lord GOD" (Ezek. 11:21).

"And I will purge out from among you the rebels, and them that transgress against me …" (Ezek. 20:38).

D. To separate the sheep from the goats

"When the Son of Man comes in His glory, and all the holy angels with Him, then He will sit on the throne of His glory. All the nations will be gathered before Him, and He will separate them one from another, as a shepherd divides his sheep from the goats. And He will set the sheep on His right hand, but the goats on the left. Then the King will say to those on His right hand, 'Come, you blessed of My Father, inherit the kingdom prepared for you from the foundation of the world: for I was hungry and you gave Me food; I was thirsty and you gave Me drink; I was a stranger and you took Me in; I was naked and you clothed Me; I was sick and you visited Me; I was in prison and you came to Me.'

"Then the righteous will answer Him, saying, 'Lord, when did we see You hungry and feed You, or thirsty and give You drink? When did we see You a stranger and take You in, or naked and clothe You? Or when did we see You sick, or in prison, and come to You?' And the King will answer and say to them, 'Assuredly, I say to you, inasmuch as you did it to one of the least of these My brethren, you did it to Me.'

"Then He will also say to those on the left hand, 'Depart from Me, you cursed, into the everlasting fire prepared for the devil and his angels: for I was hungry and you gave Me no food; I was thirsty and you gave Me no drink; I was a stranger and you did not take Me in, naked and you did not clothe Me, sick and in prison and you did not visit Me.'

"Then they also will answer Him, saying, 'Lord, when did we see You hungry or thirsty or a stranger or naked or sick or in prison, and did not minister to You?' Then He will answer them, saying, 'Assuredly, I say to you, inasmuch as you did not do it to one of the least of these, you did not do it to Me.' And these will go away into everlasting punishment, but the righteous into eternal life" (Matt. 25:31-46).

1. The false views of this judgment

   a. That this sheep and goat judgment is the same as the Great White Throne Judgment of Revelation 20:11-15. They are not the same, for one takes place at the end of the Tribulation while the other occurs at the end of the Millennium.

   b. That the sheep and goat judgment deals only with entire nations. Some have imagined the nations of the world lined up before God. At his command, Russia steps forward and is judged, then America, then Cuba, etc. This is not the case. The word translated "nations" in Matthew 25:32 should be rendered "Gentiles."

2. The basis of this judgment

The test in this judgment is how those Gentiles who survive the Tribulation have treated faithful Israel (here referred to by Christ as "my brethren"). In Nazi Germany, during the Second World War, escaping Jews were on a number of occasions befriended and protected by various German families who, in spite of their nationality, did not agree with Adolf Hitler. Apparently the same thing will happen during the Tribulation. Gentiles from all nations will hear the message of faithful Israel and believe it and, at the risk of their own lives, will protect the messengers. This, then, would seem to be the nature of the sheep and goat judgment. See also Matthew 13:38-43, 47-50; Genesis 12:1-3.

E. To bind Satan

"And the God of peace shall bruise Satan under your feet shortly" (Rom. 16:20).

"Then I saw an angel coming down from heaven, having the key to the bottomless pit and a great chain in his hand. He laid hold of the dragon, that serpent of old, who is the Devil and Satan, and bound him for a thousand years; and he cast him into the bottomless pit, and shut him up, and set a seal on him, so that he should deceive the nations no more till the thousand years were finished" (Rev. 20:1-3).

Oliver Wendell Holmes once poked fun at God's eternal plan by composing a limerick which read:

> *God's plan had a hopeful beginning;*
> *But man ruined all this by his sinning;*
> *We trust that the story*
> *Will end in God's glory*
> *But at the present the other side's winning!*

However, as this passage in Rev. 20 demonstrates, while Satan was allowed to win a few battles, God Himself has determined to win the war!

F. To resurrect Old Testament and tribulational saints

It is the view of this study guide that at the Rapture of the church God will raise only those believers who have been saved from Pentecost till the Rapture. According to this view, all other believers will be resurrected just prior to the Millennium at this time.

1. The fact of this resurrection

At least nine passages bring out this resurrection.

a. Job 19:25-26

"For I know that my redeemer liveth, and that he shall stand at the latter day upon the earth: And though after my skin worms destroy this body, yet in my flesh shall I see God."

b. Psalm 49:15

"But God will redeem my soul from the power of the grave: for he shall receive me."

c. Isaiah 25:8

"He will swallow up death in victory ..."

d. Isaiah 26:19

"*Thy dead men shall live, together with my dead body shall they arise....*"

e. Daniel 12:2

"*And many of them that sleep in the dust of the earth shall awake, some to everlasting life, and some to shame and everlasting contempt.*"

f. Hosea 13:14

"*I will ransom them from the power of the grave; I will redeem them from death: O death, I will be thy plagues; O grave, I will be thy destruction....*"

g. John 5:28-29

"*Marvel not at this: for the hour is coming, in the which all that are in the graves shall hear his voice, and shall come forth; they that have done good, unto the resurrection of life; and they that have done evil, unto the resurrection of damnation.*"

h. Hebrews 11:35

"*...and others were tortured, not accepting deliverance; that they might obtain a better resurrection.*"

i. Revelation 20:4-5

"*...and I saw the souls of them that were beheaded for the witness of Jesus, and for the word of God, and which had not worshipped the beast, neither his image, neither had received his mark upon their foreheads, or in their hands; and they lived and reigned with Christ a thousand years. But the rest of the dead lived not again until the thousand years were finished....*"

2. The order of this resurrection

This is the third of four major biblical resurrections. These are:

a. The resurrection of Christ (1 Cor. 15:23)

b. The resurrection of believers at the Rapture (1 Thess. 4:16; 1 Cor. 15:51-53)

c. The resurrection of Old Testament and tribulational saints

d. The resurrection of the unsaved (Rev. 20:5, 11-14)

Thus one of the reasons for the Second Coming will be to resurrect those non-church-related saints. For many long centuries Father Abraham has been patiently awaiting that city "*which hath foundations, whose builder and maker is God*" (Heb. 11:10). God will not let him down.

Dr. Clarence Mason has written:

Resurrection! What a magic word.

It has always been the dream of man. In the artifacts of the tomb of Queen Shubad at the University of Pennsylvania Museum, are the crushed skulls of her bodyguards and ladies-in-waiting. These servants were by this means presumptively sent along to accompany the queen from Abraham's hometown of Ur into the future life. That was about the third millennium before Christ.

Philosophers have conjectured and yearned. Rationalists have drawn a blank with their nihilism about the future. This is one area in which their writings show poignant despair. The early church had a unique message. They preached 'Jesus and the resurrection.' Other religions had their salvation schemes, their lofty ethics, their colorful rites and ceremonies. They had their great men, saints, and alleged miracles, even including virgin births. They had their millions of devotees. Their founders were wreathed in extravagant claims.

But none of them claimed to have a resurrected founder who had come forth from the grave. In this, Christianity is unique among religions. It was this message that startled the philosophers on Mars Hill, accustomed though they were to hearing 'some new thing.' This was really new! (*Prophetic Problems*, Moody Press, 1973, p. 129)

G. To judge fallen angels

"*Know ye not that we shall judge angels?*" (1 Cor. 6:3).

All fallen angels are of course included in this judgment. But they fall into two main categories: chained and unchained.

1. Unchained fallen angels

"*And Jesus asked him, saying, What is thy name? And he said, Legion: because many devils were entered into him. And they besought him that he would not command them to go out into the deep*" (Luke 8:30, 31).

"*And there was in their synagogue a man with an unclean spirit; and he cried out, Saying, Let us alone; what have we to do with thee, thou Jesus of Nazareth? art thou come to destroy us? I know thee who thou art, the Holy One of God*" (Mark 1:23, 24).

"*For we wrestle not against flesh and blood, but against principalities, against powers, against the rulers of the darkness of this world, against spiritual wickedness in high places*" (Eph. 6:12).

The point of these three passages is simply this—there is a group of fallen angels (demons) who have freedom of movement, and can therefore possess the bodies of both men and animals. Their one sin was that of following Satan in his foul rebellion against God. See Isa. 14:12-17; Ezek. 28:12-19.

2. Chained fallen angels

Christ also suffered. He died once for the sins of all us guilty sinners, although He Himself was innocent of any sin at any time, that he might bring us safely home to God. But though his body died, his spirit lived on, and it was in the spirit that he visited the spirits in prison, and preached to them—spirits of those who, long before in the days of Noah, had refused to listen to God, though he waited patiently for them while Noah was building the ark. Yet only eight persons were saved from drowning in that terrible flood (1 Peter 3:18-20, TLB).

And the angels which kept not their first estate, but left their own habitation, he hath reserved in everlasting chains under darkness unto the judgment of the great day (Jude 6).

According to the above passages these fallen angels do not have the freedom the previous angels do, but are right now in "solitary confinement" awaiting their judgment at the end of the tribulation. Why the difference? Many Bible scholars believe that this group of angels was guilty of two grievous sins—not only did they join Satan's revolt, but they also committed sexual perversion with "*the daughters of men*" before the flood. See Gen. 6:2.

■ **The time interval following His return**

According to Dan. 12:11, 12, there will be a period of seventy-five days between the Second Coming of Christ and the Millennial reign. Dr. S. Franklin Logsdon has written:

We in the United States have a national analogy. The President is elected in the early part of November, but he is not inaugurated until January 20th. There is an interim of 70-plus days. During this time, he concerns himself with the appointment of Cabinet members, foreign envoys and others who will comprise his government. In the period of 75 days between the termination of the Great Tribulation and the Coronation, the King of glory likewise will attend to certain matters. (*Profiles of Prophecy*, Zondervan, 1970, p. 81)

It would therefore appear that the seventy-five days will be spent in accomplishing seven basic things already mentioned under "Purposes of the Second Coming."

Dr. Mark Hitchcock overviews Jesus's coming as follows:

A. He will come personally (Acts 1:10, 11).
B. He will come literally (Rev. 19:11-13).
C. He will come visibly (Matt. 24:23-27).
D. He will come suddenly (Matt. 24:27; Rev. 3:3).
E. He will come dramatically (Matt. 24:29; Luke 21:25-26).
F. He will come gloriously (Matt. 24:30; 2 Thess. 1:7).
G. He will come triumphantly (Rev. 19:19-21).
   (*The End*, pp. 389-391, Tyndale House Publishers)

Perhaps no other musical piece more graphically described Jesus' return than can be found in Charles Wesley's magnificent hymn entitled, *Lo, He Comes with Clouds Descending.*

Lo, He comes with clouds descending, Once for favored sinners slain;
Thousand thousand saints attending, Swell the triumph of His train;
Alleluia! Alleluia! God appears on earth to reign.

Every eye shall now behold Him, Robed in dreadful majesty;

Those who set at naught and sold Him, Pierced and nailed Him to the tree,
Deeply wailing, deeply wailing, Shall the true Messiah see.

Now redemption, long expected, See in solemn pomp appear;
All His saints, by men rejected, Now shall meet Him in the air;
Alleluia! Alleluia! See the day of God appear.

Yea, Amen! Let all adore Thee, High on Thine eternal throne;
Savior, take the power and glory, Claim the kingdom for Thine own:
O, come quickly, O, come quickly! Everlasting God, come down. Amen.

One final observation: On July 20, 1969, the then-American President, Richard M. Nixon, stated on national television that, in his opinion, this day, July 20, was the greatest day in human history! While no Christian would have agreed with this, all could have understood his excitement, for at that very moment, two human beings were standing on the moon, and what's more, both were Americans!

However, July 20, 1969, was not the greatest day in human history. Nor would it rank as the second, or third, or fourth, or even fifth. Most Bible students would probably agree that the *fifth* greatest day took place when a young virgin mother gave birth to a Son and laid Him in a manger.

The *fourth* greatest day may have occurred when this babe, upon reaching 33 years of age, was nailed to a cruel cross, dying for our sins, as He cried out with His final breath, *"It is finished."*

The *third* greatest day would then transpire a few days later when some grieving women at His tomb were told … *"He is risen!"*

The *second* day would involve eleven men standing on a mountain top overlooking the Holy City, watching with amazement, as their beloved Master was transported to heaven by a glorious cloud!

But, Mr. President, the greatest day in human history is *yet* to come and *will* come at the sounding of the seventh trumpet!

> *Then the seventh angel sounded: And there were loud voices in heaven, saying, "The kingdoms of this world have become the kingdoms of our Lord and of His Christ, and He shall reign forever and ever!"* (Rev. 11:15).

> *Then to Him was given dominion and glory and a kingdom, that all peoples, nations, and languages should serve Him. His dominion is an everlasting dominion, which shall not pass away, And His kingdom the one which shall not be destroyed.* (Dan. 7:14).

> *He will be great, and will be called the Son of the Highest; and the Lord God will give Him the throne of His father David. And He will reign over the house of Jacob forever, and of His kingdom there will be no end."* (Luke 1:32-33).

EVENT 12 THE MILLENNIAL REIGN OF JESUS CHRIST_____

" … and they lived and reigned with Christ a thousand years" (Rev. 20:4)

Some 250 years ago, Isaac Watts wrote a hymn based on the truths found in Psalm 98. The name of this world-famous hymn is *"Joy to the World!"* At Christmas it is sung all across the world by millions of Christians and non-Christians alike. But a close study of the words of this hymn reveal that Watts did not have in mind the Bethlehem coming of Christ, but rather the millennial coming of our Lord! Observe his words:

> *Joy to the world! The Lord is come!*
> *Let earth receive her King.*
> *Let every heart prepare him room,*
> *And heaven and nature sing.*
>
> *No more let sins and sorrows grow,*
> *Nor thorns infest the ground;*
> *He comes to make his blessings flow,*
> *Far as the curse is found.*
>
> *He rules the world with truth and grace,*
> *And makes the nations prove*
> *The glories of his righteousness,*
> *And wonders of his love.*

Dr. J. Dwight Pentecost writes:

> A larger body of prophetic Scripture is devoted to the subject of the Millennium, developing its character and conditions, than any other one subject. The millennial age, in which the purposes of God are fully realized on the earth, demands considerable attention. An attempt will be made to deduce from the Scriptures themselves the essential facts and features of this theocratic kingdom. While much has been written on the subject of the Millennium, that which is clearly revealed in the Word can be our only true guide as to the nature and character of that period. (*Things to Come*, Dunham Press, 1959, p. 476)

Thus, in a nutshell, the word *millennium* is a Latin term which signifies "a thousand years."

■ **The scriptural record involved**

No less than nineteen Old Testament and New Testament books give testimony to the millennial reign of Christ.

A. Old Testament
1. Psalms 2:6-8; 98:4, 9
2. Isaiah 2:2-4; 9:6, 7; 11:6-9; 25:8; 29:18, 19; 30:23-26; 35:5-10; 40:4, 5, 10, 11; 42:16; 45:6; 49:10, 11; 55:13; 60:1, 3, 11, 19, 20, 22; 65:19, 20, 25
3. Jeremiah 23:5, 6

4. Ezekiel 34:23, 24

5. Daniel 2:44; 7:13, 14

6. Joel 3:18

7. Amos 9:11, 13

8. Micah 4:1-6

9. Zephaniah 3:9

10. Zechariah 6:12, 13; 8:3-5; 14:8, 9, 16, 20

B. New Testament

1. Matthew 19:28; 25:31

2. Luke 1:31-33; 22:30

3. Acts 2:30

4. Romans 8:21

5. First Corinthians 15:24-28

6. Philippians 2:10, 11

7. Second Timothy 2:12

8. Hebrews 1:8

9. Revelation 3:21; 5:13; 11:15; 19:15; 20:4-6

C. Selected key passages

1. *"Shout joyfully to the Lord, all the earth; Break forth in song, rejoice, and sing praises. For He is coming to judge the earth. With righteousness He shall judge the world, and the peoples with equity"* (Psa. 98:4, 9).

2. *"Now it shall come to pass in the latter days that the mountain of the Lord's house shall be established on the top of the mountains, and shall be exalted above the hills; and all nations shall flow to it. Many people shall come and say, 'Come, and let us go up to the mountain of the Lord, to the house of the God of Jacob; He will teach us His ways, and we shall walk in His paths.' For out of Zion shall go forth the law, and the word of the Lord from Jerusalem. He shall judge between the nations, and rebuke many people; they shall beat their swords into plowshares, and their spears into pruning hooks; nation shall not lift up sword against nation, neither shall they learn war anymore"* (Isa. 2:2-4).

3. *"Every valley shall be exalted and every mountain and hill brought low; the crooked places shall be made straight and the rough places smooth; the glory of the Lord shall be revealed, and all flesh shall see it together; for the mouth of the Lord has spoken. 'Behold, the Lord God shall come with a strong hand, and His arm shall rule for Him; behold, His reward is with Him, and His work before Him"* (Isa. 40:4, 5, 10).

4. *"Arise, shine; for your light has come! And the glory of the Lord is risen upon you"* (Isa. 60:1).

5. *"'Behold, the days are coming,' says the LORD, 'That I will raise to David a Branch of righteousness; a King shall reign and prosper, and execute judgment and righteousness in the earth'"* (Jer. 23:5).

6. *"Then to Him was given dominion and glory and a kingdom, that all peoples, nations, and languages should serve Him. His dominion is an everlasting dominion, which shall not pass away, and His kingdom the one which shall not be destroyed"* (Dan. 7:14).

7. *"And the Lord shall be King over all the earth. In that day it shall be—"The Lord is one, and His name one"* (Zech. 14:9).

8. *"So Jesus said to them, 'Assuredly I say to you, that in the regeneration, when the Son of Man sits on the throne of His glory, you who have followed Me will also sit on twelve thrones, judging the twelve tribes of Israel'"* (Matt. 19:28).

9. *"And He will reign over the house of Jacob forever, and of His kingdom there will be no end"* (Luke 1:33).

10. *"Then the seventh angel sounded: And there were loud voices in heaven, saying, 'The kingdoms of this world have become the kingdoms of our Lord and of His Christ, and He shall reign forever and ever!'"* (Rev. 11:15).

■ **The three different views involved**

A. Postmillennialism

This theory says that through the preaching of the gospel the world will eventually embrace Christianity and become a universal "society of saints." At this point Christ will be invited to assume command and reign over man's peaceful planet. A lofty concept indeed! However, postmillennialism is confronted with a two-fold problem:

1. The testimony of the scriptures—The Bible clearly teaches the world situation will become worse and worse prior to Christ's return, not better and better. Jesus, Paul, Peter and Jude warn of this. Note their words:

   a. Jesus: *" … when the Son of Man cometh, shall He find faith on the earth?"* (Luke 18:8).

   b. Paul: *"Now the Spirit expressly says that in latter times some will depart from the faith, giving heed to deceiving spirits and doctrines of demons"* (1 Tim. 4:1).

      "But know this, that in the last days perilous times will come: For men will be lovers of themselves, lovers of money, boasters, proud, blasphemers, disobedient to parents, unthankful, unholy, unloving, unforgiving, slanderers, without self-control, brutal, despisers of good, traitors, headstrong, haughty, lovers of pleasure rather than lovers of God, having a form of godliness but denying its power. And from such people turn away!" (2 Tim. 3:1-5).

"*I charge you therefore before God and the Lord Jesus Christ, who will judge the living and the dead at His appearing and His kingdom: Preach the word! Be ready in season and out of season. Convince, rebuke, exhort, with all longsuffering and teaching. For the time will come when they will not endure sound doctrine, but according to their own desires, because they have itching ears, they will heap up for themselves teachers; and they will turn their ears away from the truth, and be turned aside to fables*" (2 Tim. 4:1-4).

   c.   Peter: "*…knowing this first: that scoffers will come in the last days, walking according to their own lusts, and saying, 'Where is the promise of His coming? For since the fathers fell asleep, all things continue as they were from the beginning of creation'*" (2 Peter 3:3, 4).

   d.   Jude: "*But you, beloved, remember the words which were spoken before by the apostles of our Lord Jesus Christ: how they told you that there would be mockers in the last time who would walk according to their own ungodly lusts*" (vv. 17, 18).

2.   The testimony of history—Never in the human experience has a kingdom produced a king. It is always the opposite. There would have never been a Babylonian or Persian kingdom without a Nebuchadnezzar or a Cyrus! In the biological world it is the mother who gives birth to the baby. Not the other way around!

This position was popularized by a Unitarian minister named Daniel Whitby (1638-1726), and it flourished until the early part of the twentieth century. Then came World War I, and men began to wonder. Finally, the postmillennial theory was quietly laid to rest amid Hitler's gas ovens during the Second World War!

However, in recent times it seems to be making a comeback, thanks to the efforts of Christian Reconstruction theologians.

B.   Amillennialism

The prefix "a" means *no*. Thus, this view teaches there will be no thousand-year reign at all and that the New Testament church inherits all the spiritual promises and prophecies of Old Testament Israel. In this view, Isaiah's prophecy of the bear and the cow lying together and the lion eating straw like the ox (Isa. 11:7) simply does not mean what it says at all. However, if the eleventh chapter of Isaiah cannot be taken literally, what proof do we have that the magnificent fifty-third chapter should not likewise be allegorized away?

Dr. H. Wayne House defines it as follows:

The Bible predicts a continuous parallel growth of good and evil in the world between the first coming of Christ and the second coming of Christ. The kingdom of God is now present in the world through his Word, his Spirit, his church. This position has also been called "realized millennialism." (*Charts of Christian Theology and Doctrine*, p. 136)

Many reformed theologians and the Roman Catholic Church hold this view. Thus we are even now in the millennial age which began some 2,000 years ago with the birth of the church at Pentecost! However, this approach, like the post-millennial one has some very serious problems!

1. How do we reassure these survivors of Hitler's death camps, or those who are at present suffering from terminal cancer? Do we dare tell them this is the Golden Age the Bible speaks of?

2. What exactly did John the Apostle mean in Revelation 20 when he stated no less than six times that the Savior will rule and reign for one thousand years? To defend their position, the amillennialist points to a verse in the Psalms and a passage in 2 Peter:

    > *"For a thousand years in Your sight are like yesterday when it is past, and like a watch in the night"* (Psa. 90:4). *"But, beloved, do not forget this one thing, that with the Lord one day is as a thousand years, and a thousand years as one day"* (2 Peter 3:8).

These verses, it is claimed, show that the phrase "thousand years" need not always refer to a literal ten century period of time. But this interpretation completely misses the point of both authors. They were simply declaring that the eternal God who *created* time is *above* time, and not *governed by* time.

On a personal note:

> During my first semester at Dallas Seminary, the students in our Tuesday/Thursday theological class were shocked one morning when the professor walked in, sat down, and made the following announcement: "Gentlemen," he began, "I have a confession to make. Around 6:30 a.m. today, I have become an amillennialist!"

> Well, we all gasped in amazement, for after all, Dallas Theological Seminary was the theological flagship for pre-millennialism! But he continued, "Let me now explain the circumstances leading to my conversion. This morning I woke up with a splitting headache. After dressing and waiting for breakfast, I scanned the local newspaper which recorded in vivid detail the murders, rapes, robberies, and other acts of violence which had occurred during the night. So, discarding the newspaper, I glanced at the TV screen only to learn concerning universal unrest among the nations, threats of war, etc. Well, I concluded, today was not at all promising. But maybe a hearty breakfast would lift my spirits. However, this was not to be. For starters, the eggs were runny, the toast was burnt, and most important, there was no cream for my coffee!

> "But regardless of how I felt, my schedule called for me to teach two classes today—this class, and one overviewing the book of Isaiah. However, as I began my review concerning the notes on Isaiah, things soon began to change for the better. The prophet described in glowing terms the 1000-year reign

of Christ! He predicted a glorious time of no murders, rapes, sin, sickness, evil, bloodshed, wars or death! But most exciting of all, King Jesus Himself would reign over the planet from the city of Jerusalem.

"Well, after a brief review of all this, I slowly leaned back in my chair, and, in spite of my headache, the local and world bad news, and a half-eaten breakfast, a broad smile appeared on my face, as I slowly repeated, ahhh … millennium!"

Needless to say, the prof's conversion was approved by the students enrolled in both classes!

C. Premillennialism

This view teaches that Christ will return just prior to the Millennium and will personally rule during this glorious thousand-year reign. This position is the oldest of these three views. From the apostolic period on, the premillennial position was held by the early church fathers.

1. Theologians who held it during the first century A.D.

   a. Clement of Rome—40-100

   b. Ignatius—50-115

   c. Polycarp—70-167

2. Theologians who held it during the second century A.D.

   a. Justin Martyr—100-168

   b. Irenaeus—140-202

   c. Tertullian—150-200

   H. Wayne House summarizes this view:

   Adherents of this school are represented by those who generally hold to the concept of two stages in the coming of Christ. He will come *for* his church (Rapture) and then *with* his church (revelation). The two events are separated by a seven-year Tribulation. There is a consistent distinction between Israel and the church throughout history. (*Charts of Christian Theology*, p. 134)

   Dr. Rene Pache writes the following helpful words:

   Let us notice again this fact: the teaching of the Old Testament concerning the millennium is so complete that the Jews in the Talmud succeeded in developing it entirely themselves, without possessing the gifts furnished later by the New Testament. For example, they had indeed affirmed before the Apocalypse that the messianic kingdom would last one thousand years. One should not, therefore, claim (as some have done) that without the famous passage of Rev. 20:1-10 the doctrine of the millennium would not exist" (*The Return of Jesus Christ*, Moody Press, 1955, p. 380).

■ The titles involved

A. The world to come (Heb. 2:5)

B. The kingdom of heaven (Matt. 5:10)

C. The kingdom of God (Mark 1:14)

D. The last day (John 6:40)

E. The times of refreshing (Acts 3:19)

F. The restitution of all things (Acts 3:21)

G. The day of Christ—This is by far the most common biblical name for the Millennium (see 1 Cor. 1:8, 5:5, 2 Cor. 1:14; Phil. 1:6; 2:16)

Thus, during the Millennium our blessed Lord will have the opportunity to exercise His rightful and eternal four-fold Sonship:

1. His *racial* Sonship—Son of Abraham (Gen. 17:8; Matt. 1:1; Gal. 3:16)

2. His *royal* Sonship—Son of David (Isa. 9:7; Matt. 1:1; Luke 1:32, 33)

3. His *human* Sonship—Son of Man (John 5:27; Acts 1:11)

4. His *divine* Sonship—Son of God (Isa. 66:15-18, 23; Psa. 46:1, 5; 86:9; Zech. 14:16-19)

H. The regeneration (Matt. 19:28)

"*So Jesus said to them, 'Assuredly I say to you, that in the regeneration, when the Son of Man sits on the throne of His glory, you who have followed Me will also sit on twelve thrones, judging the twelve tribes of Israel'*" (Matt. 19:28).

The word "regeneration" is found only twice in the English Bible, here and in Titus 3:5, where Paul is speaking of the believer's new birth. The word literally means "re-creation." Thus the Millennium will be to the earth what salvation is to the sinner.

At this point allow me to insert a little sanctified imagination:

Let us suppose that on the seventy-fifth and final day between the end of the Great Tribulation and beginning of the glorious Millennium, we are surprised to witness a group of work angels setting up a massive canvas tent located near the Holy City itself, followed by an explanation that earth's final revival would be conducted within this hour.

Furthermore, King Jesus Himself would be preaching! So, at the designated time all the redeemed enter, walk down the sawdust aisles and are seated in the fold-up chairs. After a choir of angels sing, "*How Great Thou Art*," the Savior begins His sermon. It is immediately clear that the burning theme of the message would center on repentance and regeneration! Finally, at the conclusion a special invitation is given as the celestial choir begins singing "*Just As I Am*."

For a moment, all is absolutely silent. No one moves. Then suddenly we witness a sorrowful and sobbing woman, as she stumbles forward. Who is she, all want to know. The woman looks familiar although we have never met her. Then, suddenly, she is recognized! The woman in question is none other than Mother Nature herself!

No, she is not coming to repent of her own sins, but rather those of earth's first two sinners, Adam and Eve! They were responsible for her record of terrible earthquakes, uncontrolled forest fires, hurricanes, tsunamis, tornadoes, snow, ice, and dust storms, etc.

Yes, these all happened on her watch, but she grieved over each tragic event! In the New Testament the apostle Paul summarizes this sad tale:

> *"For all creation is waiting patiently and hopefully for that future day when God will resurrect his children. For on that day thorns and thistles, sin, death, and decay—the things that overcame the world against its will at God's command—will all disappear, and the world around us will share in the glorious freedom from sin which God's children enjoy. For we know that even the things of nature, like animals and plants, suffer in sickness and death as they await this great event"* (Rom. 8:19-22, *The Living Bible*).

Suddenly it dawns on us: We are witnessing that "great event" predicted by the apostle! Before our very eyes, Ma Nature has been transformed! Wow! What could possibly follow to top this incredible event?

Maybe, just maybe, it could be for all creatures to join with all creation in the singing one of the oldest hymns in Christendom, written by St. Francis of Assisi nearly 900 years ago. It is titled, *All Creatures of Our God and King.* Note the words of this sublime song:

All creatures of our God and King
Lift up your voice and with us sing,
Alleluia! Alleluia!
Thou burning sun with golden beam,
Thou silver moon with softer gleam!

Refrain
O praise Him! O praise Him!
Alleluia! Alleluia! Alleluia!

Thou rushing wind art that so strong
Ye clouds that sail in Heaven along,
O praise Him! Alleluia!
Thou rising morn, in praise rejoice,
Ye lights of evening, find a voice!

Refrain

Thou flowing water, pure and clear,
Make music for thy Lord to hear,
O praise Him! Alleluia!
Thou fire so masterful and bright,
That givest man both warmth and light.

Refrain

And all ye men of tender heart,
Forgiving others, take your part,

O sing ye! Alleluia!
Ye who long pain and sorrow bear,
Praise God and on Him cast your care!

Refrain

Let all things their Creator bless,
And worship Him in humbleness,
O praise Him! Alleluia!
Praise, praise the Father, praise the Son,
And praise the Spirit, Three in One!

■ **The wedding involved**

"'*Let us be glad and rejoice and give Him glory, for the marriage of the Lamb has come, and His wife has made herself ready. And to her it was granted to be arrayed in fine linen, clean and bright, for the fine linen is the righteous acts of the saints. Then he said to me, 'Write: Blessed are those who are called to the marriage supper of the Lamb!' And he said to me, 'These are the true sayings of God'*" (Rev. 19:7-9).

Here it should be observed there is a chronological and geographical contrast between the marriage *service* of Christ and His church and the marriage *supper*:

A. The Marriage Service takes place in heaven shortly after the Rapture and is a private affair.

B. The Marriage Supper takes place on earth at the beginning of the Millennium and is a public affair.

■ **The Old Testament examples involved**

A. The Sabbath

This word literally means "rest." In Old Testament times God wisely set aside a Sabbath or rest time after a period of activity. A rest was to be observed:

1. After six work days (Exod. 20:8-11; Lev. 23:3)

2. After six work weeks (Lev. 23:15, 16)

3. After six work months (Lev. 23:24, 25, 27, 34)

4. After six work years (Lev. 25:2-5)

B. Jubilee year (Lev. 25:10-12)

C. The tabernacle—because God's glory dwelt in the Holy of Holies (Exod. 25:8; 29:42-46; 40:34)

D. The feast of tabernacles (Lev. 23:33-43)

E. The Promised Land (Deut. 6:3; Heb. 4:8-10)

F. The reign of Solomon

1. Because of the vastness of his kingdom (1 Kings 4:21)

2. Because of its security (1 Kings 4:25)

3. Because of his great wisdom (1 Kings 4:29, 34)
4. Because of the fame of his kingdom (1 Kings 10:7)
5. Because of the riches of his kingdom (1 Kings 10:2)

■ **The characters involved**

Dr. Randall Price has prepared this helpful chart overviewing the millennial characteristics:

Geographical	Social	Spiritual	Environmental
Increase in territory (Ge 15:18; Isa 26:15; Ob 1:17-21)	Universal knowledge of Lord (Isa 11:9; 54:13; Hab 2:14)	Universal worship (Isa 19:21; 52:1, 7-10; Mal 1:11; Zec 8:23)	Conditions of holiness (Isa 1:26-27; 35:8-10; Zep 3:11)
Topographical changes (Eze 47:8-12; Isa 2:2; Zec 14:4, 8, 10)	Reproduction by saints (Isa 65:23; Eze 47:21-22; Zec 10:8)	Rebuilt temple (Eze 37:26-28; Eze 40-48; Hag 2:7-9; Joel 3:18)	Restoration of Edenic conditions (Isa 11:6-9, 65:25)
Jerusalem as center of world's worship (Isa 2:2-3; Mic 4:1-2; Zec 8:3; 14:16-21)	Unimpaired labor (Eze 48:18-19; Isa 62:8-9; 65:21-23)	Return of the Shekinah glory (Eze 43:1-7; 48:35; Zec 2:10-13; Jer 3:17)	Removal of harmful effects (Isa 33:24; 35:5-7; Zep 3:19)
Enlargement of Jerusalem (Eze 48:35; Jer 3:17)	Universal language (Zep 3:9)	Revival of sacrificial system (Eze 43:13-27; 45:13-25; Isa 56:7)	Restoration of longevity (Isa 65:20)
Name of Jerusalem changed (Isa 62:2-4)	Freedom from war/enemies (Isa 2:4; 14:3-7; Zec 9:8; 14:10-11; Am 9:15)	Restoration of Sabbath and ritual feasts (Eze 44:24; Zec 14:16)	Increase in daylight (Isa 4:5-6; 30:26; 60:19-20; Zec 2:5)
Jews return and live in Land (Eze 36:24; 37:25)	Peaceful society (Isa 11:6-9; 65:21; Hos 2:18; Zec 9:10)	Spiritual obedience under new covenant (Eze 36: 25-28; 37; Jer 31:31-34)	Economic prosperity (Isa 30:23-25; 35:1-7; Am 9:13-15; Joel 2:21-27)
Reversal of Land's desolate condition (Eze 36:33-36; Isa 62:4)	Justice (Isa 9:6-7; 32:16; Jer 30:9; Eze 34:23; Hos 3:5)	Satan/demons bound; no spiritual deception (Rev 20:1-3)	Universal access to Israel (Isa 2:2-3; 11:16; 56:6; Jer 3:14-15)

(*Jerusalem in Prophecy*, Harvest House, Chart #88)

■ **The reasons involved**

At least five can be listed:

A. To reward the saints of God

"*Verily there is a reward for the righteous*" (Psa. 58:11). "*To him that soweth righteousness shall be a sure reward*" (Prov. 11:18). "*Behold, the Lord God will come with strong hand, and his arm shall rule for him: behold, his reward is with him*" (Isa. 40:10). "*Rejoice, and be exceeding glad: for great is your reward in heaven*" (Matt. 5:12). "*For the Son of man shall come in the glory of his Father with his angels; and then he shall reward every man according to his works*" (Matt. 16:27). "*Then shall the King say…, Come, ye blessed of my Father, inherit the kingdom prepared for you from the foundation of the world*" (Matt. 25:34). "*Knowing that of the Lord ye shall receive the reward of the inheritance*" (Col. 3:24). "*And, behold, I come quickly; and my reward is with me*" (Rev. 22:12).

B. To answer the oft-prayed model prayer

In Luke 11:1-4 and Matthew 6:9-13 our Lord, at the request of His disciples, suggested a pattern prayer to aid all believers in their praying. One of the guidelines was this: "*Thy kingdom come.*" Here the Savior was inviting his followers to pray for the Millennium. Someday He will return to fulfill the untold millions of times these three little words have wafted their way to heaven by Christians: "*Thy kingdom come.*"

C. To fulfill three important Old Testament covenants

1. The Abrahamic Covenant—God promised Abraham two basic things:
   a. That his seed (Israel) would become a mighty nation (Gen. 12:1-3; 13:16; 15:5; 17:7; 22:17-18)
   b. That his seed (Israel) would someday own Palestine forever (Gen. 12:7; 13:14, 15, 17; 15:7, 18-21; 17:8)

2. The Davidic Covenant (2 Sam. 7:12-16; 23:5; 2 Chron. 13:5)

   Here the promise was threefold:
   a. That from David would come an everlasting throne
   b. That from David would come an everlasting kingdom
   c. That from David would come an everlasting King

   In a very real sense many of the conditions within these first two covenants have already come to pass. For example, concerning the Abrahamic Covenant, God did form a mighty nation from Abraham and today approximately 25 percent of that nation lives in the promised land. Then, in the fullness of time, God sent a babe from the seed of David to rule over the seed of Abraham in the land. (See Luke 1:30-33.) But a problem soon arose, for when the ruler from David presented Himself, He was rejected by Abraham's seed (Luke 23:18, 21; John 19:15). Thus, a third covenant was needed that would bring to completion the blessings of the first two. This God will wondrously accomplish through the New Covenant.

3. The New Covenant (Isa. 42:6; Jer. 31:31-34; Heb. 8:7-12)

   This promise was also threefold:
   a. That He would forgive their iniquity and forget their sin
   b. That He would give them new hearts
   c. That He would use Israel to reach and teach the Gentiles

D. To prove a point

This is the point: Regardless of his environment or heredity, mankind apart from God's grace, will inevitably fail. For example:

1. The age of innocence ended with willful disobedience (Gen. 3).
2. The age of conscience ended with universal corruption (Gen. 6).
3. The age of human government ended with devil-worshipping at the Tower of Babel (Gen. 11).

4. The age of promise ended with God's people out of the promised land and enslaved in Egypt (Exod. 1).

5. The age of the Law ended with the creatures killing their Creator (Matt. 27).

6. The age of the Church will end with worldwide apostasy (1 Tim. 4).

7. The age of the Tribulation will end with the battle of Armageddon (Rev. 19).

8. The age of the Millennium will end with an attempt to destroy God Himself (Rev. 20).

    (Note: Just where and how Satan will gather this unsaved human army at the end of the Millennium will be discussed later in this chapter.)

    Dr. J. Dwight Pentecost writes:

    > The millennial age is designed by God to be the final test of fallen humanity under the most ideal circumstances, surrounded by every enablement to obey the rule of the king, from whom the outward sources of temptation have been removed, so that man may be found and proved to be a failure in even this last testing of fallen humanity. (*Things to Come*, p. 538)

E. To fulfill the main burden of biblical prophecy

All Bible prophecy concerning the Lord Jesus Christ is summarized in one tiny verse by the Apostle Peter: *"the sufferings of Christ, and the glory that should follow"* (1 Pet. 1:11).

Here Peter connects Christ's first coming (the sufferings) with His second coming (the glory). This in a nutshell is a panorama of the purpose, plan, and program of almighty Jehovah God. Note this beautiful outline as we trace it through the Word of God.

1. The sufferings—a Baby, wrapped in swaddling clothes (Luke 2:12)
   The glory—a King, clothed in majestic apparel (Psa. 93:1)

2. The sufferings—He was the wearied traveler (John 4:6)
   The glory—He will be the untiring God (Isa. 40:28-29)

3. The sufferings—He had nowhere to lay His head (Luke 9:58)
   The glory—He will become heir to all things (Heb. 1:2)

4. The sufferings—He was rejected by tiny Israel (John 1:11)
   The glory—He will be accepted by all the nations (Isa. 9:6, 7)

5. The sufferings—wicked men took up stones to throw at Him (John 8:59)
   The glory—wicked men will cry for stones to fall upon them to hide them from Him (Rev. 6:16).

6. The sufferings—a lowly Savior, acquainted with grief (Isa. 53:3)
   The glory—the mighty God, anointed with the oil of gladness (Heb. 1:9)

7. The sufferings—He was clothed with a scarlet robe in mockery (Luke 23:11)
   The glory—He will be clothed with a vesture dipped in the blood of His enemies (Rev. 19:13).

8. The sufferings—He was smitten with a reed (Matt. 27:30)

   The glory—He will rule the nations with a rod of iron (Rev. 19:15).

9. The sufferings—wicked soldiers bowed their knee and mocked (Mark 15:19)

   The glory—every knee shall bow and acknowledge Him (Phil. 2:10).

10. The sufferings—He wore a crown of thorns (John 19:5)

    The glory—He will wear a crown of gold (Rev. 14:14).

11. The sufferings—His hands were pierced with nails (John 20:25)

    The glory—His hands will carry a sharp sickle (Rev. 14:14).

12. The sufferings—His feet were pierced with nails (Psa. 22:16)

    The glory—His feet will stand on the Mount of Olives (Zech. 14:4).

13. The sufferings—He had no form or comeliness (Isa. 53:2)

    The glory—He will be the fairest of ten thousand (Psa. 27:4).

14. The sufferings—He delivered up His spirit (John 19:30)

    The glory—He is alive forevermore (Rev. 1:18).

15. The sufferings—He was laid in the tomb (Matt. 27:59-60)

    The glory—He will sit on His throne (Heb. 8:1).

■ **The citizens and geography involved**

A. The citizens

1. Considered negatively

   No unsaved persons will enter the Millennium (Isa. 35; Jer. 31:33-34; Ezek. 20:37-38; Zech. 13:9; Matt. 18:3; 25:30, 46; John 3:3). However, millions of babies will evidently be reared during the Millennium. They will be born of saved but mortal Israelite and Gentile parents who survived the Tribulation and entered the Millennium in that state of mortality (thus the possible reason for the tree of life in Rev. 22:2). As they mature, some of these babies will refuse to submit their hearts to the new birth, though outward acts will be subjected to existing authority. Thus Christ will rule with a rod of iron (Rev. 2:27; 12:5; 19:15).

   Dr. Rene Pache writes concerning this:

   > As beautiful as the Millennium is, it will not be heaven … Sin will still be possible during the thousand years (Isa. 11:4; 65:20). Certain families and certain nations will refuse to go up to Jerusalem to worship the Lord (Zech. 14:17-19). Such deeds will be all the more inexcusable because the tempter will be absent and because the revelations of the Lord will be greater … Those who have been thus smitten will serve as examples to all those who would be tempted to imitate them (Isa. 66:24). (*The Return of Jesus Christ*, Moody Press, 1955, pp. 428, 429).

2. Considered positively

a. Saved Israel

    (1) Israel will once again be related to God by marriage (Isa. 54; 62:2-5; Hos. 2:14-23).

    (2) Israel will be exalted above the Gentiles (Isa. 14:1-2; 49:22-23; 60:14-17; 61:6-7).

    (3) Israel will become God's witnesses during the Millennium (Isa. 44:8; 61:6; 66:21; Jer. 16:19-21; Micah 5:7; Zeph. 3:20; Zech. 4:1-7; 8:3).

b. Saved Old Testament and Tribulational Gentiles (Isa. 2:4; 11:12 ; Rev. 5:9-10)

c. The Church (1 Cor. 6:2; 2 Tim. 2:12; Rev. 1:6; 2:26-27; 3:21)

d. The elect angels (Heb. 12:22)

B. The geography

  1. Palestine

    a. To be greatly enlarged and changed (Isa. 26:15; Obad. 1:17-21)—For the first time Israel will possess all the land promised to Abraham in Genesis 15:18-21.

    b. A great fertile plain to replace the mountainous terrain

    c. A river to flow east-west from the Mount of Olives into both the Mediterranean and the Dead seas—The following passages from The Living Bible bear this out:

"The Mount of Olives will split apart, making a very wide valley running from east to west, for half the mountain will move toward the north and half toward the south.... Life-giving waters will flow out from Jerusalem, half toward the Dead Sea and half toward the Mediterranean, flowing continuously both in winter and in summer.... All the land from Geba (the northern border of Judah) to Rimmon (the southern border) will become one vast plain" (Zech. 14:4, 8, 10).

"Sweet wine will drip from the mountains, and the hills shall flow with milk. Water will fill the dry stream beds of Judah, and a fountain will burst forth from the Temple of the Lord to water Acacia valley" (Joel 3:18).

"He told me: 'This river flows east through the desert and the Jordan Valley to the Dead Sea, where it will heal the salty waters and make them fresh and pure. Everything touching the water of this river shall live. Fish will abound in the Dead Sea, for its waters will be healed.... All kinds of fruit trees will grow along the river banks. The leaves will never turn brown and fall, and there will always be fruit. There will be a new crop every month—without fail! For they are watered by the river flowing from the Temple. The fruit will be for food and the leaves for medicine'" (Ezek. 47:8-9, 12).

  2. Jerusalem

    a. The city will become the worship center of the world

"But in the last days Mount Zion will be the most renowned of all the mountains of the world, praised by all nations; people from all over the world will make pilgrimages there" (Micah 4:1).

In the last days Jerusalem and the Temple of the Lord will become the world's greatest attraction, and people from many lands will flow there to worship the Lord.

"Come," everyone will say, "Let us go up the mountain of the Lord, to the Temple of the God of Israel; there he will teach us his laws, and we will obey them. For in those days the world will be ruled from Jerusalem" (Isa. 2:3, TLB).

b. The city will occupy an elevated site (Zech. 14:10).

c. The city will be six miles in circumference (Ezek. 48:35). (In the time of Christ the city was about four miles.)

d. The city will be named "Jehovah-Shammah," meaning "the Lord is there" (Ezek. 48:35), and "Jehovah Tsidkenu," meaning, "the Lord our righteousness" (Jer. 23:6; 33:16).

These two will be the final names for God's beloved city. It has been called by many titles in the Bible.

(1) The city of David (2 Sam. 6:12)

(2) The city of the great King (Matt. 5:35)

(3) The Holy City (Isa. 48:2; Matt. 4:5)

(4) Salem (Gen. 14:18)

(5) The city of God (Psa. 46:4; 48:1; 87:3)

(6) The city of the Lord of Hosts (Psa. 48:8)

(7) The city of righteousness (Isa. 1:26)

(8) The city of truth (Zech. 8:3)

(9) The city of the Lord (Isa. 60:14)

(10) The perfection of beauty (Lam. 2:15)

(11) The joy of the whole earth (Lam. 2:15)

Dr. Henry Morris observes:

> In the meantime, with Satan bound for a thousand years, the world will be freed from its most virulent source of evil. The awful physical trauma through which the earth had just passed during the seven years of its tribulation will not only have purged it of its human demonic corruption but also, in considerable measure, of its natural deformities. Thus it will be prepared to serve appropriately as the physical setting of the great millennial messianic kingdom.
>
> The violent earthquakes and upheavals will have leveled all the polluted cities of a sinful world, the better to facilitate the erection of

new, clean, peaceful communities at the beginning of the millennium. These great land movements will also have eliminated the great mountain ranges and islands of the world, billing up the ocean depths and restoring gentle, globally habitable topography and geography all over the world, as it had been in the antediluvian age, before the cataclysmic upheavals of the great Deluge. As Isaiah the prophet had foretold, 'Every valley shall be exalted, and every mountain and hill shall be made low: and the crooked shall be made straight, and the rough places plain' (Isa. 40:4).

Quite probably, the immense tectonic movements, eruptions, and landslides may also have trapped vast quantities of water beneath fresh sedimentary and volcanic deposits, reinstating in partial degree the primeval pressurized reservoirs of 'the great deep,' facilitating the birth of copious artesian springs, including one which will feed the vast river emerging from the millennial temple in Jerusalem (Ezek. 47:1-12; Zech. 14:8).

Thus the seas of the millennial world will be relatively narrow and shallow once again, as in primeval days. Furthermore, the restoration of the vapor canopy should, in large measure, restore the globally pleasant warm climate of the antediluvian period to the earth again. No longer will great atmospheric movements generate violent rainstorms, blizzards, hurricanes, and tornadoes, because the uniform temperatures of the global greenhouse will inhibit air mass movements of more than local extent.

In the original world, the only rains were gentle mists, from localized daily evaporation and precipitation (Gen. 2:6), keeping the world everywhere at comfortable temperatures and humidities, and supporting an abundance of plant and animal life in all regions of the globe. There were no deserts or ice caps or uninhabitable mountain heights. It was all 'very good' (Gen. 1:31). The cataclysm of the great Flood destroyed the beautiful world, but the global upheavals of the great tribulation will restore it, at least in measure.

For example, note Joel's prophecy: "Fear not, O land; be glad and rejoice: for the LORD will do great things. Be not afraid, ye beasts of the field: for the pastures of the wilderness do spring, for the tree beareth her fruit, the fig tree and the vine do yield their strength. Be glad then, ye children of Zion, and rejoice in the LORD your God: for he hath given you the former rain moderately, and he will cause to come down for you the rain, the former rain, and the latter rain in the first month" (Joel 2:21-23; see also Hosea 6:3; and Zech. 10:1).

The redistribution of earth's topography and restoration of its vapor canopy will soon result in an elimination of many, if not all, of its wastelands and deserts: *'The wilderness and the solitary place shall be glad for them; and the desert shall rejoice, and blossom as the rose ... for in the wilderness shall waters break out, and streams in the desert. And the parched ground shall become a pool, and the thirsty land springs of water'* (Isa. 35:1-7; note also Isa. 30:23; 32:15; 51:3; Ezek. 34:26; 36:33-35; etc.).

Somehow there will also come a great healing of the lands and waters of the earth. Before the great Flood, the soils were rich in all needed nutrients, and the drinking waters all came pure and fresh from artesian springs fed from deep underground reservoirs. The destruction of these deep fountains and the devastating land erosion of the great Flood largely destroyed God's primeval terrestrial ecology, leaving the lands depleted and waters polluted. Originally all animals, as well as man, were to derive nourishment only from plant foods (Gen. 1:29, 30), but under the far more rigorous conditions of the postdiluvian environment, God authorized man to eat animal flesh as well (Gen. 9:2-4). Evidently for the same reason many animals also had to become carnivorous.

These conditions were further aggravated during the long centuries after the Flood, with the lands becoming further impoverished and the waters further contaminated, requiring increasingly great expenditures on fertilization and purifications to a climax, with devastating famine conditions and with terrestrial waters so depleted and poisoned that all the animals of the sea had perished. Had such conditions been allowed to persist much longer, all life on earth would soon have become impossible.

In some marvelous way, however, God will use the physical convulsions of that awful period of purging to cleanse the lands and waters of the earth as well as its moral and spiritual climate. Possibly the tectonic and volcanic upheavals, and perhaps even the atmospheric bombardments, will implant new supplies of needed nutrients and trace elements in the soils. Even the multitudes of dead animals and plants in the lands and oceans, as well as the skeletons of the millions of dead men and horses at Armageddon and elsewhere, may well become fertilizing agents for the lands as their remains are scattered far and wide.

The unprecedented global earthquakes and eruptions will trigger vast and violent landslides and showers of dirt and rocks, entrapping tremendous volumes of ocean waters beneath great overburdens of solid materials which will rapidly become pressurized, lithified, and partially sealed.

This will likely produce at last two important effects. In the first place, the sea bottoms will be raised to higher elevations than at present, compensating for the great losses of water caused by the restoration of the atmospheric canopy and by the entrapment of vast volumes beneath the huge landslides and rock showers. The entire crust itself will, to some unknown extent, have shifted and slipped over the earth's mantle, rearranging the various continental plates to a more nearly uniform distribution of land and sea surface areas, but with relatively greater land areas than at present.

Second, this extensive rearrangement of topography and formation of large pressurized subterranean water pockets will facilitate the development of a new terrestrial system of springs and spring-fed rivers, the waters of which will be purified by the processes of heating and percolation. *'I will open rivers in high places, and fountains in the midst of the valleys: I will make the wilderness a pool of water, and the dry land springs of water'* (Isa. 41:18). (*The Revelation Record*, Tyndale House Publishers, pp. 409-411).

■ The four oft-asked questions involved

Many have inquired in regards to these four questions about the Millennium:

A. Will children be born during the Millennium?

"And the streets of the city shall be full of boys and girls playing in the streets thereof" (Zech. 8:5).

In a word, yes! Those believers who survive the Great Tribulation will enter the Millennium in their physical bodies and beget children throughout the age. The earth's population will soar (Jer. 30:20; Ezek. 47:22; Zech. 10:8).

B. What kind of bodies will people have during the Millennium?

In essence, there will be two kinds:

1. Glorified bodies
    a. Those belonging to raptured saints (1 Cor. 15:51-53)
    b. Those belonging to resurrected Old Testament and Tribulational saints (Heb. 11:35; Rev. 20:5, 6)
2. Non-glorified bodies
    a. Those belonging to believers who survive the Great Tribulation and enter the kingdom
    b. Jewish believers (Matt. 25:10)

    c. Gentile believers (Matt. 25:34)

    d. Those belonging to children who will be born during the Millennium (Zech. 8:5)

C. Will people die during the Millennium? If so, why?

Yes, but only for overt rebellion against King Jesus. This is implied by both Isaiah and Zechariah.

    1. Isaiah (Isa. 11:4; 65:20)

    2. Zechariah (Zech. 14:17-19)

D. What language will we speak during the Millennium?

"For then will I turn to the people a pure language, that they may all call upon the name of the Lord, to serve him with one consent" (Zeph. 3:9).

Consider the following possible illustrative suggestion:

Mankind's original language may be likened to a full-length language mirror which perfectly reflected the one looking into it. Thus, Adam and Eve may have possessed both a vocabulary and communication skills we can only imagine today. But at the Tower of Babel, God caused this language mirror to crash down upon humanity (Gen. 11:7-9), breaking into hundreds of smaller and ragged pieces of glass. The various groups at Babel were then allowed to possess one of these pieces (i.e., English, French, Russian, etc.) which still reflected, but were severely limited in their usefulness as compared with the original unbroken mirror.

If this be true, then the pieces will be divinely regathered and reassembled!

As has been previously noted, on four separate occasions heaven's celestial choir, composed of both angels and the redeemed, have been heard sounding forth their glorious voices, praising the Lamb, for *who* He is, and *what* He has done!

1. *"Then I looked, and I heard the voice of many angels around the throne, the living creatures, and the elders; and the number of them was ten thousand times ten thousand, and thousands of thousands, saying with a loud voice: 'Worthy is the Lamb who was slain to receive power and riches and wisdom, and strength and honor and glory and blessing!' And every creature which is in heaven and on the earth and under the earth and such as are in the sea, and all that are in them, I heard saying: Blessing and honor and glory and power be to Him who sits on the throne, and to the Lamb, forever and ever!"* (Rev. 5:11-13)

2. *"So the great dragon was cast out, that serpent of old, called the Devil and Satan, who deceives the whole world; he was cast to the earth, and his angels were cast out with him. Then I heard a loud voice saying in heaven, 'Now salvation, and strength, and the kingdom of our God, and the power of His Christ have come, for the accuser of our brethren, who accused them before our God day and night, has been cast down. And they overcame him by the blood of the Lamb and by the word of their testimony, and they did not love their lives to the death. Therefore rejoice, O heavens, and you who dwell*

in them! Woe to the inhabitants of the earth and the sea! For the devil has come down to you, having great wrath, because he knows that he has a short time'" (Rev. 12:9-12).

3. "Then the seventh angel sounded: And there were loud voices in heaven, saying, 'The kingdoms of this world have become the kingdoms of our Lord and of His Christ, and He shall reign forever and ever!' And the twenty-four elders who sat before God on their thrones fell on their faces and worshiped God, saying, 'We give You thanks, O Lord God Almighty, the One who is and who was and who is to come, because You have taken Your great power and reigned'" (Rev. 11:15-17).

4. "After these things I heard a loud voice of a great multitude in heaven, saying, 'Alleluia! Salvation and glory and honor and power belong to the Lord our God! For true and righteous are His judgments, because He has judged the great harlot who corrupted the earth with her fornication; and He has avenged on her the blood of His servants shed by her.' Again they said, 'Alleluia! Her smoke rises up forever and ever!' And the twenty-four elders and the four living creatures fell down and worshiped God who sat on the throne, saying, 'Amen! Alleluia!' Then a voice came from the throne, saying, 'Praise our God, all you His servants and those who fear Him, both small and great!' And I heard, as it were, the voice of a great multitude, as the sound of many waters and as the sound of mighty thunderings, saying, 'Alleluia! For the Lord God Omnipotent reigns!'" (Rev. 19:1-6).

Charles Wesley may well have had all this in mind when he penned the following hymn:

> O for a thousand tongues to sing
> My great Redeemer's praise,
> The glories of my God and King,
> The triumphs of His grace!
>
> Jesus! The name that charms our fears,
> That bids our sorrows cease,
> 'Tis music in the sinner's ears,
> 'Tis life and health and peace.
>
> He breaks the power of canceled sin,
> He sets the prisoner free;
> His blood can make the foulest clean,
> His blood availed for me.
>
> Hear Him, ye deaf; His praise, ye dumb,
> Your loosened tongues employ;
> Ye blind, behold your Savior come,
> And leap, ye lame, for joy.
>
> My gracious Master and my God,
> Assist me to proclaim,

To spread through all the earth abroad
The honors of Thy name.

■ **In regards to David and Jesus**

What will the Millennium mean to Israel's earthly king, and that of earth's ultimate King?

A. In regards to King David

The Lord Jesus Christ will of course be King supreme, but there are passages that suggest He will graciously choose to rule through a vice-regent, and that vice-regent will be David. Note the following Scripture:

> *"But they shall serve the Lord their God, and David their king, whom I will raise up unto them"* (Jer. 30:9).

Jeremiah wrote those words some 400 years after the death of David, so he could not have been referring to his earthly reign here.

> *"And I will set up one shepherd over them, and he shall feed them, even my servant David; he shall feed them, and he shall be their shepherd"* (Ezek. 34:23). (See also Ezek. 37:24.)

> *"Afterward shall the children of Israel return, and seek the Lord their God, and David their king; and shall fear the Lord and his goodness in the latter days"* (Hos. 3:5).

1. If we take these passages literally, David will once again sit upon the throne of Israel. He will thus be aided in his rule by:

   a. The church (1 Cor. 6:3)

   b. The apostles (Matt. 19:28)

   c. Nobles (Jer. 30:21)

   d. Princes (Isa. 32:1; Ezek. 45:8-9)

   e. Judges (Zech. 3:7; Isa. 1:26)

   George Peters has observed:

   > " ... some writers ... endeavor to make the Theocracy a Republic, but the Theocracy, in the nature of the case, is not a republic. While it is not monarchy in the sense adverted to by Samuel, viz.: of a purely human origin, yet it is a monarchy in the highest sense. It is not a Republic, for the legislative, executive, and judicial power is not potentially lodged in the people, but in God the King; and yet it embraces in itself the elements both of a Monarchy and of a Republic; a Monarchy in that the absolute Sovereignty is lodged in the person of the One great King, to which all the rest are subordinated, but Republican in this, that it embraces a Republican element in preserving the rights of every individual, from the lowest to the highest ... In other words, by a happy combination, Monarchy under divine direction, hence infallible, brings in the blessings that would result from a well-directed ideally Republican form of government, but which the latter can never fully, of itself, realize owing to the depravity and diversity of man." (*Theocratic Kingdom*, Vol. 1, p. 221)

2. The scriptures involved

   Four Old Testament passages predict David will someday serve as a vice-regent of sort during the Millennium.

   a. The testimony of Jeremiah (Jer. 30:9).

   b. The testimony of Hosea (Hos. 3:5).

   c. The testimony of Ezekiel (Ezek. 34:23; 37:24).

3. The significance involved

   a. An everlasting kingdom (2 Sam. 7:16; Psa. 89:3, 4).
      This is to say the throne of David would continue forever! This prophecy will someday be fulfilled in spite of the fact that David's original kingdom was destroyed by the Babylonians in 586 B.C. (Jer. 39, 52).

   b. An everlasting king (Luke 1:32, 33). This is to say King Jesus will sit on David's throne forever!

B. In regards to King Jesus

1. It will totally vindicate His sufferings!

   a. The grief He once endured (Psa. 22:1, 2, 6-8, 14-18; Isa. 53:1-9; Phil. 2:5-8).

   b. The glory He will enjoy (Psa. 24:7-10; Isa. 9:6, 7; Phil. 2:9-11).

2. It will fulfill His two-fold earthly ministry!

   a. He once came as the Lamb of God (John 1:29).

   b. He will come as the Lion of Judah (Rev. 5:5).

3. It will complete His three-fold assignment from the Father!

   a. That of a prophet (Deut. 18:18).

   b. That of a priest (Psa. 110:4).

   c. That of a king (Rev. 19:16).

4. It will finalize the account concerning Him!

   a. The Old Testament records the preparation for the life of Jesus.

      (1) That we might be aware of His coming (Luke 24:27; John 5:39).

      (2) That we might be assured by His coming (Rom. 15:4; 1 Cor. 10:11).

   b. The Gospels record the manifestation of the life of Christ.

      (1) The fact of His birth (Luke 2:1-20).

      (2) The fact of His death (Matt. 27; Mark 15; Luke 23; John 19).

      (3) The fact of His resurrection (Matt. 28; Mark 16; Luke 24; John 20).

      (4) The fact of His ascension (Mark 16:19; Luke 24:51).

   c. The book of Acts records the propagation of the life of Jesus.

      (1) The origin of the early church (Acts 2:1-13).

      (2) The obedience of the early church

(a) Its message (Acts 5:42)

(b) Its ministers—Serving in Jerusalem, Judea, and Samaria, led by Peter, James the half-brother of Christ, John the apostle, Philip the evangelist, and Stephen (Acts 1-12).

(c) Its missionaries—Serving throughout the known world, led by Paul, Barnabas, Timothy, Titus, and Silas (Acts 13-28).

d. The Epistles record the *interpretation* of the life of Jesus.

(1) The reason for His birth (1 Tim. 1:15; Heb. 10:4-7).

(2) The reason for His death (Rom. 4:25a; 5:8, 9; Heb. 2:14, 15).

(3) The reason for His resurrection (Rom. 4:25b; 1 Cor. 15:20).

(4) The reason for His ascension (Rom. 8:34; Heb. 4:14-16; 9:24).

e. The book of Revelation records the *coronation* of King Jesus.

This glorious event is referred to no less than five times in scripture's final book:

"Then the seventh angel sounded: And there were loud voices in heaven, saying, 'The kingdoms of this world have become the kingdoms of our Lord and of His Christ, and He shall reign forever and ever!' And the twenty-four elders who sat before God on their thrones fell on their faces and worshiped God" (Rev. 11:15, 16).

"Then I heard a loud voice saying in heaven, Now salvation, and strength, and the kingdom of our God, and the power of His Christ have come, for the accuser of our brethren, who accused them before our God day and night, has been cast down" (Rev. 12:10).

"They sing the song of Moses, the servant of God, and the song of the Lamb, saying: 'Great and marvelous are Your works, Lord God Almighty! Just and true are Your ways, O King of the saints!'" (Rev. 15:3)

"These will make war with the Lamb, and the Lamb will overcome them, for He is Lord of lords and King of kings; and those who are with Him are called, chosen, and faithful" (Rev. 17:14).

"Now I saw heaven opened, and behold, a white horse. And He who sat on him was called Faithful and True, and in righteousness He judges and makes war. And He has on His robe and on His thigh a name written: KING OF KINGS AND LORD OF LORDS" (Rev. 19:11, 16).

It should be observed that this passage speaks of many crowns!

Matthew Bridges' beautiful hymn, *Crown Him With Many Crowns*, celebrates this great future event in a majestic musical format:

Crown Him with many crowns, the Lamb upon His throne;
Hark! How the heav'nly anthem drowns all music but its own!

Awake, my soul and sing of Him Who died for thee,
And hail Him as thy matchless King through all eternity.

Crown Him the Lord of love! Behold His hands and side—
Rich wounds, yet visible above, in beauty glorified.
No angel in the sky can fully bear that sight,
But downward bends His wond'ring eye at mysteries so bright.

Crown Him the Lord of life! Who triumphed o'er the grave,
Who rose victorious in the strife for those He came to save.
His glories now we sing, who died, and rose on high,
Who died eternal life to bring, and lives that death may die.

Crown Him the Lord of heav'n! One with the Father known,
One with the Spirit through Him giv'n from yonder glorious throne,
To Thee be endless praise, for Thou for us hast died;
Be Thou, O Lord, through endless days adored and magnified.

■ **In regards to the Shekinah glory cloud of God**

Dr. Tommy Ice observes:

"The Shekinah glory is the visible manifestation of the presence of God, often showing up in the form of a cloud, light, fire, or combinations of these. The Jewish rabbis coined this extrabiblical expression. Shekinah is a form of a Hebrew word that literally means "he caused to dwell," signifying that when God's glory appeared in this way it was a divine visitation of the presence or dwelling of God. In order to see the significance of the Shekinah glory for future Bible prophecy, a survey of past appearances is necessary.

"The following events are believed to be manifestations of the Shekinah glory in history:

A. The Garden of Eden—The Lord's presence in the garden and the flaming sword (Gen. 3:8, 23, 24)

B. The Abrahamic Covenant—The flaming torch that passed between the sacrificial pieces (Gen. 15:12-18).

C. The burning bush—The burning that did not consume the bush (Exod. 3:1-5)

D. The exodus—The pillar of cloud by day and the pillar of fire by night (Exod. 13:21, 22; 14:19, 20, 24; 16:6; 6-12).

E. Mount Sinai—The Ten Commandments written by the finger of God; thunder, lightning, and a thick cloud (Exod. 19:16-20; 24:15-18; Deut. 5:22-27)

F. The special meeting with Moses—The afterglow on Moses' face as a result of his meeting with the Lord (Exod. 33:17-23; 34:5-9, 29-35).

G. The Tabernacle and the Ark of the Covenant—The glory cloud presence often associated with these items (Exod. 29:42-46; 40:34-38).

H. The book of Leviticus—The authentication of the law and residence in the holy of Holies (Lev. 9).

I. The book of Numbers—The Shekinah glory rendered judgment for sin and disobedience (Num. 13:30-14:45; 16:1-50; 20:5-13).

J. The period of Joshua and Judges—The continued dwelling of the Shekinah glory in the tabernacle (1 Sam. 4:21, 22).

K. The Solomonic Temple—The transfer of the Shekinah glory from the tabernacle to the temple (2 Chron. 5:2-7:3).

L. The departure in Ezekiel—Ezekiel watches the Shekinah glory depart the temple in preparation for judgment upon the nation (Ezek. 1:28; 3:12, 23; 8:3, 4; 9:3; 10:4, 18, 19; 11:22, 23).

M. The second temple—The Shekinah glory was not present, but a promise was given that it will be greater in the future than in the past (Hag. 2:3, 9).

N. The appearance to the shepherds—The glory of the Lord shone around them (Luke 2:8, 9).

O. The star of Bethlehem—The star or glory-cloud that guided the magi to Jesus (Matt. 2:1-12).

P. Jesus: The glory of the Lord—The incarnation was a manifestation for the Shekinah glory (John 1:1-14).

Q. The transfiguration—the Shekinah glory appears to the three disciples (Matt. 17:1-8; Mark 9:2-8; Luke 9:28-36; Heb. 1:1-3; 2 Peter 1:16-18).

R. The book of Acts—the cloven tongues of fire on Pentecost and the blinding light shone upon Paul at his conversion (Acts 2: 1-3; 9:3-8; 22:6-11; 26:13-18).

S. The revelation—Jesus Christ is dressed in the Shekinah glory (Rev. 1:12-16).

"The following is an overview of future events relating to the Shekinah glory:

A. The Tribulation—The Shekinah glory is connected with the bowl judgments (Rev. 15:8).

B. The Second Coming of Christ—The Shekinah glory is the sign of the Son of Man and the cloud upon which He returns (Matt. 16:27; 24:30; Mark 13:26; Luke 21:27).

C. The Millennium—The Shekinah glory will be present in its greatest manifestation in history because of Christ's physical presence on earth (Ezek. 43:1-7; 44:1, 2; Isa. 4:5, 6; 11:10; 35:1, 2; 40:5; 58:8, 9; 60:1-3; Zech. 2:4, 5; 11:10)."
(*Fast Facts On Bible Prophecy*, Tommy Ice, Harvest House, pp. 193-195)

Undoubtedly the saddest appearance of the Shekinah glory was witnessed by Ezekiel around 586 B.C. just prior to the Babylonian destruction of the temple and Jerusalem. The heartbroken prophet watches as it hovers over:

A. The Ark of the Covenant (Ezek. 10:18).

B. The City of Jerusalem (Ezek. 11:23).

C. The Eastern Gate (Ezek. 10:19).

D. The Mount of Olives (Ezek. 11:23).

From there it disappears into the heavens. At that point one could write the word ICHABOD (meaning "the glory has departed") over the skies of Jerusalem!

However, inasmuch as Ezekiel was forced to see God's glory depart, he will be the first to see it return!

"And the glory of Jehovah came into the house by the way of the gate whose prospect is toward the east. And the Spirit took me up, and brought me into the inner court; and, behold, the glory of Jehovah filled the house" (Ezek. 43:4, 5).

The Eastern Gate will then be forever shut signifying that God's glory would never leave Jerusalem again (Ezek. 44:2).

■ **In regards to the temple**

The biblical order—The Millennial temple is the last of great scriptural temples. These are:

A. Physical buildings

1. The Tabernacle was built by Moses around 1445 B.C.

"And it came to pass in the first month in the second year, on the first day of the month, that the tabernacle was reared up... Then a cloud covered the tent of the congregation, and the glory of the LORD filled the tabernacle... For the cloud of the LORD was upon the tabernacle by day, and fire was on it by night, in the sight of all the house of Israel, throughout all their journeys" (Exod. 40:17, 34, 38).

2. The first temple was built by Solomon around 959 B.C.

"So was ended all the work that king Solomon made for the house of the LORD. And Solomon brought in the things which David his father had dedicated; even the silver, and the gold, and the vessels, did he put among the treasures of the house of the LORD" (1 Kings 7:51).

3. The second temple was begun by Zerubbabel around 516 B.C. and later completed by King Herod around 10 B. C.

"And the elders of the Jews builded, and they prospered through the prophesying of Haggai the prophet and Zechariah the son of Iddo. And they builded, and finished it according to the commandment of the God of Israel, and according to the commandment of Cyrus, and Darius, and Artaxerxes king of Persia. And this house was finished on the third day of the month Adar, which was in the sixth year of the reign of Darius the king" (Ezra 6:14, 15).

4. The third temple will be built (perhaps by the Antichrist) following the Rapture of the church.

"And there was given me a reed like unto a rod: and the angel stood, saying, Rise, and measure the temple of God, and the altar, and them that worship therein. But the court

which is without the temple leave out, and measure it not; for it is given unto the Gentiles: and the holy city shall they tread under foot forty and two months" (Rev. 11:1, 2).

5. The Millennial temple will be built by Christ Himself at the beginning of the Millennium.

"And speak unto him, saying, Thus speaketh the LORD of hosts, saying, Behold the man whose name is The BRANCH; and he shall grow up out of his place, and he shall build the temple of the LORD: Even he shall build the temple of the LORD; and he shall bear the glory, and shall sit and rule upon his throne; and he shall be a priest upon his throne: and the counsel of peace shall be between them both" (Zech. 6:12, 13).

   a. The Millennial Temple will be the most massive of all the temples.

   b. It will be the only temple having its own river.

   "In connection with the temple, Ezekiel predicted that there will be a great river flowing from the temple to the south, having sufficient volume so that one will not be able to wade across (47:3-6). The river banks will be covered with trees (vv. 7-9), and the river will have fish and other living creatures in it. Fresh water will apparently replace the salty Dead Sea, and the river will continue to flow to the south of Israel until it reaches the Gulf of Arabah." (*The Truth About The Millennium*, Harvest House, p. 27)

   c. It will be the only temple built by Jesus Himself (Zech. 6:11-13).

   d. It will be the only temple to service both the church and Israel.

   e. It will be the most durable of all, lasting for 1000 years.

   f. It will (apparently) never be destroyed (as were the other temples), but quietly phased out by God at the end of the Millennium (Rev. 21:22).

   g. It will be the most glorious of all the temples (Hag. 2:9).

B. Fleshly and spiritual buildings

1. The body of Jesus prepared by the Father at Bethlehem

"Wherefore when he cometh into the world, he saith, Sacrifice and offering thou wouldest not, but a body hast thou prepared me" (Heb. 10:5).

The wicked Pharisees were confused concerning this temple:

"So the Jews answered and said to Him, 'What sign do You show to us, since You do these things?' Jesus answered and said to them, 'Destroy this temple, and in three days I will raise it up.' Then the Jews said, 'It has taken forty-six years to build this temple, and will You raise it up in three days?' But He was speaking of the temple of His body" (John 2:18-21).

   a. The bride/body/temple of Christ, prepared by the Holy Spirit at Pentecost (Acts 2:1; Eph. 2:19-22; 5:30; 1 Cor. 6:15; 12:12-14)

   b. The body of the believer prepared by the Holy Spirit at the moment of conversion.

"Know ye not that ye are the temple of God, and that the Spirit of God dwelleth in you?" (1 Cor. 3:16)

2. Its holy oblation

   Palestine will be redistributed among the twelve tribes of Israel during the Millennium. The land itself will be divided into three areas. Seven tribes will occupy the northern area and five the southern ground. Between these two areas there is a section called "the holy oblation," that is, that portion of ground which is set apart for the Lord.

3. Its priesthood

   On four specific occasions we are told that the sons of Zadok will be assigned the priestly duties (Ezek. 40:46; 43:19; 44:15; 48:11). Zadok was a high priest in David's time (the eleventh in descent from Aaron). His loyalty to the king was unwavering. Because of this, he was promised that his seed would have this glorious opportunity (1 Sam. 2:35; 1 Kings 2:27, 35).

4. Its prince

   In his description of the temple, Ezekiel refers to a mysterious "prince" some seventeen times. Whoever he is, he occupies a very important role in the temple itself, apparently holding an intermediary place between the people and the priesthood. We are sure that he is not Christ, since he prepares a sin offering for himself (Ezek. 45:22), and is married and has sons (Ezek. 46:16). Some suggest that the prince is from the seed of King David, and that he will be to David what the false prophet was to the Antichrist.

5. Its negative aspects

   Several articles and objects present in the temples of Moses, Solomon, and Herod will be absent from the millennial temple.

   a. There will be no veil.

      This was torn in two from top to bottom (Mt. 27:51) and will not reappear in this temple. Thus there will be no barrier to keep man from the glory of God.

   b. There will be no table of shewbread.

      This will not be needed, for the Living Bread Himself will be present.

   c. There will be no lampstands.

      These will not be needed either, since the Light of the World Himself will personally shine forth.

   d. There will be no Ark of the Covenant.

      This will also be unnecessary, since the Shekinah Glory Himself will hover over all the world, as the glory cloud once did over the Ark.

   e. The east gate will be closed. Observe the words of Ezekiel—

      "This gate shall be shut, and no man shall enter in by it; because the Lord, the

God of Israel, hath entered in by it, therefore it shall be shut" (Ezek. 44:2).

This gate, it has been suggested, will remain closed for the following reasons:

a.   This will be the gate by which the Lord Jesus Christ enters the temple. As a mark of honor to an eastern king, no person could enter the gate by which the king entered.

b.   It was from the eastern gate that the glory of God departed for the last time in the Old Testament (Ezek. 10:18, 19).

By sealing the gate, God reminds all those within that His glory will never again depart from His people. A history of this gate makes interesting reading:

> It is both the most famous and important of Jerusalem's gates. It overlooks the Kidron Valley and faces the rising sun. The crusaders called it the Golden Gate. Entrance through this walled gate leads to the Beautiful Gate of the temple itself; see Acts 3:2. Tradition says sections of this gate were donated by the Queen of Sheba. The Arabs call this the Eternal northern portal, the Gate of Repentance, and the southern portal, the Gate of Mercy. It is mentioned by Nehemiah (3:29).

■ **In regards to a possible heavenly tabernacle/temple**

A.   Is there a tabernacle in heaven?

It would appear an actual tabernacle does indeed exist in heaven. This is testified to by the following:

1.   Moses (Exod. 25:9, 40; Num. 8:4)

2.   David (1 Chron. 28:11, 12)

3.   Isaiah (Isa. 6:1-8)

4.   Stephen (Acts 7:44)

5.   Author of Hebrews (Heb. 8:2, 5; 9:11, 23, 24)

6.   John the Apostle himself (Rev. 11:19; 14:15; 15:5, 6, 8; 16:1, 17)

However, in the eternal New Jerusalem the tabernacle is not to be seen (Rev. 21:22).

B.   Why is it there?

At least four reasons have been suggested:

1.   To serve as a pattern for both the earthly tabernacle and temple

a.   The tabernacle (Exod. 25:9, 40; Num. 8:4)

b.   The temple (1 Chron. 28:11, 12)

2.   To serve as a final stop for angels enroute to performing their assignments on earth (Rev. 15:5-8)

3.   To serve as a center for our prayers (Rev. 5:8; 8:3, 4)

4.   To serve as that special place where Christ could pour out His shed blood. Some, but not all, would offer this as the fourth reason because of the following:

a. Jesus told the disciples that His resurrected body consisted of flesh and bone (Luke 24:39). He did not refer to blood.

b. Jesus told Mary Magdalene to inform the disciples that He was ascending to the Father (John 20:17).

c. The book of Hebrews (some believe) suggests the reason for this initial Easter Sunday ascension was to sprinkle His blood upon the heavenly Ark of the Covenant Mercy Seat (Heb. 6:18-20; 8:1, 2; 9:11, 12; Rev. 11:19; 15:5).

C. How does John describe the tabernacle?

"Then one of the four living creatures gave to the seven angels seven golden bowls full of the wrath of God who lives forever and ever. The temple was filled with smoke from the glory of God and from His power, and no one was able to enter the temple till the seven plagues of the seven angels were completed" (Rev. 15:7-8).

John Phillips writes:

"Since Calvary, the way into the holiest in heaven has been opened to all, because the blood of Christ has blazed a highway to the heart of God. But now, for a brief spell, that royal road is barred. God's wrath, once poured upon His Son on man's behalf is to be outpoured again.

The world which crucified the Lamb and which now has crowned its rebellions with the worship of the beast, is to be judged to the full. So bright glory burns within the temple, filling it with smoke and standing guard at the door. The way into the holiest is barred again for a while." (*Exploring Revelation*, Moody Press, 1974, p. 198)

■ **In regards to its sacrifices**

As we have already seen, several pieces of furniture in the Old Testament temple will be missing in the millennial edifice. However, the brazen altar of sacrifice will again be present. There are at least four Old Testament prophecies which speak of animal sacrifices in the millennial temple: Isa. 56:6, 7; 60:7; Zech. 14:16-21. But why the need of these animal blood sacrifices during the golden age of the Millennium?

To answer this, one must attempt to project himself into this fabulous future period. Here is an age of no sin, sorrow, sufferings, sickness, Satan, or separation. During the Millennium even the vocabulary will be different. For example, today respectable and decent society shuns certain filthy four-letter words, and well they should!

This will doubtless also be practiced during the Millennium, but how the words will change! Below is a sampling of some four-letter "cuss words" to be shunned during the thousand-year reign: *fear, pain, jail, hate, dope.*

These words are so much a part of our sinful society that it is utterly impossible to avoid or ignore them! The point is simply this: during the Millennium millions of children will be born and reared by saved Israelite and Gentile parents who survived the Tribulation. In spite of their perfect environment, however, these "kingdom kids" will need the new birth. As sons and daughters of Adam they, too, as all others, will require eternal salvation (Rom. 3:23; John 3:3). But how can these children be reached? What object lessons can be used? Here is a generation which will grow up without knowing fear, experiencing pain, witnessing hatred, taking dope, or seeing a jail. This is one reason that the sacrificial system will be reinstituted during the Millennium. These sacrifices will function as:

A. A reminder to all of the necessity of the new birth

B. An object lesson of the costliness of salvation

C. An example of the awfulness of sin

D. An illustration of the holiness of God

Imagine the following conversation in the millennial temple as a group of school children from Berlin visit the Holy City and witness the slaying of a lamb.

> *Kurt:* Sir, why did you kill that little lamb?
>
> *Priest:* Because the sin in our hearts must be paid for by innocent blood.
>
> *Kurt:* Oh, then did that lamb die to pay for my sin?
>
> *Priest:* No, Kurt, it is simply a reminder that God's Lamb did once died for all our sins!
>
> *Kurt:* Why, I didn't know God ever had a Lamb. Whatever happened to God's Lamb?
>
> *Priest:* Kurt, you've already seen God's Lamb?
>
> *Kurt:* When did we see God's Lamb? I don't remember seeing God's Lamb.
>
> *Priest:* Okay, let me ask you a question. What did your group do this morning?
>
> *Kurt:* Oh, we had a wonderful time! We visited the palace and saw Prince Immanuel, King Jesus Himself!
>
> *Priest:* (Slowly, with great emphasis) Then, Kurt, you saw God's Lamb! Kurt, you've already seen God's Lamb!

Can you imagine the eyes of those German children bulging and their small chins dropping in amazement as they are told this tremendous fact? This is perhaps the Father's most precious secret: that His blessed Son, the Mighty Monarch of the Millennium, once came as the Lowly Lamb of Bethlehem!

Dora Greenwell's beautiful hymn, *"My Savior"* serves as a fitting summary of His past pain on the cross and His future reign on the throne!

> *I am not skilled to understand*
> *What God hath willed, what God hath planned;*
> *I only know that at His right hand*
> *Is One Who is my Savior!*
>
> *I take Him at His word indeed;*
> *"Christ died for sinners"—this I read;*
> *For in my heart I find a need*
> *Of Him to be my Savior!*

That He should leave His place on high
And come for sinful man to die,
You count it strange? So once did I,
Before I knew my Savior!

And oh, that He fulfilled may see
The travail of His soul in me,
And with His work contented be,
As I with my dear Savior!

Yea, living, dying, let me bring
My strength, my solace from this Spring;
That He Who lives to be my King
Once died to be my Savior!

▶ EVENT 13 THE FINAL REVOLT OF SATAN

■ **In regards to the record involved**

"*And when the thousand years are expired, Satan shall be loosed out of his prison, and shall go out to deceive the nations which are in the four quarters of the earth, Gog and Magog, to gather them together to battle: the number of whom is as the sand of the sea. And they went up on the breadth of the earth, and compassed the camp of the saints about, and the beloved city*" (Rev. 20:7-9).

Dr. J. Vernon McGee writes the following words concerning these verses:

> When the late Dr. Chafer (founder of Dallas Theological Seminary) was once asked why God loosed Satan after he once had him bound, he replied, "If you will tell me why God let him loose in the first place, I will tell you why God lets him loose the second time." Apparently Satan is released at the end of the Millennium to reveal that the ideal conditions of the kingdom, under the personal reign of Christ, do not change the human heart. This reveals the enormity of the enmity of man against God. Scripture is accurate when it describes the heart as "desperately wicked" and incurably so. Man is totally depraved. The loosing of Satan at the end of the 1,000 years proves it. (*Reveling Through Revelation*, pp. 74, 75)

■ **In regards to the rebels involved**

We have already discussed the purposes accomplished by the sacrifices during the Millennium. Apparently millions of maturing children will view these sacrifices and hear the tender salvation plea of the priests, but will stubbornly harden their sinful hearts. The fact that earth's mighty King at Jerusalem once bled as a lowly lamb at Calvary will mean absolutely nothing to them. Outwardly they will conform, but inwardly they will despise.

Finally, at the end of the Millennium, the world will be offered for the first time in ten centuries "a choice, and not an echo." Millions will make a foolish and fatal choice.

Dr. J. Dwight Pentecost quotes F. C. Jennings, who writes:

> Has human nature changed, at least apart from sovereign grace? Is the carnal mind at last in friendship with God? Have a thousand years of absolute power and absolute benevolence, both in unchecked activity, done away with all war forever and forever? These questions must be marked by a practical test. Let Satan be loosed once more from his prison. Let him range once more earth's smiling fields that he knew of old. He saw them last soaked with blood and flooded with tears, the evidence and accompaniments of his own reign; he sees them now "laughing with abundance." But as he pursues his way further from Jerusalem, the center of this blessedness, these tokens become fainter, until, in the far-off "corner of the earth," they cease altogether, for he finds myriads who have instinctively shrunk from close contact with that holy center, and are not unprepared once more to be deceived. (*Things to Come*, Dunham Press, 1959, p. 549)

▪ **In regards to the results involved**

A. This insane and immoral insurrection is doomed to utter and complete failure. As a war correspondent, the Apostle John duly records this final battle:

> "And fire came down from God out of heaven, and devoured them. And the devil that deceived them was cast into the lake of fire and brimstone, where the beast and the false prophet are, and shall be tormented day and night for ever and ever" (Rev. 20:9-10).

Obviously, this battle referred to as Gog and Magog is not the same as the one in Ezekiel 38-39.

Dr. J. Vernon McGee writes concerning this:

> Because the rebellion is labeled "Gog and Magog," many Bible students identify it with Gog and Magog of Ezekiel 38 and 39. This, of course, is not possible, for the conflicts described are not parallel as to time, place, or participants—only the name is the same. The invasion from the north by Gog and Magog of Ezekiel 38 and 39 breaks the false peace of the Antichrist and causes him to show his hand in the midst of the Great Tribulation. That rebellion of the godless forces from the north will have made such an impression on mankind that after 1,000 years the last rebellion of man bears the same label. We have passed through a similar situation in this century. World War I was so devastating that when war again broke out in Europe, it was labeled again "World War," but differentiated by the number 2. Now World War III is being predicted! Likewise the war in Ezekiel 38 and 39 is Gog and Magog I, while this reference in verse 8 is Gog and Magog II. (*Thru the Revelation*, p. 77)

B. Note the difference between those two battles

1. The Gog and Magog of Ezekiel

"Son of man, set thy face against Gog of the land of Magog . . ." (38:2).
This battle occurs during the middle of the Great Tribulation.

  a. It is led by Gog (Russian leader?)
  b. The attack comes from the North.
  c. It involves the entire land of Israel.
  d. It is utterly crushed by God.

2. The Gog and Magog of Revelation

    "And when the thousand years are expired, Satan shall be loosed out of his prison … And shall go out to deceive the nations which are in the four quarters of the earth, Gog and Magog, to gather them together to battle: the number of whom is the sand of the sea" (Rev. 20:7, 8).

    This battle occurs at the end of the Millennium.

    a. It is led by Satan himself.
    b. The attack comes from all directions.
    c. It involves the city of Jerusalem.
    d. It is utterly crushed by God.

■ **In regards to the reader involved**

All believers should often remind themselves that we are not fighting *for* a victory, but rather *from* a victory! The final battle has been fought! The war is over! Jesus wins! So then, what should be our game plan until then? Two hymn writers, Reginald Heber and George Heath, provide the answer in beautiful musical fashion:

The Son of God Goes Forth to War
(Reginald Heber)

The Son of God goes forth to war, A kingly crown to gain;
His blood-red banner streams afar: Who follows in His train?
Who best can drink his cup of woe, Triumphant over pain,
Who patient bears his cross below, He follows in His train.

The martyr first, whose eagle eye, Could pierce beyond the grave,
Who saw his Master in the sky, And called on Him to save—
Like Him, with pardon on his tongue, In midst of mortal pain,
He prayed for them that did the wrong: Who follows in his train?

A glorious band, the chosen few, On whom the Spirit came,
Twelve valiant saints, their hope they knew, And mocked the cross and flame—
They met the tyrant's brandished steel, The lion's gory mane,
They bowed their necks the death to feel: Who follows in their train?

A noble army, men and boys, The matron and the maid,
Around the Savior's throne rejoice, In robes of light arrayed –
They climbed the steep ascent of heav'n, Thru peril, toil, and pain:
O God, to us may grace be giv'n, To follow in their train!

My Soul, Be on Thy Guard
(George Heath)

My soul, be on thy guard;
Ten thousand foes arise;
The hosts of sin are pressing hard
To draw thee from the skies.

O watch, and fight, and pray;
The battle ne'er give o'er;
Renew it boldly every day,
And help divine implore.

Never think the victory won,
Nor lay thine armor down;
The work of faith will not be done,
Till thou obtain the crown.

Fight on, my soul, till death
Shall bring thee to thy God;
He'll take thee, at thy parting breath,
To his divine abode.

EVENT 14 THE GREAT WHITE THRONE JUDGMENT

"Rejoice, O young man, in your youth, And let your heart cheer you in the days of your youth; Walk in the ways of your heart, And in the sight of your eyes; But know that for all these God will bring you into judgment" (Eccles. 11:9).

"For God will bring every work into judgment, Including every secret thing, Whether good or evil" (Eccles. 12:14).

"But I say to you that for every idle word men may speak, they will give account of it in the day of judgment" (Matt. 12:36).

"And as it is appointed for men to die once, but after this the judgment" (Heb. 9:27).

"And the angels who did not keep their proper domain, but left their own abode, He has reserved in everlasting chains under darkness for the judgment of the great day" (Jude 6).

INTRODUCTION

A prophet and an apostle were permitted to witness this, the grandfather of all judgments. Thus, these two divinely appointed men serve as court reporters. Here is that description as follows:

- ▪ **In regards to the judicial proceedings**
  - A. According to Daniel the prophet

    "I watched till thrones were put in place, and the Ancient of Days was seated; His garment was white as snow, and the hair of His head was like pure wool. His throne was a fiery flame, Its wheels a burning fire; a fiery stream issued and came forth from before Him. A thousand thousands ministered to Him; ten thousand times ten thousand stood before Him. The court was seated, and the books were opened" (Dan. 7:9, 10).

  - B. According to John the apostle

    "Then I saw a great white throne and Him who sat on it, from whose face the earth and the heaven fled away. And there was found no place for them. And I saw the dead, small and great, standing before God, and books were opened. And another book was opened, which is the Book of Life. And the dead were judged according to their works, by the things which were written in the books. The sea gave up the dead who were in it, and Death and Hades delivered up the dead who were in them. And they were judged, each one according to his works. Then Death and Hades were cast into the lake of fire. This is the second death. And anyone not found written in the Book of Life was cast into the lake of fire" (Rev. 20:11-15).

- ▪ **In regards to the Judge**

  He is none other than the Honorable Lord Jesus Christ!

  "For the Father judges no one, but has committed all judgment to the Son, and has given Him authority to execute judgment also, because He is the Son of Man" (John 5:22, 27).

  "Him God raised up on the third day, and showed Him openly, and He commanded us to preach to the people, and to testify that it is He who was ordained by God to be Judge of the living and the dead" (Acts 10:40, 42).

  "...because He has appointed a day on which He will judge the world in righteousness by the Man whom He has ordained. He has given assurance of this to all by raising Him from the dead" (Acts 17:31).

  " I charge you therefore before God and the Lord Jesus Christ, who will judge the living and the dead at His appearing and His kingdom" (2 Tim. 4:1).

- ▪ **In regards to the jury—five sets of books**
  - A. The book of conscience

Although man's conscience is not an infallible guide, he will nevertheless be condemned by those occasions when he deliberately violated it.

"…who, being past feeling, have given themselves over to lewdness, to work all uncleanness with greediness" (Eph. 4:19).

"…speaking lies in hypocrisy, having their own conscience seared with a hot iron" (1 Tim. 4:2).

"To the pure all things are pure, but to those who are defiled and unbelieving nothing is pure; but even their mind and conscience are defiled" (Titus 1:15).

"Let us draw near with a true heart in full assurance of faith, having our hearts sprinkled from an evil conscience and our bodies washed with pure water" (Heb. 10:22).

"…for when Gentiles, who do not have the law, by nature do the things in the law, these, although not having the law, are a law to themselves, who show the work of the law written in their hearts, their conscience also bearing witness, and between themselves their thoughts accusing or else excusing them" (Rom. 2:14-15).

B. The book of words

"But I say to you that for every idle word men may speak, they will give account of it in the day of judgment. For by your words you will be justified, and by your words you will be condemned" (Matt. 12:36, 37).

"He who rejects Me, and does not receive My words, has that which judges him—the word that I have spoken will judge him in the last day" (John 12:48).

C. The book of secret works

"In the day when God shall judge the secrets of men by Jesus Christ according to my gospel" (Rom. 2:16).

"For God shall bring every work into judgment, with every secret thing, whether it be good, or whether it be evil" (Eccles. 12:14).

D. The book of public works

"For the Son of man shall come in the glory of his Father with his angels; and then he shall reward every man according to his works" (Matt. 16:27).

" … whose end shall be according to their works" (2 Cor. 11:15).

E. The book of life

(See Exod. 32:32, 33; Psa. 69:28; Dan. 12:1; Phil. 4:3; Rev. 3:5; 13:8; 17:8; 20:12, 15; 21:27; 22:19.)

Note: There is controversy, and indeed some confusion, concerning these verses. The common theory is that two books are described, namely, the book of human life and the book of everlasting life. Thus:

1. Verses referring to human life: Exod. 32:31-33; Psa. 69:28

2. Verses referring to eternal life: Dan. 12:1; Phil. 4:3; Rev. 3:5; 13:8; 17:8; 20:12, 15; 21:27

- **In regards to the judged**

  Here it must be observed that this judgment is not the same as the Judgment Seat of Christ. Only the saved will appear before this judgment, the purpose being to determine the amount of rewards each believer will receive.

  However, only the unsaved will stand before the Great White Throne Judgment, the purpose being to determine the amount of punishment each unbeliever will receive.

  Note: Perhaps the most troubling thing to be experienced at this time will occur for all members belonging to the major world religions, along with the various cults of Christianity, to suddenly with horror realize the very founders of these false religious systems are standing alongside them, awaiting the same fate as all members!

- **In regards to the judgment**

  "The eternal lake of fire" (Rev. 20:14, 15; Matt. 25:41, 46)

  "Many will say to me in that day, Lord, Lord, have we not prophesied in thy name? and in thy name have cast out devils? And in thy name done many wonderful works? And then will I profess unto them, I never knew you: depart from me, ye that work iniquity" (Matt. 7:22, 23).

  "Then shall he say also unto them on the left hand, Depart from me, ye cursed, into everlasting fire, prepared for the devil and his angels: And these shall go away into everlasting punishment: but the righteous into life eternal" (Matt. 25:41, 46).

EVENT 15 THE DESTRUCTION OF THIS PRESENT EARTH AND HEAVEN

INTRODUCTION

No less than six biblical sources give testimony to this future fact.

- **In regards to the *who* involved**

  A. According to David

  "Of old You laid the foundation of the earth, and the heavens are the work of Your hands. They will perish, but You will endure; yes, they will all grow old like a garment; like a cloak You will change them, and they will be changed" (Psa. 102:25, 26).

  B. According to Isaiah

  "Lift up your eyes to the heavens, and look on the earth beneath. For the heavens will vanish away like smoke, the earth will grow old like a garment, and those who dwell in it will die in like manner; but My salvation will be forever, and My righteousness will not be abolished" (Isa. 51:6).

C. According to Jesus

"Heaven and earth will pass away, but My words will by no means pass away" (Matt. 24:35).

D. According to Peter

"But the day of the Lord will come as a thief in the night, in which the heavens will pass away with a great noise, and the elements will melt with fervent heat; both the earth and the works that are in it will be burned up. Therefore, since all these things will be dissolved, what manner of persons ought you to be in holy conduct and godliness, looking for and hastening the coming of the day of God, because of which the heavens will be dissolved, being on fire, and the elements will melt with fervent heat?" (2 Peter 3:10-12).

E. According to the author of Hebrews

"And: 'You, Lord, in the beginning laid the foundation of the earth, and the heavens are the work of Your hands. They will perish, but You remain; and they will all grow old like a garment; like a cloak You will fold them up, and they will be changed. But You are the same, and Your years will not fail'" (Heb. 1:10-12).

F. According to John

"Do not love the world or the things in the world. If anyone loves the world, the love of the Father is not in him. For all that is in the world—the lust of the flesh, the lust of the eyes, and the pride of life—is not of the Father but is of the world. And the world is passing away, and the lust of it; but he who does the will of God abides forever" (1 John 2:15-17)

■ **In regards to the *how* involved**

Dr. Henry Morris writes the following in regards to 2 Peter 3:10:

The day of the Lord will be terminated at the end of the Millennium with the long-awaited renovation of the old earth by fire. The earth will not be annihilated, any more than it was annihilated at the time of the Flood, but will be completely changed and purified, made new, as it were. All the elements themselves have been under God's curse (Gen. 3:17-19), so they must be burned up, along with the vast evidences of decay and death now preserved as fossils in the earth's crust. Possibly this will be a global atomic fission reaction (note the word 'dissolved' in 2 Peter 3: 11), or else simply a vast explosive disintegration involving transformation of the chemical energy of the elements into heat, light and sound energy. What remains after the global fiery disintegration will be other forms of energy so that, although God's principle of conservation still holds, the solid earth will seem to have 'fled away' (Rev. 20:11). *The Defender's Study Bible*, World Publishing, Inc., Grand Rapids, Michigan, 1995, p. 1407).

■ **In regards to the *why* involved**

At this stage in the Bible the final rebellion has been put down, the false prophet, the Antichrist, and the devil himself are all in the lake of fire forever, and the wicked dead have been judged. In light of this, why the necessity for this awesome destruction? To help illustrate, consider the following: let us suppose that some crackpot breaks into the money vaults of Fort Knox, Kentucky, and begins pouring filthy crankcase oil on the stacked bars of gold and silver. Upon leaving, however, he is caught, tried, and confined to prison. The authorities thereupon close their books on the Fort Knox case. But the gunk on the gold and silver remains. In this illustration, the vandal would represent the devil, the crankcase oil would stand for sin, and the gold and silver for God's perfect creation. God will someday arrest the devil, of course, and forever confine him to prison. But what about the oily sin stains that remain on his gold and silver creation? To solve the problem, God does what the Fort Knox authorities might consider doing—he purges the stains in a fiery wash. And it works. For the hotter the flame, the more rapidly the oil evaporates and the brighter the gold becomes. God will someday do to creation what He did to His beloved Israel in the Old Testament: *"Behold, I have refined thee... I have chosen thee in the furnace of affliction"* (Isa. 48:10).

EVENT 16 THE CREATION OF A NEW EARTH & HEAVEN

"For behold, I create new heavens and a new earth; and the former shall not be remembered or come to mind" (Isa. 65:17).

"'For as the new heavens and the new earth which I will make shall remain before Me,' says the LORD, *'So shall your descendants and your name remain'"* (Isa. 66:22).

"Nevertheless we, according to His promise, look for new heavens and a new earth in which righteousness dwells" (2 Peter 3:13).

"Now I saw a new heaven and a new earth, for the first heaven and the first earth had passed away. Also there was no more sea" (Rev. 21:1).

- ▪ **In regards to the chronological order involved**

   The New World will be the final of eight biblical worlds. These are:

   A. The original world (Gen. 1:1-2:25)

   B. The pre-flood world (following man's sin) (Gen. 3:1-7:9)

   C. The flood world (Gen. 7:10-8:14; 2 Peter 3:5, 6)

   D. The present world (2 Peter 3:7)

      Note: The Hebrew and Greek words translated as *age* and *world* appear hundreds of times in the scriptures. The vast majority of these refer to this world, the present one. Thus:

      1. This world and the Trinity

         a. The Father loves its inhabitants (John 3:16).

      b. Jesus died for its inhabitants (1 Peter 3:18; Rev. 13:8).

      c. Jesus came to deliver us from this evil world (Gal. 1:4).

      d. Jesus has overcome this world (John 16:33).

      e. Jesus is the light of this world (John 8:12; 9:5; 12:46).

  2. This world and the devil

      a. He is the prince of darkness who presents himself to the world as an angel of light (2 Cor. 4:4; 11:14; Eph. 6:12).

      b. He deceives the whole world (Rev. 12:9).

      c. He sows tares in God's field of wheat (Matt. 13:24-25).

  3. This world and the Christian

      a. We are not to be conformed to it (Rom. 12:2).

      b. We are to serve as the lights of this world (Matt. 5:14; Phil. 2:15).

      c. We are to deny all ungodliness and worldly lusts (Titus 2:12).

      d. Above all, we are not to love the world (2 Tim. 4:10; 1 John 2:15-17).

E. The tribulational world (Rev. 6-18)

F. The millennial world (Isa. 2:2-4; 11:6-9; 35:1-10)

G. The purged world (2 Peter 3:10, 12)

H. The new world (Isa. 65:17; 66:22; 2 Peter 3:13; Rev. 21:1)

In regards to the contrasts involved

Note the major differences between the old creation with that of the new creation:

A. The old creation

  1. Featured the first Adam who was made in the image of God (Gen. 1:26)

  2. Associated with four rivers (Gen. 2:10-14)

  3. The Tree of Life was soon denied to mankind (Gen. 3:22-24)

  4. The sun illuminated the first creation (Gen. 1:14-17)

  5. Life centered in a garden planted by God (Gen. 2:8)

  6. Introduced history's first bride (Gen. 2:23)

  7. Sin, sorrow, and death loomed ahead in the future (Gen. 2:17)

  8. Angels were instructed to keep man from Paradise (Gen. 3:24)

  9. Followers only heard the voice of God (Gen. 3:10)

  10. Records the first name for Jesus: "the seed of the woman" (Gen. 3:15)

  11. Contains the first warning from God: "Don't eat from the tree of the knowledge of good and evil" (Gen. 2:16-17)

  12. It presents believers as pilgrims (Heb. 11:8-9; 13:14; 1 Peter 2:11)

B. The new creation

1. Will feature the second Adam, who was made in the image of man (John 1:14)
2. Will be associated with an eternal river of life (Rev. 22:1)
3. The Tree of Life will be forever accessible to mankind (Rev. 22:2, 14)
4. The Son will illuminate the second creation (Rev. 21:23)
5. Life will center in a city built by Jesus (John 14:2)
6. Will introduce history's final bride (Rev. 21:9)
7. Sin, sorrow, and death will be forever banished to the past (Rev. 21:4).
8. Angels will be instructed to usher man into Paradise (Rev. 21:9).
9. Followers will *see* the very face of God (Rev. 22:4).
10. Records the final name for Jesus: "the bright and morning star" (Rev. 22:16)
11. Contains the final warning from God: "Don't add to or take from His word" (Rev. 22:18-19)
12. It presents believers as homesteaders (Psa. 23:6; 1 Thess. 4:17).

EVENT 17 THAT SHINING CITY AMONG THE STARS

INTRODUCTION

The year was around 1140 A.D. The hymn writer was Bernard of Cluny. The song was "*Jerusalem the Golden.*" Here are the lyrics:

Jerusalem the golden, with milk and honey blest
Beneath your contemplation sink heart and voice oppressed
I know not, O I know not, what joys await me there,
What radiancy of glory, what bliss beyond compare!

They stand, those hall of Zion, till jubilant with song,
And bright with many an angel, and all the martyr throng.
The Prince is ever in them, the daylight is serene;
The pastures of the blessed are deck in glorious sheen.

There is the throne of David, and there, from care released,
The shout of them that triumph, the song of them that feast;
And they who, with their Leader, have conquered in the fight,
Forever and forever are clad in robes of white.

O sweet and blessed country, the home of God's elect!
O sweet and blessed country, that eager hearts expect!

Jesus, in mercy bring us to that dear land of rest;
Who art, with God the Father, and Spirit, ever blest.

Question: Should we view our final heavenly home as a city? In a word, *yes!*

For all intents and purposes, the believer, in contemplating his or her final heavenly home, should think of it in terms of a literal, physical, incredibly large and costly, dazzling bright, and blessed city located among the stars.

- ■ **The declaration in regards to this city**
  - A. It is anticipated in the Old Testament
    1. By Abraham

       "*For he waited for the city which has foundations, whose builder and maker is God*" (Heb. 11:10).
    2. By David

       "*There is a river whose streams shall make glad the city of God, the holy place of the tabernacle of the Most High*" (Psa. 46:4). "*Glorious things are spoken of you, O city of God!*" (Psa. 87:3)
    3. By Old Testament men and women of faith

       "*These all died in faith, not having received the promises, but having seen them afar off, and were persuaded of them, and embraced them, and confessed that they were strangers and pilgrims on the earth ... But now they desire a better country, that is, an heavenly: wherefore God is not ashamed to be called their God: for he hath prepared for them a city*" (Heb. 11:13, 16).
  - B. It is promised in the Gospels

    "*Let not your heart be troubled: ye believe in God, believe also in me. In my Father's house are many mansions: if it were not so, I would have told you. I go to prepare a place for you. And if I go and prepare a place for you, I will come again, and receive you unto myself; that where I am, there ye may be also*" (John 14:1-3).
  - C. It is referred to in the Epistles

    "*Jerusalem which is above...*" (Gal. 4:26). "*But ye are come unto mount Sion, and unto the city of the living God, the heavenly Jerusalem, and to an innumerable company of angels*" (Heb. 12:22). "*For here have we no continuing city, but we seek one to come*" (Heb. 13:14).
  - D. It is described in the book of Revelation

    "*And I John saw the holy city, new Jerusalem, coming down from God out of heaven, prepared as a bride adorned for her husband*" (Rev. 21:2).
- ■ **The details in regards to this city**
  - A. The size

"And he measured the city with the reed, twelve thousand furlongs. The length and the breadth and the height of it are equal" (Rev. 21:16b).

According to our present-day measurements this city would be roughly 1,400 miles long, high, and wide. If placed in America, it would reach from New York City to Denver, Colorado, and from Canada to Florida.

How big is a city this size? Our earth has approximately 120 million square miles of water surface and 60 million square miles of land surface. If one multiplies 1,400 by 1,400 by 1,400 (the dimensions of the New Jerusalem), he arrives at the total cubic miles of the city, a staggering figure of 2.744 billion. This is some fourteen times the combined surface of the entire earth, including both land and water area.

It has been estimated that approximately 40 billion people have lived on our planet since the creation of Adam. Of this number, over 7 billion are living today. Density studies of city populations assure us that every single one of these 40 billion could easily be accommodated upon just the first "foundational floor" of this marvelous 1,400-layer metropolis.

Taking a different approach, heaven will consist of 396,000 stories (at 20 feet per story) each having an area as big as half the size of the United States.

B. The shape

"And the city lieth foursquare, and the length is as large as the breadth... The length and the breadth and the height of it are equal" (Rev. 21:16).

This description allows for two possibilities, namely, that the new Jerusalem is either in the shape of a tetragon (a perfect cube) or of a vast pyramid.

1. Arguments for a cubical city

    John's statement in Rev. 21:3 seems to indicate it. *"Behold, the tabernacle of God is with men."*

    Gary Cohen writes in *"Some Questions Concerning the New Jerusalem"*:

    > It is interesting to note that the Holy of Holies inside the Tabernacle is cubical-shaped (20 x 20 x 20 cubits). The suggestion that the entire city is a huge Holy of Holies, cubical in shape as was the sacred inner sanctuary of the Temple (1 Kings 6:20), perfectly fits the truth that this city will be the very place in which God makes His dwelling. (*Grace Journal*, vol. 6, 24)

2. Arguments for a triangular city

    H. A. Ironside writes:

    > I rather think of that holy city as the mountain of God, a vast pyramid resting on a foursquare base, 12 thousand furlongs each way, and rising to a height as great as its length and breadth, and the throne of God and of the Lamb, the very apex of it, from which flows the river of the water of life, winding about the mountain, in the midst of the one street of gold on either side of that river. But in either case, whether we think of a cube or a pyramid, the thought is the same: it is a city of absolute perfection. (*Revelation*, p. 357)

3. Arguments for another shape

Dr. J. Vernon McGee, however, takes a different approach from the two above views:

> The shape of this city is difficult to describe.... Some have envisioned it as a cube, others as a pyramid. In view of the fact that it is hanging in space as a planet or star, it seems that it would be a globe.... The city is inside the globe.... The light would shine through the 12 foundations, giving a fantastic and startling coloring to the new universe.... From the outside, the city looks like a diamond. The gold is transparent and the diamond is the setting for the gold on the inside.... We live on the outside of the planet called Earth, but the Bride will dwell within the planet called the New Jerusalem. The glory of light streaming through this crystal clear prism, will break up into a polychromed rainbow of breathtaking beauty. The sphere will have the circumference of 8,164 miles. The diameter of the moon is about 2,160 miles and that of the New Jerusalem sphere is about 2,600 miles: thus the New Jerusalem will be about the size of the moon. And it will be a sphere, as are the other heavenly bodies.
>
> While the Bible definitely pictures the New Jerusalem as floating in space, it should not be thought of as a satellite city to the earth, but rather the opposite, that is, the earth as a satellite planet encircling the New Jerusalem. (*Reveling through Revelation*, pp. 86-97, 105)

C. The names

At least seven names and titles are given for this celestial city.

1. New Jerusalem (Rev. 3:12; 21:2)
2. The Holy City (Rev. 21:2; 22:19)
3. The heavenly Jerusalem (Heb. 11:16; 12:22)
4. Mount Zion (Heb. 12:22)
5. The Bride, the Lamb's wife (Rev. 21:9)
6. Paradise

"He that hath an ear, let him hear what the Spirit saith unto the churches; To him that overcometh will I give to eat of the tree of life, which is in the midst of the paradise of God" (Rev. 2:7).

Judson Cornwall observes:

> Both the Old and the New Testaments speak of paradise. In the King James version of the Old Testament the Hebrew word for paradise is translated as, "an orchard" (Song of Solomon 4:13; Eccles. 2:5), and "a forest" (Neh. 2:8), probably because it is actually a Persian word that was coined to describe the magnificent parks and gardens that were designed for the Persian kings. Later this word was picked up by the Latin scholars who produced the Septuagint version of the Old Testament scriptures (a trans-

lation from Hebrew into Greek) who used this word as a name for the garden of Eden. Whereas our English Bible calls the first habitation of God's special creation "Eden," the Greek translation calls Adam's home "paradise." (Judson Cornwall, *Heaven*, p. 32)

    7.   The Father's house (John 14:2)

D. The foundations (Rev. 21:14, 19-20)

The city rests upon twelve layers of foundation stones, with each layer being inlaid with a different precious gem.

These twelve foundations were not only inlaid with costly gems, but each foundational layer carried the name of one of the twelve apostles of the New Testament. *"And the wall of the city had twelve foundations, and in them the names of the twelve apostles of the Lamb"* (Rev. 21:14).

It should be noted that these jewels roughly parallel the twelve stones in the breastplate of the high priest (Exod. 28:17-20).

Half of these stones also characterized the first earth before Satan's fall in Ezekiel 28:13. The new earth will enjoy all the perfections of the first earth plus double.

E. The walls

The walls of the New Jerusalem are some 216 feet high and are made of jasper (Rev. 21:17-18). The wall is obviously not for protection, but for design and beauty only. In comparison to size, a 216-foot wall around a 1,400-mile-high city would be like a one-inch curb around the Empire State building. However, some advocated the 216 feet measurement refers to the thickness of the walls, not the height. The circumference of this wall will be 5600 miles!

F. The gates

There are twelve gates to this city, three gates on each side. On each gate is the name of one of the tribes of Israel. Each gate is composed of a beautiful solid white pearl (Rev. 21:12-13, 21).

It has been observed that the "coat of arms" in the New Jerusalem is not the twelve jeweled foundation (Rev. 21:19-20), nor the jasper wall (Rev. 21:18), nor the streets of gold (Rev. 21:21), nor the ivory towers (indicated by Psa. 45:8), but rather the gates of pearl. In reality the believer will literally be surrounded by pearls. Whether one looks to the north, south, east, or west, the prominent object catching the eye will be the pearl! Why is this? Several suggestions have been offered.

The pearl was the precious gem God selected to depict the church (Matt. 13:45, 46).

The pearl comes from a body of water, which is often used to symbolize Gentile peoples. The church will consist mostly of Gentiles.

The pearl is created (unlike a diamond or piece of gold) by a living organism—an oyster experiences a grain of sand in its side. To protect itself, the little creature coats the foreign object with layer upon layer of its own substance until finally a beautiful pearl is formed. Thus, the gates of heaven may be made of pearl to remind the redeemed that each person was once a tiny little grain of sinful sand in the sight and side of almighty God. To solve this problem He forgave our iniquities by coating us with layer upon layer of his own love. We thus become "the pearl of great price" by the marvelous grace of God.

G. The main street

The central boulevard of the New Jerusalem is composed of pure transparent gold. *"…and the street of the city was pure gold, as it were transparent glass"* (Rev. 21:21b). When one considers the price of gold, the total worth of this city becomes incomprehensible.

H. The throne

"The Lord hath prepared his throne in the heavens; and his kingdom ruleth over all" (Psa. 103:19).

1. At least three biblical men were allowed to gaze upon the awesome sight of God's throne:

   a. Isaiah

   "In the year that king Uzziah died I saw also the Lord sitting upon a throne, high and lifted up, and his train filled the temple. Above it stood the seraphims: each one had six wings; with twain he covered his face, and with twain he covered his feet, and with twain he did fly. And one cried unto another, and said, Holy, holy, holy, is the Lord of hosts: the whole earth is full of his glory" (Isa. 6:1-3).

   b. Daniel

   "I beheld till the thrones were cast down, and the Ancient of days did sit, whose garment was white as snow, and the hair of his head like the pure wool: his throne was like the fiery flame, and his wheels as burning fire. A fiery stream issued and came forth from before him: thousand thousands ministered unto him, and ten thousand times ten thousand stood before him: the judgment was set, and the books were opened" (Dan. 7:9-10).

   c. John

   "And immediately I was in the spirit: and, behold, a throne was set in heaven, and one sat on the throne…. And before the throne there was a sea of glass like unto crystal: and in the midst of the throne, and round about the throne, were four beasts full of eyes before and behind" (Rev. 4:2, 6).

2. God's throne is referred to more than forty times in the New Testament alone.

I. The river of life

"And he shewed me a pure river of water of life, clear as crystal, proceeding out of the throne of God and of the Lamb" (Rev. 22:1).

The Holy Spirit doubtless meant to make at least some reference to this river when he inspired David to write: *"And he shall be like a tree planted by the rivers of water, that bringeth forth his fruit in his season; his leaf also shall not wither; and whatsoever he doeth* shall prosper" (Psa. 1:3). "There is a river, the streams whereof shall make glad the city of God, the holy place of the tabernacles of the most High" (Psa. 46:4).

J. The tree of life

"In the midst of the street of it, and on either side of the river, was there the tree of life, which bare twelve manner of fruits, and yielded her fruit every month: and the leaves of the tree were for the healing of the nations" (Rev. 22:2).

When God created man and placed him in the Garden of Eden, He placed at Adam's disposal (among many other things) the tree of life. But when man sinned, he was driven from Eden and from this tree (Gen. 2:9; 3:24). At this point in human history the tree of life disappears, but here in the New Jerusalem it will blossom and bloom as never before.

55 FUTURE EVENTS
Chronological Chart of Coming Events

Paul, Peter, and John describe the first of these future events. There message is, "Look for New and Glorified Bodies!"

Isaiah, Peter, and John describe the final of these future events. There message is, "Look for New Heavens and Earth!"

In this unique prophetical study, all the relevant scriptures (some 750 verses) have been printed out, accompanied by a helpful chart, thus allowing God Himself to summarize each of the 55 future events in the divine program.

A Chronological Chart of Coming Events

1 The Rapture of the Church—I Thessalonians 4:16,17

2 The Judgment Seat of Christ—2 Corinthians 5:10

3 The Marriage Service of the Lamb—2 Corinthians 11:2

4 The Singing of Two Special Songs—Revelation 4:11; 5:9

5 Appearance of Antichrist and the False Prophet—Revelation 13:1, 11, 12

6 The Organization of the Super Harlot Church—Revelation 17:4, 5

7 Revival of the Old Roman Empire—Daniel 7:23, 24

8 Antichrist's 7-Year Peace Treaty with Israel—Daniel 9:27

9 The Mass Return of the Jews to Israel—Ezekiel 37:12

10 Ministry of the Two Witnesses—Revelation 11:3

11 Ministry of the 144,000—Revelation 7:4

12 Rebuilding of the Third Jewish Temple—Revelation 11:1, 2

13 Rebuilding of Babylon?—Jeremiah 51:7

14 First Seal Judgment—Revelation 6:2

15 Second Seal Judgment—Revelation 6:3, 4

16 Third Seal Judgment—Revelation 6:5, 6

17 Fourth Seal Judgment—Revelation 6:7, 8

18 Fifth Seal Judgment—Revelation 6:9-11

A Chronological Chart of Coming Events

19   **Sixth Seal Judgment**—Revelation 6:12-14

20   **Gog and Magog Invasion Into Israel**—Ezekiel 38:10,11

21   **Martyrdom of the Two Witnesses**—Revelation 11:7

22   **Casting of Satan Out of Heaven**—Revelation 12:9

23   **Abomination of Desolation in the Temple**—Matthew 24:15, 16

24   **Full Manifestation of the Antichrist**—2 Thessalonians 2:8-10

25   **Worldwide Persecution of Israel**—Matthew 24:21

26   **Destruction of Religious Babylon**—Revelation 17:16

27   **First Trumpet Judgment**—Revelation 8:7

28   **Second Trumpet Judgment**—Revelation 8:8, 9

29   **Third Trumpet Judgment**—Revelation 8:10, 11

30   **Fourth Trumpet Judgment**—Revelation 8:12

31   **Fifth Trumpet Judgment**—Revelation 9:1-3

32   **Sixth Trumpet Judgment**—Revelation 9:13-16

33   **Seventh Trumpet Judgment**—Revelation 11:15

34   **First Bowl Judgment**—Revelation 16:2

35   **Second Bowl Judgment**—Revelation 16:3

36   **Third Bowl Judgment**—Revelation 16:4

37   **Fourth Bowl Judgment**—Revelation 16:8

A Chronological Chart of Coming Events

38 Fifth Bowl Judgment—Revelation 16:10

39 Sixth Bowl Judgment—Revelation 16:12

40 Seventh Bowl Judgment—Revelation 16, 18, 20, 21

41 Destruction of Economic and Political Babylon—Revelation 18:9

42 The Battle of Armageddon—Isaiah 34:2, 3

43 The Second Coming of Christ—Revelation 19:11-13

44 The Regathering and Regenerating of Faithful Israel—Matthew 24:31

45 The Judgment and Punishment of Faithless Israel—Matthew 24:48-51

46 The Judgment of the Nations—Matthew 25:31, 32

47 The Judgment of Angels—I Corinthians 6:3

48 The Resurrection of O.T. and Tribulational Saints—Isaiah 26:19

49 Casting of Satan Into the Bottomless Pit—Revelation 20:2, 3

50 The Marriage Supper of the Lamb—Revelation 19:7-9

51 The Millennial Reign of Christ—Isaiah 11:6-9

52 Satan's Final Revolt—Revelation 20:7, 8

53 The Great White Throne Judgment—Revelation 20:11, 12

54 The Destruction of this Present Earth and Heaven—2 Peter 3:10

55 The Creation of a New Earth and Heaven—Revelation 21:1

John 14:1-3

¹ Let not your heart be troubled: ye believe in God, believe also in me.

² In my Father's house are many mansions: if it were not so, I would have told you. I go to prepare a place for you.

³ And if I go and prepare a place for you, I will come again, and receive you unto myself; that where I am, there ye may be also.

1 Corinthians 1:7, 8

⁷ So that ye come behind in no gift; waiting for the coming of our Lord Jesus Christ:

⁸ Who shall also confirm you unto the end, that ye may be blameless in the day of our Lord Jesus Christ.

1 Corinthians 4:5

⁵ Therefore judge nothing before the time, until the Lord come, who both will bring to light the hidden things of darkness, and will make manifest the counsels of the hearts: and then shall every man have praise of God.

1 Corinthians 15:23

²³ But every man in his own order: Christ the first-fruits; afterward they that are Christ's at his coming.

1 Corinthians 15:51-53

⁵¹ Behold, I shew you a mystery; We shall not all sleep, but we shall all be changed,

⁵² In a moment, in the twinkling of an eye, at the last trump: for the trumpet shall sound, and the dead shall be raised incorruptible, and we shall be changed.

⁵³ For this corruptible must put on incorruption, and this mortal must put on immortality.

1 Thessalonians 1:10

¹⁰ And to wait for his Son from heaven, whom he raised from the dead, even Jesus, which delivered us from the wrath to come.

1 Thessalonians 2:19

¹⁹ For what is our hope, or joy, or crown of rejoicing? Are not even ye in the presence of our Lord Jesus Christ at his coming?

1 Thessalonians 3:13

13 To the end he may stablish your hearts unblameable in holiness before God, even our Father, at the coming of our Lord Jesus Christ with all his saints.

1 Thessalonians 4:13-18

13 But I would not have you to be ignorant, brethren, concerning them which are asleep, that ye sorrow not, even as others which have no hope.

14 For if we believe that Jesus died and rose again, even so them also which sleep in Jesus will God bring with him.

15 For this we say unto you by the word of the Lord, that we which are alive and remain unto the coming of the Lord shall not prevent them which are asleep.

16 For the Lord himself shall descend from heaven with a shout, with the voice of the archangel, and with the trump of God: and the dead in Christ shall rise first:

17 Then we which are alive and remain shall be caught up together with them in the clouds, to meet the Lord in the air: and so shall we ever be with the Lord.

18 Wherefore comfort one another with these words.

1 Thessalonians 5:23

23 And the very God of peace sanctify you wholly; and I pray God your whole spirit and soul and body be preserved blameless unto the coming of our Lord Jesus Christ.

Philippians 3:20, 21

20 For our conversation is in heaven; from whence also we look for the Saviour, the Lord Jesus Christ:

21 Who shall change our vile body, that it may be fashioned like unto his glorious body, according to the working whereby he is able even to subdue all things unto himself.

Colossians 3:4

4 When Christ, who is our life, shall appear, then shall ye also appear with him in glory.

2 Timothy 4:8

8 Henceforth there is laid up for me a crown of righteousness, which the Lord, the righteous judge, shall give me at that day: and not to me only, but unto all them also that love his appearing.

Titus 2:12, 13

12 Teaching us that, denying ungodliness and worldly lusts, we should live soberly, righteously, and godly, in this present world;

[13] Looking for that blessed hope, and the glorious appearing of the great God and our Saviour Jesus Christ.

Hebrews 9:28

[28] So Christ was once offered to bear the sins of many; and unto them that look for him shall he appear the second time without sin unto salvation.

Hebrews 10:25

[25] Not forsaking the assembling of ourselves together, as the manner of some is; but exhorting one another: and so much the more, as ye see the day approaching.

Hebrews 10:37

[37] For yet a little while, and he that shall come will come, and will not tarry.

James 5:8

[8] Be ye also patient; stablish your hearts: for the coming of the Lord draweth nigh.

1 Peter 5:2

[2] Feed the flock of God which is among you taking the oversight thereof, not by constraint, but willingly; not for filthy lucre, but of a ready mind.

1 Peter 5:4

[4] And when the chief Shepherd shall appear, ye shall receive a crown of glory that fadeth not away.

1 John 2:28

[28] And now, little children, abide in him; that, when he shall appear, we may have confidence, and not be ashamed before him at his coming.

1 John 3:2

[2] Beloved, now are we the sons of God, and it doth not yet appear what we shall be: but we know that, when he shall appear, we shall be like him; for we shall see him as he is.

Revelation 2:25

[25] But that which ye have already hold fast till I come.

Revelation 3:10, 11

[10] Because thou hast kept the word of my patience, I also will keep thee from the hour of temptation, which shall come upon all the world, to try them that dwell upon the earth.

[11] *Behold, I come quickly: hold that fast which thou hast, that no man take thy crown.*

Revelation 4:1

[1] *After this I looked, and, behold, a door was opened in heaven: and the first voice I heard was as it were of a trumpet talking with me; which said, Come up hither, and I will shew thee things which must be hereafter.*

2 — THE JUDGMENT SEAT OF CHRIST

Romans 14:10-12

[10] *But why dost thou judge thy brother? or why dost thou set at nought thy brother? for we shall all stand before the judgment seat of Christ.*

[11] *For it is written, As I live, saith the Lord, every knee shall bow to me, and every tongue shall confess to God.*

[12] *So then every one of us shall give account of himself to God.*

1 Corinthians 3:11-15

[11] *For other foundation can no man lay than that is laid, which is Jesus Christ.*

[12] *Now if any man build upon this foundation gold, silver, precious stones, wood, hay, stubble;*

[13] *Every man's work shall be made manifest: for the day shall declare it, because it shall be revealed by fire; and the fire shall try every man's work of what sort it is.*

[14] *If any man's work abide which he hath built thereupon, he shall receive a reward.*

[15] *If any man's work shall be burned, he shall suffer loss: but he himself shall be saved: yet so by fire.*

1 Corinthians 9:24

[24] *Know ye not that they which run in a race run all, but one receiveth the prize? So run, that ye may obtain the prize.*

2 Corinthians 5:10

[10] *For we must all appear before the judgment seat of Christ; that every one may receive the things done in his body, according to that he hath done, whether it be good or bad.*

Galatians 6:7-9

[7] *Be not deceived; God is not mocked: for whatsoever a man soweth, that shall he also reap.*

8 For he that soweth to his flesh shall of the flesh reap corruption; but he that soweth to the Spirit shall of the Spirit reap life everlasting.

9 And let us not be weary in well doing: for in due season we shall reap, if we faint not.

Colossians 3:24, 25

24 Knowing that of the Lord ye shall receive the reward of the inheritance: for ye serve the Lord Christ.

25 But he that doeth wrong shall receive for the wrong which he hath done: and there is no respect of persons.

2 Timothy 4:8

8 Henceforth there is laid up for me a crown of righteousness, which the Lord, the righteous judge, shall give me at that day: and not to me only, but unto all them also that love his appearing.

Hebrews 10:30

30 For we know him that hath said, Vengeance belongeth unto me, I will recompense, saith the Lord. And again, The Lord shall judge his people.

Hebrews 13:17

17 Obey them that have the rule over you, and submit yourselves: for they watch for your souls, as they that must give account, that they may do it with joy, and not with grief: for that is unprofitable for you.

1 Peter 1:7

7 That the trial of your faith, being much more precious than of gold that perisheth, though it be tried with fire, might be found unto praise and honour and glory at the appearing of Jesus Christ.

1 Peter 4:17

17 For the the time is come that judgment must begin at the house of God: and if it first begin at us,what shall the end be of them that obey not the gospel of God?

1 John 4:17

17 Herein is our love made perfect, that we may have boldness in the day of judgment: because as he is, so are we in this world.

3   THE MARRIAGE SERVICE OF THE LAMB

2 Corinthians 11:2

² For I am jealous over you with godly jealousy: for I have espoused you to one husband, that I may present you as a chaste virgin to Christ.

Ephesians 5:25-32

²⁵ Husbands, love your wives, even as Christ also loved the church, and gave himself for it;

²⁶ That he might sanctify and cleanse it with the washing of water by the word,

²⁷ That he might present it to himself a glorious church, not having spot, or wrinkle, or any such thing; but that it should be holy and without blemish.

²⁸ So ought men to love their wives as their own bodies. He that loveth his wife loveth himself.

²⁹ For no man ever yet hated his own flesh; but nourisheth and cherisheth it, even as the Lord the church:

³⁰ For we are members of his body, of his flesh, and of his bones.

³¹ For this cause shall a man leave his father and mother, and shall be joined unto his wife, and they two shall be one flesh.

³² This is a great mystery: but I speak concerning Christ and the church.

4   THE SINGING OF TWO SPECIAL SONGS

Revelation 4:10, 11

¹⁰ The four and twenty elders fall down before him that sat on the throne, and worship him that liveth for ever and ever, and cast their crowns before the throne, saying,

¹¹ Thou art worthy, O Lord, to receive glory and honour and power: for thou hast created all things, and for thy pleasure they are and were created.

Revelation 5:9, 10

⁹ And they sung a new song, saying, Thou art worthy to take the book, and to open the seals thereof: for thou wast slain, and hast redeemed us to God by thy blood out of every kindred, and tongue, and people, and nation;

¹⁰ And hast made us unto our God kings and priests: and we shall reign on the earth.

Revelation 14:3

[3] *And they sung as it were a new song before the throne, and before the four beasts, and the elders: and no man could learn that song but the hundred and forty and four thousand, which were redeemed from the earth.*

Psalm 96:1-2

[1] *O sing unto the LORD a new song: sing unto the LORD, all the earth.*

[2] *Sing unto the LORD, bless his name; shew forth his salvation from day to day.*

Psalm 98:1-2

[1] *O sing unto the LORD a new song; for he hath done marvellous things: his right hand, and his holy arm, hath gotten him the victory.*

[2] *The LORD hath made known his salvation: his righteousness hath he openly shewed in the sight of the heathen.*

Psalm 100:1-2

[1] *Make a joyful noise unto the LORD, all ye lands.*

[2] *Serve the LORD with gladness: come before his presence with singing.*

5 THE APPEARANCE OF THE ANTICHRIST & THE FALSE PROPHET

Daniel 7:24, 25

[24] *And the ten horns out of this kingdom are ten kings that shall arise: and another shall rise after them; and he shall be diverse from the first, and he shall subdue three kings.*

[25] *And he shall speak great words against the most High, and shall wear out the saints of the most High, and think to change times and laws: and they shall be given into his hand until a time and times and the dividing of time.*

2 Thessalonians 2:2-3

[2] *That ye be not soon shaken in mind, or be troubled, neither by spirit, nor by word, nor by letter as from us, as that the day of Christ is at hand.*

[3] *Let no man deceive you by any means: for that day shall not come, except there come a falling away first, and that man of sin be revealed, the son of perdition.*

Revelation 6:2

² And I saw, and behold a white horse: and he that sat on him had a bow; and a crown was given unto him: and he went forth conquering, and to conquer.

Revelation 13:1

¹ And I stood upon the sand of the sea, and saw a beast rise up out of the sea, having seven heads and ten horns, and upon his horns ten crowns, and upon his heads the name of blasphemy.

Revelation 13:8

⁸ And all that dwell upon the earth shall worship him, whose names are not written in the book of life of the Lamb slain from the foundation of the world.

Revelation 13:11-12

¹¹ And I beheld another beast coming up out of the earth; and he had two horns like a lamb, and he spake as a dragon.

¹² And he exerciseth all the power of the first beast before him, and causeth the earth and them which dwell therein to worship the first beast, whose deadly wound was healed.

6 THE ORGANIZATION OF THE SUPER HARLOT CHURCH

Acts 20:29, 30

²⁹ For I know this, that after my departing shall grievous wolves enter in among you, not sparing the flock.

³⁰ Also of your own selves shall men arise, speaking perverse things, to draw away disciples after them.

l Timothy 4:1

¹ Now the Spirit speaketh expressly, that in the latter times some shall depart from the faith, giving heed to seducing spirits, and doctrines of devils.

2 Timothy 3:1-5

¹ This know also, that in the last days perilous times shall come.

² For men shall be lovers of their own selves, covetous, boasters, proud, blasphemers, disobedient to parents, unthankful, unholy,

³ Without natural affection, trucebreakers, false accusers, incontinent, fierce, despisers of those that are good,

4 Traitors, heady, highminded, lovers of pleasures more than lovers of God;

5 Having a form of godliness, but denying the power thereof: from such turn away.

2 Timothy 4:1-4

1 I charge thee therefore before God, and the Lord Jesus Christ, who shall judge the quick and the dead at his appearing and his kingdom.

2 Preach the word; be instant in season, out of season; reprove, rebuke, exhort with all long-suffering and doctrine.

3 For the time will come when they will not endure sound doctrine; but after their own lusts shall they heap to themselves teachers, having itching ears;

4 And they shall turn away their ears from the truth, and shall be turned unto fables.

2 Peter 2:1

1 But there were false prophets also among the people, even as there shall be false teachers among you, who privily shall bring in damnable heresies, even denying the Lord that bought them, and bring upon themselves swift destruction.

1 John 2:18, 19

18 Little children, it is the last time: and as ye have heard that antichrist shall come, even now are there many antichrists; whereby we know that it is the last time.

19 They went out from us, but they were not of us; for if they had been of us, they would no doubt have continued with us: but they went out, that they might be made manifest that they were not all of us.

Jude 4

For there are certain men crept in unawares, who were before of old.

Revelation 17:1-6

1 And there came one of the seven angels which had the seven vials, and talked with me, saying unto me, Come hither; I will shew unto thee the judgment of the great whore that sitteth upon many waters:

2 With whom the kings of the earth have committed fornication, and the inhabitants of the earth have been made drunk with the wine of her fornication.

3 So he carried me away in the spirit into the wilderness: and I saw a woman sit upon a scarlet coloured beast, full of names of blasphemy, having seven heads and ten horns.

4 And the woman was arrayed in purple and scarlet colour, and decked with gold and precious stones and pearls, having a golden cup in her hand full of abominations and filthiness of her fornication:

5 And upon her forehead was a name written,

> *MYSTERY, BABYLON THE GREAT,*
> *THE MOTHER OF HARLOTS AND*
> *ABOMINATIONS OF THE EARTH.*

6 And I saw the woman drunken with the blood of the saints, and with the blood of the martyrs of Jesus: and when I saw her, I wondered with great admiration.

7   REVIVAL OF THE ROMAN EMPIRE

Daniel 2:41

41 And whereas thou sawest the feet and toes, part of potters' clay, and part of iron, the kingdom shall be divided; but there shall be in it of the strength of the iron, forasmuch as thou sawest the iron mixed with miry clay.

Daniel 7:23, 24

23 Thus he said, The fourth beast shall be the fourth kingdom upon earth, which shall be diverse from all kingdoms, and shall devour the whole earth, and shall tread it down, and break it in pieces.

24 And the ten horns out of this kingdom are ten kings that shall arise: and another shall rise after them; and he shall be diverse from the first, and he shall subdue three kings.

Revelation 12:3

3 And there appeared another wonder in heaven; and behold a great red dragon, having seven heads and ten horns, and seven crowns upon his heads.

Revelation 13:1

1 And I stood upon the sand of the sea, and saw a beast rise up out of the sea, having seven heads and ten horns, and upon his horns ten crowns, and upon his heads the name of blasphemy.

Revelation 17:12

12 And the ten horns which thou sawest are ten kings, which have received no kingdom as yet; but receive power as kings one hour with the beast.

8 **ANTICHRIST'S 7-YEAR PEACE TREATY WITH ISRAEL**

Isaiah 28:18

18 And your covenant with death shall be disannulled, and your agreement with hell shall not stand; when the overflowing scourge shall pass through, then ye shall be trodden down by it.

Daniel 9:27

27 And he shall confirm the covenant with many for one week: and in the midst of the week he shall cause the sacrifice and the oblation to cease, and for the overspreading of abominations he shall make it desolate, even until the consummation, and that determined shall be poured upon the desolate.

9 **THE MASS RETURN OF THE JEWS TO ISRAEL**

Isaiah 43:5, 6

5 Fear not: for I am with thee: I will bring thy seed from the east, and gather thee from the west;

6 I will say to the north, Give up; and to the south, Keep not back: bring my sons from far, and my daughters from the ends of the earth.

Ezekiel 37:1-12

1 The hand of the LORD was upon me, and carried me out in the spirit of the LORD, and set me down in the midst of the valley which was full of bones,

2 And caused me to pass by them round about: and, behold, there were very many in the open valley; and, lo, they were very dry.

3 And he said unto me, Son of man, can these bones live? And I answered, 0 Lord GOD, thou knowest.

4 Again he said unto me, Prophesy upon these bones, and say unto them, 0 ye dry bones, hear the word of the LORD.

5 Thus saith the Lord GOD unto these bones; Behold, I will cause breath to enter into you, and ye shall live:

6 And I will lay sinews upon you, and will bring up flesh upon you, and cover you with skin, and put breath in you, and ye shall live; and ye shall know that I am the LORD.

7 So I prophesied as I was commanded: and as I prophesied, there was a noise, and behold a shaking, and the bones came together, bone to his bone.

8 *And when I beheld, lo, the sinews and the flesh came up upon them, and the skin covered them above: but there was no breath in them.*

9 *Then said he unto me, Prophesy unto the wind, prophesy, son of man, and say to the wind, Thus saith the Lord GOD; Come from the four winds, 0 breath, and breathe upon these slain, that they may live.*

10 *So I prophesied as he commanded me, and the breath came into them, and they lived, and stood up upon their feet, an exceeding great army.*

11 *Then he said unto me, Son of man, these bones are the whole house of Israel: behold, they say, Our bones are dried, and our hope is lost: we are cut off for our parts.*

12 *Therefore prophesy and say unto them, Thus saith the Lord GOD; Behold, 0 my people, I will open your graves, and cause you to come up out of your graves, and bring you into the land of Israel.*

Ezekiel 38:8

8 *After many days thou shalt be visited: in the latter years thou shalt come into the land that is brought back from the sword, and is gathered out of many people, against the mountains of Israel, which have been always waste: but it is brought forth out of the nations, and they shall dwell safely all of them.*

10   MINISTRY OF THE TWO WITNESSES

Malachi 4:5, 6

5 *Behold, I will send you Elijah the prophet before the coming of the great and dreadful day of the LORD:*

6 *And he shall turn the heart of the fathers to the children, and the heart of the children to their fathers, lest I come and smite the earth with a curse.*

Revelation 11:3-6

3 *And I will give power unto my two witnesses, and they shall prophesy a thousand two hundred and threescore days, clothed in sackcloth.*

4 *These are the two olive trees, and the two candlesticks standing before the God of the earth.*

5 *And if any man will hurt them, fire proceedeth out of their mouth, and devoureth their enemies: and if any man will hurt them, he must in this manner be killed.*

6 *These have power to shut heaven, that it rain not in the days of their prophecy: and have power over waters to turn them to blood, and to smite the earth with all plagues, as often as they will.*

Matthew 24:14

[14] *And this gospel of the kingdom shall be preached in all the world for a witness unto all nations; and then shall the end come.*

Mark 13:10

[10] *And the gospel must first be published among all nations.*

Revelation 7:1-8

[1] *And after these things I saw four angels standing on the four corners of the earth, holding the four winds of the earth, that the wind should not blow on the earth, nor on the sea, nor on any tree.*

[2] *And I saw another angel ascending from the east, having the seal of the living God: and he cried with a loud voice to the four angels, to whom it was given to hurt the earth and the sea,*

[3] *Saying, Hurt not the earth, neither the sea, nor the trees, till we have sealed the servants of our God in their foreheads.*

[4] *And I heard the number of them which were sealed: and there were sealed an hundred and forty and four thousand of all the tribes of the children of Israel.*

[5] *Of the tribe of Juda were sealed twelve thousand. Of the tribe of Reuben were sealed twelve thousand. Of the tribe of Gad were sealed twelve thousand.*

[6] *Of the tribe of Aser were sealed twelve thousand. Of the tribe of Nephthalim were sealed twelve thousand. Of the tribe of Manasses were sealed twelve thousand.*

[7] *Of the tribe of Simeon were sealed twelve thousand. Of the tribe of Levi were sealed twelve thousand. Of the tribe of Issachar were sealed twelve thousand.*

[8] *Of the tribe of Zabulon were sealed twelve thousand. Of the tribe of Joseph were sealed twelve thousand. Of the tribe of Benjamin were sealed twelve thousand.*

Revelation 14:1-5

[1] *And I looked, and, lo, a Lamb stood on the mount Sion, and with him an hundred forty and four thousand, having his Father's name written in their foreheads.*

[2] *And I heard a voice from heaven, as the voice of many waters, and as the voice of a great thunder: and I heard the voice of harpers harping with their harps:*

[3] *And they sung as it were a new song before the throne, and before the four beasts, and the elders: and no man could learn that song but the hundred and forty and four thousand, which were redeemed from the earth.*

[4] These are they which were not defiled with women; for they are virgins. These are they which follow the Lamb whithersoever he goeth. These were redeemed from among men, being the firstfruits unto God and to the Lamb.

[5] And in their mouth was found no guile: for they are without fault before the throne of God.

12   REBUILDING OF THE THIRD JEWISH TEMPLE

Daniel 9:27

[27] And he shall confirm the covenant with many for one week: and in the midst of the week he shall cause the sacrifice and the oblation to cease, and for the overspreading of abominations he shall make it desolate, even until the consummation, and that determined shall be poured upon the desolate.

Daniel 12:11

[11] And from the time that the daily sacrifice shall be taken away, and the abomination that maketh desolate set up, there shall be a thousand two hundred and ninety days.

Matthew 24:15

[15] When ye therefore shall see the abomination of desolation, spoken of by Daniel the prophet, stand in the holy place, (whoso readeth, let him understand).

2 Thessalonians 2:4

[4] Who opposeth and exalteth himself above all that is called God, or that is worshipped; so that he as God sitteth in the temple of God, shewing himself that he is God.

Revelation 11:1, 2

[1] And there was given me a reed like unto a rod: and the angel stood, saying, Rise, and measure the temple of God, and the altar, and them that worship therein.

[2] But the court which is without the temple leave out, and measure it not; for it is given unto the Gentiles: and the holy city shall they tread under foot forty and two months.

13   REBUILDING OF BABYLON?

Jeremiah 51:7

[7] Babylon hath been a golden cup in the LORD's hand, that made all the earth drunken: the nations have drunken of her wine; therefore the nations are mad.

Revelation 18:3

3 *For all nations have drunk of the wine of the wrath of her fornication, and the kings of the earth have committed fornication with her, and the merchants of the earth are waxed rich through the abundance of her delicacies.*

Revelation 18:5

5 *For her sins have reached unto heaven, and God hath remembered her iniquities.*

Revelation 18:7

7 *How much she hath glorified herself, and lived deliciously, so much torment and sorrow give her: for she saith in her heart, I sit a queen, and am no widow, and shall see no sorrow.*

Revelation 18:24

24 *And in her was found the blood of prophets, and of saints, and of all that were slain upon the earth.*

14 FIRST SEAL JUDGMENT

Revelation 6:2

2 *And I saw, and behold a white horse: and he that sat on him had a bow; and a crown was given unto him: and he went forth conquering, and to conquer.*

Matthew 24:5

5 *For many shall come in my name, saying, I am Christ; and shall deceive many.*

Mark 13:6

6 *For many shall come in my name, saying, I am Christ; and shall deceive many.*

Luke 21:8

8 *And he said, Take heed that ye be not deceived: for many shall come in my name, saying, I am Christ; and the time draweth near: go ye not therefore after them.*

15 SECOND SEAL JUDGMENT

Revelation 6:3, 4

3 *And when he had opened the second seal, I heard the second beast say, Come and see.*

4 *And there went out another horse that was red: and power was given to him that sat thereon*

to take peace from the earth, and that they should kill one another: and there was given unto him a great sword.

Matthew 24:6

6 And ye shall hear of wars and rumours of wars: see that ye be not troubled: for all these things must come to pass, but the end is not yet.

Mark 13:7

7 And when ye shall hear of wars and rumours of wars, be ye not troubled: for such things must needs be; but the end shall not be yet.

Luke 21:9, 10

9 But when ye shall hear of wars and commotions, be not terrified: for these things must first come to pass; but the end is not by and by.

10 Then said he unto them, Nation shall rise against nation, and kingdom against kingdom.

16   THIRD SEAL JUDGMENT

Revelation 6:5, 6

5 And when he had opened the third seal, I heard the third beast say, Come and see. And I beheld, and lo a black horse; and he that sat on him had a pair of balances in his hand.

6 And I heard a voice in the midst of the four beasts say, A measure of wheat for a penny, and three measures of barley for a penny; and see thou hurt not the oil and the wine.

Matthew 24:7

7 For nation shall rise against nation, and kingdom against kingdom: and there shall be famines, and pestilences, and earthquakes, in divers places.

Mark 13:8

8 For nation shall rise against nation, and kingdom against kingdom: and there shall be earthquakes in divers places, and there shall be famines and troubles: these are the beginnings of sorrows.

Luke 21:11

11 And great earthquakes shall be in divers places, and famines, and pestilences; and fearful sights and great signs shall there be from heaven.

17   FOURTH SEAL JUDGMENT

Revelation 6:7, 8

[7] *And when he had opened the fourth seal, I heard the voice of the fourth beast say, Come and see.*

[8] *And I looked, and behold a pale horse: and his name that sat on him was Death, and Hell followed with him. And power was given unto them over the fourth part of the earth, to kill with sword, and with hunger, and with death, and with the beasts of the earth.*

Matthew 24:9

[9] *Then shall they deliver you up to be afflicted, and shall kill you: and ye shall be hated of all nations for my name's sake.*

Ezekiel 14:21

[21] *For thus saith the Lord God; How much more when I send my four sore judgments upon Jerusalem, the sword, and the famine, and the noisome beast, and the pestilence, to cut off from it man and beast?*

18   FIFTH SEAL JUDGMENT

Revelation 6:9-11

[9] *And when he had opened the fifth seal, I saw under the altar the souls of them that were slain for the word of God, and for the testimony which they held:*

[10] *And they cried with a loud voice, saying, How long, O Lord, holy and true, dost thou not judge and avenge our blood on them that Then shall they deliver you up to be afflicted, dwell on the earth?*

[11] *And white robes were given unto everyone of them; and it was said unto them, that they should rest yet for a little season, until their fellowservants also and their brethren, that should be killed as they were, should be fulfilled.*

Matthew 24:9

[9] *Then shall they deliver you up to be afflicted, and shall kill you: and ye shall be hated of all nations for my name's sake.*

Mark 13:12

[12] *Now the brother shall betray the brother to death, and the father the son; and children shall rise up against their parents, and shall cause them to be put to death.*

HE'S STILL COMING

Luke 21:16

[16] And ye shall be betrayed both by parents, and brethren, and kinsfolks, and friends; and some of you shall they cause to be put to death.

19 SIXTH SEAL JUDGMENT

Revelation 6:12-17

[12] And I beheld when he had opened the sixth seal, and, lo, there was a great earthquake; and the sun became black as sackcloth of hair, and the moon became as blood;

[13] And the stars of heaven fell unto the earth, even as a fig tree casteth her untimely figs, when she is shaken of a mighty wind.

[14] And the heaven departed as a scroll when it is rolled together; and every mountain and island were moved out of their places.

[15] And the kings of the earth, and the great men, and the rich men, and the chief captains, and the mighty men, and every bondman, and every free man, hid themselves in the dens and in the rocks of the mountains;

[16] And said to the mountains and rocks, Fall on us, and hide us from the face of him that sitteth on the throne, and from the wrath of the Lamb:

[17] For the great day of his wrath is come; and who shall be able to stand?

Mark 13:25

[25] And the stars of heaven shall fall, and the powers that are in heaven shall be shaken.

Luke 21:25

[25] And there shall be signs in the sun, and in the moon, and in the stars; and upon the earth distress of nations, with perplexity; the sea and the waves roaring.

20 GOG AND MAGOG INVASION INTO ISRAEL

Ezekiel 38:1-6

[1] And the word of the LORD came unto me, saying,

[2] Son of man, set thy face against Gog, the land of Magog, the chief prince of Meshech and Tubal, and prophesy against him,

[3] And say, Thus saith the Lord GOD; Behold, I am against thee, 0 Gog, the chief prince of Meshech and Tubal:

⁴ And I will turn thee back, and put hooks into thy jaws, and I will bring thee forth, and all thine army, horses and horsemen, all of them clothed with all sorts of armour, even a great company with bucklers and shields, all of them handling swords:

⁵ Persia, Ethiopia, and Libya with them; all of them with shield and helmet:

⁶ Gomer, and all his bands; the house of Togarmah of the north quarters, and all his bands: and many people with thee.

Ezekiel 38:8-11

⁸ After many days thou shalt be visited: in the latter years thou shalt come into the land that is brought back from the sword, and is gathered out of many people, against the mountains of Israel, which have been always waste: but it is brought forth out of the nations, and they shall dwell safely all of them.

⁹ Thou shalt ascend and come like a storm, thou shalt be like a cloud to cover the land, thou, and all thy bands, and many people with thee.

¹⁰ Thus saith the Lord GOD; It shall also come to pass, that at the same time shall things come into thy mind, and thou shalt think an evil thought:

¹¹ And thou shalt say, I will go up to the land of unwalled villages; I will go to them that are at rest, that dwell safely, all of them dwelling without walls, and having neither bars or gates.

Ezekiel 39:1-12

¹ Therefore, thou son of man, prophesy against Gog, and say, Thus saith the Lord GOD; Behold, I am against thee, 0 Gog, the chief prince of Meshech and Tubal:

² And I will turn thee back, and leave but the sixth part of thee, and will cause thee to come up from the north parts, and will bring thee upon the mountains of Israel:

³ And I will smite thy bow out of thy left hand, and will cause thine arrows to fall out of thy right hand.

⁴ Thou shalt fall upon the mountains of Israel, thou, and all thy bands, and the people that is with thee: I will give thee unto the ravenous birds of every sort, and to the beasts of the field to be devoured.

⁵ Thou shalt fall upon the open field: for I have spoken it, saith the Lord GOD.

⁶ And I will send a fire on Magog, and among them that dwell carelessly in the isles: and they shall know that I am the LORD.

⁷ So will I make my holy name known in the midst of my people Israel; and I will not let them pollute my holy name any more: and the heathen shall know that I am the LORD, the Holy One in Israel.

[8] Behold, it is come, and it is done, saith the Lord GOD; this is the day whereof I have spoken.

[9] And they that dwell in the cities of Israel shall go forth, and shall set on fire and burn the weapons, both the shields and the bucklers, the bows and the arrows, and the handstaves, and the spears, and they shall burn them with fire seven years:

[10] So that they shall take no wood out of the field, neither cut down any out of the forests; for they shall burn the weapons with fire: and they shall spoil those that spoiled them, and rob those that robbed them, saith the Lord GOD.

[11] And it shall come to pass in that day, that I will give unto Gog a place there of graves in Israel, the valley of the passengers on the east of the sea: and it shall stop the noses of the passengers: and there shall they bury Gog and all his multitude: and they shall call it The valley of Hamongog.

[12] And seven months shall the house of Israel be burying of them, that they may cleanse the land.

21   MARTYDOM OF THE TWO WITNESSES

Revelation 11:7-13

[7] And when they shall have finished their testimony, the beast that ascendeth out of the bottomless pit shall make war against them, and shall overcome them, and kill them.

[8] And their dead bodies shall lie in the street of the great city, which spiritually is called Sodom and Egypt, where also our Lord was crucified.

[9] And they of the people and kindreds and tongues and nations shall see their dead bodies three days and an half, and shall not suffer their dead bodies to be put in graves.

[10] And they that dwell upon the earth shall rejoice over them, and make merry, and shall send gifts one to another; because these two prophets tormented them that dwelt on the earth.

[11] And after three days and an half the Spirit of life from God entered into them, and they stood upon their feet; and great fear fell upon them which saw them.

[12] And they heard a great voice from heaven saying unto them, Come up hither. And they ascended up to heaven in a cloud; and their enemies beheld them.

[13] And the same hour was there a great earthquake, and the tenth part of the city fell, and in the earthquake were slain of men seven thousand: and the remnant were affrighted, and gave glory to the God of heaven.

22   CASTING OF SATAN OUT OF HEAVEN

Revelation 12:7-12

7 And there was war in heaven: Michael and his angels fought against the dragon; and the dragon fought and his angels,

[8] *And prevailed not; neither was their place found any more in heaven.*

[9] *And the great dragon was cast out, that old serpent, called the Devil, and Satan, which deceiveth the whole world: he was cast out into the earth, and his angels were cast out with him.*

[10] *And I heard a loud voice saying in heaven, Now is come salvation, and strength, and the kingdom of our God, and the power of his Christ: for the accuser of our brethren is cast down, which accused them before our God day and night.*

[11] *And they overcame him by the blood of the Lamb, and by the word of their testimony; and they loved not their lives unto the death.*

[12] *Therefore rejoice, ye heavens, and ye that dwell in them. Woe to the inhabiters of the earth and of the sea! for the devil is come down unto you, having great wrath, because he knoweth that he hath but a short time.*

23 | ABOMINATION OF DESOLATION IN THE TEMPLE

Matthew 24:15-20

[15] *When ye therefore shall see the abomination of desolation, spoken of by Daniel the prophet, stand in the holy place, (whoso readeth, let him understand:)*

[16] *Then let them which be in Judaea flee into the mountains:*

[17] *Let him which is on the housetop not come down to take any thing out of his house:*

[18] *Neither let him which is in the field return back to take his clothes.*

[19] *And woe unto them that are with child, and to them that give suck in those days!*

[20] *But pray ye that your flight be not in the winter, neither on the sabbath day.*

Mark 13:14-18

[14] *But when ye shall see the abomination of desolation, spoken of by Daniel the prophet, standing where it ought not, (let him that readeth understand,) then let them that be in Judaea flee to the mountains:*

[15] *And let him that is on the housetop not go down into the house, neither enter therein, to take any thing out of his house:*

[16] *And let him that is in the field not turn back again for to take up his garment.*

[17] *But woe to them that are with child, and to them that give suck in those days!*

[18] *And pray ye that your flight be not in the winter.*

2 Thessalonians 2:3, 4

³ Let no man deceive you by any means: for that day shall not come, except there come a falling away first, and that man of sin be revealed, the son of perdition;

⁴ Who opposeth and exalteth himself above all that is called God, or that is worshipped; so that he as God sitteth in the temple of God, shewing himself that he is God.

Revelation 13:11-15

¹¹ And I beheld another beast coming up out of the earth; and he had two horns like a lamb, and he spake as a dragon.

¹² And he exerciseth all the power of the first beast before him, and causeth the earth and them which dwell therein to worship the first beast, whose deadly wound was healed.

¹³ And he doeth great wonders, so that he maketh fire come down from heaven on the earth in the sight of men,

¹⁴ And deceiveth them that dwell on the earth by the means of those miracles which he had power to do in the sight of the beast; saying to them that dwell on the earth, that they should make an image to the beast, which had the wound by a sword, and did live.

¹⁵ And he had power to give life unto the image of the beast, that the image of the beast should both speak, and cause that as many as would not worship the image of the beast should be killed.

24   FULL MANIFESTATION OF THE ANTICHRIST

Daniel 7:25

²⁵ And he shall speak great words against the most High, and shall wear out the saints of the most High, and think to change times and laws: and they shall be given into his hand until a time and times and the dividing of time.

Daniel 11:36-37

³⁶ And the king shall do according to his will; and he shall exalt himself, and magnify himself above every god, and shall speak marvellous things against the God of gods, and shall prosper till the indignation be accomplished: for that that is determined shall be done.

³⁷ Neither shall he regard the God of his fathers, nor the desire of women, nor regard any god: for he shall magnify himself above all.

Daniel 8:23-25

²³ And in the latter time of their kingdom, when the transgressors are come to the full, a king of fierce countenance, and understanding dark sentences, shall stand up.

[24] *And his power shall be mighty, but not by his own power: and he shall destroy wonderfully, and shall prosper, and practise, and shall destroy the mighty and the holy people.*

[25] *And through his policy also he shall cause craft to prosper in his hand; and he shall magnify himself in his heart, and by peace shall destroy many: he shall also stand up against the Prince of princes; but he shall be broken without hand.*

2 Thessalonians 2:8-10

[8] *And then shall that Wicked be revealed, whom the Lord shall consume with the spirit of his mouth, and shall destroy with the brightness of his coming:*

[9] *Even him, whose coming is after the working of Satan with all power and signs and lying wonders,*

[10] *And with all deceivableness of unrighteousness in them that perish; because they received not the love of the truth, that they might be saved.*

Revelation 13:5-8

[5] *And there was given unto him a mouth speaking great things and blasphemies; and power was given unto him to continue forty and two months.*

[6] *And he opened his mouth in blasphemy against God, to blaspheme his name, and his tabernacle, and them that dwell in heaven.*

[7] *And it was given unto him to make war with the saints, and to overcome them: and power was given him over all kindreds, and tongues, and nations.*

[8] *And all that dwell upon the earth shall worship him, whose names are not written in the book of life of the Lamb slain from the foundation of the world.*

25 — WORLDWIDE PERSECUTION OF ISRAEL

Daniel 12:1

[1] *And at that time shall Michael stand up, the great prince which standeth for the children of thy people: and there shall be a time of trouble, such as never was since there was a nation even to that same time: and at that time thy people shall be delivered, every one that shall be found written in the book.*

Zechariah 11:16

[16] *For, lo, I will raise up a shepherd in the land, which shall not visit those that be cut off, neither shall seek the young one, nor heal that that is broken, nor feed that that standeth still: but he shall eat the flesh of the fat, and tear their claws in pieces.*

Zechariah 13:8

[8] *And it shall come to pass, that in all the land, saith the LORD, two parts therein shall be cut off and die; but the third shall be left therein.*

Matthew 24:21

[21] *For then shall be great tribulation, such as was not since the beginning of the world to this time, no, nor ever shall be.*

Luke 21:22

[22] *For these be the days of vengeance, that all things which are written may be fulfilled.*

Revelation 7:13-14

[13] *And one of the elders answered, saying unto me, What are these which are arrayed in white robes? and whence came they?*

[14] *And I said unto him, Sir, thou knowest. And he said to me, These are they which came out of great tribulation, and have washed their robes, and made them white in the blood of the Lamb.*

Revelation 12:13

[13] *And when the dragon saw that he was cast unto the earth, he persecuted the woman which brought forth the man child.*

26 DESTRUCTION OF RELIGIOUS BABYLON

Revelation 17:15-17

[15] *And he saith unto me, The waters which thou sawest, where the whore sitteth, are peoples, and multitudes, and nations, and tongues.*

[16] *And the ten horns which thou sawest upon the beast, these shall hate the whore, and shall make her desolate and naked, and shall eat her flesh, and burn her with fire.*

[17] *For God hath put in their hearts to fulfil his will, and to agree, and give their kingdom unto the beast, until the words of God shall be fulfilled,*

27 FIRST TRUMPET JUDGMENT

Revelation 8:7

[7] *The first angel sounded, and there followed hail and fire mingled with blood, and they were cast upon the earth: and the third part of trees was burnt up, and all green grass was burnt up.*

28   SECOND TRUMPET JUDGMENT

Revelation 8:8-9

⁸ And the second angel sounded, and as it were a great mountain burning with fire was cast into the sea: and the third part of the sea became blood;

⁹ And the third part of the creatures which were in the sea, and had life, died; and the third part of the ships were destroyed.

29   THIRD TRUMPET JUDGMENT

Revelation 8:10, 11

¹⁰ And the third angel sounded, and there fell a great star from heaven, burning as it were a lamp, and it fell upon the third part of the rivers, and upon the fountains of waters;

¹¹ And the name of the star is called Wormwood: and the third part of the waters became wormwood; and many men died of the waters, because they were made bitter.

30   FOURTH TRUMPET JUDGMENT

Revelation 8:12

¹² And the fourth angel sounded, and the third part of the sun was smitten, and the third part of the moon, and the third part of the stars; so as the third part of them was darkened, and the day shone not for a third part of it, and the night likewise.

31   FIFTH TRUMPET JUDGMENT

Revelation 9:1-12

¹ And the fifth angel sounded, and I saw a star fall from heaven unto the earth: and to him was given the key of the bottomless pit.

² And he opened the bottomless pit; and there arose a smoke out of the pit, as the smoke of a great furnace; and the sun and the air were darkened by reason of the smoke of the pit.

³ And there came out of the smoke locusts upon the earth: and unto them was given power, as the scorpions of the earth have power.

⁴ And it was commanded them that they should not hurt the grass of the earth, neither any green thing, neither any tree; but only those men which have not the seal of God in their foreheads.

⁵ *And to them it was given that they should not kill them, but that they should be tormented five months: and their torment was as the torment of a scorpion, when he striketh a man.*

⁶ *And in those days shall men seek death, and shall not find it; and shall desire to die, and death shall flee from them.*

⁷ *And the shapes of the locusts were like unto horses prepared unto battle; and on their heads were as it were crowns like gold, and their faces were as the faces of men.*

⁸ *And they had hair as the hair of women, and their teeth were as the teeth of lions.*

⁹ *And they had breastplates, as it were breastplates of iron; and the sound of their wings was as the sound of chariots of many horses running to battle.*

¹⁰ *And they had tails like unto scorpions, and there were stings in their tails: and their power was to hurt men five months.*

¹¹ *And they had a king over them, which is the angel of the bottomless pit, whose name in the Hebrew tongue is Abaddon, but in the Greek tongue hath his name Apollyon.*

¹² *One woe is past; and, behold, there come two woes more hereafter.*

32 SIXTH TRUMPET JUDGMENT

Revelation 9:13-19

¹³ *And the sixth angel sounded, and I heard a voice from the four horns of the golden altar which is before God,*

¹⁴ *Saying to the sixth angel which had the trumpet, Loose the four angels which are bound in the great river Euphrates.*

¹⁵ *And the four angels were loosed, which were prepared for an hour, and a day, and a month, and a year, for to slay the third part of men.*

¹⁶ *And the number of the army of the horsemen were two hundred thousand thousand: and I heard the number of them.*

¹⁷ *And thus I saw the horses in the vision, and them that sat on them, having breastplates of fire, and of jacinth, and brimstone: and the heads of the horses were as the heads of lions; and out of their mouths issued fire and smoke and brimstone.*

¹⁸ *By these three was the third part of men killed, by the fire, and by the smoke, and by the brimstone, which issued out of their mouths.*

¹⁹ *For their power is in their mouth, and in their tails: for their tails were like unto serpents, and had heads and with them they do hurt.*

33 SEVENTH TRUMPET JUDGMENT

Revelation 11:15-19

[15] *And the seventh angel sounded; and there were great voices in heaven, saying, The kingdoms of this world are become the kingdoms of our Lord, and of his Christ; and he shall reign for ever and ever.*

[16] *And the four and twenty elders, which sat before God on their seats, fell upon their faces, and worshipped God,*

[17] *Saying, We give thee thanks, O Lord God Almighty, which art, and wast, and art to come; because thou hast taken to thee thy great power, and hast reigned.*

[18] *And the nations were angry, and thy wrath is come, and the time of the dead, that they should be judged, and that thou shouldest give reward unto thy servants the prophets, and to the saints, and them that fear thy name, small and great; and shouldest destroy them which destroy the earth.*

[19] *And the temple of God was opened in heaven, and there was seen in his temple the ark of his testament: and there were lightnings, and voices, and thunderings, and an earthquake, and great hail.*

34 FIRST BOWL JUDGMENT

Revelation 16:2

[2] *And the first went, and poured out his vial upon the earth; and there fell a noisome and grievous sore upon the men which had the mark of the beast, and upon them which worshipped his image.*

35 SECOND BOWL JUDGMENT

Revelation 16:3

[3] *And the second angel poured out his vial upon the sea; and it became as the blood of a dead man: and every living soul died in the sea.*

36 THIRD BOWL JUDGMENT

Revelation 16:4-7

[4] *And the third angel poured out his vial upon the rivers and fountains of waters; and they became blood.*

HE'S STILL COMING

⁵ And I heard the angel of the waters say, Thou art righteous, O Lord, which art, and wast, and shalt be, because thou hast judged thus.

⁶ For they have shed the blood of saints and prophets, and thou hast given them blood to drink; for they are worthy.

⁷ And I heard another out of the altar say, Even so, Lord God Almighty, true and righteous are thy judgments.

37   FOURTH BOWL JUDGMENT

Revelation 16:8, 9

⁸ And the fourth angel poured out his vial upon the sun; and power was given unto him to scorch men with fire.

⁹ And men were scorched with great heat, and blasphemed the name of God, which hath power over these plagues: and they repented not to give him glory.

38   FIFTH BOWL JUDGMENT

Revelation 16:10, 11

¹⁰ And the fifth angel poured out his vial upon the seat of the beast; and his kingdom was full of darkness; and they gnawed their tongues for pain,

¹¹ And blasphemed the God of heaven because of their pains and their sores, and repented not of their deeds.

39   SIXTH BOWL JUDGMENT

Revelation 16:12-14

¹² And the sixth angel poured out his vial upon the great river Euphrates; and the water thereof was dried up, that the way of the kings of the east might be prepared.

¹³ And I saw three unclean spirits like frogs come out of the mouth of the dragon, and out of the mouth of the beast, and out of the mouth of the false prophet.

¹⁴ For they are the spirits of devils, working miracles, which go forth unto the kings of the earth and of the whole world, to gather them to the battle of that great day of God Almighty.

40   SEVENTH BOWL JUDGMENT

Revelation 16:17-21

[17] And the seventh angel poured out his vial into the air; and there came a great voice out of the temple of heaven, from the throne, saying, It is done.

[18] And there were voices, and thunders, and lightnings; and there was a great earthquake, such as was not since men were upon the earth, so mighty an earthquake, and so great.

[19] And the great city was divided into three parts, and the cities of the nations fell: and great Babylon came in remembrance before God, to give unto her the cup of the wine of the fierceness of his wrath.

[20] And every island fled away, and the mountains were not found.

[21] And there fell upon men a great hail out of heaven, every stone about the weight of a talent: and men blasphemed God because of the hail; for the plague there was exceedingly great.

41   DESTRUCTION OF ECONOMIC & POLITICAL BABYLON

Isaiah 13:19, 20

[19] And Babylon, the glory of kingdoms, the beauty of the Chaldees' excellency, shall be as when God overthrew Sodom and Gomorrah.

[20] It shall never be inhabited, neither shall it be dwelt in from generation to generation: neither shall the Arabian pitch tent there; neither shall the shepherds make their fold there.

Jerermiah 51:8

[8] Babylon is suddenly fallen and destroyed: howl for her; take balm for her pain, if so be she may be healed.

Revelation 14:8

[8] And there followed another angel, saying, Babylon is fallen, is fallen, that great city, because she made all nations drink of the wine of the wrath of her fornication.

Revelation 18:1-2

[1] And after these things I saw another angel come down from heaven, having great power; and the earth was lightened with his glory.

[2] And he cried mightily with a strong voice, saying, Babylon the great is fallen, is fallen, and is

become the habitation of devils, and the hold of every foul spirit, and a cage of every unclean and hateful bird.

Revelation 18:9

⁹ And the kings of the earth, who have committed fornication and lived deliciously with her, shall bewail her, and lament for her, when they shall see the smoke of her burning.

Revelation 18:18, 19, 21

¹⁸ And cried when they saw the smoke of her burning, saying, What city is like unto this great city!

¹⁹ And they cast dust on their heads, and cried, weeping and wailing, saying, Alas, alas, that great city, wherein were made rich all that had ships in the sea by reason of her costliness! for in one hour is she made desolate.

²¹ And a mighty angel took up a stone like a great millstone, and cast it into the sea, saying, Thus with violence shall that great city Babylon be thrown down, and shall be found no more at all.

42 THE BATTLE OF ARMAGEDDON

Psalm 2:1-5

¹ Why do the heathen rage, and the people imagine a vain thing?

² The kings of the earth set themselves, and the rulers take counsel together, against the LORD, and against his anointed, saying,

³ Let us break their bands asunder, and cast away their cords from us.

⁴ He that sitteth in the heavens shall laugh: the Lord shall have them in derision.

⁵ Then shall he speak unto them in his wrath, and vex them in his sore displeasure.

Isaiah 13:6-13

⁶ Howl ye; for the day of the LORD is at hand; it shall come as a destruction from the Almighty.

⁷ Therefore shall all hands be faint, and every man's heart shall melt:

⁸ And they shall be afraid: pangs and sorrows shall take hold of them; they shall be in pain as a woman that travaileth: they shall be amazed one at another; their faces shall be as flames.

⁹ Behold, the day of the LORD cometh, cruel both with wrath and fierce anger, to lay the land desolate: and he shall destroy the sinners thereof out of it.

¹⁰ For the stars of heaven and the constellations thereof shall not give their light: the sun shall be darkened in his going forth, and the moon shall not cause her light to shine.

[11] *And I will punish the world for their evil, and the wicked for their iniquity; and I will cause the arrogancy of the proud to cease, and will lay low the haughtiness of the terrible.*

[12] *I will make a man more precious than fine gold; even a man than the golden wedge of Ophir.*

[13] *Therefore I will shake the heavens, and the earth shall remove out of her place, in the wrath of the LORD of hosts, and in the day of his fierce anger.*

Isaiah 24:1

[1] *Behold, the LORD maketh the earth empty, and maketh it waste, and turneth it upside down, and scattereth abroad the inhabitants thereof.*

Isaiah 24:19, 20

[19] *The earth is utterly broken down, the earth is clean dissolved, the earth is moved exceedingly.*

[20] *The earth shall reel to and fro like a drunkard, and shall be removed like a cottage; and the transgression thereof shall be heavy upon it; and it shall fall, and not rise again.*

Isaiah 26:21

[21] *For, behold, the LORD cometh out of his place to punish the inhabitants of the earth for their iniquity: the earth also shall disclose her blood, and shall no more cover her slain.*

Isaiah 34:14

[1] *Come near, ye nations, to hear; and hearken, ye people: let the earth hear, and all that is therein; the world, and all things that come forth of it.*

[2] *For the indignation of the LORD is upon all nations, and his fury upon all their armies: he hath utterly destroyed them, he hath delivered them to the slaughter.*

[3] *Their slain also shall be cast out, and their stink shall come up out of their carcases, and the mountains shall be melted with their blood.*

[4] *And all the host of heaven shall be dissolved, and the heavens shall be rolled together as a scroll: and all their host shall fall down, as the leaf falleth off from the vine, and as a falling fig from the fig tree.*

Isaiah 42:13-14

[13] *The LORD shall go forth as a mighty man, he shall stir up jealousy like a man of war: he shall cry, yea, roar; he shall prevail against his enemies.*

[14] *I have long time holden my peace; I have been still, and refrained myself: now will I cry like a travailing woman; I will destroy and devour at once.*

Isaiah 63:6

[6] *And I will tread down the people in mine anger, and make them drunk in my fury, and I will bring down their strength to the earth.*

Isaiah 66:15, 16, 24

[15] *For, behold, the LORD will come with fire, and with his chariots like a whirlwind, to render his anger with fury, and his rebuke with flames of fire.*

[16] *For by fire and by his sword will the LORD plead with all flesh: and the slain of the LORD shall be many.*

[24] *And they shall go forth, and look upon the carcases of the men that have transgressed against me: for their worm shall not die, neither shall their fire be quenched; and they shall be an abhorring unto all flesh.*

Joel 3:2

[2] *I will also gather all nations, and will bring them down into the valley of Jehoshaphat, and will plead with them there for my people and for my heritage Israel, whom they have scattered among the nations, and parted my land.*

Joel 3:9-16

[9] *Proclaim ye this among the Gentiles; Prepare war, wake up the mighty men, let all the men of war draw near; let them come up:*

[10] *Beat your plowshares into swords, and your pruninghooks into spears: let the weak say, I am strong.*

[11] *Assemble yourselves, and come, all ye heathen, and gather yourselves together round about: thither cause thy mighty ones to come down, 0 LORD.*

[12] *Let the heathen be wakened, and come up to the valley of Jehoshaphat: for there will I sit to judge all the heathen round about.*

[13] *Put ye in the sickle, for the harvest is ripe: come, get you down; for the press is full, the fats overflow; for their wickedness is great.*

[14] *Multitudes, multitudes in the valley of decision: for the day of the LORD is near in the valley of decision.*

[15] *The sun and the moon shall be darkened, and the stars shall withdraw their shining.*

[16] *The LORD also shall roar out of Zion, and utter his voice from Jerusalem; and the heavens and the earth shall shake: but the LORD will be the hope of his people, and the strength of the children of Israel.*

Micah 5:15

[15] And I will execute vengeance in anger and fury upon the heathen, such as they have not heard.

Zephaniah 1:14-17

[14] The great day of the LORD is near, it is near, and hasteth greatly, even the voice of the day of the LORD: the mighty man shall cry there bitterly.

[15] That day is a day of wrath, a day of trouble and distress, a day of wasteness and desolation, a day of darkness and gloominess, a day of clouds and thick darkness,

[16] A day of the trumpet and alarm against the fenced cities, and against the high towers.

[17] And I will bring distress upon men, that they shall walk like blind men, because they have sinned against the LORD: and their blood shall be poured out as dust, and their flesh as the dung.

Zephaniah 3:8

[8] Therefore wait ye upon me, saith the LORD, until the day that I rise up to the prey: for my determination is to gather the nations, that I may assemble the kingdoms, to pour upon them mine indignation, even all my fierce anger: for all the earth shall be devoured with the fire of my jealousy.

Zechariah 12:2-4

[2] Behold, I will make Jerusalem a cup of trembling unto all the people round about, when they shall be in the siege both against Judah and against Jerusalem.

[3] And in that day will I make Jerusalem a burdensome stone for all people: all that burden themselves with it shall be cut in pieces, though all the people of the earth be gathered together against it.

[4] In that day, saith the LORD, I will smite every horse with astonishment, and his rider with madness: and I will open mine eyes upon the house of Judah, and will smite every horse of the people with blindness.

Zephaniah 12:9

[9] And it shall come to pass in that day, that I will seek to destroy all the nations that come against Jerusalem.

Zephaniah 14:1-3

[1] Behold, the day of the LORD cometh, and thy spoil shall be divided in the midst of thee.

[2] For I will gather all nations against Jerusalem to battle; and the city shall be taken, and the

houses rifled, and the women ravished; and half of the city shall go forth into captivity, and the residue of the people shall not be cut off from the city.

³ Then shall the LORD go forth, and fight against those nations, as when he fought in the day of battle.

Zephaniah 14:12

¹² And this shall be the plague wherewith the LORD will smite all the people that have fought against Jerusalem; Their flesh shall consume away while they stand upon their feet, and their eyes shall consume away in their holes, and their tongue shall consume away in their mouth.

Matthew 24:28

²⁸ For wheresoever the carcase is, there will the eagles be gathered together.

Matthew 24:40-41

⁴⁰ Then shall two be in the field; the one shall be taken, and the other left.

⁴¹ Two women shall be grinding at the mill; the one shall be taken, and the other left.

Luke 17:34-37

³⁴ I tell you, in that night there shall be two men in one bed; the one shall be taken, and the other shall be left.

³⁵ Two women shall be grinding together; the one shall be taken, and the other left.

³⁶ Two men shall be in the field; the one shall be taken, and the other left.

³⁷ And they answered and said unto him, Where, Lord? And he said unto them, Wheresoever the body is, thither will the eagles be gathered together.

Revelation 14:14

¹⁴ And I looked, and behold a white cloud, and upon the cloud one sat like unto the Son of man, having on his head a golden crown, and in his hand a sharp sickle.

Revelation 14:20

²⁰ And the winepress was trodden without the city, and blood came out of the winepress, even unto the horse bridles, by the space of a thousand and six hundred furlongs.

Revelation 16:16

¹⁶ And he gathered them together into a place called in the Hebrew tongue Armageddon.

Revelation 19:17-21

[17] And I saw an angel standing in the sun; and he cried with a loud voice, saying to all the fowls that fly in the midst of heaven, Come and gather yourselves together unto the supper of the great God;

[18] That ye may eat the flesh of kings, and the flesh of captains, and the flesh of mighty men, and the flesh of horses, and of them that sit on them, and the flesh of all men, both free and bond, both small and great.

[19] And I saw the beast, and the kings of the earth, and their armies, gathered together to make war against him that sat on the horse, and against his army.

[20] And the beast was taken, and with him the false prophet that wrought miracles before him, with which he deceived them that had received the mark of the beast, and them that worshipped his image. These both were cast alive into a lake of fire burning with brimstone.

[21] And the remnant were slain with the sword of him that sat upon the horse, which sword proceeded out of his mouth: and all the fowls were filled with their flesh.

43 THE SECOND COMING OF CHRIST

Isaiah 25:9

[9] And it shall be said in that day, Lo, this is our God; we have waited for him, and he will save us: this is the LORD; we have waited for him, we will be glad and rejoice in his salvation.

Isaiah 11:12

[12] And he shall set up an ensign for the nations, and shall assemble the outcasts of Israel, and gather together the dispersed of Judah from the four corners of the earth.

Isaiah 40:5

[5] And the glory of the LORD shall be revealed, and all flesh shall see it together: for the mouth of the LORD hath spoken it.

Isaiah 40:10

[10] Behold, the Lord GOD will come with strong hand, and his arm shall rule for him: behold, his reward is with him, and his work before him.

Isaiah 59:20

[20] And the Redeemer shall come to Zion, and unto them that turn from transgression in Jacob, saith the LORD.

Ezekiel 43:2, 4

2 And, behold, the glory of the God of Israel came from the way of the east: and his voice was like a noise of many waters: and the earth shined with his glory.

4 And the glory of the LORD came into the house by the way of the gate whose prospect is toward the east.

Daniel 7:13-14

13 I saw in the night visions, and, behold, one like the Son of man came with the clouds of heaven, and came to the Ancient of days, and they brought him near before him.

14 And there was given him dominion, and glory, and a kingdom, that all people, nations, and languages, should serve him: his dominion is an everlasting dominion, which shall not pass away, and his kingdom that which shall not be destroyed.

Habakkuk 3:3-6

3 God came from Teman, and the Holy One from mount Paran. Selah. His glory covered the heavens, and the earth was full of his praise.

4 And his brightness was as the light; he had horns coming out of his hand: and there was the hiding of his power.

5 Before him went the pestilence, and burning coals went forth at his feet.

6 He stood, and measured the earth: he beheld, and drove asunder the nations; and the everlasting mountains were scattered, the perpetual hills did bow: his ways are everlasting.

Habakkuk 3:10-11

10 The mountains saw thee, and they trembled: the overflowing of the water passed by: the deep uttered his voice, and lifted up his hands on high.

11 The sun and moon stood still in their habitation: at the light of thine arrows they went, and at the shining of thy glittering spear.

Haggai 2:6-7

6 For thus saith the LORD of hosts; Yet once, it is a little while, and I will shake the heavens, and the earth, and the sea, and the dry land;

7 And I will shake all nations, and the desire of all nations shall come: and I will fill this house with glory, saith the LORD of hosts.

Zechariah 8:3

³ *Thus saith the LORD; I am returned unto Zion, and will dwell in the midst of Jerusalem: and Jerusalem shall be called a city of truth; and the mountain of the LORD of hosts the holy mountain.*

Zechariah 14:4

⁴ *And his feet shall stand in that day upon the mount of Olives, which is before Jerusalem on the east, and the mount of Olives shall cleave in the midst thereof toward the east and toward the west, and there shall be a very great valley; and half of the mountain shall remove toward the north, and half of it toward the south.*

Zechariah 14:8

⁸ *And it shall be in that day, that living waters shall go out from Jerusalem; half of them toward the former sea, and half of them toward the hinder sea: in summer and in winter shall it be.*

Malachi 3:1

¹ *Behold, I will send my messenger, and he shall prepare the way before me: and the Lord, whom ye seek, shall suddenly come to his temple, even the messenger of the covenant, whom ye delight in: behold, he shall come, saith the LORD of hosts.*

Malachi 4:2

² *But unto you that fear my name shall the Sun of righteousness arise with healing in his wings; and ye shall go forth, and grow up as calves of the stall.*

Matthew 24:29-30

²⁹ *Immediately after the tribulation of those days shall the sun be darkened, and the moon shall not give her light, and the stars shall fall from heaven, and the powers of the heavens shall be shaken:*

³⁰ *And then shall appear the sign of the Son of man in heaven: and then shall all the tribes of the earth mourn, and they shall see the Son of man coming in the clouds of heaven with power and great glory.*

Matthew 26:64

⁶⁴ *Jesus saith unto him, Thou hast said: nevertheless I say unto you, Hereafter shall ye see the Son of man sitting on the right hand of power, and coming in the clouds of heaven.*

Mark 13:26

²⁶ *And then shall they see the Son of man coming in the clouds with great power and glory.*

HE'S STILL COMING

Mark 14:62

[62] *And Jesus said, I am: and ye shall see the Son of man sitting on the right hand of power, and coming in the clouds of heaven.*

Luke 21:27

[27] *And then shall they see the Son of man coming in a cloud with power and great glory.*

Luke 22:69

[69] *Hereafter shall the Son of man sit on the right hand of the power of God.*

Acts 1:11

[11] *Which also said, Ye men of Galilee, why stand ye gazing up into heaven? this same Jesus, which is taken up from you into heaven, shall so come in like manner as ye have seen him go into heaven.*

Acts 3:20-21

[20] *And he shall send Jesus Christ, which before was preached unto you:*

[21] *Whom the heaven must receive until the times of restitution of all things, which God hath spoken by the mouth of all his holy prophets since the world began.*

Acts 15:16

[16] *After this I will return, and will build again the tabernacle of David, which is fallen down; and I will build again the ruins thereof, and I will set it up.*

Romans 11:26

[26] *And so all Israel shall be saved: as it is written, There shall come out of Sion the Deliverer, and shall turn away ungodliness from Jacob.*

1 Corinthians 15:24

[24] *Then cometh the end, when he shall have delivered up the kingdom to God, even the Father; when he shall have put down all rule and all authority and power.*

2 Thessalonians 1:7-8

[7] *And to you who are troubled rest with us, when the Lord Jesus shall be revealed from heaven with his mighty angels,*

[8] *In flaming fire taking vengeance on them that know not God, and that obey not the gospel of our Lord Jesus Christ.*

Revelation 1:7

[7] *Behold, he cometh with clouds; and every eye shall see him, and they also which pierced him: and all kindreds of the earth shall wall because of him. Even so, Amen.*

Revelation 2:25

[25] *But that which ye have already hold fast till I come.*

Revelation 19:11-14

[11] *And I saw heaven opened, and behold a white horse; and he that sat upon him was called Faithful and True, and in righteousness he doth judge and make war.*

[12] *His eyes were as a flame of fire, and on his head were many crowns; and he had a name written, that no man knew, but he himself.*

[13] *And he was clothed with a vesture dipped in blood: and his name is called The Word of God.*

[14] *And the armies which were in heaven followed him upon white horses, clothed in fine linen, white and clean.*

44 THE REGATHERING & REGENERATION OF FAITHFUL ISRAEL

Isaiah 10:20-23

[20] *And it shall come to pass in that day, that the remnant of Israel, and such as are escaped of the house of Jacob, shall no more again stay upon him that smote them; but shall stay upon the LORD, the Holy One of Israel, in truth.*

[21] *The remnant shall return, even the remnant of Jacob, unto the mighty God.*

[22] *For though thy people Israel be as the sand of the sea, yet a remnant of them shall return: the consumption decreed shall overflow with righteousness.*

[23] *For the Lord GOD of hosts shall make a consumption, even determined, in the midst of all the land.*

Isaiah 11:12

[12] *And he shall set up an ensign for the nations, and shall assemble the outcasts of Israel, and gather together the dispersed of Judah from the four corners of the earth.*

Isaiah 25:8

[8] *He will swallow up death in victory; and the Lord GOD will wipe away tears from off all faces; and the rebuke of his people shall he take away from off all the earth: for the LORD hath spoken it.*

Isaiah 25:9

9 And it shall be said in that day, Lo, this is our God; we have waited for him, and he will save us: this is the LORD; we have waited for him, we will be glad and rejoice in his salvation.

Isaiah 35:10

10 And the ransomed of the LORD shall return, and come to Zion with songs and everlasting joy upon their heads: they shall obtain joy and gladness, and sorrow and sighing shall flee away.

Isaiah 40:5

5 And the glory of the LORD shall be revealed, and all flesh shall see it together: for the mouth of the LORD hath spoken it.

Isaiah 43:5

5 Fear not: for I am with thee: I will bring thy seed from the east, and gather thee from the west.

Isaiah 43:6

6 I will say to the north, Give up; and to the south, Keep not back: bring my sons from far, and my daughters from the ends of the earth.

Jeremiah 16:14

14 Therefore, behold, the days come, saith the LORD, that it shall no more be said, The LORD liveth, that brought up the children of Israel out of the land of Egypt.

Jeremiah 16:15

15 But, The LORD liveth, that brought up the children of Israel from the land of the north, and from all the lands whither he had driven them: and I will bring them again into their land that I gave unto their fathers.

Jeremiah 23:3

3 And I will gather the remnant of my flock out of all countries whither I have driven them, and will bring them again to their folds; and they shall be fruitful and increase.

Jeremiah 24:6

6 For I will set mine eyes upon them for good, and I will bring them again to this land: and I will build them, and not pull them down; and I will plant them, and not pluck them up.

Jeremiah 29:14

[14] And I will be found of you, saith the LORD: and I will turn away your captivity, and I will gather you from all the nations, and from all the places whither I have driven you, saith the LORD; and I will bring you again into the place whence I caused you to be carried away captive.

Jeremiah 31:8

[8] Behold, I will bring them from the north country, and gather them from the coasts of the earth, and with them the blind and the lame, the woman with child and her that travaileth with child together: a great company shall return thither.

Jeremiah 31:33

[33] But this shall be the covenant that I will make with the house of Israel; After those days, saith the LORD, I will put my law in their inward parts, and write it in their hearts; and will be their God, and they shall be my people.

Jeremiah 32:37

[37] Behold, I will gather them out of all countries, whither I have driven them in mine anger, and in my fury, and in great wrath; and I will bring them again unto this place, and I will cause them to dwell safely.

Jeremiah 32:39

[39] And I will give them one heart, and one way, that they may fear me for ever, for the good of them, and of their children after them.

Jeremiah 32:40

[40] I will make an everlasting covenant with them: I will never stop doing good to them, and I will inspire them to fear me, so they will never turn away from me.

Jeremiah 46:27

[27] But fear not thou, 0 my servant Jacob, and be not dismayed, 0 Israel: for, behold, I will save thee from afar off, and thy seed from the land of their captivity; and Jacob shall return, and be in rest and at ease, and none shall make him afraid.

Ezekiel 11:16, 17

[16] Therefore say, Thus saith the Lord GOD; Although I have cast them far off among the heathen, and although I have scattered them among the countries, yet will I be to them as a little sanctuary in the countries where they shall come.

17 Therefore say, Thus saith the Lord GOD; I will even gather you from the people, and assemble you out of the countries where ye have been scattered, and I will give you the land of Israel.

Ezekiel 11:19-20

19 And I will give them one heart, and I will put a new spirit within you; and I will take the stony heart out of their flesh, and will give them an heart of flesh:

20 That they may walk in my statutes, and keep mine ordinances, and do them: and they shall be my people, and I will be their God.

Ezekiel 34:11-13

11 For thus saith the Lord GOD; Behold, I, even I, will both search my sheep, and seek them out.

12 As a shepherd seeketh out his flock in the day that he is among his sheep that are scattered; so will I seek out my sheep, and will deliver them out of all places where they have been scattered in the cloudy and dark day.

13 And I will bring them out from the people, and gather them from the countries, and will bring them to their own land, and feed them upon the mountains of Israel by the rivers, and in all the inhabited places of the country.

Ezekiel 36:25-28

25 Then will I sprinkle clean water upon you, and ye shall be clean: from all your filthiness, and from all your idols, will I cleanse you.

26 A new heart also will I give you, and a new spirit will I put within you: and I will take away the stony heart out of your flesh, and I will give you an heart of flesh.

27 And I will put my spirit within you, and cause you to walk in my statutes, and ye shall keep my judgments, and do them.

28 And ye shall dwell in the land that I gave to your fathers; and ye shall be my people, and I will be your God.

Ezekiel 37:12-14

12 Therefore prophesy and say unto them, Thus saith the Lord GOD; Behold, 0 my people, I will open your graves, and cause you to come up out of your graves, and bring you into the land of Israel.

13 And ye shall know that I am the LORD, when I have opened your graves, 0 my people, and brought you up out of your graves,

14 And shall put my spirit in you, and ye shall live, and I shall place you in your own land: then shall ye know that I the LORD have spoken it, and performed it, saith the LORD.

Hosea 1:10-11

¹⁰ Yet the number of the children of Israel shall be as the sand of the sea, which cannot be measured nor numbered; and it shall come to pass, that in the place where it was said unto them, Ye are not my people, there it shall be said unto them, Ye are the sons of the living God.

¹¹ Then shall the children of Judah and the children of Israel be gathered together, and appoint themselves one head, and they shall come up out of the land: for great shall be the day of Jezreel.

Hosea 3:5

⁵ Afterward shall the children of Israel return, and seek the LORD their God, and David their king; and shall fear the LORD and his goodness in the latter days.

Amos 9:14-15

¹⁴ And I will bring again the captivity of my people of Israel, and they shall build the waste cities, and inhabit them; and they shall plant vineyards, and drink the wine thereof; they shall also make gardens, and eat the fruit of them.

¹⁵ And I will plant them upon their land, and they shall no more be pulled up out of their land which I have given them, saith the LORD thy God.

Micah 7:18-19

¹⁸ Who is a God like unto thee, that pardoneth iniquity, and passeth by the transgression of the remnant of his heritage? he retaineth not his anger for ever, because he delighteth in mercy.

¹⁹ He will turn again, he will have compassion upon us; he will subdue our iniquities; and thou wilt cast all their sins into the depths of the sea.

Zechariah 12:10

¹⁰ And I will pour upon the house of David, and upon the inhabitants of Jerusalem, the spirit of grace and of supplications: and they shall look upon me whom they have pierced, and they shall mourn for him, as one mourneth for his only son, and shall be in bitterness for him, as one that is in bitterness for his firstborn.

Zechariah 13:1

¹ In that day there shall be a fountain opened to the house of David and to the inhabitants of Jerusalem for sin and for uncleanness.

Matthew 24:31

¹¹ And he shall send his angels with a great sound of a trumpet, and they shall gather together his elect from the four winds, from one end of heaven to the other.

Mark 13:27

27 And then shall he send his angels, and shall gather together his elect from the four winds, from the uttermost part of the earth to the uttermost part of heaven.

45 THE JUDGMENT & PUNISHMENT OF FAITHLESS ISRAEL

Ezekiel 11:21

21 But as for them whose heart walketh after the heart of their detestable things and their abominations, I will recompense their way upon their own heads, saith the Lord GOD.

Ezekiel 20:38

38 And I will purge out from among you the rebels, and them that transgress against me: I will bring them forth out of the country where they sojourn, and they shall not enter into the land of Israel: and ye shall know that I am the LORD.

Amos 9:9, 10

9 For, lo, I will command, and I will sift the house of Israel among all nations, like as corn is sifted in a sieve, yet shall not the least grain fall upon the earth.

10 All the sinners of my people shall die by the sword, which say, The evil shall not overtake nor prevent us.

Zechariah 13:8

8 And it shall come to pass, that in all the land, saith the LORD, two parts therein shall be cut off and die; but the third shall be left therein.

Malachi 4:1

1 For, behold, the day cometh, that shall burn as an oven; and all the proud, yea, and all that do wickedly, shall be stubble: and the day that cometh shall burn them up, saith the LORD of hosts, that it shall leave them neither root nor branch.

Matthew 24:48-51

48 But and if that evil servant shall say in his heart, My lord delayeth his coming;

49 And shall begin to smite his fellowservants, and to eat and drink with the drunken;

50 The lord of that servant shall come in a day when he looketh not for him, and in an hour that he is not aware of,

51 And shall cut him asunder, and appoint him his portion with the hypocrites: there shall be weeping and gnashing of teeth.

Matthew 25:7-10

[7] *Then all those virgins arose, and trimmed their lamps.*

[8] *And the foolish said unto the wise, Give us of your oil; for our lamps are gone out.*

[9] *But the wise answered, saying, Not so; lest there be not enough for us and you: but go ye rather to them that sell, and buy for yourselves.*

[10] *And while they went to buy, the bridegroom came; and they that were ready went in with him to the marriage: and the door was shut.*

Matthew 25:24-30

[24] *Then he which had received the one talent came and said, Lord, I knew thee that thou art an hard man, reaping where thou hast not sown, and gathering where thou hast not strawed:*

[25] *And I was afraid, and went and hid thy talent in the earth: lo, there thou hast that is thine.*

[26] *His lord answered and said unto him, Thou wicked and slothful servant, thou knewest that I reap where I sowed not, and gather where I have not strawed:*

[27] *Thou oughtest therefore to have put my money to the exchangers, and then at my coming I should have received mine own with usury.*

[28] *Take therefore the talent from him, and give it unto him which hath ten talents.*

[29] *For unto every one that hath shall be given, and he shall have abundance: but from him that hath not shall be taken away even that which he hath.*

[30] *And cast ye the unprofitable servant into outer darkness: there shall be weeping and gnashing of teeth.*

Luke 21:34-35

[34] *And take heed to yourselves, lest at any time your hearts be overcharged with surfeiting, and drunkenness, and cares of this life, and so that day come upon you unawares.*

[35] *For as a snare shall it come on all them that dwell on the face of the whole earth.*

Romans 9:6

[6] *Not as though the word of God hath taken none effect. For they are not all Israel, which are of Israel.*

1 Thessalonians 2:14-16

[14] *For ye, brethren, became followers of the churches of God which in Judaea are in Christ Jesus: for ye also have suffered like things of your own countrymen, even as they have of the Jews:*

HE'S STILL COMING

¹⁵ *Who both killed the Lord Jesus, and their own prophets, and have persecuted us; and they please not God, and are contrary to all men:*

¹⁶ *Forbidding us to speak to the Gentiles that they might be saved, to fill up their sins alway: for the wrath is come upon them to the uttermost.*

Revelation 3:9

⁹ *Behold, I will make them of the synagogue of Satan, which say they are Jews, and are not, but do lie; behold, I will make them to come and worship before thy feet, and to know that I have loved thee.*

46   THE JUDGMENT OF THE NATIONS

Matthew 13:40, 41

⁴⁰ *As therefore the tares are gathered and burned in the fire; so shall it be in the end of this world.*

⁴¹ *The Son of man shall send forth his angels, and they shall gather out of his kingdom all things that offend, and them which do iniquity.*

Matthew 13:47-49

⁴⁷ *Again, the kingdom of heaven is like unto a net, that was cast into the sea, and gathered of every kind:*

⁴⁸ *Which, when it was full, they drew to shore, and sat down, and gathered the good into vessels, but cast the bad away.*

⁴⁹ *So shall it be at the end of the world: the angels shall come forth, and sever the wicked from among the just.*

Matthew 25:31-46

³¹ *When the Son of man shall come in his glory, and all the holy angels with him, then shall he sit upon the throne of his glory:*

³² *And before him shall be gathered all nations: and he shall separate them one from another, as a shepherd divideth his sheep from the goats:*

³³ *And he shall set the sheep on his right hand, but the goats on the left.*

³⁴ *Then shall the King say unto them on his right hand, Come, ye blessed of my Father, inherit the kingdom prepared for you from the foundation of the world:*

³⁵ *For I was an hungred, and ye gave me meat: I was thirsty, and ye gave me drink: I was a stranger, and ye took me in:*

³⁶ *Naked, and ye clothed me: I was sick, and ye visited me: I was in prison, and ye came unto me.*

³⁷ *Then shall the righteous answer him, saying, Lord, when saw we thee an hungred, and fed thee? or thirsty, and gave thee drink?*

³⁸ *When saw we thee a stranger, and took thee in? or naked, and clothed thee?*

³⁹ *Or when saw we thee sick, or in prison, and came unto thee?*

⁴⁰ *And the King shall answer and say unto them, Verily I say unto you, Inasmuch as ye have done it unto one of the least of these my brethren, ye have done it unto me.*

⁴¹ *Then shall he say also unto them on the left hand, Depart from me, ye cursed, into everlasting fire, prepared for the devil and his angels:*

⁴² *For I was an hungred, and ye gave me no meat: I was thirsty, and ye gave me no drink:*

⁴³ *I was a stranger, and ye took me not in: naked, and ye clothed me not: sick, and in prison, and ye visited me not.*

⁴⁴ *Then shall they also answer him, saying, Lord, when saw we thee an hungred, or athirst, or a stranger, or naked, or sick, or in prison, and did not minister unto thee?*

⁴⁵ *Then shall he answer them, saying, Verily I say unto you, Inasmuch as ye did it not to one of the least of these, ye did it not to me.*

⁴⁶ *And these shall go away into everlasting punishment: but the righteous into life.*

47 — THE JUDGMENT OF ANGELS

Mark 1:23-24

²³ *And there was in their synagogue a man with an unclean spirit; and he cried out,*

²⁴ *Saying, Let us alone; what have we to do with thee, thou Jesus of Nazareth? art thou come to destroy us? I know thee who thou art, the Holy One of God.*

1 Corinthians 6:3

³ *Know ye not that we shall judge angels? how much more things that pertain to this life?*

2 Peter 2:4

⁴ *For if God spared not the angels that sinned, but cast them down to hell, and delivered them into chains of darkness, to be reserved unto judgment;*

Jude 1:6

⁶ *And the angels which kept not their first estate, but left their own habitation, he hath reserved in everlasting chains under darkness unto the judgment of the great day.*

Job 19:25-26

[25] *For I know that my redeemer liveth, and that he shall stand at the latter day upon the earth:*

[26] *And though after my skin worms destroy this body, yet in my flesh shall I see God.*

Psalm 49:15

[15] *But God will redeem my soul from the power of the grave: for he shall receive me. Selah.*

Isaiah 25:8-9

[8] *He will swallow up death in victory; and the Lord GOD will wipe away tears from off all faces; and the rebuke of his people shall he take away from off all the earth: for the LORD hath spoken it.*

[9] *And it shall be said in that day, Lo, this is our God; we have waited for him, and he will save us: this is the LORD; we have waited for him, we will be glad and rejoice in his salvation.*

Isaiah 26:19

[19] *Thy dead men shall live, together with my dead body shall they arise. Awake and sing, ye that dwell in dust: for thy dew is as the dew of herbs, and the earth shall cast out the dead.*

Daniel 12:2-3

[2] *And many of them that sleep in the dust of the earth shall awake, some to everlasting life, and some to shame and everlasting contempt.*

[3] *And they that be wise shall shine as the brightness of the firmament; and they that turn many to righteousness as the stars for ever and ever.*

Hosea 13:14

[14] *I will ransom them from the power of the grave; I will redeem them from death: O death, I will be thy plagues; O grave, I will be thy destruction: repentance shall be hid from mine eyes.*

John 5:28-29

[28] *Marvel not at this: for the hour is coming, in the which all that are in the graves shall hear his voice,*

[29] *And shall come forth; they that have done good, unto the resurrection of life; and they that have done evil, unto the resurrection of damnation.*

John 11:23-27

[23] *Jesus saith unto her, Thy brother shall rise again.*

[24] *Martha saith unto him, I know that he shall rise again in the resurrection at the last day.*

[25] *Jesus said unto her, I am the resurrection, and the life: he that believeth in me, though he were dead, yet shall he live:*

[26] *And whosoever liveth and believeth in me shall never die. Believest thou this?*

Hebrews 11:35

[35] *Women received their dead raised to life again: and others were tortured, not accepting deliverance; that they might obtain a better resurrection.*

Revelation 6:9-11

[9] *And when he had opened the fifth seal, I saw under the altar the souls of them that were slain for the word of God, and for the testimony which they held:*

[10] *And they cried with a loud voice, saying, How long, O Lord, holy and true, dost thou not judge and avenge our blood on them that dwell on the earth?*

[11] *And white robes were given unto every one of them; and it was said unto them, that they should rest yet for a little season, until their fellowservants also and their brethren, that should be killed as they were, should be fulfilled.*

Revelation 20:4-6

[4] *And I saw thrones, and they sat upon them, and judgment was given unto them: and I saw the souls of them that were beheaded for the witness of Jesus, and for the word of God, and which had not worshipped the beast, neither his image, neither had received his mark upon their foreheads, or in their hands; and they lived and reigned with Christ a thousand years.*

[5] *But the rest of the dead lived not again until the thousand years were finished. This is the first resurrection.*

[6] *Blessed and holy is he that hath part in the first resurrection: on such the second death hath no power, but they shall be priests of God and of Christ, and shall reign with him a thousand years.*

(49) CASTING OF SATAN INTO THE BOTTOMLESS PIT

Romans 16:20

[20] *The God of peace will soon crush Satan under your feet. The grace of our Lord Jesus be with you.*

Romans 20:1-3

[1] And I saw an angel come down from heaven, having the key of the bottomless pit and a great chain in his hand.

[2] And he laid hold on the dragon, that old serpent, which is the Devil, and Satan, and bound him a thousand years,

[3] And cast him into the bottomless pit, and shut him up, and set a seal upon him, that he should deceive the nations no more, till the thousand years should be fulfilled: and after that he must be loosed a little season.

50   THE MARRIAGE SUPPER OF THE LAMB

Isaiah 61:10

[10] I will greatly rejoice in the LORD, my soul shall be joyful in my God; for he bath clothed me with the garments of salvation, he bath covered me with the robe of righteousness, as a bridegroom decketh himself with ornaments, and as a bride adorneth herself with her jewels.

Isaiah 22:2

[2] The kingdom of heaven is like unto a certain king, which made a marriage for his son,

Isaiah 25:1

[1] Then shall the kingdom of heaven be likened unto ten virgins, which took their lamps, and went forth to meet the bridegroom.

Luke 12:35-36

[35] Let your loins be girded about, and your lights burning;

[36] And ye yourselves like unto men that wait for their lord, when he will return from the wedding; that when he cometh and knocketh, they may open unto him immediately.

Revelation 19:6-9

[6] And I heard as it were the voice of a great multitude, and as the voice of many waters, and as the voice of mighty thunderings, saying, Alleluia: for the Lord God omnipotent reigneth.

[7] Let us be glad and rejoice, and give honour to him: for the marriage of the Lamb is come, and his wife hath made herself ready.

[8] And to her was granted that she should be arrayed in fine linen, clean and white: for the fine linen is the righteousness of saints.

[9] And he saith unto me, Write, Blessed are they which are called unto the marriage supper of the Lamb. And he saith unto me, These are the true sayings of God.

Psalm 2:6-8

⁶ *Yet have I set my king upon my holy hill of Zion.*

⁷ *I will declare the decree: the LORD hath said unto me, Thou art my Son; this day have I begotten thee.*

⁸ *Ask of me, and I shall give thee the heathen for thine inheritance, and the uttermost parts of the earth for thy possession.*

Psalm 98:4, 9

⁴ *Make a joyful noise unto the LORD, all the earth: make a loud noise, and rejoice, and sing praise.*

⁹ *Let them sing before the Lord, for He comes to judge the earth. He will judge the world in righteousness and the peoples with equity.*

Isaiah 2:2-4

² *And it shall come to pass in the last days, that the mountain of the LORD's house shall be established in the top of the mountains, and shall be exalted above the hills; and all nations shall flow unto it.*

³ *And many people shall go and say, Come ye, and let us go up to the mountain of the LORD, to the house of the God of Jacob; and he will teach us of his ways, and we will walk in his paths: for out of Zion shall go forth the law, and the word of the LORD from Jerusalem.*

⁴ *And he shall judge among the nations, and shall rebuke many people: and they shall beat their swords into plowshares, and their spears into pruninghooks: nation shall not lift up sword against nation, neither shall they learn war any more.*

Isaiah 9:6-7

⁶ *For unto us a child is born, unto us a son is given: and the government shall be upon his shoulder: and his name shall be called Wonderful, Counsellor, The mighty God, The everlasting Father, The Prince of Peace.*

⁷ *Of the increase of his government and peace there shall be no end, upon the throne of David, and upon his kingdom, to order it, and to establish it with judgment and with justice from henceforth even for ever. The zeal of the LORD of hosts will perform this.*

Isaiah 11:6-9

⁶ *The wolf also shall dwell with the lamb, and the leopard shall lie down with the kid; and the calf and the young lion and the fatling together; and a little child shall lead them.*

[7] *And the cow and the bear shall feed; their young ones shall lie down together: and the lion shall eat straw like the ox.*

[8] *And the sucking child shall play on the hole of the asp, and the weaned child shall put his hand on the cockatrice' den.*

[9] *They shall not hurt nor destroy in all my holy mountain: for the earth shall be full of the knowledge of the LORD, as the waters cover the sea.*

Isaiah 25:8

[8] *He will swallow up death in victory; and the Lord GOD will wipe away tears from off all faces; and the rebuke of his people shall he take away from off all the earth: for the LORD hath spoken it.*

Isaiah 29:18, 19

[18] *And in that day shall the deaf hear the words of the book, and the eyes of the blind shall see out of obscurity, and out of darkness.*

[19] *The meek also shall increase their joy in the LORD, and the poor among men shall rejoice in the Holy One of Israel.*

Isaiah 30:23-26

[23] *Then shall he give the rain of thy seed, that thou shalt sow the ground withal; and bread and plenteous: in that day shall thy cattle feed in large pastures.*

[24] *The oxen likewise and the young asses that ear the ground shall eat clean provender, which hath been winnowed with the shovel and with the fan.*

[25] *And there shall be upon every high mountain, and upon every high hill, rivers and streams of waters in the day of the great slaughter, when the towers fall.*

[26] *Moreover the light of the moon shall be as the light of the sun, and the light of the sun shall be sevenfold, as the light of seven days, in the day that the LORD bindeth up the breach of his people, and healeth the stroke of their wound.*

Isaiah 35:5-10

[5] *Then the eyes of the blind shall be opened, and the ears of the deaf shall be unstopped.*

[6] *Then shall the lame man leap as an hart, and the tongue of the dumb sing: for in the wilderness shall waters break out, and streams in the desert.*

[7] *And the parched ground shall become a pool, and the thirsty land springs of water: in the habitation of dragons, where each lay, shall be grass with reeds and rushes.*

[8] *And an highway shall be there, and a way, and it shall be called The way of holiness; the unclean shall not pass over it; but it shall be for those: the wayfaring men, though fools, shall not err therein.*

⁹ No lion shall be there, nor any ravenous beast shall go up thereon, it shall not be found there; but the redeemed shall walk there:

¹⁰ And the ransomed of the LORD shall return, and come to Zion with songs and everlasting joy upon their heads: they shall obtain joy and glad ness, and sorrow and sighing shall flee away.

Isaiah 40:4-5

⁴ Every valley shall be exalted, and every mountain and hill shall be made low: and the crooked shall be made straight, and the rough places plain:

⁵ And the glory of the LORD shall be revealed, and all flesh shall see it together: for the mouth of the LORD hath spoken it.

Isaiah 40:10-11

¹⁰ Behold, the Lord GOD will come with strong hand, and his arm shall rule for him: behold, his reward is with him, and his work before him.

¹¹ He shall feed his flock like a shepherd: he shall gather the lambs with his arm, and carry them in his bosom, and shall gently lead those that are with young.

Isaiah 42:16

¹⁶ And I will bring the blind by a way that they knew not; I will lead them in paths that they have not known: I will make darkness light before them, and crooked things straight. These things will I do unto them, and not forsake them.

Isaiah 45:6

⁶ That they may know from the rising of the sun, and from the west, that there is none beside me. I am the LORD, and there is none else.

Isaiah 49:10, 11

¹⁰ They shall not hunger nor thirst; neither shall the heat nor sun smite them: for he that hath mercy on them shall lead them, even by the springs of water shall he guide them.

¹¹ And I will make all my mountains a way, and my highways shall be exalted.

Isaiah 55:13

¹³ Instead of the thorn shall come up the fir tree, and instead of the brier shall come up the myrtle tree: and it shall be to the LORD for a name, for an everlasting sign that shall not be cut off.

Isaiah 60:1

¹ Arise, shine; for thy light is come, and the glory of the LORD is risen upon thee.

Isaiah 60:3

³ And the Gentiles shall come to thy light, and kings to the brightness of thy rising.

Isaiah 60:11

¹¹ Therefore thy gates shall be open continually; they shall not be shut day nor night; that men may bring unto thee the forces of the Gentiles, and that their kings may be brought.

Isaiah 60:19-20

¹⁹ The sun shall be no more thy light by day; nei ther for brightness shall the moon give light unto thee: but the LORD shall be unto thee an everlasting light, and thy God thy glory.

²⁰ Thy sun shall no more go down; neither shall thy moon withdraw itself: for the LORD shall be thine everlasting light, and the daysof thy mourning shall be ended.

Isaiah 60:22

²² A little one shall become a thousand, and a small one a strong nation: I the LORD will hasten it in his time.

Isaiah 65:19-20

¹⁹ And I will rejoice in Jerusalem, and joy in my people: and the voice of weeping shall be no more heard in her, nor the voice of crying.

²⁰ There shall be no more thence an infant of days, nor an old man that hath not filled his days: for the child shall die an hundred years old; but the sinner being an hundred years old shall be accursed.

Isaiah 65:25

²⁵ The wolf and the lamb shall feed together, and the lion shall eat straw like the bullock: and dust shall be the serpent's meat. They shall not hurt nor destroy in all my holy mountain, saith the LORD.

Jeremiah 23:5-6

⁵ Behold, the days come, saith the LORD, that I will raise unto David a righteous Branch, and a King shall reign and prosper, and shall execute judgment and justice in the earth.

⁶ In his days Judah shall be saved, and Israel shall dwell safely: and this is his name whereby he shall be called, THE LORD OUR RIGHTEOUSNESS.

Ezekiel 34:23-24

²³ And I will set up one shepherd over them, and he shall feed them, even my servant David; he

shall feed them, and he shall be their shepherd.

²⁴ And I the LORD will be their God, and my servant David a prince among them; I the LORD have spoken it.

Daniel 2:44

⁴⁴ And in the days of these kings shall the God of heaven set up a kingdom, which shall never be destroyed: and the kingdom shall not be left to other people, but it shall break in pieces and consume all these kingdoms, and it shall stand for ever.

Daniel 7:13,14

¹³ I saw in the night visions, and, behold, one like the Son of man came with the clouds of heaven, and came to the Ancient of days, and they brought him near before him.

¹⁴ And there was given Him dominion, and glory, and a kingdom, that all people, nations, and languages should serve Him; His dominion is an everlasting dominion, which shall not pass away, this kingdom that which shall not be destroyed.

Joel 3:18

¹⁸ And it shall come to pass in that day, that the mountains shall drop down new wine, and the hills shall flow with milk, and all the rivers of Judah shall flow with waters, and a fountain shall come forth of the house of the LORD, and shall water the valley of Shittim.

Amos 9:11, 13

¹¹ In that day will I raise up the tabernacle of David that is fallen, and close up the breaches thereof; and I will raise up his ruins, and I will build it as in the days of old:

¹³ Behold, the days come, saith the LORD, that the plowman shall overtake the reaper, and the treader of grapes him that soweth seed; and the mountains shall drop sweet wine, and all the hills shall melt.

Micah 4:1-6

¹ But in the last days it shall come to pass, that the mountain of the house of the LORD shall be established in the top of the mountains, and it shall be exalted above the hills; and people shall flow unto it.

² And many nations shall come, and say, Come, and let us go up to the mountain of the LORD, and to the house of the God of Jacob; and he will teach us of his ways, and we will walk in his paths: for the law shall go forth of Zion, and the word of the LORD from Jerusalem.

³ And he shall judge among many people, and rebuke strong nations afar off; and they shall beat their swords into plowshares, and their spears into pruninghooks: nation shall not lift up a sword against nation, neither shall they learn war any more.

[4] But they shall sit every man under his vine and under his fig tree; and none shall make them afraid: for the mouth of the LORD of hosts hath spoken it.

[5] For all people will walk every one in the name of his god, and we will walk in the name of the LORD our God for ever and ever.

[6] In that day, saith the LORD, will I assemble her that halteth, and I will gather her that is driven out and her that I have afflicted.

Habakkuk 2:14

[14] For the earth shall be filled with the knowledge of the glory of the LORD, as the waters cover the sea.

Zephaniah 3:9

[9] For then will I turn to the people a pure language, that they may all call upon the name of the LORD, to serve him with one consent.

Zephaniah 3:15

[15] The LORD hath taken away thy judgments, he hath cast out thine enemy: the king of Israel, even the LORD, is in the midst of thee: thou shalt not see evil any more.

Zephaniah 3:17

[17] The LORD thy God in the midst of thee is mighty; he will save, he will rejoice over thee with joy; he will rest in his love, he will joy over thee with singing.

Zechariah 6:12-13

[12] And speak unto him, saying, Thus speaketh the LORD of hosts, saying, Behold the man whose name is The BRANCH; and he shall grow up out of his place, and he shall build the temple of the LORD:

[13] Even he shall build the temple of the LORD; and he shall bear the glory, and shall sit and rule upon his throne; and he shall be a priest upon his throne: and the counsel of peace shall be between them both.

Zechariah 8:3-5

[3] Thus saith the LORD; I am returned unto Zion, and will dwell in the midst of Jerusalem: and Jerusalem shall be called a city of truth; and the mountain of the LORD of hosts the holy mountain.

⁴ Thus saith the LORD of hosts; There shall yet old men and old women dwell in the streets of Jerusalem, and every man with his staff in his hand for very age.

⁵ And the streets of the city shall be full of boys and girls playing in the streets thereof.

Zechariah 14:8-9

⁸ And it shall be in that day, that living waters shall go out from Jerusalem; half of them toward the former sea, and half of them toward the hinder sea: in summer and in winter shall it be.

⁹ And the LORD shall be king over all the earth: in that day shall there be one LORD, and his name one.

Zechariah 14:16

¹⁶ And it shall come to pass, that every one that is left of all the nations which came against Jerusalem shall even go up from year to year to worship the King, the LORD of hosts, and to keep the feast of tabernacles.

Zechariah 14:20

²⁰ In that day shall there be upon the bells of the horses, HOLINESS UNTO THE LORD; and the pots in the LORD's house shall be like the bowls before the altar.

Matthew 19:28

²⁸ And Jesus said unto them, Verily I say unto you, That ye which have followed me, in the regeneration when the Son of man shall sit in the throne of his glory, ye also shall sit upon twelve thrones, judging the twelve tribes of Israel.

Matthew 25:31

³¹ When the Son of man shall come in his glory, and all the holy angels with him, then shall he sit upon the throne of his glory:

Luke 1:31-33

³¹ And, behold, thou shalt conceive in thy womb, and bring forth a son, and shalt call his name JESUS.

³² He shall be great, and shall be called the Son of the Highest: and the Lord God shall give unto him the throne of his father David:

³³ And he shall reign over the house of Jacob for ever; and of his kingdom there shall be no end.

Luke 22:30

[30] That ye may eat and drink at my table in my kingdom, and sit on thrones judging the twelve tribes of Israel.

Acts 2:30

[30] Therefore being a prophet, and knowing that God had sworn with an oath to him, that of the fruit of his loins, according to the flesh, he would raise up Christ to sit on his throne;

Romans 8:21

[21] Because the creature itself also shall be delivered from the bondage of corruption into the glorious liberty of the children of God.

1 Corinthians 15:24-28

[24] Then cometh the end, when he shall have delivered up the kingdom to God, even the Father; when he shall have put down all rule and all authority and power.

[25] For he must reign, till he hath put all enemies under his feet.

[26] The last enemy that shall be destroyed is death.

[27] For he hath put all things under his feet. But when he saith, all things are put under him, it is manifest that he is excepted, which did put all things under him.

[28] And when all things shall be subdued unto him, then shall the Son also himself be subject unto him that put all things under him, that God may be all in all.

Philippians 2:10-11

[10] That at the name of Jesus every knee should bow, of things in heaven, and things in earth, and things under the earth;

[11] And that every tongue should confess that Jesus Christ is Lord, to the glory of God the Jather.

2 Timothy 2:12

[12] If we suffer, we shall also reign with him: if we deny him, he also will deny us.

Hebrews 1:8

[8] But unto the Son he saith, Thy throne, 0 God, is for ever and ever: a sceptre of righteousness is the sceptre of thy kingdom.

Revelation 3:21

[21] To him that overcometh will I grant to sit with me in my throne, even as I also overcame, and am set down with my Father in his throne.

Revelation 5:13

¹³ And every creature which is in heaven, and on the earth, and under the earth, and such as are in the sea, and all that are in them, heard I saying, Blessing, and honour, and glory, and power, be unto him that sitteth upon the throne, and unto the Lamb for ever and ever.

Revelation 11:15

¹⁵ And the seventh angel sounded; and there were great voices in heaven, saying, The kingdoms of this world are become the kingdoms of our Lord, and of his Christ; and he shall reign for ever and ever.

Revelation 19:15

¹⁵ And out of his mouth goeth a sharp sword, that with it he should smite the nations: and he shall rule them with a rod of iron: and he treadeth the winepress of the fierceness and wrath of Almighty God.

Revelation 20:4-6

⁴ And I saw thrones, and they sat upon them, and judgment was given unto them: and I saw the souls of them that were beheaded for the witness of Jesus, and for the word of God, and which had not worshipped the beast, neither his image, neither had received his mark upon their foreheads, or in their hands; and they lived and reigned with Christ a thousand years.

⁵ But the rest of the dead lived not again until the thousand years were finished. This is the first resurrection.

⁶ Blessed and holy is he that hath part in the first resurrection: on such the second death hath no power, but they shall be priests of God and of Christ, and shall reign with him a thousand years.

52 — SATAN'S FINAL REVOLT

Revelation 20:7-10

⁷ And when the thousand years are expired, Satan shall be loosed out of his prison,

⁸ And shall go out to deceive the nations which are in the four quarters of the earth, Gog and Magog, to gather them together to battle: the number of whom is as the sand of the sea.

⁹ And they went up on the breadth of the earth, and compassed the camp of the saints about, and the beloved city: and fire came down from God out of heaven, and devoured them.

¹⁰ And the devil that deceived them was cast into the lake of fire and brimstone, where the beast and the false prophet are, and shall be tormented day and night for ever and ever.

Psalm 9:17

17 The wicked shall be turned into hell, and all the nations that forget God.

Ecclesiastes 12:14

14 For God will bring every deed into judgement, including every hidden thing, whether it is good or evil.

Daniel 7:9, 10

9 I beheld till the thrones were cast down, and the Ancient of days did sit, whose garment was white as snow, and the hair of his head like the pure wool: his throne was like the fiery flame, and his wheels as burning fire.

10 A fiery stream issued and came forth from before him: thousand thousands ministered unto him, and ten thousand times ten thou sand stood before him: the judgment was set, and the books were opened.

Matthew 7:21-23

21 Not every one that saith unto me, Lord, Lord, shall enter into the kingdom of heaven; but he that doeth the will of my Father which is in heaven.

22 Many will say to me in that day, Lord, Lord, have we not prophesied in thy name? and in thy name have cast out devils? and in thy name done many wonderful works?

23 And then will I profess unto them, I never knew you: depart from me, ye that work iniquity.

Matthew 12:36, 37

36 But I say unto you, That every idle word that men shall speak, they shall give account thereof in the day of judgment.

37 For by thy words thou shalt be justified, and by thy words thou shalt be condemned.

John 5:22

22 For the Father judgeth no man, but hath committed all judgment unto the Son.

John 5:27

27 And hath given him authority to execute judgment also, because he is the Son of man.

John 12:48

48 He that rejecteth me, and receiveth not my words, hath one that judgeth him: the word that I have spoken, the same shall judge him in the last day.

Acts 10:42

42 And he commanded us to preach unto the people, and to testify that it is he which was ordained of God to be the Judge of quick and dead.

Acts 17:31

31 Because he hath appointed a day, in the which he will judge the world in righteousness by that man whom he hath ordained; whereof he hath given assurance unto all men, in that he hath raised him from the dead.

2 Timothy 4:1

1 I charge thee therefore before God, and the Lord Jesus Christ, who shall judge the quick and the dead at his appearing and his kingdom.

Hebrews 9:27

27 And as it is appointed unto men once to die, but after this the judgment.

Revelation 20:11-15

11 I saw a great white throne, and him that sat on it, from whose face the earth and the heaven fled away; and there was found no place for them.

12 I saw the dead, small and great, stand before God; and the books were opened: and another book was opened, which is the book of life: and the dead were judged out of those things which were written in the books, according to their works.

13 the sea gave up the dead which were in it; and death and hell delivered up the dead which were in them: and they were judged every man according to their works.

14 death and hell were cast into the lake of fire. This is the second death.

15 whosoever was not found written in the book of life was cast into the lake of fire.

54 THE DESTRUCTION OF THIS PRESENT EARTH AND HEAVEN

Isaiah 51:6

6 Lift up your eyes to the heavens, and look upon the earth beneath: for the heavens shall vanish away like smoke, and the earth shall wax old like a garment, and they that dwell therein shall die in like manner: but my salvation shall be for ever, and my righteousness shall not be abolished.

Matthew 24:35

[35] *Heaven and earth shall pass away, but my words shall not pass away.*

Hebrews 1:10-12

[10] *And, Thou, Lord, in the beginning hast laid the foundation of the earth; and the heavens are the works of thine hands:*

[11] *They shall perish; but thou remainest; and they all shall wax old as doth a garment.*

[12] *And as a vesture shalt thou fold them up, and they shall be changed: but thou art the same, and thy years shall not fail.*

2 Peter 3:10-12

[10] *But the day of the Lord will come as a thief in the night; in the which the heavens shall pass away with a great noise, and the elements shall melt with fervent heat, the earth also and the works that are therein shall be burned up.*

[11] *Seeing then that all these things shall be dissolved, what manner of persons ought ye to be in all holy conversation and godliness,*

[12] *Looking for and hasting unto the coming of the day of God, wherein the heavens being on fire shall be dissolved, and the elements shall melt with fervent heat?*

1 John 2:17

[17] *And the world passeth away, and the lust thereof: but he that doeth the will of God abideth for ever.*

55   THE CREATION OF A NEW EARTH AND HEAVEN

Isaiah 65:17

[17] *For, behold, I create new heavens and a new earth: and the former shall not be remembered, nor come into mind.*

Isaiah 66:22

[22] *As the new heavens and new earth that I make will endure before me, declares the Lord, so will your name and their decendants endure.*

2 Peter 3:13

¹³ Nevertheless we, according to his promise, look for new heavens and a new earth, wherein dwelleth righteousness.

Revelation 21:1

¹ And I saw a new heaven and a new earth: for the first heaven and the first earth were passed away; and there was no more sea.

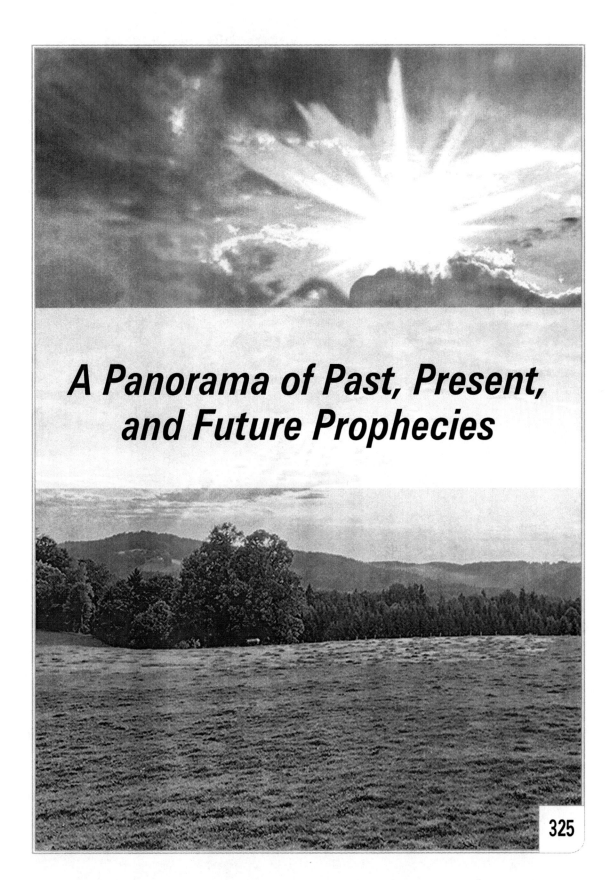

A Panorama of Past, Present, and Future Prophecies

A PANORAMA OF PAST, PRESENT, AND FUTURE PROPHECIES

"Known unto God are all his works from the beginning of the world" (Acts 15:18).

Here they are—key prophecies regarding individuals, cities, nations, last day conditions, the Great Tribulation, Battle of Armageddon, the Millennium, and of supreme significance, those prophecies relating to the person and work of the Lord Jesus Christ.

" . . . worship God; for the testimony of Jesus is the spirit of prophecy" (Rev. 19:10).

Complete ■ Concise ■ Certain ■ Christ-centered

"But the day of the Lord will come as a thief in the night; in the which the heavens shall pass away with a great noise, and the elements shall melt with fervent heat, the earth also and the works that are therein shall be burned up. Seeing then that all these things shall be dissolved, what manner of persons ought ye to be in all holy conversation and godliness, Looking for and hastening unto the coming of the day of God, wherein the heavens being on fire shall be dissolved, and the elements shall melt with fervent heat? Nevertheless we, according to his promise, look for new heavens and a new earth, wherein dwelleth righteousness. Wherefore, beloved, seeing that ye look for such things, be diligent that ye may be found of him in peace, without spot, and blameless" (2 Peter 3:10-14).

100 OF THE MOST IMPORTANT OR WELL-KNOWN PREDICTIONS IN THE BIBLE

PREDICTIONS REGARDING INDIVIDUALS—Old Testament

1. Abraham
   a. That God would father a great nation through him (Gen. 12:2; 15:5)
   b. That God would reward or punish nations according to their treatment of Israel (Gen. 12:3)
   c. That God would give Abraham and his seed a land (Gen. 12:7; 15:18-21; 17:8)
   d. That Abraham would have a son in his old age (Gen. 15:4; 18:10, 14)
   e. That the nation Abraham founded would serve in a foreign land for 400 years (Gen. 15:13)

    f.   That God would lead them out with great riches (Gen. 15:14)

    g.   That God would destroy Sodom (Gen. 18:20-21)

2. **Adam**

    a.   That he would die spiritually if he disobeyed God (Gen. 2:17; 3:3)

    b.   That he would die physically if he disobeyed God (Gen. 2:17; 5:5)

3. **Alexander the Great**

    a.   The he would utterly defeat the Persians and establish a world empire (Dan. 2:32-39; 7:6; 8:5-8, 21; 11:3)

    b.   That he would suddenly die and his kingdom would be divided into four parts (Dan. 8:8, 22; 11:4)

4. **Antiochus Epiphanes**

    a.   That this Syrian Jew-hater would persecute the Jews and profane their temple (Dan. 8:9-13)

    b.   That the temple would be cleansed after a period of 2,300 days (Dan. 8:14)

5. **Barak**

    a.   That he would defeat Sisera through the help of a woman (Judg. 4:6-9)

6. **Belshazzar**

    a.   That God would judge this wicked Babylonian ruler by immediately allowing the Persians to take his kingdom (Dan. 5:25-28)

7. **Cyrus**

    a.   That this Persian warrior would be allowed to build a world empire (Isa. 45:1-4)

    b.   That he would permit the Jews to return to Jerusalem and rebuild both their temple and city, which were previously destroyed by Nebuchadnezzar (Isa. 44:28; 45:13)

8. **David**

    a.   That both sword and sorrow would be a part of his household because of his sins of adultery and murder (2 Sam. 12:9-12)

    b.   That Bathsheba's first infant son would die (2 Sam. 12:14)

    c.   That David's kingdom would eventually be established forever (2 Sam. 7:16)

    d.   That Solomon, not David, would build the temple (1 Chron. 17:1-12; 22:8-10; 28:2-6)

9. **Elijah**

    a.   That it would not rain for three and one-half years (1 Kings 17:1)

    b.   That a starving widow and her son would be supernaturally fed by God (1 Kings 17:14)

    c.   That wicked King Ahab would have his blood shed and die in the same place where he had godly Naboth killed (1 Kings 21:19)

    d.   That Ahab's wife, Jezebel, would be eaten by dogs (1 Kings 21:23)

10. **Elisha**
    a. That a widow's oil would be supernaturally increased (2 Kings 4:1-4)
    b. That a barren Shunammite woman would have a son (2 Kings 4:16)
    c. That Naaman's leprosy would be healed by washing in the Jordan River (2 Kings 5:10)
    d. That the starving citizens of besieged Samaria would enjoy an abundance of food within 24 hours (2 Kings 7:1)
    e. That the skeptic who ridiculed the abundant food prediction would live to see it fulfilled but would not eat the food (2 Kings 7:2)

11. **Gideon**
    a. That he would defeat a mighty Midianite army with but 300 soldiers (Judg. 6:14; 7:7)

12. **Hezekiah**
    a. That a divine plague would supernaturally deliver both King Hezekiah and the people of Jerusalem from Assyrian troops who had surrounded the city (2 Kings 19:6-7a; Isa. 37:33-35)
    b. That the Assyrian king Sennacherib would be killed upon returning to Nineveh (Isa. 37:7)
    c. That God would heal and add an additional 15 years to the life of Hezekiah (2 Kings 20:1-6; 2 Chron. 32:24; Isa. 38:1-5)

13. **Jacob**
    a. That he and his seed would be served by Esau and his seed (Gen. 25:23)
    b. That God would bring him back to the land of Canaan (Gen. 28:15)
    c. Jacob predicted the lifestyle of his 12 sons and the tribes they would found (Gen. 49)

14. **Jehoshaphat**
    a. That God would save the hopelessly outnumbered people of Judah from a threatened Moabite and Ammonite invasion (2 Chron. 20:14-17)

15. **Joseph**
    a. That his 11 brothers would someday bow down to him (Gen. 37:5-7)
    b. That the Middle East would experience seven years of bumper crops, followed by seven years of famine (Gen. 41:29-31)

16. **Josiah**
    a. That this godly Judean king would burn the decayed bones of ungodly Israelite king Jeroboam's pagan priests upon the false altar the wicked ruler had once constructed (1 Kings 13:1-3)

17. **Joshua**
    a. That Joshua would be given victory over his enemies in Canaan (Josh. 1:1-9)
    b. That the Jordan River would be parted (Josh. 3:13)
    c. That the walls of Jericho would fall after the sounding of trumpets (Josh. 6:5)

18. **Moses**
    a. That he would deliver Israel from the Egyptian captivity (Exod. 3:10)
    b. That the deliverance would be effected by divine miracles (Exod. 3:20)
    c. That Israel would leave Egypt with great wealth (Exod. 3:21-22)
    d. That God would divide the Red Sea waters, bringing escape for Israel and death for the Egyptians (Exod. 14:16-17)
    e. That God would feed Israel with manna (Exod. 16:4)
    f. That the Sabbath would be observed by Israel throughout the ages (Exod. 31:16-17)
    g. That Moses, because of a previous sin, would not enter the promised land (Num. 20:12; Deut. 3:23-26)
    h. That Moses, however, would be allowed to see it (Deut. 3:27)

19. **Nebuchadnezzar**
    a. That Nebuchadnezzar would lose his mind and live like an animal for seven years because of his pride (Dan. 4:24-25)
    b. That after seven years, Nebuchadnezzar would have his kingdom restored (Dan. 4:26)

20. **Noah**
    a. That God would destroy the earth but save him and his family (Gen. 6:13, 18)
    b. That God would never again destroy the world by a flood (Gen. 8:21; 9:11)
    c. That God would preserve the four seasons and the day and night arrangements (Gen. 8:22)

21. **Solomon**
    a. That he would be given much wisdom, riches, and honor (1 Kings 3:10-13)
    b. That God would rend the kingdom from his son because of Solomon's sin (1 Kings 11:11-13)

22. **Zedekiah**
    a. That Judah's final and wicked king would be forced to look into the eyes of Nebuchadnezzar (Jer. 32:4-5)
    b. That he would not see the land of Babylon even though he would be carried there (Ezek. 12:13)

PREDICTIONS REGARDING INDIVIDUALS—New Testament

23. **John the Baptist**
    a. That he would be a Spirit-filled Nazarite (Lk. 1:15)
    b. That he would be the forerunner of the Messiah (Isa. 40:3-5; Mal. 3:1a; Lk. 1:17, 76)

24. **Judas**
    a. That he would be possessed and controlled by Satan (Jn. 6:70, 71)

HE'S STILL COMING

b. That he would betray Christ (Matt. 26:21-25; Mk. 14:18-21; Lk. 22:21-23; Jn. 13:18, 21-27)

25. **Paul**
   a. That he would suffer much for Jesus (Acts 9:16)
   b. That he would serve as a minister to the Gentiles (Acts 9:15)
   c. That he would preach before kings (Acts 9:15)
   d. That he would be arrested by the Jews when he arrived in Jerusalem (Acts 21:4, 11)
   e. That he would eventually go to Rome (Acts 23:11)
   f. That all the 276 people (including Paul) would safely leave a sinking ship, caused by a terrible storm at sea (Acts 27:22, 26, 37)

26. **Peter**
   a. That he would deny Jesus (Matt. 26:34; Mk. 14:30; Lk. 22:34; Jn. 13:38)
   b. That Peter would suffer martyrdom for Jesus (Jn. 21:18-19; 2 Pet. 1:12-14)

27. **Zacharias**
   a. That his barren wife Elisabeth would give him a son whose name would be John (Lk. 1:13)
   b. That he would be unable to speak until that son was born (Lk. 1:20)

PREDICTIONS REGARDING JESUS—Those Old Testament Predictions Jesus Fulfilled

28. **In regard to His birth**
   a. That He would be called Emmanuel (Isa. 7:14)
   b. That He would be born in Bethlehem (Mic. 5:2)
   c. That He would be worshipped by wise men and presented with gifts (Psa. 72:10; Isa. 60:3, 6, 9)
   d. That He would be in Egypt for a season (Num. 24:8; Hos. 11:1)
   e. That His birthplace would suffer a massacre of infants (Jer. 31:15)
   f. That He would be called a Nazarene (Isa. 11:1)

29. **In regard to His human ancestry**
   a. That He would be born of a woman (Gen. 3:15)
   b. That He would be from the line of Abraham (Gen. 12:3, 7; 17:7)
   c. That He would be from the tribe of Judah (Gen. 49:10)
   d. That He would be from the house of David (2 Sam. 7:12-13)
   e. That He would be born of a virgin (Isa. 7:14)

30. **In regard to His nature (Isa. 9:6)**
   a. That He would be the Son of man: *"For unto us a child is born..."*

b. That He would be the Son of God: *"unto us a son is given ... and his name shall be called ... The Mighty God ..."*

31. **In regard to His forerunner**
    a. That John the Baptist would serve as His forerunner (Isa. 40:3-5; Mal. 3:1)

32. **In regard to His relationship with the Father**
    a. That He would be zealous for the Father (Psa. 69:9; 119:139)
    b. That He would be filled with God's Spirit (Psa. 45:7; Isa. 11:2; 61:1-2)

33. **In regard to His earthly ministry**
    a. That He would heal many (Isa. 53:4-5)
    b. That He would deal gently with the Gentiles (Isa. 9:1-2; 42:1-3)
    c. That He would speak in parables (Isa. 6:9-10)

34. **In regard to His triumphal entry**
    a. That He would make a triumphal entry into Jerusalem (Zech. 9:9)
    b. That He would be praised by little children (Psa. 8:2)

35. **In regard to His sufferings**
    a. That He would be a man of sorrows (Isa. 53:3)
    b. That He would be rejected by His own (Psa. 69:8; Isa. 53:3)
    c. That He would be the rejected cornerstone (Psa. 118:22-23)
    d. That His miracles would not be believed (Isa. 53:1)
    e. That He would be forsaken by His disciples (Zech. 13:7)
    f. That His friend would betray Him for 30 pieces of silver (Psa. 41:9; 55:12-14; Zech. 11:12-13)
    g. That He would be sold for 30 pieces of silver which would later be used to buy a potter's field (Zech. 11:12)
    h. That He would be scourged and spat upon (Isa. 50:6)

36. **In regard to His crucifixion**
    a. That He would be crucified between two thieves (Isa. 53:12)
    b. That He would be given vinegar to drink (Psa. 69:21)
    c. That He would thirst (Psa. 22:15)
    d. That He would be surrounded and ridiculed by His enemies (Psa. 22:7-8)
    e. That He would suffer the piercing of His hands and feet (Psa. 22:16; Zech. 12:10)
    f. That His garments would be parted and gambled for (Psa. 22:18)

37. **In regard to His death**
    a. That He would die at the end of the 69th "week" as predicted by Daniel the prophet (Dan. 9:24-27)
    b. That He would commend His spirit to the Father (Psa. 31:5)

    c.   That His bones would not be broken (Ex. 12:46; Num. 9:12; Psa. 34:20)

    d.   That He would be stared at in death (Zech. 12:10)

38. **In regard to His burial**

    a.   That He would be buried with the rich (Isa. 53:9)

39. **In regard to His resurrection**

    a.   That He would be raised from the dead (Psa. 16:10)

40. **In regard to His ascension**

    a.   That He would ascend (Psa. 24:7-10)

41. **In regard to His high priestly ministry**

    a.   That He would then become a greater high priest than Aaron (Psa. 110:4)

42. **In regard to His exaltation**

    a.   That He would be seated at God's right hand (Psa. 110:1)

43. **In regard to His victory at Armageddon**

    a.   That He would become a smiting scepter (Num. 24:17; Dan. 2:44-45)

44. **In regard to His millennial reign**

    a.   That He would be given the throne of David (2 Sam. 7:11-12; Psa. 132:11; Isa. 9:6-7; 16:5; Jer. 23:5; Lk. 1:31-32)

    b.   That this throne would be an eternal throne (Dan. 2:44; 7:14, 27; Mic. 4:7; Lk. 1:32-33)

    c.   That He would rule the heathen (Psa. 2:8)

PREDICTIONS REGARDING JESUS—Those New Testament Predictions Jesus Foretold

45. **In regard to the church**

    a.   That He would establish it, protect it, and give it its authority (Mt. 16:13-19)

46. **In regard to Himself**

    a.   His transfiguration (Mt. 16:28)

    b.   His sufferings (Mt. 16:21a; 17:12b)

    c.   His betrayal by Judas (Mt. 26:21-25; Mk. 14:18-21; Lk. 22:21-23; Jn. 13:21-26)

    d.   His denials by Peter (Mt. 26:30-35; Mk. 14:26-31; Lk. 22:31-34; Jn. 13:36-38)

    e.   His death (Mt. 17:23a; 20:18; Jn. 3:14; 12:32-33)

    f.   His resurrection (Mt. 17:23b; Mk. 9:31b)

    g.   His return (Mt. 24:30; Jn. 14:3)

47. **In regard to the resurrection of Lazarus** (Jn. 11:11)

48. **In regard to the destruction of Jerusalem and the temple** (Lk. 19:43-44; Mk. 13:1-2)

49. **In regard to the martyrdom of Peter** (Jn. 21:18-19)

50. **In regard to the Day of Pentecost** (Acts 1:4-5)

51. **In regard to the nation Israel**
    a. That Israel would be set aside for awhile in favor of the Gentiles (Mt. 21:43)
    b. That Israel would later recognize Jesus as her Messiah (Mt. 23:39)
52. **In regard to the coming Great Tribulation** (Mt. 24:21)
53. **In regard to the Battle of Armageddon** (Mk. 24:28)
54. **In regard to the resurrection of the dead** (Jn. 5:28-29)
55. **In regard to future rewards** (Mt. 10:41-42; 19:29)
56. **In regard to the glorious Millennium** (Mt. 8:11; 13:43; 19:28; 25:34)

PREDICTIONS REGARDING NATIONS

57. **Edom**
    a. That its commerce would cease, its land to become desolate and its very race to become extinct (Obadiah; Jer. 49:17-18; Ezek. 35:3-7; Mal. 1:4)
58. **Egypt**
    a. It was to experience seven years of plenty and seven years of famine (Gen. 41:1-7, 17-24; 45:6, 11)
    b. It was to host Israel for 400 years and afflict them (Gen. 15:13)
    c. Egypt would be judged for this by the ten plagues (Gen. 15:14; Exod. 3:20; 6:1; 7:5)
    d. It would decline from its exalted position and become a base nation (Ezek. 29:1-2, 15)
    e. It will be restored and blessed by God along with Assyria and Israel during the Millennium (Isa. 19:21-25)
59. **Assyria**
    a. It would conquer the ten northern Israelite tribes (Mic. 1)
    b. It would suffer the death of many of its troops outside the city of Jerusalem (2 Kings 19:6-7a; Isa. 37:33-35)
    c. It would be overthrown by the Babylonians (Isa. 10:12; 14:24-27; Nah. 1-3)
60. **Babylonia**
    a. It would defeat the Egyptians (Jer. 46)
    b. It would defeat the Assyrians (Nahum)
    c. It would be defeated by the Medes and Persians (Dan. 5)
61. **Persia**
    a. It would defeat the Babylonians (Dan. 2:39; 7:5)
    b. It would be defeated by the Greeks (Dan. 8:5-8, 21-22)
62. **Greece**
    a. Alexander the Great would conquer Greece and establish a world empire (Dan. 7:6; 8:5-8, 21; 11:3)

b. It would be divided into four parts following Alexander's death (Dan. 8:8, 22; 11:4)

63. **Rome**

    a. It would defeat the Greeks (Dan. 2:40; 7:7)

    b. It would destroy Jerusalem (Mt. 23:37-39)

    c. It will be revived during the Tribulation (Dan. 2:41; 7:7-8; Rev. 13:1; 17:12)

    d. It will be destroyed by Jesus at the Second Coming (Dan. 2:34-35, 44; 7:14, 27)

64. **Gog and Magog—Russia**

    a. To invade Israel during the Tribulation (Ezek. 38:1-3)

    b. To be joined by various allies (Ezek. 38:4-7)

    c. To come down for a spoil (Ezek. 38:12)

    d. To suffer a disastrous defeat at the hand of God, losing some 83 percent of its troops (Ezek. 39:2)

65. **Israel: Past Predictions**

    a. A great nation would come from Abraham (Gen. 12:2)

    b. This nation would exist forever (Jer. 31:35-37)

    c. Israel's kings would come from the tribe of Judah (Gen. 49:10)

    d. Canaan will be given to Israel forever (Gen. 13:15)

    e. Israel would sojourn in another land (Egypt) for 400 years, there to serve and be afflicted (Gen. 15:13)

    f. This oppressive nation (Egypt) would be judged by God (Gen. 15:14)

    g. Israel would leave Egypt with great substance (Gen. 15:14)

    h. Israel would return to Canaan from Egypt in the fourth generation (Gen. 15:16)

    i. Israel would set a king over them (Deut. 17:14-20)

    j. Israel would suffer a tragic civil war after the death of Solomon (1 Kings 11:11, 31)

    k. The Northern Kingdom would be carried away into Assyrian captivity (1 Kings 14:15-16; Hos. 1:5; 10:1, 6)

    l. The Southern Kingdom would be carried away into Babylonian captivity (Jer. 13:19; 20:4-5; 21:10; Mic. 4:10)

    m. The temple would be destroyed (1 Kings 9:7; 2 Chron. 7:20-21; Jer. 7:14)

    n. The length of the Babylonian captivity would be 70 years (Jer. 25:11; 29:10)

    o. Israel would then return to the land (Jer. 29:10)

    p. The temple vessels once carried into Babylon would be brought back to the land (2 Kings 25:14-15; Jer. 28:3; Dan. 5:1-4)

    q. Israel eventually would be scattered among the nations of the world (Lev. 26:33; Deut. 4:27-28; 28:25-68; Hos. 9:17)

    r. Israel would reject her Messiah (Isa. 53:1-9)

66. **Israel: Present Predictions**
    a. Israel would "abide many days" without a king, an heir apparent, the Levitical offerings, the temple, or the Levitical priesthood (Hos. 3:4)
    b. Israel also would be free from idolatry during this terrible time (Hos. 3:4)
    c. Israel would become a byword among the nations (Deut. 28:37)
    d. Israel would loan to many nations, but borrow from none (Deut. 28:12)
    e. Israel would be hounded and persecuted (Deut. 28:65-67)
    f. Israel nevertheless would retain her identity (Lev. 26:44; Jer. 46:28)
    g. Israel would remain alone and aloof among the nations (Num. 23:9)

67. **Israel: Future Predictions**
    a. Israel would return to Palestine in the latter days prior to the Second Coming of Jesus (Deut. 30:3; Ezek. 36:24; 37:1-14)
    b. Israel will be deceived into signing a seven-year peace treaty with the Western leader (Antichrist) during the Great Tribulation (Isa. 28:18; Dan. 9:27)
    c. Israel will experience a hellish onslaught by Satan himself (Rev. 12:13, 17)
    d. Israel will recognize Christ as its Messiah (Zech. 12:10; 13:9b)
    e. Israel will be regenerated, regathered, and restored to the land following the Great Tribulation (Jer. 33:8; Ezek. 11:17)
    f. Israel will become God's witnesses during the Millennium (Isa. 44:8; 61:6)

PREDICTIONS REGARDING CITIES

68. **Sodom**
    a. That God would destroy it for its terrible wickedness (Gen. 18:20-21)

69. **Tyre**
    a. The city was to be scraped and made flat, like the top of a rock (Ezek. 26:4)
    b. It was to become a place for the spreading of nets (Ezek. 26:5)
    c. Its stones and timber were to be laid in the sea (Ezek. 26:12; Zech. 9:3-4)
    d. The city was never to be rebuilt (Ezek. 26:21)

70. **Jericho**
    a. That the city walls would be supernaturally destroyed by God (Josh. 6:2-5)
    b. That the city would later be rebuilt by one man (Josh. 6:26a)
    c. That the builder's oldest son would die when the work on the city had begun (Josh. 6:26b)
    d. That the builder's youngest son would die when the work was completed (Josh. 6:26c)

71. **Nineveh**
    a. That the city would be destroyed by the Babylonians (Nahum)

72. **Babylon**
   a. That the city would be given over to the Medes and Persians (Dan. 5:26-28)

73. **Jerusalem: Past Predictions**
   a. It would become God's chosen place (Deut. 12:5-6, 11; 26:2; Josh. 9:27; 1 Kings 8:29; 11:36; 15:4; 2 Kings 21:4, 7; 2 Chron. 7:12; Psa. 78:68)
   b. It would be spared from invasion by the Assyrians (Isa. 37:33-35)
   c. It would be destroyed by the Babylonians (Isa. 3:8; Jer. 11:23; 26:18; Mic. 3:12)
   d. It would be rebuilt by the Jews after spending 70 years in Babylonian captivity (Isa. 44:28; Jer. 25:11-12; 29:10)
   e. It would have its streets and walls rebuilt during a period of trouble (Dan. 9:25)
   f. The walls would be rebuilt 483 years prior to the crucifixion of Jesus (Dan. 9:26)
   g. It would be destroyed by the Romans (Lk. 19:41-44)
   h. The temple of Herod would also be burned at this time (Mt. 24:1-2)

74. **Jerusalem: Present Prediction**
   a. It would be trodden down by Gentiles until the Second Coming (Lk. 21:24)

75. **Jerusalem: Future Predictions**
   a. It will be occupied by the Antichrist during the Tribulation (Zech. 12:2; 14:2)
   b. It will become the worship center of the world during the Millennium (Isa. 2:2-3; Mic. 4:1)

PREDICTIONS REGARDING CONDITIONS JUST PRIOR TO CHRIST'S RETURN

76. **A departure from the Christian faith caused by Christ-hating and truth-denying false religious teachers** (1 Tim. 4:1a; 2 Tim. 4:3; 2 Peter 2:1-2)

77. **An increase of demonic activity** (1 Tim. 4:1b)

78. **A godless and powerless form of religion** (2 Tim. 3:5)

79. **The rise of lust-controlled mockers, totally devoid of natural human affection** (2 Tim. 3:3; 2 Peter 3:3-4; Jude 18-19)

80. **Blasphemers who will be self-centered, arrogant, greedy, and lawless** (2 Tim. 3:2)

PREDICTIONS REGARDING THOSE EVENTS ACCOMPANYING CHRIST'S RETURN

81. **Rapture of the Church** (1 Cor. 15:51-53; 1 Thess. 4:13-17)

82. **The Judgment Seat of Christ** (Rom. 14:10-12; 2 Cor. 5:10)

83. **The singing of heaven's two songs, praising God for His work in creation and redemption** (Rev. 4:10-11; 5:8-10)

84. **The Marriage Service of the Lamb** (2 Cor. 11:2)

85. **The Great Tribulation: Part One** (first 3 ½ years)

a. Appearance of the antichrist and his peace treaty with Israel (Rev. 13:1-2; Dan. 9:27; Isa. 28:18)

b. Organization of the super harlot church (Rev. 17)

c. Revival of the Old Roman Empire (Dan. 2:41; 7:7-8; Rev. 13:1; 17:12)

d. Mass return of the Jews to Israel (Ezek. 37:1-14)

e. Ministries of the 144,000 and two witnesses (Rev. 7:1-4; 11:3-13)

f. Rebuilding of the third temple (2 Thess. 2:4; Rev. 11:1-2)

g. Possible rebuilding of Babylon (Isa. 13-14; Jer. 50-51)

h. Pouring out of the first six seals (Rev. 6:1-17)

86. **The Great Tribulation: Part Two** (middle, brief undetermined period)

a. The Gog and Magog invasion into Israel and subsequent destruction (Ezek. 38-39)

b. The martyrdom of the two witnesses (Rev. 11:7)

c. The song of the 144,000 (Rev. 14:1-5)

d. The casting out of Satan from heaven (Rev. 12:3-15)

e. The destruction of the false church (Rev. 17:16)

87. **The Great Tribulation: Part Three** (final 3 ½ years)

a. Full manifestation of the Antichrist (Rev. 13:16-18; 2 Thess. 2:3-4)

b. Worldwide persecution of Israel (Dan. 12:1; Zech. 11:16; Mt. 24:21; Rev. 12:13)

c. Pouring out of the last seal judgment (Rev. 8-9; 11:15-19)

d. Pouring out of the seven bowls (or vials) of judgment (Rev. 16)

e. Destruction of the city of Babylon (Rev. 18)

88. **The Second Coming of Christ** (Mt. 24:29-30; Rev. 11:15; 19:11-14)

89. **Battle of Armageddon** (Zech. 12:9; Rev. 16:15-21)

90. **Regathering of saved Israel** (Isa. 43:5-6; Mt. 24:31)

91. **Regathering of unsaved Israel** (Ezek. 20:38)

92. **Judgment of the Gentile nations** (Mt. 25:31-46)

93. **Resurrection of saved Old Testament and martyred tribulational believers** (Dan. 12:2; Jn. 5:28-29; Rev. 6:9-11; 20:4-5)

94. **Judgment of the fallen angels** (1 Cor. 6:3)

95. **Imprisonment of Satan for 1000 years** (Rev. 20:1-3)

96. **Marriage Supper of the Lamb** (Rev. 19:7-9)

97. **The Millennium** (Isa. 2:2-4; Rev. 20:4)

98. **Satan's final revolt** (Rev. 20:7-8)

99. **Destruction of this present earth and heaven** (2 Peter 3:10-12)

100. **Creation of a new heaven and earth** (2 Peter 3:13; Rev. 21:1)

CPSIA information can be obtained at www.ICGtesting.com
Printed in the USA
BVOW01s0840131214

378704BV00003B/6/P